Welcoming the Undesirables

D1458341

Welcoming the Undesirables

Brazil and the Jewish Question

Jeffrey Lesser

UNIVERSITY OF CALIFORNIA PRESS
Berkeley · Los Angeles · London

University of California Press
Berkeley and Los Angeles, California

University of California Press, Ltd.
London, England

Library of Congress Cataloging-in-Publication Data

Lesser, Jeff.
    Welcoming the undesirables : Brazil and the Jewish question /
Jeffrey Lesser.

      p. cm.
    Includes bibliographical references and index.
    ISBN 0-520-08412-8. — ISBN 0-520-08413-6 (pbk.)
    1. Jews—Brazil—History—20th century. 2. Immigrants—Brazil—History—20th
century. 3. Antisemitism—Brazil. 4. Nationalism—Brazil. 5. Brazil—Ethnic
relations. 6. Brazil—Emigration and immigration—History—20th century.
I. Title.
F2659.J5L54   1994
981'.004924—dc20   93-21199
                                               CIP

Printed in the United States of America
9 8 7 6 5 4 3 2 1

Dedicated to the memory of my father,
Dr. William Morris Lesser, ל"ז

Contents

Photographs follow page 82.

Tables

A Note on Spelling

Portuguese: I have modernized all Portuguese spellings in the text and footnotes *except* for book titles. Any exceptions to this rule are noted.

Yiddish: I have used the modern (YIVO) transliteration system for all Yiddish words *except* for those newspapers in which a transliteration appears on the masthead. In those cases I have reproduced the transliteration faithfully.

Abbreviations Used in the Text and Notes

AAJDC-NY	Archives of the American Jewish Joint Distribution Committee, New York
ADSS	Vatican, Secrétairie d'État de Sa Sainteté, *Actes et documents du Saint Siège relatifs à la seconde guerre mondiale*
AESP	Archive of *O Estado de São Paulo*, São Paulo
AHI-R	Arquivo Histórico Itamaraty, Rio de Janeiro (Archive of the Brazilian Foreign Ministry)
AHJB-SP	Arquivo Histórico Judaico Brasileiro, São Paulo (Brazilian-Jewish Historical Archive)
AHRS-PA	Arquivo Histórico do Rio Grande do Sul, Porto Alegre (Rio Grande do Sul Historical Archive)
AIB	Ação Integralista Brasileira (Brazilian Integralist Action Party)
AJA-C	American Jewish Archives, Cincinnati
AJYB	American Jewish Committee, *American Jewish Yearbook*
ALV-SP	Archives of the Lar dos Velhos, São Paulo (Archives of the Jewish Old Age Home, São Paulo)

ANL   Aliança Nacional Libertadora
               (National Liberation Alliance)

AN-R   Arquivo Nacional, Rio de Janeiro
               (Brazilian National Archives)

BODBJ-L   Board of Deputies of British Jews, London

CIC   Conselho de Imigração e Colonização
               (Immigration and Colonization Council)

CIP   Congregação Israelita Paulista
               (Jewish Congregation of São Paulo)

CPDOC-R   Centro de Pesquisa e Documentação de História
               Contemporânea do Brasil (Center for Research and
               Documentation on the Contemporary History of Bra-
               zil), Fundação Getúlio Vargas, Rio de Janeiro

CZA-J   Central Zionist Archives, Jerusalem

DNI   Departamento Nacional de Imigração
               (National Department of Immigration)

DNP   Departamento Nacional de Povoamento
               (National Colonization Department)

DTCI   Directoria de Terras, Colonização e Imigração
               (Land, Colonization, and Immigration Directorate)

Emigdirect   Berlin United Committee for Jewish Migration

FRUS   United States, Department of State, *Foreign Relations
               of the United States, Diplomatic Papers*

GV   Getúlio Vargas

HIAS   Hebrew Immigrant Aid and Sheltering Society

HICEM   An umbrella group of the HIAS, the ICA, and Emig-
               direct

HL-NY   Herbert Lehman Papers, Columbia University

HUC/JIR-C   Hebrew Union College/Jewish Institute of Religion
               Library, Cincinnati

ICA   Yidishe kolonizatsye gezelshaft
               (Jewish Colonization Association)

JCA-L   Archives of the Jewish Colonization Association,
               London

JCA	Jewish Colonization Association
JM	James G. McDonald Papers
LP	Letters to Paris
NARC-W	National Archives and Record Center, Washington, D.C.
OA	Oswaldo Aranha
PRCNE	Presidência da República—Fundo Conselho Nacional de Economia (National Economic Council)
PRO-L	Public Record Office, London
PRR	Partido Republicano Rio-grandense (Rio Grande do Sul Republican Party)
PRRE	Secretaria da Presidência da República—Relações Exteriores (Secretary of the President of the Republic—Foreign Relations)
RACCA	Jewish Colonization Association, *Rapport de l'administration centrale au conseil d'administration* (Report of the central administration of the administrative council)
RIC	*Revista de Imigração e Colonização* (Journal of Immigration and Colonization)
SCA	Séance du Conseil d'Administration (Meeting of the Administrative Council), Archives of the Jewish Colonization Association, London
SMML-NJ	Seeley G. Mudd Manuscript Library, Princeton University Archives
SRBI	*Livro de Atas de "Sociedade Religiosa e Beneficente Israelita, São Paulo,"* Archives of the Lar dos Velhos, São Paulo
YIVO-NY	Institute for Jewish Research, New York

Preface

A study of the Jewish Question in Brazil bridges two scholarly disciplines that have been traditionally seen as mutually exclusive but in fact are closely related. To be sure, no one has ever claimed that Jews never lived in Latin America. Even so, Latin American historians have tended, at least until recently, to see the study of Jews as really a part of Jewish history, implicitly relegating Jews to a space in which they were not real Latin Americans. At the same time, Jewish historians have tended to lump all but the largest numerical communities into the category of "exotica," and thus not worthy of careful study. Yet again Brazil's Jews, and their interactions with each other and non-Jews, were seen as not "real." These tendencies have left studies of Brazil's Jewish Question out of both the Latin American and Jewish historiography. This situation has been reinforced by the fact that documents are unorganized and scattered throughout the world, and that the number of languages needed to conduct research is daunting. Even so, this study shows, if nothing else, that the assumption that Latin American history and Jewish history are two separate disciplines is, at least in some cases, misleading. Indeed, I hope my research serves to demonstrate that the Jewish Question is as critical to understanding race and ethnicity in modern Brazil as Brazilian notions of race and ethnicity are to understanding the vision of Jews, by Jews and others.

A number of foundations were extraordinarily generous in providing the money I needed to travel and write over the past few years. To those organizations committed to encouraging scholarly research go my

thanks: the American Council of Learned Societies, the American Jewish Archives, the Dorot Foundation at Brown University, the Jewish
Communal Fund of New York, the Lucius N. Littauer Foundation, the
Memorial Foundation for Jewish Culture, the National Foundation for
Jewish Culture, the New York University Humanities Council, the
Dean of the Graduate School of Arts and Sciences and the History Department of New York University, the Social Science Research Council,
and the YIVO Institute for Jewish Research. Connecticut College aided
the completion of this project by allowing me to take a leave of absence
in order to accept a grant from the American Council of Learned Societies and has consistently funded my research through the R. Francis
Johnson Faculty Development Fund.

The wide scope of my research put me at the mercy of archivists,
librarians, bureaucrats, and colonels who control access to documentation. These people, however, were uniformly helpful and kind, not only
showing me their collections but often helping me dig through unorganized materials in search of that single crucial item of interest. My
thanks go to Dona Betty and Sr. Eliseu of the Arquivo Nacional in Rio
de Janeiro; Dona Lúcia Monte Alto Silva, the director of the Itamaraty
Archives; the staff of the Centro de Pesquisa e Documentação de História Contemporânea at Rio de Janeiro's Fundação Getúlio Vargas; and
the staff of the Arquivo Histórico Judaico Brasileiro in São Paulo. Sub-
scribers to the international computer network BrasNet were kind and
quick in responding to linguistic and bibliographic queries. Vera Roubi-
cek, the librarian of the Alfred Hirschberg Library of the Congregação
Israelita Paulista, was always generous and good spirited, and Julian
Kay and Michael L. Richman of the Jewish Colonization Association
gave me free rein with the archives they preside over. At Connecticut
College, reference librarians James McDonald, Lorrie Knight, and Ash-
ley Powell Hanson spent hours helping me scour through computer
data bases. The rest of the Charles Shain Library staff was always gra-
cious and friendly in putting up with what must have seemed like a
never-ending list of strange requests. Individuals opened their homes,
and their private papers, to me. Too many other people, in too many
other places, were extremely helpful and kind, and this brief note of
thanks cannot show my gratitude to them.

The completion of this book has been encouraged by a number of
friends and colleagues. Warren Dean, who advised my doctoral disser-
tation, has had a huge influence on my career, both as a scholar and as
a teacher. If anything good comes from my research, and the presenta-

tion of it, it is because of his insistence on the highest academic and moral standards. Many in Brazil, the United States, Europe, and Israel have supported me, including Rabbi Henry I. Sobel and the directorate of the Congregação Israelita Paulista, Roney Cytrynowicz, Anani Dzidzienyo, Judith L. Elkin, Abraham Faermann and the staff and directorate of the Instituto Cultural Judaico Marc Chagall (Porto Alegre), Luiza H. Schmitz Kleimann, Marlene Kulkes, Rabbi Michael Leipziger, José Carlos Sebe Bom Meihy, Abraham J. Peck, Kevin Proffitt and the staff of the American Jewish Archives, Frieda Wolff and her late husband, Egon, and Susanne Worcman.

The American Jewish Archives, the Columbia University Seminar on Brazil, the Instituto Cultural Judaico Marc Chagall, the Latin American Studies Association, the Nucleo de Estudos de População of Campinas University, the Universidade Federal do Rio Grande do Sul, the Pontifícia Universidade Católica of Porto Alegre, the Tokyo University of Foreign Studies, and Berlin's Ibero-American Institute all provided me with the opportunity to present my work publicly. The Instituto de Estudos Brasileiros of the University of São Paulo was kind enough to invite me to spend a year as a visiting researcher.

A number of my colleagues commented on chapters of this book or read the entire manuscript in various forms. My friend and colleague Marc Forster encouraged me, cajoled me, and always left me a few steps behind on the basketball court and in the pool. His comments on an often incomprehensible early draft improved it and prevented a number of bizarre "Lesserisms" from creeping into the text. Roger Brooks was always available for phone consultations as I struggled to translate powerful emotions into words. Robert Levine graciously and rapidly made detailed comments on the manuscript, and his willingness to read rewritten chapters taught me a great deal about the real meaning of both scholarship and collegiality. My editor at the University of California Press, Eileen McWilliam, was always supportive, good-humored, and willing to endure long phone conversations that were more psychoanalytic than analytical. The Press's Betsey Scheiner and Carl Walesa were invaluable in editing the manuscript and making it into a book. Roney Cytrynowicz, Judith L. Elkin, Thomas Holloway, Samy Katz, Elizabeth Mahan, and Benjamin Orlove each read the entire manuscript, making perceptive and helpful comments. George Reid Andrews, Gabriel Bolaffi, Ralph Della Cava, Sandra McGee Deutsch, John W. F. Dulles, Boris Fausto, Stanley E. Hilton, Herbert Klein, Ignacio Klich, Joseph Love, Frederick S. Paxton, Ken Serbin, Thomas Skidmore, and

Shigeru Suzuki all provided insights on various chapters. David Hirsch provided invaluable bibliographical and orthographic help, and John W. F. Dulles, Samy Katz, Maria Luiza Tucci Carneiro, and Cliff Welch each shared documents with me that their own research uncovered. Julie Berins, Sueann Caulfield, Maureen O'Dougherty, Tony Pereira, Marisa Sanematsu, and Michael Shavitt generously helped proofread the final version of the manuscript.

Of course, this work is ultimately the result of the support of my friends and family. To Irma, Peter, and Suzanne Lesser and the Lesser, Friedlander, and Shavitt families goes my great love. Special thanks go to Rabbi Uri and Peppy Goren, Ilton and Hannah Gitz and their families, and Gabriel and Clelia Bolaffi. The Jewish communities of São Paulo, Rio de Janeiro, and Porto Alegre opened their doors for me and never failed to provide stimulus.

Finally, this book is dedicated to Eliana Shavitt Lesser, who has endured long nights, cross-hemispheric relocations, and numerous adventures with grace, good humor, and love. Eliana's help makes this book as much hers as mine. Yet whatever collective pride we have in this project, it pales in comparison with that which we have for our twin sons, Gabriel Zev Shavitt Lesser and Aron Yossef Shavitt Lesser.

AUTHOR'S NOTE

During the very last stages of editing *Welcoming the Undersirables,* I received word of Warren Dean's tragic death in an accident in Chile, where he was conducting research on the ecological history of Latin America. As my mentor he inspired me to be creative; as a friend he taught me much about respect for other cultures. For his students, colleagues, and friends, Warren Dean provided a model of courtesy, kindness, and seriousness. He changed the way people thought about Brazil by opening new areas of study and challenged us to constantly reevaluate our own research. His influence will be felt for generations and his presence will be missed by all.

São Paulo, July 1994

Introduction: Brazil and the Jews

On September 25, 1947, Oswaldo Aranha, the influential former Brazilian foreign minister and an ex-ambassador to the United States, was elected president of the General Assembly of the United Nations; one of his charges was the partitioning of Palestine. Aranha and the Brazilian representative to the United Nations, João Carlos Muniz, former director of Brazil's powerful Immigration and Colonization Council, actively supported the resolution, and two months later the State of Israel was established.[1] Jews and Gentiles around the world viewed Israel's creation as a triumph of democracy in international politics. Brazil and Aranha, both crucial to the decision, were considered friends of Israel, Zionism, and all Jews. In Tel Aviv a street was named after Aranha, as was a cultural center in a kibbutz settled by Brazilian Jews.

The honors accorded to Brazil following the United Nations vote might have been tempered if it had been widely known that fourteen years earlier Brazilian president Getúlio Vargas and his policymakers, including Aranha and Muniz, had proposed to prevent the entry of Jewish refugees. Following two years of informal restriction, on June 7, 1937, five months before the establishment of the fascist-inspired *Estado Novo* (New State), Brazil's Ministry of Foreign Relations (known as Itamaraty) issued a secret circular that banned the granting of visas to all persons of "Semitic origin." Jewish relief organizations, many of whose leaders were important U.N. lobbyists in 1947, knew of the secret circular. The British and United States diplomatic corps were also aware of its existence. Yet all of this was diplomatically ignored in the

1

wake of Israel's creation. Even Aranha's reported comment that the creation of Israel meant that the Rio de Janeiro neighborhood of Copacabana would be returned to the Brazilians passed unnoticed.[2]

Why did Jews, a small part of a large immigrant stream from Europe and the Middle East, cause such consternation that they were eventually banned from entering Brazil?[3] And why, just one year after the ban was in place, did more Jews enter Brazil legally than at any time in the past twenty years? The answer to these two questions involved a change in the way a small but extraordinarily powerful group of intellectuals and politicians looked at Brazilian national identity and the role immigrants, and thus residents and potential citizens, would play in shaping it. They represented a new generation in Brazilian politics whose influence was formalized in 1930 following a Getúlio Vargas–led coup. While the general politics of the group ranged from far right to far left, almost all agreed with the social notion, frequently learned in one of Brazil's law schools, that social Darwinism and scientific racism formed the backbone of an appropriate analysis of Brazilian cultural and economic development.

The foreign ministers, justice ministers, diplomats, journalists, and intellectuals who provide the cast of characters for this book struggled to combine the pseudoscientific social categorizations so prominent among the educated in twentieth-century Europe and the Americas with a new nationalist sentiment. This fused with omnipresent traditional Christian motifs so that attempts to engender devotion to "*a patria*" (patriotism) put non-Christian groups, and particularly those who had been attacked through the ages, in a precarious position.[4] No immigrant group tested the new attitudes more than Jews. Many in the Brazilian intelligentsia and political elite considered Jews culturally undesirable even while believing that they had a special, inherited relationship to financial power and could thus help Brazil to develop industrially. Jewish immigration therefore challenged policymakers who deemed Jews a non-European race but also desired to create a Brazilian society that mirrored the industry of the United States or Germany. By the mid-1930s the Jewish Question or Jewish Problem (both terms were used regularly) was high on the Brazilian political and social agenda.[5]

The existence of a Jewish Question in Brazil should not lead readers to assume that its formulation or application was similar to that in Argentina or Europe, where popular and official anti-Semitism ran rampant. In these cases, anti-Semitism was based on convoluted images of real Jews with whom the Gentile population had regular contact. In Brazil, however, influential individuals attacked images of *imaginary* Jews who were presumed to be simultaneously communists and capitalists whose degenerate life-styles were formed in putrid and poverty-stricken European ethnic enclaves. The harsh and unrealistic judgments were framed in an unsophisticated reading of European anti-Semitism and Jew hatred applied to an inaccurate image of Jewish life outside of Brazil. The surprise in all this, however, is that *real* Jews living in Brazil, were they citizens or refugees, faced few daily or structural impediments to achieving either social or economic goals. Thus Brazil's Jewish Question was really a struggle by Brazil's leaders to fit the bigoted images of Jews that filtered in from Europe with the reality that the overwhelming majority of Jewish immigrants were neither very rich nor very poor, were rarely active politically, and rapidly acculturated to Brazilian society. Unlike in thirteenth-century Europe, where Augustinian ambivalence toward images of biblical Jews clashed with Dominican and Franciscan attacks on actual Talmudic Jews, or in twentieth-century Europe, where long-held stereotypes of Jews reinforced an angry scapegoating in times of economic, political, and social crisis, in Brazil the imagined Jew, not the real one, was considered the danger.[6]

If the combination of nationalism and racism led to the creation of a Jewish Question by those at the very top of Brazil's political and intellectual worlds, the Vargas regime's facile use of nationalist discourse to achieve short-term political goals often led to expressions of nativism from state politicians who represented socially conservative urban middle-class constituencies that included members of the government and military bureaucracy, the clergy, and white-collar workers. Brazilian nativism in the 1930s and 1940s was not all that different from the same phenomenon occurring throughout the Americas. Those judged to have allegiances or concerns outside of some blurrily defined "*brasilidade*" (Brazilianness—a term regularly used by members of the Vargas regime) were a danger to society and its citizens. As was the case elsewhere, Brazilian nativism was "conscious[ly] or unconscious[ly], intimately connected with nationalism."[7] Yet nationalism and nativism, for all their classic components, co-existed with a belief that racism did not exist in Brazil. Even the way the word *raça* was used in mid-twentieth-century Brazil included both the invidious pseudoscience so popular in Europe at the time *and* the fifteenth-century notion of a "population . . . of human beings who through inheritance possessed common characteristics."[8] Brazilian politicians, often expressing ideas formulated by leading intellectuals, preached a kind of internal equality that allowed virtually any nonblack who resided within Brazil's borders to be "Brazilian," while judging many outside of the territorial boundaries as unwelcome nonwhites. For Jewish immigrants and refugees, the simple act of entering Brazil, whether through legal means or not, usually transformed them from undesirable elements into welcome ones.

Benedict Anderson, in reference to eighteenth- and nineteenth-century Latin America, has rightly asked, "Why did . . . colonial provinces, usually containing large, oppressed . . . populations, produce creoles who consciously redefined these populations as fellow-nationals?"[9] If we think of the "oppressed populations" as immigrants and the "creoles" as Brazil's federal elites, we are forced to take Anderson's provocation a step further and ask why Brazil's national leaders sought to define Jews who wanted to settle in Brazil as unwelcome even while accepting Jews, be they born in Brazil or naturalized, immigrants or refugees, as equal enough to be chosen for positions ranging from finance minister to the head of the census bureau. The reasons are numerous. From an ideological perspective, the agreement among most federal politicians and intellectuals that a "Brazilian race" existed meant that they considered foreigners as detracting from a homogeneous society that was actually extremely diverse. This allowed the elites on whom this study focuses to speak a language of exclusion that gave them nativist credentials in a time of economic crisis.[10] It also implied that anyone in Brazil, regardless of background, could be part of this nation striving for prosperity by following the rules set out by an increasingly authoritarian regime. Simply residing in Brazil and not causing trouble made a person a component of Brazilian "racial" homogeneity. Thus, the language of Brazilian nativism could attack foreigners of all physical types and ethnic and religious backgrounds while still expressing a belief that there was no racism in Brazil.

An important issue that cannot remain untouched surrounds the relation of the Jewish Question to the African one. Put more broadly, how did Brazilian racial ideology relate to groups who seem to have been judged neither white (European) nor black (African)? The answers, as it turns out, are numerous and often contradictory. At the theoretical level, it is clear that looking at blacks and whites leaves gaps in our understanding of Brazilian society, since Brazil's twentieth-century political leaders and intelligentsia used the word *European* not as a descriptive adjective related to region of birth but as a racial synonym for *white*. This meant that European groups (like Jews) or Caucasian phenotypes (like Arabs and East Indians) were judged neither "black" nor "white." Second, it is important to make a clear distinction between long-term residents of Brazil, who had to be dealt with in one way, and potential residents (immigrants), over whom elites had a different kind of influence. Since the debates in Brazil over those of African descent always took place with the knowledge that Afro-Brazilian society existed, the ban on African immigration could not have been intended to prevent the existence of Afro-Brazilian society. Rather, the prohibition was a way of guaranteeing that the numbers of Africans would not increase—in the hope that miscegenation would make that community disappear. The African Question, then, always revolved around Brazilian residents and how to deal with them. The Jewish Question, on the other hand, had a number of very different components. Few Jews lived in Brazil before 1920, and thus discussions of Jewish immigration were potentially more absolute because the group could be banned or encouraged to enter. This increased the stakes, because Brazilian leaders now had the responsibility for creating minority communities.

The established paradigm of black/white race relations is not sufficient for dealing with the Jewish Question, since it assumes that all those judged as not black were considered white, and vice versa. Analyzing who was considered "nonblack" or "nonwhite," however, leads to very different conclusions than examining who is "white" or "black." While those involved in Jewish studies are familiar with the analysis of why Jews were categorized as a race from at least the fifteenth century, most of those studying Brazilian race relations have accepted the modern social scientific definitions of the term, thus focusing on whites, blacks, mulattos, and occasionally Asians, but not Jews.[11] While many academics have challenged Brazil's "racial democracy" by pointing to the disadvantaged position that most people of color face in Brazil, they have often assumed that all Europeans, including Jews, were considered desirable members of the "acceptable" white category. The presumption that those of European descent were universally privileged has even led some to claim that anti-Jewish sentiment does not exist in modern Brazil.[12] Looking at Brazil in terms of "nonwhite" and "nonblack," however, makes explicit the operational connections between ethnic and racial labels. Revising the terms of analysis thus provides the tools for understanding why Jews living in Brazil were ac-

cepted as "nonblack," and thus represented a privileged component of
the social hierarchy, at the same time that Jews wishing to immigrate
were judged "nonwhite" and thus a social danger.

In the same way that the categories of "black" and "white" have led
many scholars to ignore the Jewish Question in Brazil, an assumption
that anti-Semites despised all Jews all the time has skewed the analysis
of the few scholars who have tackled the issue. This misconception has
usually manifested itself in an assumption that Brazil's twentieth-century anti-Jewish immigration policies could be linked ideologically to
the Portuguese Inquisition and that the existence of significant numbers
of Jews and New Christians in colonial Brazil is an indication of an
unbroken line between that community and the modern one.[13] One
scholar categorizes the anti-Jewish immigration policy of the Estado
Novo as a "Nova Inquisição," a New Inquisition.[14] A rabbi visiting
Brazil in 1940 commented that some Jews were "following in the very
footsteps of their Marrano brothers of the fifteenth and sixteenth century," sentiments echoed more recently by a Brazilian historian who
defines European Jewish refugees who converted to Catholicism during
the 1930s in order to escape Nazism as "20th Century New Christians."[15]

The revival of colonial terminology to explain modern Brazilian ethnic relations implies an unwarranted influence from sixteenth-century
Iberia. Yosef Hayim Yerushalmi has convincingly argued that although
there are "some phenomenological affinities between . . . assimilation
and anti-Semitism in the Iberian Peninsula in the fifteenth to the eigh-
teenth centuries, and in Germany of the nineteenth and twentieth,"
there was little historical continuity between the two periods.[16] As such,
the assumption that a continuous theoretical and legislative line between colonial and modern Brazil made Jews unacceptable as immigrants or citizens is not viable. Brazilian anti-Semites in the 1920s,
1930s, and 1940s, however, were extraordinarily derivative. They
rarely, if ever, looked any further than nineteenth- and twentieth-
century Western Europe to find intellectual justifications for their positions.

Inquisitional anti-Semitism viewed Jews as the enemy within. In
twentieth-century Brazil this was not the case. The fluctuating relationship between Iberian and Central European anti-Semitism is important
to emphasize. Thus, while a notion of *limpeza de sangue* (purity of
blood) can be found in both models, it was independently developed by
Germans and Portuguese. Furthermore, the question of whether that

purity was immutable was not answered in the same way in Germany and the Iberian Peninsula. Conversion to Catholicism was initially encouraged by the Spanish and Portuguese crowns, a policy that was also followed by the Vatican during the 1930s and 1940s. The Nazis, the Brazilian government, and many modern Brazilian racists, however, rejected the idea that a Jew could convert. The theories of de Gobineau and Chamberlain, more than Torquemada, informed the bigotry of twentieth-century Brazil.

It is, therefore, useful to define Brazilian society as "ethnic" in addition to "racial." This redefinition leads to a whole series of new questions about the relationships among immigrant groups, immigration policy, and national identity. Certainly future studies of those judged neither black nor white (Arabs, Asians, East Indians) are necessary to complete the complex picture I propose to begin painting. Even so, a study of the Jewish Question helps to illuminate the ideology that elites used to define who was a Brazilian and what role immigrants would play in Brazil. One aspect was intimately related to modifications in how many members of the Vargas regime connected notions of development and ethnicity. For those federal politicians who wished to recast Brazil along industrial lines, industry and culture were related. Yet how this cultural component of economic change would operate was widely debated among large landowners, industrialists, and nativist intellectuals and politicians. All increasingly sought to limit immigration, reflecting their own disappointment that the ambitious state and federal programs to subsidize European immigration launched in the 1870s and 1880s had not created a "tropical Belle Époque" based on Central and Northern European labor.[17] The growing working and middle classes, especially in Rio de Janeiro but to some extent in São Paulo and Brazil's other urban centers as well, were just as concerned by immigration. Increasingly frightened by economic difficulties in the decades after World War I, they perceived immigrants primarily as competitors for education, jobs, and social rank.[18]

Jewish immigration became a focus of attention among Brazilian intellectuals and members of the government in the 1920s and 1930s in part because of what Daphne Patai has termed surplus visibility.[19] Not only did immigrants from Eastern Europe swell Brazil's Jewish population from perhaps fifteen thousand in 1920 to about five times that number just two decades later, but many Jewish immigrants and refugees also successfully climbed the economic ladder in Brazilian cities. In the academy, in editorial offices, and in the halls of government, complaints echoed. Jews were both greedy capitalists and evil communists. Jews lived in cities and could never be farmers. Jews were criminals. In addition, Jews were too successful. For Jews (and many other immigrants) Brazil was *o país do futuro* (the country of the future), but for many powerful Brazilians, Jews were imagined to be one of the least desirable of all immigrant groups.

Jews struggled with the *ambiguity* of Brazilian minority status more than many other immigrant groups. Africans and Chinese, for example, were unambiguously undesirable, and a constitutional ban on their entry was enacted in the late nineteenth century.[20] Japanese immigrants, although never able to hide their racial differences, usually lived and worked in the countryside, somewhat away from the scrutiny of intellectuals and politicians, who used nativism to appeal to a growing urban middle class who aspired to enter the elite and shared many of that group's values.[21] Jews, on the other hand, caused a problem since they were judged a separate race that could not easily be distinguished physically. Brazilian elites thus struggled with the tension created by the presence of a minority group that was simultaneously the same and different. One resolution was an intellectual attempt to encourage policies that would separate members of the Jewish "race" from Europeans. Those considered Jewish by their country of origin were defined as Jews, as were all who identified themselves as Jewish. Beginning in 1937, anyone judged by a consular officer or diplomat to have a "Jewish name" was also defined as a Jew, regardless of his or her actual religious or ethnic background. Even some who converted to Catholicism, and who had Vatican baptismal certificates and the weight of the Holy See diplomatic corps behind them, were judged to be Jews.

The ambiguous images did not always have a negative impact on Jews, often opening spaces for refugees to remake their lives after the horrors they had faced in Eastern and Western Europe and the Middle East. By actively manipulating bigotry and crafting an image that played on prejudice, Jewish leaders convinced Brazilian policymakers that Jewish immigration had economic and political value. More importantly, Jews were able to pry open Brazil's doors, even if for only a few years, at a moment when European Jewry was engaged in a life-and-death struggle. Consequently, between 1933 and 1942 almost twenty-five thousand Jews, primarily Germans and Poles fleeing Nazism, legally entered Brazil, despite the fact that most members of the Vargas regime considered Jewish immigration undesirable. Even while Jews entered in relatively steady numbers between 1922 and 1942, the ambiguous position of "nonwhite" European immigrants in Brazil led to a wartime immigration policy that was anti-Jewish.

How anti-Jewish images and stereotypes affected policy, and the attempts to twist these prejudices to the advantage of desperate refugees, is one focus of this book.[22] My analysis of why federal policymakers reacted as they did to the idea of Jewish immigration, however, should not suggest that minority groups exist exclusively, or even primarily, in reaction to societal bigotry.[23] Indeed, as will be evident throughout, most Jewish residents saw Brazil as a country where social and economic advancement was likely. Furthermore, my discussion of Jewish stereotypes in Brazil should not imply that this work is primarily about anti-Semitism. Neither is it a psychological study of the roots of bigotry among influential Brazilian policymakers, nor does it pretend to analyze the roots of the anti-Semitic ideologies among notable Brazilian racists. Such studies have been attempted elsewhere.[24] What I have tried to do is distinguish between Judeophobes (those who hate all Jews) and anti-Semites (those who hold some or many group negative stereotypical notions about Jews). Those who hold group positive stereotypes of Jews I have termed *philo-Semites,* but, as I argue throughout, both philo- and anti-Semitic notions were often held simultaneously since many Brazilians who described ethnic and racial groups in stereotypical ways often linked both negative and positive notions.

While Jews began to immigrate to Brazil in large numbers in the mid-1920s, political leaders and intellectuals began to ask the Jewish Question only in the 1930s. One of the reasons for the time lag was the slow realization that Jews were entering Brazil in such large numbers, in part because immigration statistics categorized only Catholics and non-Catholics. More important, however, was the Revolution of 1930, which represented an abrupt political shift that ended the large landowners' hegemony as Brazil's *only* political power brokers. When Getúlio Vargas became provisional president, Brazil embarked on a new economic path whose goal was industrialization and urbanization. Following traditional patterns, many in the Vargas regime argued that immigrants should be expected to help the economy by transferring technology, capital, and industrial labor experience to Brazil. These new immigrants were expected, as in the past, to help transform Brazilian culture. Yet it was not the ethnic or racial aspects of Brazilian culture that elites now primarily hoped to change. On the contrary, the cultural role of immigrants had little to do with the whitening of "black" and mixed-race rural society, but rather with bringing an in-

dustrial spirit to the urban centers. Significant segments of the middle
class, who were sometimes less well trained, sometimes without the
pressure to succeed felt by many immigrants, and sometimes without
even minimal amounts of capital to invest, saw immigrants as competitors. For this group, which also feared the industrial aspirations of the
elites, assimilation became a catchword. The idea that immigrants
should assimilate into a Brazilian urban culture primarily formed by
mass migration simultaneously represented a glorification of the nineteenth-century ideal of the white European immigrant and a twentieth-
century notion of what the literary critic Roberto Schwarz calls "Nationalism by Elimination"—that is, a tendency to define an authentic
Brazilian culture by denying the viability of supposedly foreign elements.[25] As Vargas himself wrote, "The immigrant must be . . . a force
for progress . . . [but] we must guard ourselves against the infiltration
of elements that could be transformed into ideological or racial dissenters."[26] By designating acceptable immigrants as those who would not
modify the European ethnic and racial balance in Brazil's cities, the
middle class could speak the language of economic development without favoring a change in the population. Such sentiments dovetailed
neatly with the increasing influence of European scientific racialist
thought among intellectuals to make nationalism and xenophobia powerful political tools.

Within months of the coup that brought Vargas to power, federal
leaders transformed the immigration debate into one that revolved
around whether state and federal immigration policies should emphasize cultural "improvement" or economic development. All of the
groups involved (except the immigrants) were in general agreement that
Brazil's open immigration policy had to be changed, and the discussion
of how to do so took place in the halls of Congress, in the press, in the
general's quarters, and occasionally even in the streets. The aspect of
this tense debate that most galvanized politicians and those they represented was how to deal with immigrants who were considered simultaneously economically desirable and culturally undesirable. Prior to
1920 this was rarely an issue (except in the case of Japanese immigration) because the federal government represented large landowners who
generally presumed that all immigrants were white Europeans and either Catholic or Protestant. They favored the "Europeanization" of
Brazil, which meant more than just replacing slave labor with wage
labor; it meant the literal whitening of what was considered a degenerate "black" and mixed-race culture. While many elites looked at Bra-

zil's population and found both economic and cultural faults, they were extremely optimistic that an influx of European immigrants would provide labor while ethnically and racially changing rural society.

After the 1930s the general agreement on immigration policy that existed among Brazil's power brokers fell apart as the federal government began its attempt to centralize power by invoking new ideologies that supported federal political authoritarianism. This led to a split between those who had previously held power and the new regime. The traditional elites, generally large landowners in states like Rio Grande do Sul and São Paulo, continued to favor cheap labor above all and were even occasionally willing to support the entry of culturally undesirable groups like the Japanese.[27] Yet the "cheap labor" position was increasingly opposed by a coalition of groups that looked to restrict immigration as much as possible. The military, heavily imbued with racist ideas popular among European authoritarians and fearful that foreign communities would bring communism to Brazil, argued for an almost complete stoppage. Politicians who represented middle-class urban constituencies, most notably in Rio de Janeiro, used antiforeigner rhetoric as a regular part of almost all political discourse and fought for restrictive immigration legislation. Middle-class sentiments were reinforced by nativist groups, especially following the economic crash of 1929. Such organizations, including one that claimed a million members, looked for a return to an immigration policy that placed European Christian culture above all else.

The Brazilian response to Jewish immigrants in the 1920s, 1930s, and 1940s was extraordinarily modern and nationally specific. Yet Jews were merely one group enmeshed in a larger "immigrant question" that had increasingly plagued intellectuals and policymakers at both the federal and state levels since the early nineteenth century. In the waning years of Portugal's colonial rule of Brazil in the early nineteenth century, immigration policy aimed to populate frontier areas with European immigrants who would help build the agricultural economy. Such plans, however, were limited in scope, and the two colonies of Swiss, German, and Austrian citizens that were established in 1812 and 1819 in the states of Espírito Santo and Rio de Janeiro were not successful in encouraging large-scale immigration or colonization.

Brazil ended its colonial relationship with Portugal and established its own empire in 1822. There can be no doubt that religion was an important issue to imperial leaders, who promulgated a constitution "in the name of the holy Trinity" and made Roman Catholicism the state religion.[28] At the same time, fear of Argentine imperialism and Botucudo indigenous populations led the new imperial regime to make immigration and colonization a priority. Political and economic elites (often the same people) set out to populate Brazil's southern frontier by encouraging the immigration of Europeans with the promise of land. Many potential immigrants, however, were Protestants cautious about entering a nation whose official religion was Catholicism and where the public practice of other religions was illegal. Even simple religious life-events, like marriage, could take place only within the confines of the Catholic Church. The existence of an official religion did not mean that the Empire demanded Catholicism as a condition of entry, though, and in 1824 the imperial government began subsidizing the entry of Protestant Central European immigrants, mainly poor farmers and former soldiers from the Napoleonic Wars.[29] Although they were forced to worship in private and were denied the right to vote, many Protestant farmers did set up colonies in southern Brazil.[30]

The discussion of the religious background of immigrants in the imperial era revolved around a simple bipartite distinction between Catholics and non-Catholics. The non-Catholic group, however, never included all those who were not Catholic. Indeed, the idea that Muslims, Buddhists, or Jews would immigrate to Brazil was rarely even considered. To most members of the Brazilian elite, non-Catholics were simply Protestants. Such an idea was reinforced by the reality of immigration patterns to Brazil, where, prior to the 1880s, virtually every non-Catholic immigrant was indeed a white European Protestant.[31]

In spite of official encouragement, few immigrants actually came to Brazil prior to 1872, because the United States was winning an international competition for immigrants. Brazil's negative image as a disease-infested jungle with little real economic opportunity was accentuated by the racist fears engendered among potential immigrants by the large numbers of slaves. This combined with the fact that large landholders, in spite of the desires of Dom Pedro II, treated immigrant farmers badly, seeing European immigrants simply as white replacements for black slaves. In 1859 Prussia prohibited companies from promoting Brazilian colonization, a ban that in 1871 was extended to all of Germany and that, in this comprehensive form, would continue in effect until 1896.

In the 1870s Brazil's empire began crumbling in the face of a new regional order. As the emperor's power was eclipsed by modernizing landowners, especially in the prosperous and politically powerful cof-

fee-growing state of São Paulo, immigration policy took on new importance.[32] Landowners began pressuring the imperial government to create a mass colonization policy that would fill São Paulo with European
workers who, it was believed, were better workers than slaves and ex-
slaves, would re-create Brazil in Europe's image, and would transform
the economy from slave to wage labor.[33] In 1888 the abolition of slavery took place, and in 1891 Brazil's first republican constitution, which
included a guarantee of religious freedom, was promulgated. The societal changes, and a new system that subsidized transportation to Brazil
for immigrants, made the republican model far more attractive than the
imperial one. Between 1890 and 1919 more than 2.6 million immigrants entered the nation, the majority of them Southern European
Catholics (usually Italians) who stayed permanently.[34]

At the end of the nineteenth century many elites believed that the
question of immigration was nearly resolved. Brazil was in intense competition for immigrants, and politicians did not wonder about the wisdom of an open policy for Europeans.[35] In the early twentieth century,
however, elites increasingly voiced concerns about a perceived failure
of early republican policy to attract workers who would remain on the
land. Some began to wonder if European labor was too politicized, too
lazy, or too greedy, and emphasized the need to find a compliant work
force. The Japanese, perceived as docile yet hard workers, seemed to
fit the bill, and a reformulation of racial notions and their relation to
immigration took place. When the Japanese were denied entry rights by
the United States in 1908, a Japanese-Brazilian agreement led Japanese
immigrants to move to Brazil on a large scale.[36] The debates over the
wisdom of Japanese immigration provided intellectuals and politicians
with a new forum with which to express their notions of Brazilian economic and social development. During the 1920s, as a series of economic crises hit Brazil, immigrants began to find themselves the targets
of growing nativist movements. Brought to Brazil to produce wealth,
immigrants, white and nonwhite, seemed to have failed.

Because immigrants were at least partially blamed for many of Brazil's ills, those entering the country in significant numbers in the 1920s
and 1930s, especially after the depression, became especially vulnera-
ble. Thus, while few Jews had immigrated to Brazil in the nineteenth
century, after 1920 their growing numbers, perhaps as much as 50 percent of a rapidly growing Eastern European stream, made them targets
for nativists. Although Japanese immigrants were often attacked for
their racial and ethnic differences, large landowners who desired rural

workers continued to support them. Jews, on the other hand, challenged the long-held assumptions that all European immigrants were Christian and that all immigrants should work on the land.

Most Brazilians knew little about Jews in the nineteenth and early twentieth centuries. Most Jews knew just as little about Brazil. If any images existed among either group, these were not the result of human contact: there had been no major Jewish migration to Brazil since the Inquisition, when Jews had fled the Iberian Peninsula.[37] These Jews, variously called Judaizantes, Marranos, Conversos, and Cristãos Novos (New Christians), came in small numbers to escape the economic, social, and religious persecution of the church and crown. Their presence, however, never encouraged large-scale Jewish immigration to colonial Brazil, even though New Christians may have made up as much as 20 percent of the white population of the colonial capital of Salvador, Bahia.[38]

Independence, achieved in 1822, ended official persecution of Jews, even though the Catholic Church remained established and non-Catholics were not permitted public exercise of their faith. Limitations of religious freedom were relaxed in the later years of the Empire to encourage Protestant immigration. Although the census of 1872 recorded no Jewish inhabitants in Brazil, perhaps two thousand Jews did enter during the imperial era, and made significant social and economic progress in the capital of Rio de Janeiro.[39] They formed some communal institutions, but their small numbers did not compare with the masses arriving in other American nations.[40] Dom Pedro II, Brazil's emperor from 1841 to 1889, although a friend and admirer of Gobineau, has been described by some as a philo-Semite, but the Hebrew liturgical poems he translated into French are not fully convincing evidence.[41] Even with few Jews, however, some instances of anti-Semitism remained. In 1852 Robert Schenck, Millard Fillmore's minister plenipotentiary and envoy extraordinary to Brazil, reported that the use of Judas effigies on Good Friday was an "occasion of insulting poor Jews."[42]

Brazil had a negative image among Europeans, including Jews, in the mid to late nineteenth century. Indeed, the first proposal for planned Jewish colonization in Brazil, in 1881, was never even completed.[43] A decade later, more serious thought was given to mass settlement when Czar Nicholas II expelled all Jews from Moscow as part of his "Russification" plan, an important component of which was the compulsory practice of the Russian Orthodox religion.[44] In Germany, Jewish communal leaders, fearful that the Russian Jews might resettle among them and interfere with the process of acculturation begun so auspiciously under Napoléon's emancipation decree, set out to find some alternate places of residence for the refugees. They quickly set up an agency, the Deutsches Zentral Komitee für die Russischen Juden (German Central Committee for Russian Jews), and sent Oswald Boxer, a Viennese journalist and friend of the Zionist leader Theodore Herzl, to Brazil to investigate possibilities for the resettlement of Russian Jewry as farmers.[45] Notions of return to the land, then popular among European Jewish intellectuals, led many in the Deutsches Zentral Komitee to ignore the fact that most Muscovite Jews were urban tradespeople and not farmers. Regardless of this difficulty, Boxer reported enthusiastically to the committee after visiting São Paulo and Rio in May 1891.[46] The high hopes were dashed when a series of political changes, including the "revolution" that transformed Brazil into a republic and the subsequent coup that removed General Deodoro da Fonseca from the ruling junta, discouraged the Deutsches Zentral Komitee from sending any immigrants to Brazil. The secular nature of the new Brazilian Republic, and the end of all legal distinction of religious affiliation, did not soothe other fears that were confirmed in 1892 when Oswald Boxer died of yellow fever in Rio de Janeiro.[47]

At the end of the nineteenth century Brazil's Jewish population was small, officially consisting of only three hundred people.[48] It is more likely, however, that the number was somewhat closer to three thousand.[49] Some were the descendants of Haquitia and Ladino-speaking Sephardic North Africans who had migrated to the Amazon to participate in the emerging rubber economy of the mid to late nineteenth century.[50] Others were single men from rural Bessarabia who "came with the idea of making money and returning home."[51] Jews from England, Alsace-Lorraine, Germany, and the United States made up part of an immigrant middle class of tradespeople, skilled workers, and professionals who dominated commerce and manufacturing in Rio de Janeiro.[52] Members of neither the urban class nor the rural laboring class, most had settled in Brazil for professional reasons.

In the early twentieth century, few European Jews went to Brazil, since more desirable locations, such as the United States and Canada, constructed no barriers to Jewish entry. As the numbers of Jews leaving Europe increased after 1900, however, Baron Maurice de Hirsch de Gereuth (Moritz Baron Hirsch), a Bavarian-born Jewish philanthropist living in Brussels, decided "to stake my wealth and intellectual powers

. . . to give a portion of my companions in faith the possibility of finding a new existence, primarily as farmers and also as artisans, in those lands where the laws and religious tolerance permit them to carry on the struggle for existence. . . . "[53] Finding that money was available from a number of European sources, the baron founded the Jewish Colonization Association, or ICA (in Yiddish, the Yidishe Kolonizatsye Gezelshaft), in 1891 with the specific purpose of aiding poverty-stricken Eastern European and Balkan Jewry by establishing Jewish farming colonies in the Americas.[54] In 1893 the ICA set up its first colony in Moisesville, Argentina, to provide for Russian Jews already in the area.[55] Consequently boatloads of ICA-sponsored Jews arrived in the country.[56] In 1896 Hirsch died, bequeathing the funds needed to expand the organization's scope of activity. In early 1901 the ICA began to investigate expansion into Brazil, and the state of Rio Grande do Sul, because of its proximity to the Argentine colonies and the state government's desire for new colonists, was thought to be a good home for Russian Jews.[57] It was also attractive because the Positivist-influenced Rio Grande do Sul Republican Party (PRR) was tolerant in matters of religion, an important factor for immigrants being persecuted for religious reasons in the Russian Empire.[58] PRR leader Júlio de Castilhos believed that guaranteed freedom of religion fostered spontaneous immigration and was required in a scientifically based state in which religion had no political or important social role to play.[59]

Between 1904 and 1924 the ICA formed two Jewish agricultural colonies on the frontier of Rio Grande do Sul.[60] The Eastern European Jewish colonists who settled in Brazil never amounted to more than a few thousand people, yet they played two critical roles. First, the mere existence of the agricultural colonies challenged images of Jews as exclusively and insidiously oriented toward finance and capital in urban areas. Furthermore, residents of the colonies committed themselves to life in Brazil. This challenged notions that Jews were a closed group, uninterested in becoming citizens of countries where they resided. The two farming colonies were the first step in the regular and organized migration of Jews to Brazil. As the victims of czarist "Russification" policy, these Jews fled daily persecution and accepted farming, with which they had little or no experience, only as a condition of their escape. Jews never shared the dream of returning wealthy—the dream of *fazer a América*. Immigration to Brazil was the start of a new life that could never include a return home.

The ICA brought Jewish immigration to the official attention of Bra-

zilian leaders for the first time since the Inquisition. This occurred for a
number of reasons. First, the association enjoyed the diplomatic support of a British government committed to ensuring that emigrating
Russian Jewry would resettle outside of the United Kingdom. Thus in
times of crisis, the Rio Grande do Sul government would often find the
Jewish colonies represented by extremely powerful English diplomats.
Furthermore, some of the ICA's most powerful directors were also
heavy investors in the Brazilian economy. Thus the ICA provided legitimate refugee relief even while representing foreign interests in Brazil.
As a result, a particularly strong relationship developed between the
ICA, committed to Jewish resettlement, and the Rio Grande do Sul government, interested in subsidizing and sponsoring agricultural colonization and encouraging foreign investment.[61]

There is no doubt that the Jewish colonies held special meaning for
gaúcho (the term for residents of Rio Grande do Sul) leaders. When the
Rio Grande do Sul government decided to promote colonization at the
St. Louis International Exhibition of 1904, the official English-language
Descriptive Memorial of the State of Rio Grande do Sul singled out the
Jewish colonies, and no others, as examples of the positive results of
colonization in the area.[62] This initial interest in Jewish immigration
was important since many members of the Rio Grande do Sul government in the first few decades of the twentieth century would become
federal leaders when Getúlio Vargas (himself a politician from Rio
Grande do Sul) led the coup that made him president of Brazil in 1930.
Indeed, these politicians had positive images of Jewish immigration that
were unrelated to ethnic or religious factors. Simply by chance, the ICA
began setting up its colonies during a period when immigration to Brazil
fell significantly, a situation generated in large part because of a crisis
in the coffee industry generated by overproduction. Furthermore, a general recuperation of the Italian economy decreased the entry of Italians,
a group that provided almost 60 percent of all immigrants to Brazil
between 1880 and 1900.[63]

Since few people knew much about Jews in early twentieth-century
Brazil, politicians and large landowners were happy to support any
group that would work the land in frontier regions. The positive attitude, however, was to change as more Jews entered Brazil in the next
three decades. Those opposed to Brazil's changing economic order
claimed that Jews were unacceptable in Brazilian society because many
had left the colonies for the city, a seeming confirmation of a number
of anti-Semitic accusations. Nativists pointed to the regular migration

of Jews from the Rio Grande do Sul colonies to urban areas as evidence that Jews could not fit into Brazil's agricultural orientation. Some on the left pointed to the European-based ICA as an example of an alleged international Jewish capitalist conspiracy. For those on the right, the ICA's international and domestic connections gave the impression of an insular, powerful, and not easily identifiable group. Surprisingly, in 1942, when Brazil entered the war on the Allied side, the Jewish colonies (with only tiny Jewish populations at the time) were again pointed to, this time as positive examples of how well immigrant groups had integrated into Brazilian society. Jewish colonization, then, set the initial parameters for the discussion of Jewish immigration during the first decades of the twentieth century.

The pattern of immigration to Brazil, both general and Jewish, changed when the violence and dislocation of World War I was unleashed upon the world. Although not militarily involved, Brazil suffered inflation, shortages, and capital market shifts that scarred its already troubled social and economic face. Yet a quieter, more subtle change also occurred with the coming of global war. Throughout the Americas the streams of immigrants that had poured from Europe to new, promised lands were shut off. In Europe, World War I temporarily strengthened local economies, demanded men to fill its armies, and commandeered shipping and passenger space for military purposes. With the end of the war, immigration restriction became the rule, and as nativist movements arose throughout the Western Hemisphere, immigration decreased.

Such was almost the case in Brazil. The number of migrants entering Brazil's ports fell by over 50 percent between 1913 and 1914 and by another 60 percent the year after. In 1918 fewer than twenty thousand immigrants entered Brazil, a low that would not again be approached until 1936.[64] But with the end of World War I, large numbers of people renewed their migration, in part because Brazil did not respond to its local nationalist movements with immigration quotas. Between 1918 and 1919 the number of arrivals to Brazil's ports almost doubled, and in 1920 almost doubled again, reaching sixty-nine thousand.[65] These postwar immigrants differed in many ways from the prewar group, both in national origin and in their view of success and opportunity. Although Portuguese, Italian, Spanish, and German immigrants continued to predominate, two new groups now entered in growing numbers: Japanese and Eastern Europeans.[66] Population pressure on Japan's islands, and the growing unrest it caused among Japanese rural folk, led the Meiji regime and its Taisho successors to encourage emigration.[67] These "push" factors combined with growing legislative and popular anti-Asian movements throughout the Americas. When Japanese entry into the U.S. was banned in 1908, Brazil became the center of an ever-growing Japanese diaspora.[68] In the two decades following World War I, more than one hundred fifty thousand Japanese immigrants entered Brazil.[69]

East Europeans also began entering Brazil in large numbers after the war. The upheavals created by the establishment of the new state of Poland encouraged this emigration, as did restrictive quotas in the United States.[70] Argentina and Canada also increasingly closed their doors to foreigners, and between 1924 and 1934 Eastern European im-migration to Brazil increased almost ten times as more than ninety-three thousand entered.[71] The frequently destitute Eastern European immi-grants to Brazil rarely enjoyed the support of their often powerless gov-ernments. As late as 1927, a contract between the Polish government and Brazil's secretary of agriculture for the transportation of two thou-sand Polish families was based on a notion that the mixing of Eastern Europeans with other immigrants would "go a long way to obviate any labor trouble that might otherwise occur." [72] Whatever positive attri-butes the Eastern Europeans might have presented to Brazilian elites in terms of "dividing and conquering," the Lithuanian government com-plained that the condition of its twenty thousand immigrants was "so pitiable . . . that [we] might be forced to repatriate them." [73]

Jews made up about 45 to 50 percent of those immigrants arriving in Brazil from Eastern Europe.[74] Like all Eastern Europeans, Jews re-evaluated Brazil's potential as a country of resettlement as the economy seemed increasingly prosperous in the face of a shift toward industrial development after World War I. Jews, however, were not simply pulled toward Brazil; their increasingly precarious position in Eastern Europe provided encouragement to leave. By the mid-1920s more than 10 per-cent of the Jews emigrating from Europe chose Brazil as their destina-tion, and by the early 1930s the Jewish population of Brazil approached sixty thousand.

The Eastern European Jews who arrived in Brazil after World War I and the Russian Revolution settled primarily in the states of São Paulo, Rio Grande do Sul, and Rio de Janeiro and achieved a level of economic success matched by only a few other immigrant groups in Brazil. This occurred because Jewish immigrants usually settled in or near urban centers, although they were no more city-based than any other immigrant group prior to migration. Jews, unlike other immigrant groups, did rely on international relief organizations, whose main offices were uniformly in port cities, to provide them with passage out of Europe and a start in their new homes. Thus, new Jewish arrivals settled where aid was most available, and soon family members, friends, and former neighbors who had previously migrated added a series of relief and communal institutions for newcomers.[75] This urban placement was fortuitous since the cities provided, in the 1920s and 1930s, economic opportunities that may never have been available in rural areas. The ability to quickly earn an income combined with the communal and ethnic-based nature of the immigration process to lead Jewish immigrants into establishing burial societies, youth groups, schools, and synagogues. With the establishment of Jewish institutions, Jewish families were more likely to invest their time and capital in a Brazilian future and less likely to leave. By the mid-1920s, Brazil was an attractive nation of relocation for Jews.

Jewish immigrants to Brazil rarely saw their move as an attempt to get rich overseas and return home. Economic opportunity, however, was an important component of the migratory process. Many Jews had lived in towns prior to migration and thus had some experience in small business and trade. An ever-increasing match between Eastern European economic skills and the demands of the Brazilian economy for commercial and industrial activity helped Jews rise to positions of economic security. Jews found that peddling and textiles, not farming, gave them access to economic success. By the end of the 1920s European Jews saw that Brazil provided positive options for both secular and religious life. As other American republics restricted immigration through legislation, Brazil, with its huge expanses of underpopulated land, growing urban centers, relatively open immigration laws, and seeming lack of anti-Semitism, did indeed seem *o país do futuro*.

Between 1920 and 1930 about thirty thousand Jews immigrated to Brazil, making it the third most important receiving country in the Americas after the United States and Argentina. In one five-year period almost 13 percent of all Jews leaving their countries of origin went to Brazil. The sharp increase in Jewish migration to Brazil did not go unnoticed, and some relief workers believed that "the European Jew has adopted a new slogan: 'Go South, young man, go South!' "[76] These immigrants, for the most part, actively maintained many aspects of their premigration culture and were an extremely visible "other" in the mélange of immigrants who inhabited Brazil.

The combination of economic success and cultural difference made Jews particular targets of nativists after the Depression. Immigrants had been expected to save Brazil's agricultural economy and Europeanize the culture at the same time. Jews seemed to do neither. By 1934 immigration quotas had been established via a new constitution, and criticism of Jewish immigration was becoming a regular component of political discourse. It is this clash between the elite's expectations of immigrants and the Jews' nonconformity to these expectations that provides the background for the longest part of this study. As popular and political nationalism grew, Jews found themselves singled out for negative treatment by the Brazilian government.[77] Yet unlike the Japanese, whose diplomats took a very active role in the lives of their nationals, Jews had no official diplomatic representation and were thus an easy target.[78]

The growing Jewish immigrant population, a worsening economy, and rising nativism made the Jewish Question an important topic among intellectuals, state politicians from urban areas, and federal leaders. This was reinforced when the rise of National Socialism in Germany and Fascism in Italy simultaneously provided a model for anti-Semitism and forced even more Jews to look to Brazil and other American republics for refuge. Beginning in 1935, Brazil began to deny visas to Jews. The existence of Nazi ideology made anti-Semitism respectable, and this surely played a role in how Brazilian policymakers reacted when confronted with growing pressure to accept Jewish immigrants and refugees. Modern European racial theories encouraged the view of Jews as an undesirable race. My research, however, has not produced any evidence that suggests that restrictions on Jewish immigration were related to conscious attempts to curry favor with the Hitler regime.[79] In one case, a group of Jews given special certificates of moral conduct by the Nazis in order to facilitate their entry into Brazil was even prohibited from entering.

Anti-Semitism was rampant among Brazilian intellectuals and federal policymakers in the 1930s. Yet only 11 percent more Jews, representing about three thousand people, entered Brazil between 1920 and 1930 than did between 1930 and 1940. (See appendixes 2 and 5.) In other words, the growing public discourse opposing Jewish entry, and the resulting prohibition on Jewish entrances, neither stopped Jewish entry nor particularly changed its pattern. There are a number of reasons for this. Complaints to senators, members of parliament, and congressmen by Jewish tourists and businesspeople from the United States,

Canada, Britain, and South Africa led those governments to put pressure on Brazil to modify its restrictions. Furthermore, the appointment
of former ambassador to the United States Oswaldo Aranha as foreign
minister helped a philo-Semitic vision of "the Jew" to gain credence
within the government. From this perspective German, Italian, and Austrian Jewish refugees were increasingly seen as bringing skills and capital to Brazil. International pressure to accept refugees was matched by
a change in perception among some of Brazil's most important immigration policymakers.[80] By 1938 new rules regarding Jewish immigration reopened Brazil's gates to such an extent that more Jews were to
enter than in any of the ten years previously.

Jews, in spite of their perceived undesirability, were often welcomed
in Brazil. Fluid perceptions of Jews held by Brazilian political leaders
and intellectuals, and the manipulation of these notions in order to save
the lives of refugees, explain why restrictive laws were enacted in the
1930s in spite of a desire for immigrants and why Jewish immigration
continued in spite of restrictions to the contrary. The story, however,
begins in the 1920s, when a change in Brazil's image and increasingly
restrictive immigration laws in the United States, Canada, and Argentina led large numbers of Eastern European Jews to choose Brazil as a
new home.

CHAPTER ONE

The "Other" Arrives

With the end of World War I, Jews began arriving in Brazil in ever-growing numbers.[1] This was partly a result of changes in immigration legislation in the United States, Canada, Argentina, and South Africa, where restrictive immigration acts reduced Jewish entrances.[2] The National Origins Act, which enacted a quota system in the United States in 1921 that was strengthened in 1924, provided a model for countries desiring to restrict immigrants. Similar Canadian legislation led to a 75 percent drop in Jewish immigration between 1922 and 1923, and later increases never again approached the 1922 high.[3] The Argentine government significantly decreased Jewish immigration in late 1922 by withdrawing permission from the Jewish Colonization Association, and all other immigration and colonization organizations, to certify immigrants for passport visas. Another law instructed Argentine consuls to issue visas to emigrants only in their countries of birth, making it virtually impossible for large segments of the Jewish refugee population to obtain visas.[4]

Why did Jews start migrating to Brazil in large numbers after World War I? One answer, commonly heard among those in the business of refugee relief, was that only "when the gates of the United States were closed against immigration, the more or less regular immigration of families to Brazil commenced."[5] This interpretation, in addition to implying a certain passivity, explains only why Jews were unable to enter other American nations and why Jewish international relief groups put a new emphasis on Brazil. It does not explain why Jewish immigrants

TABLE 1.1

JEWISH AND GENERAL IMMIGRATION TO BRAZIL, 1925–1929

Year	General	% Change	Jewish	% Change
1925	82,547	—	1,690	—
1926	118,686	44	3,154	87
1927	97,974	−17	3,175	0
1928	78,128	−19	3,167	0
1929	96,186	23	4,874	54

SOURCES "Discriminação por nacionalidade dos imigrantes entrando no Brasil no período 1924–1933 e 1934–1939," *RIC* 1:3 (July 1940), 633–38. SCA 1926–1935, JCA-L.

began to accept Brazil as a nation for relocation after previously rejecting it. A better explanation, perhaps, has to do with the immigrants themselves. Active choices played a critical role, and Brazil's new popularity lay, at least in part, in the expectations immigrants had about the chances of future success.

There were a number of reasons Brazil's image began to improve in the 1920s. One was location. For those wishing to establish themselves in well-known Argentina, Brazil was a strategically placed and convenient way station out of Eastern Europe.[6] Yet even if significant numbers intended to move elsewhere, Brazil's relatively strong economy was attractive. Newly formed communal and religious institutions provided funding and social help for newcomers. As Jews prospered in small and large cities throughout the states of Rio Grande do Sul, São Paulo, Rio de Janeiro, and Paraná, they sent a new message back to Europe. Brazil was no longer the *land fun di mahlpes* (land of the monkeys) but a land of prosperity and little religious conflict. Substantial post–World War I industrial economic growth provided jobs, and, for Jews encountering economic restrictions in Eastern Europe, Brazil's developing economy acted as a magnet.

At the same time that Jewish migration to Brazil was increasing, Brazil began to tighten its own immigration procedures, although not to the extent of other American nations. In 1921 Epitácio Pessoa's government mandated that immigrants prove they could financially survive in Brazil as a condition of entrance.[7] Even so, Brazil continued to be one of the few large American republics without quotas. The Jewish Colonization Association, while continuing to target Brazil as a nation of relocation, realized that the federal government was increasingly restricting

immigration. The ICA thus decided to appoint Rabbi Isaiah Raffalovich, formerly the director of a large Jewish relocation center in Liverpool, as head of operations in Brazil in December 1923. Raffalovich
was a superb choice for the job: he was an experienced politician who
worked well with Jewish and non-Jewish political leaders and social
organizations.[8]

One of Raffalovich's first decisions was to urge the relocation of the
ICA central office to Brazil's political capital, Rio de Janeiro, where he
could deal directly with those involved in making, and making exceptions to, Brazil's increasingly complicated immigration laws. Visas, for
example, could no longer be issued without specific approval from Rio
de Janeiro, and many Jewish applicants were waiting in cities like Warsaw and Bucharest.[9] As a result, Jews had "a tendency for immigration
into Uruguay [even though] none of these immigrants have anybody to
join [but] their only reason being the difficulty in obtaining the Brazilian
Consul's visa."[10] Finding the situation intolerable, the new ICA director hoped to "obtain the goodwill of the Brazilian Government Authorities, in order that restrictions on immigration may be removed and, if
possible, concessions procured for future immigrants."[11] Raffalovich's
political experience paid off. He befriended Arthur Haas, a well-con-
nected French Jewish immigrant who lived in Belo Horizonte and had
cofounded the Siderúrgica Belgo-Mineira ironworks as well as intro-
ducing the first windmill and Ford automobile to the state. Through
Haas, Raffalovich was introduced into high political circles.[12] Pleading
his case directly to the ministers of foreign affairs and of agriculture,
both of whom became "very interested in our work," the rabbi was able
to garner special concessions for immigrants sponsored by the ICA.[13] A
few months later, the minister of foreign affairs pledged that those holding ICA certificates of recommendation would be assured a Brazilian
visa.[14]

Raffalovich's growing connections worked particularly well in 1924,
when Brazil tightened its immigration laws even further. Only federally
approved navigation companies could now bring immigrants to Brazil.[15] Second- and third-class non-Brazilian passengers were all defined
as immigrants and allowed disembarkation only if possessing a series
of documents including police good-conduct certificates.[16] Entries were
restricted to specific ports, and all immigrants entering through Rio de
Janeiro were required to pass a health inspection.[17] None of this
stopped Raffalovich, who responded by making applicants for visas
seem to fit the immigration categories set up by the legislation. Skirting

laws intended to promote the entry of farmers, the Jewish Colonization Association subsidized the fares of family members of colonists without requiring them to work on the Rio Grande do Sul colonies.[18] This worked only in a limited way, and Raffalovich believed that "without an agricultural basis we cannot hope for any appreciable immigration into Brazil."[19] Claiming erroneously that Brazil had no industries in which to employ factory workers, Raffalovich believed that the arrival of Jews without agricultural skills was dangerous: "We shall not only be overwhelmed with an indigent mass with whom we shall not be able to cope, but a howl will be raised in the familiar tone of European anti-semitism."[20]

Raffalovich was correct in his assessment. Following notices in Rio de Janeiro's major newspapers of a meeting between the rabbi and the minister of agriculture, one journal, "in the orthodox fashion of the Jew baiters," printed a series of articles warning against Jewish immigration.[21] In response Raffalovich befriended the editors of local newspapers in order to keep anti-Semitic articles from appearing. Furthermore, he believed that the only way to gain "the sympathy and cooperation of the Government [and] of the Brazilian people" was to demonstrate that the objective of the Jewish Colonization Association was to "plant on Brazilian soil workers and producers."[22] Such statements endeared the rabbi to many in the Brazilian government, and the mid-twenties marked a high point in the relationship between the government and the ICA. The immigration department, part of the Ministry of Agriculture, was "constantly at our service and at our request grants free passages into the interior to our immigrants." In 1926 consuls at Riga, Danzig, Paris, Warsaw, and Galatz were ordered by the Foreign Ministry to grant visas to ICA-sponsored holders of Russian passports in spite of a special order denying visas to Russians.[23] Similar service was granted by the intendant of the state of São Paulo.[24]

By the early 1920s, Brazil was so popular that some Eastern European Jews had even concocted a complicated scheme to gain passages and visas. First, they applied to work on one of the Jewish colonies in Rio Grande do Sul, thus garnering a free passage from the ICA. Once in Rio Grande do Sul, they would quickly find a free train ride from Porto Alegre to São Paulo by agreeing to work on a São Paulo coffee plantation. Many then jumped train, since they were "artisans such as carpenters, blacksmiths and shoemakers who can find work in São Paulo and its environs."[25] After arriving in São Paulo they presented themselves to local relief organizations as refugees who had arrived independently, in order to receive aid and language classes.[26]

Brazil's doors had been pried open, and one relief group, the United Evacuation Committee, sent more refugees to Brazil than to the United States or Argentina.[27] Brazil's positive image among relief groups was heightened in 1923 when the ICA received a colonization offer from a company "backed by the Brazilian Government" that would provide free transport and land for Jewish refugees moving to rural areas.[28] Although a "high official" supervised the project, nothing came of it. Even so, the putative willingness of the government to encourage Jewish immigration led the ICA to press for more immigration to Brazil. By the mid-1920s Brazil was *a tsukunftsland far idisher emigratsye*—a land of the future for Jewish emigrants.[29]

THE ROOTS OF THE ANTI-JEWISH IMMIGRANT MOVEMENT

The same forces that had led to a positive reevaluation of Brazil as a nation of relocation by European Jews also frightened many Brazilians. The population of the country was exploding, and the census of 1920 showed an increase of over 13 million people in just twenty years (from 17.3 to 30.6 million), a significant portion of it as a result of immigration.[30] Almost half of Brazil's urban population lived in just two cities, Rio de Janeiro and São Paulo, and Porto Alegre was becoming a metropolis as well. São Paulo, now Brazil's second largest city, absorbed almost 60 percent of the immigrants entering Brazil between 1901 and 1920. Immigrants represented 10 percent of the male labor force in Brazil, and many had become moderately successful, in part because they were more literate than native Brazilians and in part because the Brazilian state had invested heavily in them through the subsidized immigration policy.[31] At the same time, a growing number of native Brazilians were descending the economic ladder, expressing their frustration in riots or via organized resistance to compulsory military service or rapidly rising prices.[32]

Immigration played a major role in the development of new social conflicts in São Paulo, Rio de Janeiro, and Porto Alegre, not coincidentally the areas where Jewish immigrants concentrated.[33] As natives found their expectations for success unfulfilled, state and federal politicians soon realized that anti-immigrant rhetoric held a potent attraction

TABLE 1.2

JEWISH IMMIGRATION TO BRAZIL, BY COUNTRY OF ORIGIN, 1925–1935

Country	1925	1926	1927	1928	1929	1930	1931	1932	1933	1934	1935
Poland	802	1,009	1,095	1,290	2,765	1,168	753	931	1,920	1,746	1,130
Germany	0	0	0	0	0	0	0	0	363	835	357
Russia	225	283	286	315	0	0	0	0	0	0	0
Lithuania	0	0	0	151	60	7	0	0	0	0	0
Romania	220	283	571	43	58	0	135	0	210	292	127
Other	0	0	0	0	0	0	0	0	824	921	144
Total	1,690	3,154	3,175	3,167	4,874	3,558	1,985	2,049	3,317	3,794	1,758

SOURCES Figures on Eastern European immigration from SCA, 1925–1933, JCA-L. Figures on German immigration from "Les juifs dans l'histoire du Brésil," *Rapport d'activité pendant la période 1933–43*, HIAS-Brazil, folder 1, YIVO-NY. Totals from "Discriminação por nacionalidade dos imigrantes entrando no Brasil no período 1924–1933 e 1934–1939," *RIC* 1:3 (July 1940), 633–38. Discrepancies in totals can be attributed to different sources.

for many urban voters. In the 1920s nativists increasingly turned their attention toward attacking Jews, often using the eugenics-influenced language of Central and Western European anti-Semitism. The fact that most Jewish immigrants were from post–Russian Revolution Eastern Europe provided fodder for leading Brazilian intellectuals and politicians to confirm their prejudices of all Jews as communists and economic exploiters. The press, policymakers, and academics commented on "The Jewish Problem" more than would be expected given the relatively modest size of the community.

The specter of a "Jewish invasion" was especially apparent in discussions of immigration. In 1923 Francisco José Oliveira Vianna, a lawyer and historian who was one of Brazil's most important theoreticians of ethnicity and an architect of modern Brazilian immigration policy, testified before the Chamber of Deputies that "the intensive Aryanization of our ethnic composition" should be a priority.[34] A year later Alcibíades Delamare, an intellectual whose periodical *Gil Blas* was a self-described nationalist pamphlet, helped form the Academia Brasileira de Estudos Econômicos e Sociais in Rio de Janeiro along with Nicolau José Debané and others who in the 1930s would be associated with the anti-immigrant group the Society of the Friends of Alberto Torres. Apparently Delamare frequently attacked foreigners through references to an unpublished tract by Álvaro Bomilcar titled *A ordem militar e a ordem judaica*.[35] Rio de Janeiro's *O Brasil* (which should not be confused with the monarchist journal of the same name) agreed, printing a "virulent anti-Semitic article that warns against the immigration of Jews who are not producers but will come to [Brazil] to exploit the inhabitants."[36]

Attacks on Jews came not only from academics and the press, but from politicians as well. In 1923 Fidelis Reis, an influential and longtime federal deputy from Minas Gerais's Partido Republicano Mineiro best known for his attempts to ban all immigrants of African and Asian descent, worried that "the Jewish Colonization Association is interested in acquiring vast stretches of land in Rio Grande do Sul," even though the organization had not purchased any land in Brazil after 1912 and no longer even promoted colonization. Although only ten thousand of Brazil's approximately 30 million inhabitants were Jewish, Reis, founder of the Minas Gerais engineering faculty and former director of the Sociedade Mineira de Agricultura, demanded that Brazilian society confront what he believed was a new social danger.[37]

Reis's vision of Jews became increasingly common among Brazilian politicians in the 1920s.[38] Jewish visibility, and the fascination and disgust that went with it, were the result of the concentration of Jews in specific neighborhoods in São Paulo, Rio de Janeiro, and Porto Alegre and concomitant concerns about assimilability and integration. That many Jews spoke Yiddish and did not worship as the majority did gave the group an exotic appeal. Imaginations were inflamed, and anti-Semites found an easy target when a small group of Jewish immigrant pimps and prostitutes were discovered operating in Brazil. Yet what really separated Jews from other European immigrants in Brazil, and made them a subject of scrutiny by non-Jews, was their concentration in a series of very visible occupations, mainly peddling and the textile trades, in which they had rapid success. Their increasing affluence brought out the latent racism and anti-Semitism of the society that surrounded them.[39] Within a decade, Jews would find themselves restricted from entering Brazil.

PEDDLERS AND PROSTITUTES

Most Jews arriving in Brazil in the 1920s came from Eastern Europe, primarily from Poland. Comprising a little over 10 percent of Poland's population, Jews were relatively urbanized, and were concentrated occupationally in manufacturing and trade.[40] Those with experience and skills—such as tailors, mechanics, and shoemakers—were needed, especially in the industrializing cities of the south, but Jewish immigrants rarely had the capital to purchase a shop or factory upon arrival in one of Brazil's urban centers. These immigrants were often aided by *laispar kasses,* loan societies that provided peddlers with the initial funds to purchase goods or help open a small shop or factory. Although each Jewish loan society functioned differently, all allowed an immigrant to form a cash base.[41]

About 35 percent of the Jews arriving in Brazil had no profession or salable skills and thus entered the life of the *clientelchik* (Brazilian Yiddish for "peddler"; the Brazilian Portuguese equivalent term was *mascate*), an occupation that did not demand a large initial capital investment.[42] Peddling, although hard work, was a prototype of Jewish economic integration in Brazil. Jewish store or factory owners would sell piece goods or housewares on credit to the newcomers, often choosing agents who were relations or townspeople in their countries of origin. In cities with small Jewish populations, as many as 80 percent of the new immigrant males worked as peddlers, although the percentages

were considerably lower in Rio de Janeiro and São Paulo.[43] The willingness of Jewish immigrants to work intensely as peddlers proved so lucrative for them that it often led to their owning small shops or factories
and an even more rapid accumulation of capital. With a niche carved
out, Jews began to ascend the economic ladder, especially in the textile
industry.[44]

Brazil was fertile ground for peddling.[45] Some European immigrants
peddled clandestinely in the mid-nineteenth century, but legal peddling
began on a large scale in the very late 1800s with Syrian and Lebanese
immigrants who arrived to the wider markets created by abolition.
When more Syrians and Lebanese immigrated during the coffee boom,
they also entered the field, often carrying their goods on mules throughout the interiors of São Paulo and Paraná.[46] This set the stage for the
acceptance of Jewish peddlers a generation later as Brazil experienced
significant population growth. By the 1920s a middle class had formed,
and with it came a desire for previously unavailable goods. Yet product
distribution did not progress as efficiently as industrial growth and capital redistribution. In cities and rural areas, peddlers picked up the slack,
distributing products in an efficient and inexpensive manner.

Jewish *clientelchiks* often purchased goods wholesale from Syrian
and Lebanese former peddlers who had become wholesalers.[47] Like
these earlier immigrants, Jews "habitually travelled in groups of two, in
part because of the dangers in some places, but also to help business."[48]
An experienced peddler helped the newcomer earn some income while
teaching him Portuguese phrases and a sales pitch, and "little by little,
the neophyte acquired a rudimentary knowledge of the language, the
money, [and] how often to frequent the streets."[49] Since many Jewish
immigrants had experience in textiles prior to migration, they gravi-
tated to the peddling of cloth, clothing, and sewing implements, something that often drew negative comments from the press.[50] By the late
1930s, 54 percent of the industries in Luz, a São Paulo district with a
high Jewish population, produced clothing and cloth articles.[51]

Peddling was such an important part of immigrant life that Brazilian-
Jewish humor of the era even included "*clientelchik* stories." One of the
most popular folk tales told of Natanson:

> One day Natanson visited a client named Kalmanovitch in order to sell him
> some goods, and the following conversation was reported to have ensued:
>
> K: Thank you, my friend, but I don't need anything.
> N: Cotton? Are you sure you don't need some?
> K: No.

N: And silks?

K: No.

N: And belts?

K: No.

After responding "no" to all of Natanson's questions, Kalmanovitch asked the *clientelchik* to leave so he could go on with his work. As Natanson was leaving he suddenly stopped and in a loud voice began reciting the Kaddish, the Jewish prayer for the dead.

K: But, why are you doing this? Why are you saying Kaddish?

Natanson the *clientelchik* shot back, "Because, my friend, for me you died." [52]

In cities across Brazil, from Curitiba in the south to Natal in the northeast, Jewish immigrants worked as peddlers. [53] Saúl Givelder's story is typical. Born in 1906 in Moguilev, Russia, near the Dniester River, Givelder moved with his parents to Bessarabia when Saúl's father became manager of a small nail factory. Saúl attempted to immigrate to Palestine in his late teens but was unable to procure the necessary emigrant visa from the Soviet government. Givelder first considered moving to Brazil because he "had many friends [there], and I had heard they became rich because [it] was a country where you could earn a lot of money." [54] In 1930 he made his way to Marseille, where he purchased a passage with an advance from the Jewish Colonization Association. Upon arrival in Rio de Janeiro, he became an urban peddler after a friend arranged for him to purchase umbrellas on credit. "In truth [Givelder] was not very good" at peddling, but soon he became partners with a friend who owned a shop. This expanded the line of goods he peddled and increased his income. When Givelder's wife came to Rio ten months after his arrival, he already "had a house . . . and the basic necessities were satisfied." [55] Givelder's story was not uncommon among Jewish immigrants in Brazil's large and small cities. One Jewish leader reported that although "the Jewish immigrants have to struggle hard in order to find independent existences . . . they [can] usually start as hawkers until they succeed in establishing themselves as shop-keepers." [56]

Despite the economic support that community institutions provided for *clientelchiks,* peddling elicited ambiguous support from Jewish leaders in Brazil. Many worried that a popular association of Jews with peddling was dangerous because "the trouble is that most immigrants have no trades and to introduce a large number of *luftmenschen* [those with no visible means of support] who should swell the already too large numbers of peddlers is to run the real risk of increased anti-Semitism." [57] These fears were not unfounded. When the highly regarded poet Guilherme de Almeida, a member of Brazil's prestigious Academy of Letters, termed Bom Retiro "The Ghetto" in a series of eight articles on "impressions of our diverse foreign neighborhoods" for the mass-circulation newspaper *O Estado de São Paulo*, he probably meant to conjure up a dual image that combined the notion of a Central European urban neighborhood where Jews were segregated from the surrounding society with the poverty and otherness that non-Jews often associated with the Eastern European *shtetl*.[58] Bom Retiro, however, was neither a legislated Jewish residential area nor particularly poverty-stricken. In fact, Bom Retiro had been an immigrant neighborhood since 1881, when São Paulo's provincial assembly placed an immigrant receiving station there. Almeida's image of Bom Retiro, however, suggests that he believed Jews were somehow less than completely human: "I found myself face to face with the first face [I saw] in the São Paulo ghetto. Face? Beard: beard and nose. The first Jew." [59]

Concern about image was further provoked by the existence of a small but visible number of Jewish pimps and prostitutes in most large cities. Most often associated with Argentina, and more specifically Buenos Aires, where the trade was legalized in 1875, foreign prostitution was introduced on a large scale to Brazil only at the end of the nineteenth century. Non-Brazilian prostitutes, often brought to Buenos Aires and moved overland to Rio, were to be found throughout the country by 1900.[60] The Jewish community vociferously took part in the antiprostitution movement. The Brazilian government also showed its concern and in 1921 insisted on discussing the subject with the International Emigration Commission, a fifteen-nation group headquartered in Geneva. At the meeting, the Brazilian representative noted that "there remains the question of the protection of women and young girls and of the white slave trade. It is in the interest of Brazil to examine this question and to take all steps advisable so as to increase the efficacy of measures already adopted." [61] The various international commissions had little success in stopping the trade, and in 1926 the League of Nations created a special commission to investigate the issue, but it too was powerless.[62]

Even at its height, the number of immigrant Jewish prostitutes in Brazil was relatively small, probably less than 750. Almost 70 percent of the prostitutes registered in São Paulo in 1915 were Brazilian natives, and 35 percent were not white.[63] Of the 3,529 prostitutes arrested by the São Paulo police in 1922, more than 55 percent were Brazilians and less than 15 percent were from Eastern Europe. A study of ten thousand prostitutes published in 1936 found only 17 percent coming from Eastern Europe, certainly not the huge numbers claimed.[64] In spite of the fact that most Jewish prostitutes were thought to be Polish, the 1936 study found only four hundred with that nationality.

It is telling that Jews, who made up a tiny percentage of all prostitutes in Brazil and who, "like prostitutes of color, suffered in the bordellos of the 'red-light' districts," elicited such frequent comment from Brazilians.[65] This was the result of elite concerns about "moral hygiene" that were often expressed in attacks on prostitution among the poorer sectors of the middle class—exactly the clientele of the Jewish prostitutes.[66] Soon the popular press and anti-Semitic "intellectuals," playing upon the traditional Christian view of Judaism as a religion of ritual and not morality, created an image that associated prostitution, and moral decadence, with immigrant Jewry. One of the best examples of this was Francisco Ferreira da Rosa's series on prostitution for Rio's popular daily newspaper *O Paiz,* later used as the basis for his book *O lupanar: Estudo sobre o caftanismo e a prostituição no Rio de Janeiro* (The bordello: A study of pimping and prostitution in Rio de Janeiro), published in 1896. On the surface *O lupanar* was simply a plea for the "moral cleansing of Rio de Janeiro" that would be conducted by protecting innocent women from harmful procurers.[67] Who were these pimps who had to be stopped? "The pimp, generally speaking, is an Israelite, is a *Jew.*"[68] Ferreira da Rosa, who labeled all pimps as "degenerate Israelites" and titled his first full "analytical" chapter "The Jew—The Pimp," was really attacking Jews. Indeed, virtually every person mentioned in *O lupanar* is Jewish, and virtually every anti-Semitic stereotype is expounded. Jews "multiplied themselves in every part of the world." Jews were "petrified in their rites and mummified in their customs, they are a type of human fossil." More frightening, no group "changed more and changed less" than Jews, making them "a privileged race . . . always ready for transformation" that would allow them to infiltrate Christian society.[69]

These turn-of-the-century comments set the stage for an image that linked Jewish immigration, anti-Semitism, and prostitution.[70] A number of scholars have pointed out that in fin de siècle Brazil the word *polaca* was synonymous with prostitute, Jew, and others on the margins of polite society and that the slang word for pimp, *cafetão,* was probably a reference to the caftan, the traditional robe of Eastern European Jewish men.[71] The image of Jews as pimps and prostitutes, then, became part of a societally accepted norm that was probably transformed from one in Christian Europe that linked Jewish men to non-Jewish prostitutes because both were seen to "have but one interest, the conversion of sex into money or money into sex."[72]

The frequent references to prostitutes and pimps in Brazil as *polacas* and *cafetões* were implicitly about Jews, even if the group went unmentioned specifically. Even Gilberto Freyre, who openly defended Jews as one component of Brazilian "racial democracy," was deeply influenced by the negative stereotypes. In his discussion of prostitution in *Ordem e progresso,* Freyre uses the word *cafetão* ten times and cites *O lupanar* eleven times in just two pages.[73] Freyre, furthermore, explicitly mentions the Eastern European background of prostitutes, referring to them as *polacas* and quoting Ferreira da Rosa's comment that the white slave trade was run by "an association composed of Russian Jews, Germans, Austrians and other nationalities."[74] The association between Jewish immigrants and prostitution was not always subtle. *Vida Policial,* a weekly police journal published in Rio de Janeiro between 1925 and 1927, often claimed that white women involved in sex crimes (of which prostitution was only one) were Jewish. Frida Mystal, murdered by strangulation, was characterized in the following manner: "Polish by birth, this Jew conserved the peculiarities of race [perhaps a reference to synagogue attendance or speaking Yiddish] even while a prostitute."[75] In fact, even while articles in *Vida Policial* regularly mentioned the names of other "dishonest women," the magazine focused on the Jewish minority and discussed religion only in reference to Jews.

Jewish prostitution was usually controlled by a multinational crime syndicate founded in Poland, the Zwi Migdal.[76] The Zwi Migdal moved to Buenos Aires in 1904, and in 1909 more than 50 percent of the licensed brothels were said to be run by Jewish madams, and the percentage of Jewish prostitutes in the city may have been even higher.[77] Its network stretched throughout Europe and the Americas and was entrenched in Brazil's large cities, where it, oddly enough, was one of the main patrons of Yiddish culture, particularly the theater. In 1910 the Zwi Migdal branch in Rio de Janeiro held a public march to dedicate the Torah scrolls of its private synagogue, but members of the Jewish community attacked the marchers and took the scrolls.[78] In the 1920s the Zwi Migdal scandalized both Jews and non-Jews alike with the building of a synagogue whose president, a well-known Rio pimp, invited leaders of the Jewish and non-Jewish Brazilian community to a groundbreaking celebration and party.[79]

There is no evidence that Jewish men frequented prostitutes, Jewish or otherwise, any more or less than other immigrant men with resident families. Indeed, since so many Jewish immigrants came to Brazil in complete family units, it is not surprising that the Jewish immigrant community was not ambivalent in rejecting Jewish prostitutes and pimps in social and religious matters as *t'meim* (impure).[80] As a result, the prostitutes and pimps were forced to create a parallel Jewish society. In São Paulo, a group called the Sociedade Religiosa e Beneficente Israelita (SRBI) was formed in 1924, apparently by the prostitutes themselves, to provide a series of Jewish services that the general community refused to provide.[81] The society had fifty-six members at the end of its first year, and its social center/brothel was located in the central red-light district of São Paulo.

The major concern of the SRBI was the future, in part because most of its members died before they were twenty-five.[82] Because most rabbis refused to perform burial rites for known prostitutes, the prostitutes organized their own Jewish cemeteries. It must be emphasized that a desire among prostitutes to be buried in a traditional manner indicates how closed Eastern European Jewish society was; it does not necessarily indicate that the prostitutes were "religious" in the contemporary sense. On December 18, 1924, an "Extraordinary General Assembly" of the SRBI was held to discuss the "acquisition of land to serve as a cemetery for the members," since none desired burial in non-Jewish cemeteries.[83] The SRBI did not have enough money to buy land, and a special fund-raising drive among members was ordered by the group's president. Three years later enough money had been collected to purchase the land and provide regular medical care for all dues-paying members.[84] By 1927, the membership of the Sociedade Religiosa e Beneficente Israelita had grown to seventy-five and the brothel had moved to a larger building.[85]

Jewish law prohibits prostitution, and Brazil's Jewish community actively attempted to stop it. In response to the problem of white slavery, societies for the protection of Jewish women were formed in Brazil, usually with funding from Jewish organizations in Europe. In 1924 Brazil received special emphasis, and in 1925 London's Association for the Protection of Girls and Women singled out Brazil as a problem area.[86] The chair of the B'nai B'rith Committee against White Slavery in Hamburg even translated and abridged *O lupanar* in an attempt to further emphasize the danger to Jews if white slavery continued to be associated with Jews.[87] Brazil's immigrant Jews also took a strong stand, for reasons of morality as much as of appearance. Samuel Malamud, who to-day is still a leading member of Brazil's Jewish community, notes in his memoirs that Rio's Jewish community actually organized a committee to prevent the *mumes* (Yiddish for "aunties") from entering theaters located in Jewish residential areas.[88] Local organizations also watched the docks and prevented single Jewish girls and women from being contacted by Zwi Migdal operatives on arrival. One member of Rio's Jewish community remembered "a lot of white slaves" who were met at the port by relief workers and placed in private homes until legitimate work was found.[89] The vigilance of the Jewish community paralleled the growth of the trade. In 1927 about 100 "young women" were "protected" from pimps in Rio de Janeiro and São Paulo. In 1928 the number surpassed 250, doubling yet again the following year.[90] The community became even more vigilant after the Zwi Migdal leadership tried unsuccessfully to relocate to Rio de Janeiro following the arrest of members in Buenos Aires in 1930.[91] In 1932, the Rio case worker for the local Society for the Protection of Girls and Women met 119 ships in order to ensure that Jewish women would not enter the white slave trade.[92]

Local relief organizations were "instrumental in preventing innocent girls from being drawn into vice and shame," and often involved Rabbi Raffalovich in more serious cases.[93] Esther C., a native of Safed, Palestine, came to Rio with her brother, a merchant, at the age of sixteen. Their neighbor was a "notorious libertine, who, with the assistance of a woman of bad repute, designed the moral destruction of the girl."[94] Esther was reported missing by her brother at the end of September 1926 and traced to the interior of Brazil, where Raffalovich traveled to resolve the matter. The local judge of minors, after some persuasion, annulled a marriage that had taken place and had "the rascal arrested." Finding the girl "unable to resist the dangers of this city," Raffalovich had her repatriated to Palestine a week later. Another typical case was that of Sura F., an eighteen-year-old Polish girl brought to São Paulo with a passage paid by her sister, a local prostitute. Sura came to the attention of the São Paulo ICA office when a third sister contacted Buenos Aires's Jüdischer Emigranten Schutzverein. Upon making contact with Sura, Raffalovich had a local lawyer prepare immigration documents and had her sent to Buenos Aires in the care of another sister.[95]

By the mid-1930s the battle against prostitution was over. The Jewish community made it increasingly difficult for single Jewish women to leave the ports in the hands of pimps, and Brazilian social legislation made commercial vice an increasingly criminal act. The leading members of the Zwi Migdal were arrested in Buenos Aires in 1930, and although few convictions resulted, the organization never recovered.[96] Even the Sociedade Religiosa e Beneficente Israelita began discussing its own dissolution.[97] This never occurred, however, since new members were constantly joining the society, an indication of a concern among older prostitutes that they would not receive proper medical care and a religious burial. In 1940 the group had over 100 members and in 1945 almost 130. A rest home was established for "old and abandoned members," and in 1953, when complaints were common that the home "did not offer comfort, was unhygienic . . . and offered danger to those who lived there," it was decided to allocate funds for a new space.[98] The story of Jewish prostitution ended in 1968 when the society was dissolved and the few remaining members entered the general Jewish Old Age Home with a donation of their remaining capital.[99]

Although the Jewish community battled prostitution, its existence, even in small numbers for a limited time, created just the image that community leaders feared. Again seeming to follow the European lead, which held that Jewish sexuality, beginning with the ritual circumcision ceremony of the *brit-milah,* was a form of social deviance, Brazilian anti-Semites used prostitution as ammunition to promote notions of Jewish immorality.[100] Cezar Magalhaens summed up these views, complaining in a collection of nationalist essays entitled *Pela brazilidade* that Jews made up one of "the inexpungeable and immoral . . . currents of emigration that enter too often in nations which encourage colonization."[101] The old issue of Jewish moral turpitude meshed easily with new claims that Jews controlled the white slave trade.[102] Other writers focused attention on Poland as the center of world prostitution, arguing that Jews, "because of the proverbial beauty of their women, are the principal traffickers."[103] In a speech before the Brazilian Criminologists Society on "pimping" as a social problem in Brazil, Anésio Frota Aguiar made it clear that not all pimps and prostitutes were Jews, while at the same time suggesting that all Jews might be pimps or prostitutes.[104] Presenting a list entitled "Pimps affiliated with the 'Migdal,' all Jews, expelled from Argentina," Aguiar portrayed all immigrant Jews in Brazil as pimps.[105] Further playing on stereotypes, Aguiar complained that "the Jew . . . exploits pimping as if it were a business."[106]

The combination, even if rare, of religious ritual and prostitution struck anti-Semitic commentators as hypocritical. This was the result of a seeming incongruity of apparently religious Jews involved with crime. Many Jews involved in prostitution maintained traditions such as keeping kosher, attending regular religious services in special synagogues built by Jewish pimps, and being buried in special cemeteries for Jewish prostitutes and pimps. The tendency of non-Jews to associate such superficial aspects of Judaism with an acceptance of the moral creeds of the religion emphasized the oddity of what must have appeared an exotic immigrant subgroup, and the seeming peculiarity of traditional Jews involved in prostitution created a point of focus.[107] Not all observers, of course, were so naive. Evaristo de Moraes, for example, noted that prostitution was one of the "saddest aspects" of Jewish life in Rio but was the natural economic result of the forced social and educational segregation of Jews in Eastern Europe.[108]

INSTITUTIONS AND INTEGRATION

Swelled by the numbers and relative success of immigrants arriving after World War I, Brazilian Jewry created an extensive network of communal, social, economic, and political institutions. These included synagogues, relief agencies, libraries, old-age homes, burial societies, and restaurants. The realization that the future was in Brazil, and not elsewhere, lay behind this. The Jewish Colonization Association's boast that "it is the undisputed opinion of all that a marked difference is discernible in the moral and religious condition of local Jewry since our advent into this country" was correct in many respects.[109] The creation of ICA-sponsored institutions in Brazil, and the promotion of them abroad, gave the community the social and religious bases needed to complete Jewish life.

The rapid expansion of Jewish institutions took place not only in São Paulo, Rio de Janeiro, and Porto Alegre, the cities where the majority of Jews were settling. In 1914, the state of Bahia's first Jewish cultural organization was founded in the capital city of Salvador, where the Jewish population consisted of about twenty families, the majority working as peddlers, although some were shop owners.[110] By 1923, the Jewish population of the city had grown to 267, about 80 percent of those living in the state, and was a microcosm of Jewish life in the early interwar era. Most Jewish immigrants to Salvador chose peddling as a first occupation, although those with capital did buy furniture stores and fabric shops or establish themselves in textiles.[111] For those without a skill, peddling was a good option because an initial loan for living expenses, trade goods, and cart could be gotten from the local *laispar kasse*.

The Jews in Salvador founded a synagogue, library, banquet hall, and lecture hall by charging the members of the community a monthly fee. Their small numbers, and their isolation in the midst of a generally monolithic Catholic society, however, also encouraged the community to want to expand its size. Thus when Marcos Pereira, an ICA representative, visited Salvador in August 1923, Jewish leaders emphasized that their community had the funds and the desire to lodge new immigrants and was willing to help them find work.[112] Salvador operated on a small scale like all other Jewish communities in Brazil. A desire for immigrants and economic opportunity created a functioning aid network for arrivals. As this system grew, encouraging reports returned to Europe, stimulating more immigration, which in turn expanded the system still further.

Other factors helped establish a communal base that encouraged Jews to come to, and stay in, Brazil. In the early 1920s Jewish schools, most funded by the ICA, could be found throughout Brazil, even in such small communities as Campinas, Niterói, and Curitiba.[113] The ICA's largest school was the Gymnasio Hebreo-Brasileiro in Rio de Janeiro, with more than 250 students. By 1930 the ICA had twenty-five schools in operation for more than 1,600 Jewish students.[114] Yet it was not only the ICA that was giving education to the young. As early as 1925 the Jewish Colonization Association's educational support funding had caused a small war in Brazil between Zionists, who insisted that Hebrew be taught, and the anti-Zionist, left-wing Russian Jews, who did "not do their duty to the schools, chiefly because Yiddish is not taught."[115] Political parties created their own schools even in smaller communities like Porto Alegre. The larger Jewish communities in São Paulo and Rio de Janeiro had as many as five schools divided along political lines.

Newspapers also served the community. Brazil's first Yiddish-language newspaper, *Di Menscheit* (Humanity), began publication in 1915 in Porto Alegre to serve the growing community of ex-ICA colonists. The establishment of Jewish newspapers indicates that migrants were accepting Brazil as "home."[116] In 1916 Brazil's first Portuguese-language Jewish newspaper was founded by a Rio de Janeiro intellectual, David Perez, whose Moroccan parents had arrived in the middle of the nineteenth century as part of a small North African Jewish migration to the Amazon region. Perez, a lawyer who felt himself both a Zionist and "a Brazilian as well," founded *A Columna* to combine a Zionist line with a desire to "defend the interests of Jews in Brasil."[117] Interestingly, *A Columna*'s strident Zionism was often encouraged by its coeditor, Alvaro de Castilho, a non-Jew who believed that Zionism should be part of the Humanist movement.[118] While *A Columna* was published for only two years, its existence suggests that Brazilian Jews operating in the public arena saw Zionism as a respected ideology that would appeal widely to Jewish immigrants. Indeed, Zionism's impact reached outside of the Jewish community beginning in the 1920s, when Brazilian newspapers regularly reported on the situation in Palestine and visits to Brazil by Zionist leaders.[119]

The decade after World War I witnessed an expansion of the Jewish press in Brazil. Most newspapers were printed in Yiddish and served as political and informational tools for the growing Jewish community. Even political journals printed items that made integration into Brazilian social and economic life easier. The Jewish press also helped facilitate immigration to Brazil, because much published information was related to the bringing of family members to Brazil from Eastern Europe. Rio de Janeiro's *Dos Idische Vochenblatt* (The Jewish Weekly) is a perfect example of this phenomenon. Founded in 1923 as a Zionist weekly by Aron Kaufman, the paper ran many lead stories on the positive aspects of Jewish immigrant life in Brazil.[120] *Dos Idische Vochenblatt*'s advertisements encouraged new migration. One travel agency, A Maritima, based on Avenida Rio Branco, the main commercial street in Rio de Janeiro, recognized that new business might be stirred up among the Jewish community; less than three months after the founding of the paper it began placing large ads. These advertisements, first published in Portuguese but soon after in Yiddish, announced that prepaid tickets could be purchased in Rio for travel to Brazil from Eastern Europe.[121] The least expensive passages were from the Polish cities of Warsaw and Vilna, the two main cities of embarkation to Brazil, and cost 760 milreis, or about ninety U.S. dollars. Those traveling from Bucharest or Kishineff had to pay a higher fare of 810 milreis (ninety-six U.S. dollars). In order to encourage Jews to buy the prepaid passages, and in recognition of the fact that immigration often occurred in family units, discounts were given for children and all fares could be bought on installment.

The Yiddish newspapers connected the growing Jewish-Brazilian community with the rest of Brazil. As early as 1919, Eliezer Levy, editor of Belém do Pará's Zionist *Kol Yisroel* (Voice of Israel), had founded a school for children that taught both Portuguese and Hebrew and boasted that "the Governor of the State presided at the [inauguration] ceremony, and there were in attendance a large number of [non-Jewish] first-class families and gentlemen prominent in social and commercial circles."[122] It was *Dos Idische Vochenblatt*'s announcement of the invitation of Albert Einstein to Brazil by Rio de Janeiro's Escola Politécnica and Clube dos Engenheiros that led Isaiah Raffalovich to make the visit a means by which to unite Rio's Jewish community.[123] The pro-Zionist and leftist political slant of many of the Jewish newspapers caused a great deal of concern for those in the ICA who felt their job of refugee relief would be hampered by a virulently pro-Zionist Jewish community. As early as 1923, recognizing the growing power of the Brazilian Jewish press, Marcos Pereira suggested to the ICA Directorate that it found and maintain a magazine in Portuguese and Yiddish. As Pereira envisioned, *Illustração Israelita*'s run of 779 copies was of general interest to Brazilian Jews and stayed away from any political opinions that might "offend Brazilian national sentiments."[124]

The desire of the ICA to publish in Brazil's national language shows that it, and presumably at least some Jewish leaders, were making an attempt to acculturate Eastern European Jewry. The Jewish newspapers did serve an important role in helping immigrants to accustom themselves to their new land. Even the stridently Zionist *Dos Idische Vochenblatt* ran advertisements, sometimes in Yiddish and sometimes in Portuguese, for Fildago Beer from Brahma and goods sold by merchants outside of the Jewish community. By 1925 the newspaper had a section in Portuguese that it promoted in front-page headlines, and a government decree, which required all newspapers to print the 1925 constitutional revisions in Portuguese, was strictly followed.[125] The Yiddish press thus gave immigrant Jews the initial means, in terms of both language and economic/social life, to start becoming Brazilians and, like so many other institutions, made Brazil a positive choice, and not simply a last one, for Jewish immigrants.

The establishment of Jewish institutions made Brazil a more desirable place for Jews, which led the ICA's Isaiah Raffalovich to grow in political importance, especially in the area of refugee relief. He convinced local shipping companies to give the ICA reduced rates on prepaid tickets and free passages when space permitted. This allowed him to make special arrangements for Jews in serious trouble. A woman whose husband was killed in Rio de Janeiro and who was left penniless was repatriated along with her two children to Odessa. Aaron Weiner, a Bessarabian immigrant who contracted tuberculosis, was given free passage by the Royal Mail Steam Packet Company back to Europe, where "his disease was arrested and he is doing almost well." A young woman who arrived from Constantinople without parents "and would have most assuredly gone wrong" also received a free passage to Alexandria so that she might join her mother.[126]

Unlike earlier immigrants, many of whom had been aided financially, about two-thirds of the Jews arriving after 1925 came with passages prepaid by relatives already in Brazil.[127] These capital expenditures by new residents indicate how quickly many Jews found economic success. Jewish immigrants already in Brazil also established a relief system that helped newcomers find jobs. Those with no skills, however, swelled the number of Jewish peddlers, visibly concentrated in Rio de Janeiro and São Paulo. Raffalovich continued to worry about a negative backlash and encouraged the establishment of more loan and credit societies because he felt that "a system must be formulated and capital provided, whereby the newcomer should be able to render himself, in as short a time as possible, independent for his means of gaining a livelihood."[128] He also encouraged the ICA to send only immigrants with skills or money: "Brazil offers immense opportunities for artisans and skilled craftsmen . . . [but] the country presents few resources for intellectuals, those in the liberal professions and those involved in commerce who have no capital with which to start."[129]

In order to guarantee a "proper" migration, Raffalovich wrote a pamphlet extolling Brazil's virtues for distribution in Eastern Europe. Filled with facts and figures designed to present Brazil in a good light, *Brazilye: A tsukunftsland far idisher emigratsye* (Brazil: A land of the future for Jewish emigrants) even insisted on using the nation's proper name since "in truth the name is 'The United States of Brazil.' "[130] Perhaps Raffalovich, as had the Republican assembly that created the name, hoped to conjure favorable comparisons with another "United States" that had been popular with Jewish migrants. How much Raffalovich's book encouraged movement to Brazil cannot be measured. What is certain is that those in the ICA's Berlin office, where the pamphlet was published, knew little about Brazil. The advertisements printed on the dust jacket were for Spanish-language courses and a Spanish-Yiddish dictionary.

Throughout the 1920s the process of integrating Jewish immigrants into Brazilian society improved. An ICA-edited, multivolume history of the Jews now included a section on Brazilian Jewry and was published in Portuguese. Sermons for all major Jewish holidays were printed in both Yiddish and Portuguese, and local institutions regularly provided language lessons for new arrivals. A Portuguese-Yiddish dictionary was distributed. In 1916, the Talmud Torah Bet-Sepher Yvrit of São Paulo became Brazil's first Jewish religious school. By the early 1920s religious and nonreligious Jewish schools existed throughout Brazil. In 1928 there were twenty-two ICA-sponsored schools, and Rabbi Raffalovich reported enthusiastically that the number of children enrolled, especially outside of Rio de Janeiro and São Paulo, was growing rapidly.[131] The schools that opened in smaller communities usually succeeded in that most Jewish children attended. In the larger and wealthier communities of Rio and São Paulo, however, "the vast majority of the people neither send their children to nor assist financially the Jewish classes."[132] Political divisions, particularly between Yiddishists (who were often non-Zionist) and Hebraists (who were usually Zionist), created many schools with poor funding rather than a few schools with good financial bases.

With the influx of immigrants, the Jewish Colonization Association could no longer handle the financial and human costs of international refugee relief. As a result, the ICA joined forces with the Hebrew Immigrant Aid and Sheltering Society of New York and Emigdirect of Berlin to form HICEM (*HIAS-ICA-Em*igdirect). The group claimed that Brazil was "immensely rich [and] offered [great] possibilities for immigrants and especially Jews," and sent many migrants there.[133] The creation of HICEM increased the funding, and thus communal visibility, of already established organizations and helped encourage still more Jews to immigrate.[134] This included, for the first time, an institutional promotion of Sephardic immigration.[135] In 1926 many Jews in Constantinople were evacuated, and in the early 1930s Brazil received between 10 and 20 percent of the Jewish immigrants leaving that city.[136] The Sephardic community quickly grew in size and importance, and with this nucleus in place, a later migration, mainly from Egypt following the Suez crisis of the mid-1950s, was to find recognizable communal life already in place.[137]

By the end of the 1920s Jewish life in Brazil was well established. Many were comfortable economically, and in some cities there were "literally no poor, although very few . . . in affluent positions."[138] The Brazilian Jewish community experienced remarkable growth in the twenties, tripling in size. Raffalovich said that he thought "Brazil is destined to play an important role in the future history of Jewry," a belief reinforced by a growing communal participation in international Jewish affairs through such efforts as sending Passover food to Russia.[139] Economic problems, beginning with the drop in coffee prices in the late 1920s, changed the attitude of many Brazilians to all immigrants, and especially Jewish ones. By 1930 the world-wide depression caused a rise in prices and unemployment and further influenced immigration. Local Jewish organizations had fewer funds, and economic and political problems in Brazil discouraged potential immigrants. Overall immigration dropped over 30 percent between 1929 and 1930, and Jewish entrances fell as well.

By the early 1930s Brazil's Jewish community had changed significantly. Whereas a decade earlier Jews viewed Brazil merely as a station on their way to fortunes elsewhere, now remigration was rare. Many realized that "if it is not possible at the present juncture to make fortunes in Brazil, it is yet easier to earn a living here than in any other part of the world."[140] As a result of these changes, the ICA concentrated its work less upon arrival aid and more on the legal aspects of garnering visas and changing immigrants into Brazilian citizens. ICA-Brazil, especially under Raffalovich, was ideally suited for this task and maintained excellent relations with authorities, even after the passage of restrictive legislation. As 1933 approached, the "Country of the Future" seemed to offer great promise for Brazilian Jewry.

CHAPTER TWO

Nationalism, Nativism, and Restriction

The late 1920s were among the most tumultuous in Brazilian history. The coffee economy—based in São Paulo—declined as states out of the political mainstream began to grow in financial strength. President Washington Luís, a representative of São Paulo's large landowners, came under increasing fire from regional elites allied with the revolutionary military officers (*tenentes*) whose army revolt had been aborted in mid-decade. The presidential campaign that began in 1929 reflected these problems, creating bitter political infighting. The race pitted São Paulo State president Júlio Prestes, Luís's hand-picked successor and a representative of the coffee-based oligarchy, against Rio Grande do Sul's Getúlio Vargas, the candidate of the Liberal Alliance, a front that represented a number of not always compatible groups. These included those whose economic power was not based on coffee production and who looked to the state to modernize Brazil's economy, stridently anti-communist nationalists whose primary concern was the maintenance of order among the rural and urban working classes, and an emerging middle class that had become increasingly disenfranchised by the central government's continued favoritism toward the owners of large coffee plantations.[1]

In the midst of the violence-marred electioneering two economic crises hit Brazil, increasing already high political and social tensions. For the third year in a row a bumper crop of coffee forced prices to sink rapidly. The decline was aggravated when the New York Stock Exchange crashed at the end of October, and by December coffee prices were half of what they had been eleven months earlier.[2] It was in the midst of this failing economy that the election took place on March 1, 1930. Prestes was declared the winner by about 250,000 of the 1,750,000 votes cast, but the outcome, and the precipitous drop in Brazil's export earnings, encouraged supporters of the Liberal Alliance to challenge Prestes's victory amid accusations of widespread fraud. Brazil was rife with rumors about the possibility of a revolution in the months following the election. In early October, Vargas proclaimed the vote fraudulent and troops in Rio Grande do Sul began their revolt, led by a group of *tenentes* that included Pedro Aurélio Góis Monteiro and Oswaldo Aranha, both of whom would become important federal political leaders. The following day Congress, at the request of President Washington Luís, declared a state of siege. The Revolution of 1930 had begun.

By mid-October much of Brazil's military had revolted against the central government. On October 24, the few top-ranking generals who still supported Luís demanded his resignation and overthrew the federal government. A few days later Luís resigned, preventing the inauguration of Prestes. On October 27 Oswaldo Aranha entered the federal capital of Rio de Janeiro at the head of three thousand troops. That same day the ruling junta made it clear that Getúlio Vargas would be the new head of state, and popular demonstrations in Rio called for Vargas's assumption of the presidency. On November 4, the generals made Vargas "provisional president" of a "provisional government," thus ending the Revolution of 1930.[3]

Vargas's appointment was a watershed in Brazilian political history. By shifting the focus of the central government and the groups that it represented, the new regime changed some of the ways in which Brazilian politics worked. One area where this was especially noticeable was in the attitude toward immigrants, including Jews. After 1930 the government and its supporters increasingly used the discussion of immigration to express nationalist and nativist positions. The nationalist-authoritarians in the new regime were attracted to certain racist forms of national regeneration popular in Europe at the time and thus had ideological reasons for limiting foreign entry.[4] These leanings dovetailed with the attitudes of a small but growing urban middle class, most noticeably in Rio de Janeiro but to some extent in Brazil's other large cities as well, that desired economic and social mobility without immigrant competition. Thus, as urban unemployment grew in the early 1930s, immigrants, many of whom had worked extremely hard to become moderately successful, became easy scapegoats. It took only a few years for political attacks on foreigners to be transformed into policies based on the commonly held notion that "one of the causes of unemployment is found in the free entry of foreigners . . . [who] frequently contribute to an increase in economic disorder and social insecurity."[5] Anti-immigrant rhetoric was aimed at those immigrants who might settle in urban areas and whose occupations revolved around the distribution, and not the production, of important goods.

It was in this highly charged atmosphere that Brazilian politicians shifted their discourse on immigration and immigrants in dramatic ways between 1930 and 1935. Nationalism would transform old ideas about the "whitening" of Brazil into federal policies aimed at "Brazilianization." This would eventually lead to a full-blown anti-foreigner movement among many federal and state officials. At its start, however, nativist movements targeted only groups that, while not banned from entering Brazil, did not fit "European" ideals. Since Europe was not seen as a geographical space but rather as a social construct that included notions of color and religion, the many Jews entering Brazil from Europe were seen as part of a "non-European" group. The anti-immigrant rhetoric so prevalent in the cities, however, was not absolute. Indeed, the image of immigrants as a positive force for development continued among many large landowners who remained committed to non-Brazilian labor. As anti-immigrant sentiment became a key to election in urban areas, local representatives of the rural elite balked. Whatever political cachet nativism had, it was of only moderate concern to *fazendeiros* worried about maintaining their social status, harvesting their crops, and rounding up their cattle.

The positions in the immigration battle were plainly staked out, although not always clearly articulated. Large landowners and their representatives wanted to guarantee the continued entry of agricultural workers. Many urban politicians, on the other hand, argued that most immigrants should be banned, especially those who did not fit into the "European" category. The Vargas regime was squarely in the middle, encouraging the tension between competing political forces as a means of enhancing and consolidating its own power. This placed Jewish immigrants and refugees in a particularly precarious position. Beginning in the 1920s, Jewish immigrants to Brazil rarely came from rural areas and, as nonfarmers, had no support from large landowners. Urban nativists, generally at odds with the *fazendeiros* over immigration policy, also viewed Jews negatively, considering them an insidious nonwhite race whose racial differences were dangerously indistinguishable. The undesirability of Jews became one of the few areas of agreement among urban and rural politicians.

The growth of nativism in Brazil forced the federal government to reevaluate its traditional encouragement of immigration. This was reinforced by political changes in Europe, where many ills were being blamed on minority groups. Brazil's long tradition of European-influenced racialist thought provided the xenophobic rhetoric with which to target groups like immigrant Jews who entered in growing numbers and often settled in urban areas.[6] Jews posed a particular challenge to nativists interested in whitening Brazil through European immigration; they were considered racially distinct yet insidious since they were able to pass physically as part of the majority. Worse still, Jews seemed to insult nativists by not pressing their physical advantage and choosing to maintain their culture by dressing and worshiping differently.

The complex emotions that the growth of Jewish immigration created played directly into the hands of important state and federal politicians and intellectuals eager to establish their nativist credentials. The most significant shift in the discourse regarding Jewish immigrants was the transformation of religion into a racial category and the use of new kinds of language to relate amorphous anti-immigrant sentiment to widely accepted anti-Jewish notions.[7] Influential thinkers like the conservative social critic Francisco José Oliveira Vianna, a historian and professor at the Law Faculty in Rio de Janeiro, were attracted to European racists like Gobineau whose writings could also be used to justify the establishment of a strong central state.[8] Vianna, who was described as a mulatto by his contemporaries, classified Jews as non-Europeans, using the accepted semantic code to suggest that they were nonwhites— important in a nation where "whitening" was the code word nationalists traditionally attached to policies intended to remake Brazil in Europe's image.[9] Anti-Jewish sentiment was also implicit in intellectual support of "Aryanization," and in *Raça e assimilação* (1932) Vianna openly mimicked European racists by applauding the "new Aryan centers" of southern Brazil.[10] He even used a survey of the ethnic composition of New London, Connecticut, by Connecticut College professor Bessie Bloom Wessel as evidence for his claim that "the Jewish group is unassimilable," a conclusion not suggested by Wessel herself.[11]

Vianna was not the only intellectual who claimed that by limiting immigration, or stopping it altogether, Brazilian society would reproduce itself from within and bring white European elements to the fore.

Renato Kehl, founder of the *Boletim de Eugenia* (Bulletin of Eugenics), sympathized with the German "race hygiene" movement directed primarily against Jews and claimed that the Central Brazilian Commission of Eugenics was modeled on the German Society for Race Hygiene.[12] At the First Brazilian Eugenics Congress, held in 1929, a group including Congressman A. J. de Azevedo Amaral, the clinician (and later federal deputy) Antônio Xavier de Oliveira, and Miguel Couto, the president of the National Academy of Medicine and later a member of the 1933–34 Constitutional Assembly, proposed that Brazil should restrict the entry of non-Europeans, a motion that was only narrowly defeated. Although important academics like the geneticist Octávio Domingues and the Franz Boas–trained anthropologist Edgar Roquette-Pinto opposed the outright racism of many in the eugenics movement, the regular arrival of "non-European" immigrant groups like Jews fueled the negative judgments of Brazil's racial and ethnic heterogeneity and made "assimilation" a widely discussed topic. Yet the implication that assimilation could take place only by restricting entry to "European" immigrants shows that many intellectuals believed that Brazilian society was too culturally weak to assimilate all people. Rather, given the fine line that Brazil walked, only ethnically and racially "pure" immigrants could melt into the pot without contaminating it.

With already an established presence in Brazil, Jews, along with the Japanese, became the most important target of nativists.[13] The Japanese, however, had two important defenders: large landowners, who desired the presumed agricultural orientation of most Japanese immigrants; and the federal government, which realized that the economic, political, and military might of Japan demanded respect. Targeting Jewish immigration, on the other hand, was comparatively safe and easy. European Jewish immigrants had little international diplomatic support and, in the 1920s, rarely played the agricultural roles demanded of immigrants. This allowed politicians who represented powerful landowners to participate in the anti-immigrant movement without fear of arousing the wrath of their sponsors. At the same time, Jews made up an increasing percentage of the expanding Eastern European migratory stream, representing almost 42 percent of all Poles who immigrated to Brazil between 1926 and 1937 and a remarkable 77.7 percent of those who did so between 1931 and 1935.[14] Brazilian nativism and Jewish immigration were growing, ready to collide in the near future.

EARLY ANTI-IMMIGRANT LEGISLATION AND CHANGES IN RELIEF PLANS

Attacks on immigration were an integral part of the provisional government's agenda. Just forty-five days after the coup, broad new legislation limited the entrance of third-class passengers, all of whom were to be considered immigrants regardless of their true travel purposes.[15] Those traveling in "immigrant class" were to be denied entry unless they were (a) already resident; (b) a farmer with special permission from a state ministry of agriculture or the federal Ministry of Labor, Industry, and Commerce and with an affidavit of support from an already resident family; or (c) an agricultural immigrant family brought over by an approved company or association (of which the Jewish Colonization Association was one).[16]

Three aspects of the new legislation deserve particular attention. The first was the reworking of the 1924 law that used the class of passage to define one's status as tourist or immigrant. The linkage of passage class with social status suggests a connection of immigration to poverty, and one later Vargas-era analyst worried that restrictions on immigrant visas for third-class passengers would diminish the number of skilled workers entering Brazil, thus hindering economic development.[17] A second aspect of the 1930 immigration legislation involved money. Poor immigrants were officially considered undesirable since all needed to show proof of possession of at least "two or three contos" per person (215 to 320 U.S. dollars).[18] The third innovation mandated in 1930 came with the creation of *cartas de chamada. Chamadas*, as they were generally known, were official forms that allowed those resident in Brazil to "call" their relatives by providing them with an affidavit of support. The *chamada* system functioned to increase the bureaucratic hurdles that residents of Brazil would have to negotiate in order to bring in relatives. The actual forms first had to be approved by the police in the city where an immigrant's sponsor lived. This was not an easy task, and Jewish residents of Brazil frequently complained about "the difficulties experienced at the Police Office in the Capital in making *chamadas*."[19] The approved form would then be legalized by the Immigration Department of the Ministry of Labor, Industry, and Commerce. Only with the legalized *chamada* could a resident purchase a prepaid ticket for a foreigner. By the time a prepaid ticket had been sent, both the local police and the federal government had a file of specific information about who was entering and for what reasons.

TABLE 2.1

JEWISH AND GENERAL IMMIGRATION TO BRAZIL, 1929–1945

Year	General	% Change	Jewish	% Change	% Jewish/General
1929	96,186	—	4,874	—	5.0
1930	62,610	−35	3,558	−27	5.7
1931	27,465	−56	1,985	−44	7.2
1932	31,494	14	2,049	3	6.5
1933	46,081	48	3,317	61	7.1
1934	46,027	0	3,794	14	8.2
1935	29,585	−36	1,758	−54	5.9
1936	12,773	−57	3,418	94	26.8
1937	34,677	270	2,003	−41	5.8
1938	19,388	−45	530	−73	2.7
1939	22,668	117	4,601	768	20.3
1940	18,449	−19	2,416	−47	13.1
1941	9,938	−47	1,500	−38	15.1
1942	2,425	−76	108	−93	4.5
1943	1,308	−46	11	−90	0.84
1944	1,593	121	6	−46	0.38
1945	3,168	198	120	1,900	3.8

SOURCES "Discriminação por nacionalidade dos imigrantes entrando no Brasil no período 1924–1933 e 1934–1939," RIC 1:3 (July 1940), 633–38. SCA 1926–1935, JCA-L. Rapport d'activité pendant la période 1933–1943. HIAS-Brazil, folder 1, YIVO-NY. Mark Wischnitzer, To Dwell in Safety: The Story of Jewish Migration since 1800 (Philadelphia: The Jewish Publication Society of America, 1948), p. 293, table 6.

The new immigration requirements at first had the desired effects: Jewish immigration was reduced by almost 45 percent and general immigration by even more .[20] By making foreign entry increasingly difficult, immigration to Brazil was cut by more than half between 1930 and 1931, and remained below the mark for 1930 until 1951. Yet Jewish immigration, in spite of growing complaints from Brazil's overseas representatives, never fell as much as general immigration, and recovered to a much higher level. Whereas general entry between 1931 and 1945 never reached the mark set in 1930, Jewish immigration frequently hovered near, and occasionally exceeded, its 1930 figure and made up an increasingly large percent of all immigration to Brazil.

Given the barriers, why did Jewish entry rise so much after 1932? The most important reason was that the new restrictions did not discourage desperate Jews from going to Brazil but rather motivated them to work within the system more efficiently. Jewish relief agencies redoubled their efforts to teach residents how to "call" their relatives legally, and the ICA increasingly functioned as a *despachante* in order to help resident immigrants cut bureaucratic red tape.[21] Furthermore, Jewish leaders succeeded in countering prevailing attitudes about immigrants among influential politicians. A few months after the Revolution of 1930, for example, the ICA's Isaiah Raffalovich convinced Minister of Labor Lindolfo Collor to recognize the Jewish Colonization Association as an accredited immigration company.[22] Raffalovich was equally successful at the Foreign Ministry, and consuls in Paris, Warsaw, Galatz, Madrid, and Lisbon were told that "you can put visas in the passports of colonists or their families that present *cartas de chamada* of the JCA."[23]

The federal accreditation of the ICA was only one step in bringing immigrants to Brazil under the new restrictions. Raffalovich, who cut an imposing figure with his distinguished goatee, mustache, and riveting eyes, also successfully worked with local officials. When federally funded free passages for immigrants in transit to the interior of Brazil were cut, he convinced Rio Grande do Sul officials to pick up the tab.[24] In another instance he was introduced to the governor of Pará, a state with a third-generation Jewish community of two hundred families of mainly North African origin. This led to "an invitation to the ICA to take up activities in the State of Pará [that] the Government will do all in its power to help."[25] The outline of the plan, which never came to fruition, was presented to the editors of Pará's two major newspapers, the chief of police, and the "cream of Jewish and non-Jewish society" at a large banquet. "Newcomers from Central and Eastern Europe" believed Raffalovich "with a little capital and business acumen would be able to find a fruitful field for their energies."[26]

Between 1931 and 1932 there was a rise in Jewish entrances in spite of the extension of the 1930 legislation for a second year. In 1932 a record number of prepaid passages were purchased by Jews and sent to relatives in Europe.[27] The Jewish Society for the Protection and Aid of Immigrants "EZRA" of São Paulo, for example, aided 242 legal resident aliens to call 526 European family members in 1932 alone.[28] This group and others worked together to convince passenger shipping companies to allow local outlets to sell prepaid tickets at reduced prices when they were unable to fill ships. In 1932 the ICA purchased almost 150 of these reduced-price tickets, and many individuals did the same.[29] Within two years of the establishment of the new laws, the annual Jewish immigration rate once again reached more than three thousand.

ANTI-IMMIGRANT INFLUENCES IN THE DIPLOMATIC CORPS, 1930–1934

The rise in Jewish immigration during a period when entry was supposed to be reduced led to intense discussion in the high echelons of Brazil's diplomatic corps; the ambassadors, consuls, attachés, and legation and mission heads. These individuals represented Brazil's most important overseas decision makers, and it was their images of Jews and Jewish immigration that decision makers in Rio de Janeiro evaluated when constructing policy. Every important diplomat posted in a European country with a large Jewish population commented regularly throughout the 1930s and 1940s on Jewish immigration. Although a few took humanitarian positions or argued that Jewish refugees could help Brazil develop economically, the overwhelming majority were opposed to the unrestricted entry of Jews. As the numbers of Jews requesting visas increased, diplomats abroad were transformed from promoters of Brazil's economic expansion to protectors of Brazilian society. Indeed, the prevention of foreigners' entry was deemed so important that one of the first tasks that Vargas gave to the diplomatic corps was the enforcement of the aforementioned decree limiting the entry of third-class passengers.[30]

Approximately twenty Brazilian diplomats, most at the ambassador or consul-general level, actively argued against giving visas to Jews. All had advanced their careers most markedly after Vargas had taken power, and a number had been promoted to the ambassador or consul-general level within a year of the establishment of the Estado Novo.[31] Like foreign ministers Afrânio de Mello Franco (1930–1933), José Carlos de Macedo Soares (1934–1937), and Oswaldo Aranha (1938–1945), almost all had received their diplomas in social and legal science (Ciências Jurídicas e Sociais) from one of Brazil's prestigious law schools, over half in Rio de Janeiro. It was in this setting, where professors such as Oliveira Vianna imbued students with the spirit of scientific racists like Le Bon, Gobineau, and Chamberlain, that diplomats began to form a notion of immigration as a social issue and Jews as an undesirable component of Brazilian society.[32]

These high-level diplomats played a key role in the debate over Jewish immigration, which they saw primarily as a social issue. They argued that Jewish immigrants would lead Brazil to racial, cultural, and political ruin, and correspondence from those in the Foreign Service generally portrayed every Jewish immigrant as a potential subversive.[33] Of course, some Jewish immigrants to Brazil were communists, but many in intellectual and political circles played on traditional anti-Semitic notions by assuming that all Jews were engaged in communist activity. A well-printed 1931 pamphlet whose publication was authorized by São Paulo's Delegate of Social Order, *O comunismo e sua nefasta propaganda*, claimed that among the most active European communists operating in Brazil, "almost all are Jews."[34] What made such statements perniciously anti-Semitic was the generalization from the particular—that a sizable minority from Eastern Europe were socialists or bundists—to the group—that all Jews, by virtue of a biological defect, were prone to upset the status quo.[35] Readers of such pamphlets were not simply meant to understand that, statistically speaking, many communists happened to be Jews; they were meant to infer that all Jews were communists and therefore dangerous.

The shift from inclusionary toward exclusionist attitudes toward all immigrants was reflected throughout the entire overseas network of consulates and embassies. Finding immigrants useful to Brazil's agricultural growth was no longer the priority. Rather, a variety of undesirable immigrant groups were to be identified and kept away. Constant ideological reinforcement from influential Brazilians pushed policymakers in Rio to refine immigration restrictions further. Nabuco Gouvêa, a diplomat in Bucharest, where a few hundred Jews who met all the published immigration regulations were given visas each year, complained in all his yearly reports from 1931 to 1934 that Jews were "the worst possible" immigrants.[36] The commercial attaché in Alexandria, Egypt, believed that anti-foreigner movements in the Turkish empire would have ruinous effects on Brazil. Seven or eight thousand Armenians, so it seems, had been expelled from Turkey in 1930 and were buying Brazilian immigrant visas from local travel agents. In and of itself the arrival of such a large group of Armenians would be "a great calamity."[37] What made it even worse, according to the diplomat, was that the Armenians would add to the number of undesirable Syrians and Jews already in Brazil: "From year to year, unfortunately, there is a growing emigration of Syrians and Jews to Brazil and if the Armenian is added to this, we can proudly say that we are populating Brazil and forming our race with all that is the most repugnant in the universe."[38]

Brazil's policy toward potential South Asian immigrants was a further signal of the renewed desire for ethnic purity among diplomats. In early August 1930, Bhagwan Singh, the manager of the Indo-Brazilian Association of Calcutta, began investigating the possibility of sending five hundred rural laborers to Brazil.[39] The Revolution of 1930 was still three months in the future, and such a group neatly fit Brazil's stated development plans at the time. Realizing this, Brazil's consul general in Calcutta felt comfortable in declaring "that this Consulate has no objection what so ever regarding the Indian emigrant who may desire to leave for Brazil."[40] Singh correctly perceived this as an endorsement of the Indo-Brazilian Association as an officially approved immigration company as legislated by the 1924 immigration law.[41] Over the next eighteen months the Indo-Brazilian Association worked at attracting Indian immigrants for the voyage to Brazil, apparently never realizing the changes in policy that had taken place following the Revolution of 1930.

As final preparations were made, the company discovered that it no longer had the support or authorization of the Brazilian government. The National Population Department, attached to the Ministry of Labor, Industry, and Commerce, had the final authority over immigration and declared that it " . . . has always been opposed to the Hindu immigrant . . . [who] is undesirable . . . because of his physical incapacity, as well as other defects, that make assimilation difficult, or perhaps impossible."[42] In the space of just a year and a half the primary condition immigrants needed to satisfy had changed. Rural laborers were still needed, but only if they could assimilate into European Brazilian society.

The Foreign Ministry informed all Brazilian consulates of the prohibition of Indian immigration. Even so, the Indo-Brazilian Association, now renamed the Indo-South American Travellers Aid Society, cynically (or perhaps ignorantly) continued promoting the opportunities available and collecting registration fees from people wishing to immigrate.[43] When Bombay's *Indian Daily Mail* suggested that Indians resident in South Africa would be welcomed in Brazil, the diplomatic corps quickly set out to squelch the idea.[44] Manoel A. de Heredia, Brazil's consul general in Bombay, termed the idea "absurd" and published official responses in a number of newspapers, noting that "since 1930 all emigration [of Indians] to Brazil has been forbidden until December 31 [1933]."[45] Murillo M. de Souza, Brazil's consul in Calcutta, was furious that the group was collecting money and demanded that "you immediately stop this sort of procedure otherwise I shall be compelled to bring it to the notice of the Indian Government."[46] In fact de Souza had already used diplomatic channels to complain about the "shady purpose" the Indo-South American Travellers Aid Society served. Furthermore, knowing that the unwritten aspects of immigration legislation were as important as the written ones, de Souza told the foreign secretary to the government of India that "by a decree 19.482 of the 12th December 1930, the Brazilian Government had prohibited all immigration."[47] The decree did restrict the entry of foreigners but did not prohibit immigration outright, and even a reserved circular denying consuls the right to give visas was never meant to stop the flow entirely.[48]

THE EUROPEAN INFLUENCE

The rise of totalitarianism in Europe also contributed to the transformation of Brazil's intellectual discourse and policies on immigration. Many Brazilian political figures and intellectuals were attracted to German national socialism and the fascist movements in Italy, Portugal, and Spain—nations that, like Brazil, had been damaged by the world depression. They wondered if the democratic system, and the dissent and differences that flourished within it, were the cause of social unrest and economic difficulty. By assuming the chancellorship of Germany in 1933, Adolf Hitler provided a new, antidemocratic, political model for industrializing societies. Hitler justified his authoritarian methods with a rhetoric that blamed Jews for Germany's ills; following the German lead, many influential Brazilians started making the "Jewish Question" a regular part of their public and political discourse.

Nazism and fascism inspired numerous Brazilian nationalist movements. All had anti-immigrant and anti-foreigner ideologies, and most included an explicit anti-Jewish component. The Society of the Friends of Alberto Torres was one of the most potent. Named in memory of Alberto Torres (1865–1917), a Brazilian economic and cultural nationalist who had proposed that "immigrants and foreign minorities" were one factor causing Brazil's dissolution, the society was formed in Rio de Janeiro in 1932 by fifty intellectuals, diplomats, politicians, and *tenentes* closely tied to the Vargas regime, including Plínio Salgado, Juarez Távora, and Nicolau José Debané.[49] One aim of the "Friends" was to lobby against the immigration of "unassimilable" ethnic elements like Jews and the Japanese.[50] Such ideas were promoted by the Vargas regime, which also used the language of assimilation, and the group continually emitted "attacks on the Japanese, the League of Nations, or most any other non-nationalistic element which at the time may figure in the news."[51] Former foreign minister Felix Pacheco, owner and editor in chief of Rio de Janeiro's widely read and influential *Jornal do Comércio,* offered space in his newspaper to the "Friends" and provided extensive coverage of conferences the group held on immigration. These conferences, because of the coverage and the social and political prominence of participants, helped the "Friends" garner an importance that exceeded their numbers. The nativist thrust of the group was quite sophisticated and its anti-Semitism was often masked with nonracist rhetoric. No one could prove, argued "Friend" Nicolau Debané, author of numerous nationalist tracts and a former career diplomat who had served in Egypt and the Soviet Union, that "the Semitic race is inferior to the Aryan." Rather, "the Jews have not lost their character [as a] privileged race" and thus could never assimilate into Catholic Brazil.[52] Felix Pacheco often claimed with no irony that he was not anti-Semitic even while pointing out to foreign diplomats that "we cannot possibly have any place for [Jews] here."[53] Such feelings could be found throughout the Vargas regime. When Morris Melvin Wagner of Sacramento, California, proposed to create a "Hebrew Republic" in southern Brazil, it was rejected out of hand as "not worth considering" by the National Population Department (DNP), the agency in charge of colonization.[54]

The Nazi boycott of Jewish enterprises, and later banning of Jews from the civil service and government in the first six months of 1933, received some approval among Brazilian nativists. They also adopted the Nazi technique of dehumanizing Jews, often referring to Jews as "elements" rather than people. The Ação Integralista Brasileira (AIB) was the largest organized group with a clear anti-Semitic agenda. The AIB was fascist in orientation, with popular roots among the middle classes, the armed forces, many of Italian and German descent in southern Brazil, and a few very wealthy industrialists. Yet the intellectual roots of Integralism were not popular; rather, they sprang from Brazil's prestigious law faculties, where Integralists, like many of the diplomats in charge of making and implementing immigration policy, frequently linked communism and "international Jewish finance" in their manifestos.[55] The first public meeting of the Integralists was held on January 3, 1933, just three days after Hitler's election; its leadership included members of the traditional oligarchy, monarchists, and nationalist *gaúchos.*[56] The AIB, partly funded by the German embassy in Rio and, clandestinely, by the Italian government, had a corporatist economic and political ideology that was antiliberal, anticapitalist and anticommunist.[57] Although ideologically based upon Portuguese and Italian Fascism, the Integralistas were attracted to the trappings of Nazism—the salutes, symbols, and goose steps.[58] These embellishments helped to encourage the latent anti-Semitic component in Brazilian fascism. By early 1934 Integralism was no longer a regional phenomenon but claimed 180,000 adherents throughout the country.[59]

One important goal of the Integralistas was to combat "secret societies" linked to Judaism.[60] This echoed claims made by the European theorists, who reworked traditional anti-Semitic arguments that the Russian and French Revolutions were financed by "international Jewish capital."[61] To Integralistas, opposition groups were interchangeably and indiscriminately "Jews," "Bolsheviks," or "liberals."[62] One of the movement's founders and the head of the AIB's Department of Doctrine, the São Paulo Law School–trained jurist Miguel Reale, changed the title of his book *O operario e o integralismo* (The worker and integralism) to *O capitalismo internacional* (International capitalism) to suggest that a "physiognomy of capitalism" was linked to "foreign" German Jewish businesspeople.[63] This played on notions that Jews were members of a race that had physically distinct characteristics, thus transforming capitalism from an economic act to a racial characteristic.

One of the strengths of Integralism was its capacity to create widespread negative images of its opponents. This was done through ninety Integralist newspapers, led by Rio de Janeiro's *A Ofensiva* and São Paulo's *A Ação*. One of the critical actors in the Integralist anti-Jewish media campaign was Gustavo Barroso, a historian, a former federal deputy from Ceará, and three-time president (1931, 1932, 1950) of the Academy of Letters, Brazil's most prestigious intellectual and academic organization. Barroso was also an open admirer of Hitler and Nazism, leading Buenos Aires's pro-Nazi *Deutsche La Plata Zeitung* to call him the "Führer of Integralism."[64] Barroso had been educated at the Rio de Janeiro Law School, where he had developed his notion that capitalism was the same as communism and both were equal to Judaism.[65] All of Barroso's seventeen books on Integralism were anti-Semitic, and seven specifically charged that an international Jewish conspiracy existed. He also translated anti-Semitic works into Portuguese, and in early 1933 he published the first of many Portuguese editions of the *Protocols of the Elders of Zion*, a book circulated throughout the Americas that claimed to expose an alleged Jewish conspiracy to dominate the world.[66] The Integralist press widely reported Gustavo Barroso's anti-Semitic campaign, which took facts and molded them into larger fictions. Barroso attacked Congressman Horacio Lafer and other Jewish entrepreneurs in *A sinagoga paulista* (The Paulista synagogue) and was only rarely held accountable for his lies.[67] Other works assaulted an alleged "world Jewish capitalist conspiracy" and attacked U.S. liberalism from an anti-Semitic perspective. Hitting closer to home, Rio's few Jewish prostitutes and pimps were portrayed as the majority of those involved in vice.[68] By the mid-1930s, a number of anti-Semitic titles were easily available in Rio de Janeiro, São Paulo, and Porto Alegre, including Henry Ford's *The International Jew* and Barroso's *Brasil, colônia de banqueiros,* a publication recommended to cadets in the national Escola Militar by General José Meira de Vasconcelos, a contributor to the Integralist weekly *A Ofensiva.*[69] It is no surprise that some observers wondered if "the most serious anti-Semitic agitation [in South America] was found in Brazil."[70]

The linkage of Brazil's precarious financial situation with an international Jewish capitalist conspiracy was not the exclusive ground of the Integralists. After the prices of Brazilian export products like coffee fell in 1935, the National Liberation Alliance (ANL), the mass movement created by the then illegal Brazilian Communist Party (PCB), argued that all foreign firms should be immediately nationalized. Anti-Semites in the ANL often connected these firms, and economic imperialism in general, to Judaism. João Alberto Lins de Barros, one of the *tenentes* of 1930 and an important adviser to Getúlio Vargas, for example, complained that Brazil did not have "the courage to break with international Judaism" and "Jewish bankers."[71] Jews, so it seemed, had few friends among Brazilian political activists.

THE JEWISH COMMUNITY STRIKES BACK

Brazil's Jewish community reacted quickly to the rise in anti-Semitism in the early 1930s.[72] Pamphlets circulated among Rio's Jews suggested that it was time to defend "the legitimate interests of the Jewish Collective of Brazil," and in late March 1933, the Jewish Colonization Association's Isaiah Raffalovich organized a protest in Rio de Janeiro "against the tyrannical treatment of German Jews." The march, according to the rabbi, was peaceful. Even so, the police waded into the crowd, where they waged "a brutal aggression against the defenseless Jewish population," eventually wrecking homes in the area, attacking Jews in local cafés, and finally violating a nearby synagogue.[73]

Raffalovich immediately complained to the Minister of Justice, who launched an internal investigation.[74] This was headed by Federal Police Chief Filinto Müller, a Vargas confidant and ex-*tenente* from Mato Grosso, whose feared Political and Social Police (and undercover Serviço Secreto de Investigações—the S-2) answered only to Vargas.[75] Müller's influence was felt even by high-ranking members of the government like Ambassador to the United States Oswaldo Aranha, who complained to Vargas that police agents were regularly opening his correspondence.[76] Müller, a Brazilian of German descent, was a notorious Third Reich admirer and was closely tied to both the German embassy and the Integralist Party. Not surprisingly, his official report was at odds with Raffalovich's claims.[77] The problem, according to the police, was that many marchers were "well-known communists" (although none were so well known that they were mentioned by name) whose extremist ideas led to "confusion and disorder."[78] Fortunately, according to the police, they were able to apprehend those creating the disorder without entering into homes, cafés, or the synagogue. Regardless of the truthfulness of the police statement, another protest against "Hitlerist atrocities" scheduled for July 1933 was prohibited under pressure from the German embassy. In this case, according to Raffalovich, even antigovernment Rio newspapers "were afraid to make mention of what [had] taken place."[79]

With public protests banned, Jewish leaders took a personal approach. In October 1934, Raffalovich met with Integralist chief Plínio Salgado and received his assurance that the Integralists "would leave the Jewish question out of the program."[80] When an Integralist parade in São Paulo was attacked by communists, however, it "produced a fury against Jews, who of course are [considered] by anti-Semites the progenitors of Communism."[81] This produced widespread concern in the Jewish community, and some wealthy Jews even supplied funds to the Integralists in order to secure "an agreement to eliminate most of the anti-Semitic material from the party publications."[82] The AIB gladly took the money but persisted with its anti-Jewish propaganda.

There were also direct attacks on anti-Semitism by non-Jews. In 1933 Carlos Lacerda and a number of other intellectuals walked out of a meeting of Pró-Arte, an artistic exchange association funded by the German embassy, when the Nazis in the organization announced a plan to expel Jewish members.[83] The well-known author Antônio Baptista Pereira attacked anti-Jewish movements in *O Brasil e o anti-semitismo* (1934), finding some support in intellectual circles. Azevedo Amaral's review of this book in Samuel Wainer's *Revista Brasileira,* for example, denounced anti-Semitism in Brazil and elsewhere.[84] In *Questão judaica, questão social* (1933), the sociologist José Pérez rejected the idea that the "traditional tolerance of the country [would prevent] explosions from hateful anti-Semites." Pérez saw a link between nationalism and the new intellectuals who had risen to power with Vargas, claiming that "the new sociologists of the *pátria amada* [had] cried hysterically 'KILL THE JEWS' " during an academic conference.[85] A compilation in defense of Jews entitled *Por que ser anti-semita?: Um inquérito entre intellectuaes brasileiros* (Why be an anti-Semite?: An inquiry among Brazilian intellectuals) was produced in 1933 by another group of intellectuals.[86] This collection of articles, so it appeared, had come directly from thinkers troubled by the incompatibility between Nazi Aryan theory and Brazil's racially and ethnically mixed society. Although all the articles were genuine, the work was secretly organized by Raffalovich and funded by the Jewish Colonization Association. The book, which ranged from academic explanations to outright polemics, seems to have had little impact.

The language used in *Por que ser anti-semita?* by the Brazilian non-Jewish intellectuals in defense of Jews is worth examining. Jews were considered a distinct racial and national group and were always distinguished from "Germans" or "Brazilians." The preface clearly notes the differences: "here [in Brazil] Jews and Germans live alike—and all, Semites and Aryans, live well or badly, but live . . . and work and produce with us."[87] Some writers used traditional stereotypes of Jews even while defending them. A description of an anti-Nazi meeting included the following: "the most prestigious Jews of Paris—bankers, lawyers, writers, industrialists . . . like silver fish in the breast of the equatorial ocean."[88] This usage of anti-Semitic images suggests that many educated Brazilians, including those who defined themselves as liberal, were unable to overcome cultural stereotypes. Those in favor of Jewish immigration could never create a discourse much different from that of anti-Semites.

Ironically, the Jewish community was aided in its fight against anti-Semitism by the growing entry after 1932 of German, Austrian, and Italian Jewish refugees whose bourgeois background was less easily categorized as undesirable, in spite of their settlement in urban areas. Although politicians attacked Eastern European Jews as an integral component of post-1930 Brazilian nativism, the newcomers from Central Europe were highly acculturated, spoke languages common to non-Jewish immigrant communities in Brazil, and were moderate or conservative politically. They were also highly educated and skilled, and often arrived with some capital. As the non-Jewish Herbert V. Levy, at the time a young journalist (and later a federal deputy from São Paulo and director general of the *Gazeta Mercantil*), argued in his *Problemas actuaes da economia brasileira* (1934), Germany's "anti-Semitic campaign offers [Brazil] the opportunity to receive . . . the best in the arts, in the sciences, in economics, in letters [and] in all areas of cultural activity . . . [German Jews] are of undeniable value to progress and cultural development." [89]

In order to emphasize their similarities to other already resident groups, many Central European Jews actively disassociated themselves from what they considered the culturally inferior established Eastern European community.[90] This, they believed, would prevent them from being categorized in negative ways by nativists who attacked Jewish peddling and communal solidarity. Central European refugees were, in fact, part of the industrial European culture that many middle- and upper-class Brazilians wished to emulate. German Jewish organizations emphasized the teaching of Portuguese, something even the nativists had trouble criticizing. German Jews also created institutions specifically aimed at promoting German social and cultural life, and even among refugees there was rarely a declining attachment to German high culture.[91] A German Jewish refugee from Berlin who helped found the Brazilian-Jewish Cultural and Beneficent Society (SIBRA) of Porto Alegre also translated Thomas Mann and Herman Hesse for Livraria do Globo, a large publishing house and bookstore whose titles included a great deal of Brazilian and European anti-Semitic material.[92]

The "Jewish Question" became increasingly complicated as large numbers of Central European refugees entered Brazil. A number of influential Brazilians, without abandoning restrictions, now began to simultaneously support continued or expanded Jewish immigration. None, however, proposed a completely open policy based on humanitarian principles. Rather, like some Nazi policies in which certain Jews were allowed to maintain their positions as long as they remained economically "useful," some diplomats and journalists argued that only wealthy or skilled refugees should be permitted to enter. Rio de Janeiro's well-established *Correio da Manhã* editorialized in favor of an increased Jewish presence, noting that "the great exodus of Jewish workers from Germany . . . would bring all their technical, industrial and principally agricultural skills." [93] Ildefonso Falcão, the Brazilian consul in Cologne, Germany, approached Foreign Minister Afrânio de Mello

Franco confidentially about the possibilities of giving immigrant visas to Germans "of the Semitic race who [formerly] occupied public positions or were in the liberal professions."[94] In addition to their skills, thought Falcão, Jews would "bring part of their capital because of a special concession made by the German government." Falcão did not reach his conclusion without a push; the Jewish directors of some of Germany's largest industries, including Schürman and Tietz A.G. (furniture manufacturers) and the Ludolph Marx Group, had come to the consul with formal proposals to establish similar firms in São Paulo and Rio de Janeiro.[95]

The negatives attached to all potential Jewish immigrants, in spite of the benefits they might bring to Brazil, led Falcão to hedge his positive assessment of the situation. In his letter to Foreign Minister Mello Franco, Falcão suggested: "It is possible that I am wrong [in my assessment] and in that case Your Excellency should tell me."[96] Mello Franco, however, was even more unsure than Falcão about the wisdom of promoting Jewish immigration in a political climate so heavily imbued with nativism and anti-Semitism. He simply sent Falcão's letter on to the Minister of Labor, Industry, and Commerce, Joaquim Pedro Salgado Filho, before responding to his consul in Cologne.[97]

Although no clear policy existed with regard to the immigration of members of the Jewish bourgeoisie, Mello Franco was certain that there were no obstacles to the entrance of Jews who were "rural workers with a definite destination."[98] Jewish organizations found "a very liberal attitude in favor of Jewish refugees," and in 1933 over three hundred refugees were granted special permission to enter Brazil.[99] Jews not destined to toil on the land, however, posed a problem, although no specific restrictions against their entry existed. Itamaraty cautiously instructed a government business representative in Poland about the policy on visas for nonagricultural workers: "it has become vital that the formalities are followed . . . for the entry of immigrants in the country."[100] In other words, the lax attitude that Brazil's overseas representatives often took in granting immigrant visas was not acceptable for Jews who were not farmers.

With diplomats carefully following the rules, refugees without families already resident in Brazil found themselves in a difficult position. In December 1933, Rabbi Raffalovich attempted to convince Labor Minister Salgado Filho, who had previously been open to Jewish immigration, to continue to make exceptions for Jews. The rabbi was well prepared for the meeting: he brought letters of support from the director general of the Labor Department and from the minister of agriculture. He even invited Congressman Horacio Lafer, a Jewish friend of Salgado Filho, to attend. The meeting was a failure. Salgado Filho's power had been eclipsed by nativists, and he "would not hear of making an exception in our case. [Because of the] overpopulation of all larger cities and the insufficiency of employment he cannot allow immigration . . . to hurt the native."[101] According to Salgado Filho only new agricultural colonies could create spaces for Jewish immigrants without family members in Brazil.[102]

NATIVISM AND THE CONSTITUTION OF 1934

Immigration and assimilation featured prominently in the debates on a new constitution that began in 1933. Simple laws and decrees no longer seemed sufficient, and politicians agreed that immigration restriction needed to have the force of constitutional law. Brazil's constitutional delegates hoped to model their new immigration policy on the United States National Origins Acts, a document that "left a conviction in various quarters [in the United States] that the chief purpose . . . was to keep out Jews."[103] Although rarely mentioned as such in the debates, delegates regularly alluded to Jews. The deputy from Ceará, Antônio Xavier de Oliveira, worried that Brazil "should not be the promised land of Israel."[104] São Paulo's representative, Jorge Americano, was less concerned. He believed that "Jewish blood" could be found in everyone and suggested that worrying about it was useless.[105] Pedro Aurélio de Góis Monteiro, another delegate and one of the leaders of the Revolution of 1930, argued that "it is an error to presume that immigration brings civilization." According to Góis Monteiro, "disparate and nonassimilable races" should be excluded.[106] Others complained of those who "only go to the state capital cities to form neighborhoods of disorder and crime," a claim often directed at those who lived in Bom Retiro (São Paulo), Praça Onze (Rio de Janeiro), and Bom Fim (Porto Alegre), all traditional immigrant areas where Jews concentrated.[107] New Brazilian legislation, insisted Xavier de Oliveira, had to limit entry "to those elements judged preferable, the civilized whites of Central and Northern Europe."[108] Oliveira's rejection of Eastern European Jewish immigrants neatly combined notions of race, ethnicity, and geography. Generalized nativism had been transformed into specific anti-Semitism.

The discussion of the new Brazilian constitution came during a period of relatively open political debate in Brazil.[109] This made nativism a public issue of which anti-Semitism was one important component. Afonso Arinos de Mello Franco, a prominent and well-respected intellectual and journalist who in 1933 directed the two most influential newspapers in the state of Minas Gerais, attacked Jews in *Preparação ao nacionalismo,* published in 1934 by the highly regarded Civilização Brasileira.[110] In it he cited anti-Semitic works including Hitler's *Mein Kampf* (the original German version) and the Gustavo Barroso–translated version of Henry Ford's *The International Jew.* This racist literature was used to support Arinos's claim that "Jewish internationalists" were responsible for everything from "the German Revolution" to the French Revolution, which Arinos (like many Nazi theorists and the Integralist Barroso) claimed was inspired by "Jews" such as Danton ("David"), Robespierre ("Rubin"), and Rousseau.[111] Arinos also argued that Jews, because of the "special formation of the Hebraic psychology," were natural communists who caused the Russian Revolution.[112] Arinos castigated non-Jewish Brazilians such as Solidônio Leite, whose essay on the importance of Jews in colonial Brazil had appeared in the aforementioned *Por que ser anti-semita?,* while glorifying such Nazi favorites as the Portuguese anti-Semite Mario Saa.[113]

Nativism sold newspapers, and the debate over the new constitution gave politicians concerned about the preservation of what they termed the Brazilian "race" growing access to the press. Fidelis Reis, a longtime deputy who more than a decade earlier had tried to ban Asian and Jewish immigrants, now received more publicity for his bigotry.[114] Rio de Janeiro's frequently anti-Vargas *A Nação* entered the fray arguing that the nativist Society of the Friends of Alberto Torres "is just what we need."[115] Another powerful *carioca* (the term for residents of Rio de Janeiro) paper, the *Correio da Manhã,* agreed and opined that Brazil could not be "the great melting pot for the fusion and reform of all the world as the Jewish writer Zegwill [suggests]."[116] Federal decision makers found these articles useful for suggesting that their anti-Jewish policies had widespread support.[117] A special subfile of nativist newspaper clippings was even kept in Itamaraty's Jewish immigration files.

The constitution of 1934 simultaneously reflected the desires of Brazil's urban middle and working classes as it attempted to appeal to those groups.[118] It guaranteed free elections while centralizing and expanding the government's social and economic roles. The constitution's clear nativism also expressed the growing xenophobia that had overtaken urban Brazil.[119] An annual quota of 2 percent of the number from each nation who had arrived in the previous fifty years was fixed, and farmers were given preferential treatment.[120] The national government now had total authority over immigration, and the constitution suggested "the possibility of prohibition, total, or in relation to origin," of immigrants in order "to guarantee the ethnic integration and physical and civic capacity of the immigrant."[121] All licensed businesses needed a majority of native born Brazilians on their boards of directors.[122] Liberal professions were restricted to Brazilian citizens or those who had been naturalized *and* had served in the Brazilian armed forces. The rejection of professional diplomas granted by foreign educational institutions left many immigrants in the liberal professions unable to work legally without a degree from a Brazilian university.[123] Ten German Jewish physicians went to Brazil in 1933 after receiving assurances that they could practice after passing language and Brazilian history examinations, as well as some medical courses. All entered the University of Rio de Janeiro as students in 1933, but new restrictions a year later forced them out since they were not native born.[124]

Exclusionist sentiment had wide support in urban areas. Although relatively small, it was the middle class that seemed to hold the political balance, and with both extremes of the political spectrum blaming immigrants for Brazil's troubles, exclusion was widely appealing.[125] Those with university educations (doctors, lawyers, engineers) believed restriction was the best way to secure their social and economic status. For professionals struggling to find jobs or clients, foreign-trained professionals and urban workers were perceived as threatening. Nativism had become more than a key to election in many urban districts; it had become a generally agreed-upon position. However useful in capturing political allegiances, nativism also had a downside. The new immigration restrictions made it increasingly difficult to satisfy industry's demands for skilled immigrant labor. Furthermore, nativists were angered that restrictive policies did not close the ports entirely.

These contradictions led to an increasingly open discussion of the "Jewish Question" among Brazilian intellectuals and urban politicians. Júlio de Revorêdo of São Paulo's Department of Labor was commissioned by the agricultural secretary of the state of Minas Gerais to do a study of immigration. In his manuscript, which was financially supported by the Government Printing Office and published under the title *Immigração*, Revorêdo argued that Jews should be prohibited from entering Brazil because they were not open to assimilation given "the propaganda of the rabbis against Jewish integration."[126] Oliveira Vianna hypothesized that while Spanish and Portuguese immigrants were highly assimilable and could easily be submerged and help improve the "Brazilian race," the Jewish "miscegenation co-efficient is equal to zero."[127] Some even claimed knowledge of "the presence and activity of . . . Jewish political and religious societ[ies] in Brazil [involved in] politics, espionage, [and] crimes."[128]

EARLY INTERNATIONAL PRESSURE: THE LEAGUE OF NATIONS AND THE MCDONALD MISSION

Brazil has always been a country of exceptions, especially when it comes to policy enforcement. This, in the 1930s, was the result of the fact that many petty public officials were willing to be bribed in order not to enforce rules while those in the higher echelons consciously wrote policies that were open to wide interpretation. A single policy, then, could be pointed at as political evidence of the simultaneous dominance of contradictory ideologies. New immigration restrictions thus did not prevent Jews from entering Brazil, and when the League of Nations in 1933 appointed James G. McDonald, a diplomat from the United States whose salary and budget were funded primarily by a group of Jewish organizations, as High Commissioner for Refugees (Jewish and Other) Coming from Germany, he focused much of his energy on Brazil.[129] The League of Nations's attempt to convince Brazil to accept German Jewish refugees is important for a number of reasons. In spite of the general failure of the mission, it cemented Brazil's image among North Americans and Europeans as flexible on the refugee question, an image that informed relations with the United States and England for the next decade. The failure also made clear the depth of anti-Jewish sentiment among Brazilian federal decision makers in the mid-1930s. Finally, it was High Commissioner McDonald who helped create the philo-Semitic discourse based around Jewish economic desirability that eventually influenced the Brazilian policies allowing thousands of refugees to enter the country.

    The High Commission began its work in the midst of a growing undercurrent of anti-Jewish sentiment in Brazil in 1933 and 1934. By associating Jews with all plans for refugee relief, even ones that did not include Jews, nativists were able to give the impression that Brazil was being overrun with objectionable immigrants. Such was the case when the League of Nations suggested that Brazil accept a large group of Christian Assyrians whose claims to autonomy were not sustainable after the end of the British mandate in Iraq.[130] To combat the plan successfully, nativists realized, they could not simply attack Assyrians, a group unknown to most Brazilians. Rather, more familiar images were needed to engender a negative reaction.[131] To Costa Rego, an anti-Semitic Catholic monsignor writing for Rio's *Correio da Manhã*, Assyrians were bad but German Jews were "in certain respects even worse." [132] In an editorial published by Rio's always supportive *Jornal do Comércio*, the Society of the Friends of Alberto Torres tried hard to find a common ground between nationalist and nativist sentiments by linking immigration to war. Assyrians were like Jews, asserted the group, a military enemy that would culturally defeat Brazil if allowed to penetrate its borders.

> The threat that hovers over Brazil of an invasion of the inhabitants of Iraq, which England wished to place in Paraná, was a signal of alarm that awakened our people and warned them against certain currents of immigration that have been coming our way. We refer in particular to the Japanese and the Jews, who for good reasons are undesirable immigrants rejected today by all nations that are in need of foreign labor.
>
> Now the Jews: Although not fit for the racial formation of Brazil, they continue to disembark at Brazilian ports, filling our cities with parasites, intermediaries, secondhand buyers, installment peddlers, and dishonest elements in commercial circles. . . . Let us have sufficient courage to repel the Japanese, the Jews, and other undesirable elements and say audibly that we only want to have European immigrants who are suitable for the building of our country.[133]

Brazil's deputies rejected the League of Nations plan. This was, at least in part, a result of the influence of Raúl de Paula, secretary of the Society of the Friends of Alberto Torres and a member of a federal commission on immigration appointed by the minister of labor.[134] Rio's *Folha da Manhã* publicly thanked nativist groups for stopping the entry of Assyrians.[135] Rio's *Diário da Tarde* complimented the "patriotic attitude of Getúlio Vargas who vetoed the lamentable initiative." [136] Nativism had won out over humanitarianism.

The antirefugee climate was exaggerated by the resentment the League of Nations had created with its Assyrian proposal. This made James McDonald's mission to Brazil nearly impossible. Even so, Mc-Donald believed Brazil was an excellent place to relocate refugees, and he proposed with no irony that Brazil had an opportunity "of helping [itself] as well as helping to solve the problem of refugees from Germany." [137] Economic strength, claimed McDonald, resulted from immigrant populations, and the commissioner played on stereotypes of Jewish business acumen when he commented that "the stupidity of the German policy had driven [out] . . . her best brains and most enterprising minds . . . [T]he admission of refugees from Germany with specific capacities . . . would help [Latin American nations] to develop a more diversified national economy."[138] McDonald emphasized that current immigration policies needed to change. Brazil, along with Argentina, was asked to consider the admission of eighty to one hundred refugee families a month, and Uruguay twenty to thirty, for a trial period of six months.

In his initial investigations McDonald appears to have made three serious errors. The first was a failure to recognize that many Brazilian policymakers were nativists and anti-Semites. Second, McDonald never appreciated the serious splits between the state and federal governments over immigration. Although encouraged that Rio de Janeiro was "as full of lobbyists from various states working for Japanese agricultural immigration as Washington is of arms lobbyists during the discussion of a naval bill," the commissioner focused much of his energy on state and local officials, who had little influence over federal immigration policy.[139]

Finally, McDonald was naively optimistic that pro-immigrant sentiment outside of urban areas included Jewish refugees.[140] When São Paulo officials noted that their state "could absorb 100,000 new workers in the coffee and cotton *fazendas*" and others in Pernambuco and Rio Grande do Sul spoke of their "imperative need for new workers and [their] determination to overcome the opposition of the 'politicians,'" they were not referring to Jewish professionals, small traders, craftsmen, or minor officials and clerks never previously employed in agriculture or as manual workers.[141] A proposal drawn up in 1935 by the Land, Colonization, and Immigration Directorate (DTCI) of São Paulo's Secretary of Agriculture, Industry, and Commerce aimed at reducing the numbers of immigrants entering from countries like Poland that had both large numbers of Jews and low indices of agricultural settlement.[142] Similarly, José Antônio Flores da Cunha, military governor of Rio Grande do Sul and an adversary of Vargas, was not thinking of petit bourgeois immigrants when he "showed considerable impatience with the attitude of such nationalists as the Minister of Labour" and suggested that refugees go to Uruguay and "then come over land to Rio Grande do Sul, with no attention paid to constitutional restrictions that should never have been adopted."[143]

In spite of the negative reaction to previous League of Nations proposals, McDonald decided to target Brazil on his four-month survey trip to South America in 1935. The specific aim was to find places for twenty-six thousand refugees who had left Germany after 1933 and had resettled temporarily in other European countries.[144] The High Commission planned to resettle five thousand refugees (70 percent were Jews) during 1935. McDonald thought twenty-five hundred might be sent to Latin America even though passage there cost twice as much as to the United States or Palestine. He believed mistakenly that there would be no new German refugees after 1935 and that if Latin America absorbed those not settled in Palestine, North America, or Europe, the problem would be solved. The estimate was incorrect: the complete evacuation of German Jewry became necessary after the passage of the Nuremberg Laws in 1935. McDonald was accompanied by a longtime associate active in international affairs, Dr. Samuel Guy Inman, a North American academic who specialized in Latin America. McDonald believed Inman was "the best informed North American on the peoples and problems of South America," and Inman hoped that his "personal acquaintanceships might enable us to accomplish more than ordinary diplomatic approaches."[145] Inman, however, was more realistic than McDonald. He considered the trip "more or less a gamble, with the present extreme nationalistic spirit."[146]

The McDonald Mission concentrated its efforts on Brazil, Argentina, and Uruguay. Each had substantial Jewish populations, established refugee support organizations, and, in the High Commissioner's view, a willingness to take refugees. McDonald believed that Brazil and Argentina presented the best economic opportunities for the refugees and that his guarantee that visas would be given only to "intellectuals" would lead to a relaxation of quota restrictions. This idea was encouraged by Oswaldo Aranha, Brazilian ambassador to the United States, after Inman emphasized that only a "limited number of carefully picked people, who would contribute to Brazilian life as they thoroughly identified themselves with your civilization," would be sent.[147] Aranha sent personal letters of introduction to government officials whom "it might be to our advantage to consult," including President Getúlio Vargas.[148]

Before McDonald even set foot in Rio, the nativist press began inflaming public and political sentiment, again using a coded anti-Semitic language that never actually mentioned the word *Jews* or *Jewish*. Rio's *Diário de Notícias* sent a collective shiver down *carioca* spines with its headline "The Germans Expelled from Germany Will Come to Brazil— The Next Trip of the High Commissioner Is to Brazil."[149] McDonald "had been warned repeatedly by immigration experts . . . that these restrictions, administrative, legal, and in Brazil also constitutional, could not be overcome," but he appeared to have been surprised by the intense anti-Jewish immigration sentiment among federal bureaucrats.[150] With issues of assimilation and ethnic purity very much a part of the national discourse on immigration, McDonald should have realized that the door might be closed to most refugees. Even so he remained optimistic and continued to see Brazil as flexible in taking refugees because there, more than in any other Latin American nation, McDonald and Inman met with the government's highest representatives. Vargas and most ranking government officials discussed refugees with the two, who for almost two months "continued uninterruptedly our assaults on the Brazilian authorities."[151] This suggests that Vargas hoped to defuse international pressure by giving the impression that he would consider exceptions to Brazilian policy. McDonald was impressed with the treatment he received. After meeting with Francisco Campos, a legal scholar and politician from Minas Gerais who had founded a neofascist "black shirt" movement in Minas Gerais in 1931 and had become Brazil's first minister of education in the same year and a special consultant to President Vargas in 1933, and Carlos Drummond de Andrade, private secretary to the minister of education, McDonald commented on "how civilized these Brazilians really are as compared with so many of our cold, perfunctory Anglo-Saxon officials!"[152] The apparent friendliness did not fool the experienced Inman. He complained that "Brazilian officials have a technique in handling foreign commissions which consists of receiving them cordially with the hope that they will not be in the country more than two or three weeks. After he has gone away, charmed by his reception, nothing is done."[153] Always claiming an "unfailing willingness to participate in any great humanitarian movement," members of the regime rarely did anything concrete for refugees.[154]

Inman and McDonald met with everyone who might help their cause. A discussion with Sebastião Cardinal Leme of Rio de Janeiro, a close friend of Vargas who often dined alone with the president, regarding Catholic refugees from Germany led to the government's rapid approval of visas for this group.[155] Sir Henry Lynch, the London Rothschild Group's representative in Rio and a confidant of Vargas and other Brazilian officials, on the other hand, "emphasized the difficulty of getting around the constitution and the . . . emphasis on agricultural immigrants."[156] U.S., French, and British diplomatic representatives were cordial but extremely pessimistic about the Jewish refugee matter.[157] Even relief representatives were "close competitor[s] with the diplomats for the prize in unmitigated pessimism."[158] A British diplomat emphasized that the Brazilian government was interested only in farmers and asked McDonald if he "could describe [the refugees] as such, or even as being prepared to work on the land."[159] Since relief groups directed most Jewish farmers to Palestine, McDonald could only "stress the humanitarian issue and also the fact that refugees who had [already] entered Brazil . . . had shown themselves excellent citizens devoid of the communist taint which the press were inclined to attribute to fleers from Herr Hitler's wrath."[160] This humanitarian approach was not particularly successful, but Inman and McDonald continued to present Jewish refugees as exceptional since "unless the case could be made on the broad basis of humanity which might justify opening the doors to these victims of persecution, as it were on extraconstitutional grounds, I feared that we would probably be defeated."[161]

McDonald remained optimistic. Brazil's size and industrial plans led him to wonder "why . . . should there not be a Jewish community here . . . at least several times larger than [the one] in Argentina."[162] This view was encouraged by Aranha's support and Vargas's desire to give an impression of openness. An invitation for Inman and McDonald to meet the president in the summer capital of Petrópolis arrived and Vargas tried to charm the two diplomats, although McDonald hoped that an offhand comment that "my grandfather must have come from Ireland . . . was not meant to be uncomplimentary."[163] Vargas responded with apparent enthusiasm to McDonald's request for a special arrangement that would permit 500 Jews or 125 Jewish families a month to enter Brazil.[164] He promised "that he would speak to the Minister of Labor the next day . . . and ask for him to fix a quota"; McDonald and Inman left Petrópolis feeling confident.[165]

Getúlio Vargas was adept at promoting false hopes among international observers, a strategy he would use to deal with the refugee issue until he left power in 1945. McDonald, however, did not know this and decided to rally British support so that Vargas would be encouraged to pursue the plan.[166] The English, however, were not interested, in spite of their own desire to insure that Jewish refugees would not settle in England, a point that they wanted kept quiet.[167] Since the British government "would not be prepared to admit quantities of refugees either to this country or to the Crown colonies, we are not in a good position to urge other Governments to do so."[168] Fear of international embarrassment led the British to withhold support, and McDonald realized that no one really wanted refugees.

British support probably would not have mattered. Meeting with

Agamemnon Magalhães, a nativist who replaced the generally amenable Salgado Filho as Minister of Labor, Industry, and Commerce, two days after leaving Petrópolis, McDonald and Inman were told categorically that the German quota was 3,080 and that only 10 percent of this number could be Jews even if they were farmers.[169] Inman was infuriated. He privately wrote that Magalhães "is entirely wrong in saying that. No law has been passed interpreting the Constitution and these figures are not legally fixed."[170] Since Vargas often interpreted the constitution as he wished until specific laws were passed, some hope still remained. Magalhães, however, would be of no help; he refused to discuss circumventing the 2 percent quota, since, according to McDonald, he was "a new man from the North and intensely politically minded."[171] If any exceptions were made, Magalhães is reported to have told the two, "I would at once be attacked by the Friends of Alberto Torres and following such an attack I would have to stand an interpellation in the Chamber."[172]

Agamemnon Magalhães's lack of interest was a major defeat but was not surprising considering the general anti-immigrant sentiment in Brazil.[173] A *Jornal do Comércio* headline screamed "Itamaraty against the National Interest" when plans to accept refugees surfaced.[174] Raúl de Paula, a member of the Society of the Friends of Alberto Torres, quit the Ministry of Labor Commission on Immigration in disgust, wanting "to be free in my actions . . . to continue [my] campaign against Japanese and Jews [who are] undesirable elements for our racial mixture."[175] Sebastião Sampaio, former consul general in New York (and later consul general in Prague), feared that the entrance of German Jews would hurt negotiations with the Nazis for a new commercial treaty.[176] Others in the government rejected the plan despite the High Commissioner's guarantee that "no Communists or other radicals interested to carry on their political activities" would be included among the refugees.[177] Only the foreign minister, the lawyer and industrialist Macedo Soares, "was unqualifiedly in favor of our proposal," and promised to urge Vargas to accept it.[178]

Macedo Soares lacked influence even among the diplomatic corps he ostensibly commanded. Brazil's delegate in Bucharest argued against giving visas to Jews who "frequently expressed subversive ideas," something the "excellent Romanian Christian farmers" did not.[179] A member of the embassy staff in London had a similar opinion, telling Macedo Soares that Jews were dangerous "communist propagandists" and that they were transferring money to Brazil to help pay "for [communist] propaganda and the other necessities of the Communist Party."[180] The problem could be solved, said the diplomat, only if the issuance of the visas was contingent upon the embassy's receiving assurance that the money was coming from "authentic" sources. Such attitudes were frequently expressed by those within the regime, and the weak Macedo Soares had little choice but to follow suit.

The only way to get visas for significant numbers of German Jewish refugees, McDonald and Inman realized, was through a legal or technical formula. It was Ideolo Vaz de Mello, head of the Passport Division and a member of an interdepartmental committee on immigration, who came up with a plan that Inman termed "a brilliant idea": the creation of a quota for "stateless" individuals. The stateless had no legally defined nationality and could not enter under a national quota. Ex-quota entries might thus be a technical way of solving the problem within the confines of the law. Vaz de Mello was a *gaúcho* who had previously lobbied for the entrance of large numbers of Japanese laborers, and he enthusiastically agreed to help McDonald compose a plan that would be acceptable to both Labor and Foreign Affairs, arguing that "the policy embodied in the Constitution . . . is absurd, all the more because of Brazil's obvious need for European blood to strengthen the population here, which is so largely Negro or Indian."[181]

Vaz de Mello's plan, like a previous one he had concocted that classified only those above fourteen years of age as immigrants, fell apart when Magalhães insisted that stateless visas be given only to farmers and that any of these refugees who moved to urban areas would be deported.[182] Since the High Commission had neither the resources, the authorization, nor the refugees to set up Jewish agricultural colonies, this demand could not be met. McDonald next suggested that he would guarantee employment for refugees prior to arrival in Brazil. This proposal, however, never reached the minister of labor because of objections ranging from the lack of an ICA-sponsored agricultural project to the minister's insistence that he would read only plans presented personally. Magalhães always seemed to be out of Rio de Janeiro, and McDonald was no doubt discouraged when, after waiting for the minister to return, he was told to relax and "bring [himself] into close communion with nature."[183]

Only the Jewish Colonization Association, which had abandoned the colonization ideal in Brazil almost two decades earlier, continued to fantasize about the "very great possibilities in the immense Brazilian Republic."[184] Louis Oungre, general director of the ICA, was in Brazil when Vaz de Mello made his suggestion about creating a stateless quota that would allow Jews to settle in new farming colonies, but he would not make any commitments without the permission of the ICA directorate. The ICA, however, never formulated a colonization plan, angering many in Brazil's Jewish community. Not realizing that Jewish farmers usually went to Palestine and were not among the refugees coming to Brazil from Germany, resident Jews angrily attacked the ICA and Oungre in a public meeting. Dr. Moses Rabinovitch of Rio's Brazilian Jewish Association complained that the Jewish community was "indignant" and that the ICA should "recognize the bright future that a formidable and essential agricultural immigration of Jews would have in Brazil." [185] The lack of support did not stop new colonization plans from being hatched. In April 1935, the Center for the Promotion of Jewish Agriculture was formed with the express aim of settling Jewish farmers in rural zones near large cities.[186] Its main achievement was to put further pressure on the ICA, which, in 1936, finally set up a new Jewish farming colony near Rio. (See chapter 3.)

McDonald and Inman's hard work did bring about some results. In 1935 a plan to bring Jewish academics dismissed by the German government to Brazil was launched with some success. Alberto Bueno Neto, secretary of agriculture of the State of São Paulo, for example, regularly contracted foreign scientists at great expense to help with São Paulo's agricultural problems. When he learned that German Jewish specialists in agriculture, plant disease, and soil analysis were available "for the salary of a Brazilian professor or scientist," he was ecstatic and "practically guaranteed employment." [187] Inman remained concerned that such hirings would be waylaid by immigration restrictions but believed that "state authorities in São Paulo evidently believe that they are strong enough to force the central government to do whatever seems necessary to meet the immigration demands of the state which pays most of the federal bills." [188] Federal Minister of Agriculture Odilón Duarte Braga, although showing more restraint, was also enthusiastic about hiring German professors since "he hoped that the specialists would be satisfied with seemingly low salaries." [189] Eleven different academic institutions throughout Brazil desired displaced German scholars, including the world-renowned Butantã and Oswaldo Cruz institutes.[190] An old friend of Inman's, Anisio S. Teixeira, Rio de Janeiro's reformist secretary of education and Brazil's leading educator following completion of a master's degree at Columbia University Teachers College under the guidance of John Dewey, authorized the establishment of a new university in the city and suggested that refugees might be contracted there. The rector, Afrânio Peixoto, a regular on the Rio social circuit and "a scientist with an international reputation who loves to make whoopee," had publicly defended Jews in the aforementioned *Por que ser anti-semita?* and hired refugees for about half of the twenty new teaching positions.[191] At the recently established University of São Paulo, however, a stated desire to fill positions in chemistry and natural history with "Germans being expelled from their country by Hitlerism" did not translate into the hiring of more than a few Jews.[192]

The small victories never added up to much. In late 1935 Teixeira, Peixoto, and other reformers who opposed religious training in public schools, including Heitor Villa-Lobos, were fired following a series of anti-Vargas insurrections that took place throughout Brazil. Teixeira sought exile in France, where he became a founder of UNESCO, and was replaced by Francisco Campos, who promised to create an educational system for the "traditional, humanistic and Christian Brazil" by ridding the system of bolshevik tendencies.[193] Yet again, the anti-Jewish codes were clear in the reference to communism and the assertion that Brazil was monolithically Christian, and the Integralists leaped to support the changes.[194] Not surprisingly, Brazil steadfastly refused to admit large numbers of refugees, and a lack of international support for the High Commission for Refugees meant that few German Jews entered Brazil under League of Nations auspices. The many disappointments, and a growing realization that humanitarianism had little influence in international politics, led McDonald to resign in December 1935. The High Commissioner left his post embittered, believing that "considerations of diplomatic correctness must yield to those of common humanity" but knowing that this would never be the case.[195]

GERMAN JEWISH IMAGES OF BRAZIL

Restrictive legislation, nativism, and lack of support were not the only impediments to Jewish migration to Brazil. Another obstruction came from German Jews who wondered if Brazil might be less a place of refuge and more one of trouble and misery. According to popular wisdom Brazil lacked educational facilities and was believed to be a land of revolution and dictatorship.[196] White-collar refugees were afraid they would be forced to become day laborers and would not have the opportunity to purchase land or homes. This image of Brazil had been in the making for some time. A 1928 conference on refugees held in Buenos

Aires had portrayed Brazil specifically, and Latin America generally, as a blue-collar region unattractive for German Jewish merchants, businesspeople, and academics. According to Haim Avni, the *Korrespondenzblatt* of Berlin's Central Office for Jewish Emigration frequently warned German Jewry about the dangers of migration to South America.[197] The portrayal was so negative that between 1933 and 1936, when emigration from Germany was highest, Jews generally went to the United States, Canada, Palestine, or Argentina rather than Brazil. It was only when the Nuremberg Laws took effect and it became increasingly difficult for Jews to enter preferred nations of destination that German Jews began coming in greater numbers to Brazil. (See appendix 8.)

The most frightening vision of Brazil was produced by Dr. Arthur Ruppin, a German Jew who visited South America to examine its potential for German Jewish resettlement in late 1935. Ruppin, a committed Zionist and later the first professor of Jewish Sociology at the Hebrew University (Jerusalem), published his report in the Hebrew press in Palestine, in five articles in Berlin's *Jüdische Rundschau*, in London's *Jewish Chronicle*, and later as a book.[198] The potential for German Jewish life in Brazil, according to Ruppin, was low. Eastern European Jews had succeeded because they worked as "salesmen on the installment system [who] go from house to house like peddlers in order to find customers, and it seems that the German Jews cannot very well compete in that respect with the East European Jews."[199] The two thousand German Jews who had immigrated to Brazil before October 1935 were having trouble getting the jobs they desired. The "immigrants were ignorant of the needs of the country and belong mostly to the commercial class. While skilled workers and artisans found remunerative work very quickly, this was much more difficult for the business people, who had at first to content themselves with subordinate and poorly paid positions."[200] Ruppin failed to mention that German Jews often refused to accept help from relief organizations operated by Eastern Europeans. In 1935, for example, only 494 of the 835 German Jewish refugees who migrated to Brazil went to the local HICEM for help, even though the organization was finding jobs for about 75 percent of those who needed them.[201] Regardless of their reasons, as late as 1935 German Jewry found little reason to leave for Brazil.

Brazilian law did make it difficult for German Jews in the liberal professions. Those with European professional degrees were not allowed to practice, and one immigrant aid group reported that the test to legalize a foreign medical degree was so difficult that "none—except

TABLE 2.2

JEWISH EMIGRATION FROM GERMANY AND JEWISH
IMMIGRATION TO BRAZIL, 1933–1941

Year	Total Jewish Emigr. from Germany	German-Jewish Immig. to Brazil	German-Jewish Immig./All Jewish Immig.	
			No.	%
1933	37,000	363	1.0	10.9
1934	23,000	835	3.6	22.0
1935	21,000	357	1.7	20.0
1936	25,000	1,772	7.1	51.8
1937	23,000	1,315	5.7	65.6
1938	40,000	445	1.1	83.9
1939	78,000	2,899	3.7	63.0
1940	15,000	1,033	6.9	27.2
1941	8,000	408	5.1	3.7
Total	270,000	9,427	3.5	40.3

SOURCES Werner Rosenstock, "Exodus 1933–1939: A Survey of Jewish Emigration from Germany," *Leo Baeck Institute Yearbook* 1 (1956), 377. Herbert A. Strauss, "Jewish Emigration from Germany: Nazi Policies and Jewish Responses (I)," *Leo Baeck Institute Yearbook* 25 (1980), 326. "Les juifs dans l'histoire du Brésil," *Rapport d'activité pendant la période 1933–1943*, HIAS-Brazil, folder 1, YIVO-NY.

a single dentist—is so far known to have passed."[202] Many German Jewish physicians were unable to obtain licenses and turned to other professions. Others affiliated with Brazilians in order to work officially in unrestricted areas of medicine while unofficially (and illegally) continuing their practices on the side. Evidence of this is found in the *Crônica Israelita,* published by the Jewish Congregation of São Paulo (CIP), which was filled with advertisements for medical services by Central European Jewish immigrant practitioners.[203] Yet extralegal jobs were limited, and according to Ruppin, "even in the event of relaxations in the legal immigration restrictions in the near future the economic prospects for German Jews, unless they have a capital of at least £1,000, are limited."[204]

Arthur Ruppin believed that Brazil would never accept more than the 835 German Jews it had in 1934. He was wrong: by 1936 twice that number had entered, representing a growing percentage of all Jewish immigrants to Brazil. (See table 2.2.) Many who arrived before 1936 were young people, single or recently married, who later "called" their

TABLE 2.3

JEWISH AND GENERAL IMMIGRATION TO BRAZIL,
1933–1936

Year	General	Jewish	% Jewish/General
1933	46,081	3,317	7.1
1934	46,027	3,794	8.2
1935	29,585	1,758	5.9
1936	12,773	3,418	26.0

SOURCES "Discriminação por nacionalidade dos imigrantes entrando no Brasil no período 1924–1933 e 1934–1939," *RIC* 1:3 (July 1940), 633–38. SCA 1926–1935, JCA-L.

parents and relatives to Brazil via the *chamada* system. The majority of German Jews settled in São Paulo, Rio de Janeiro, and Porto Alegre. Some, however, went to unexpected locations like the town of Rolândia, in the northern part of the state of Paraná, where ten of the sixty German families who immigrated after 1933 were Jewish.[205]

EXCEPTIONS

In spite of the quotas set out by the 1934 constitution, Jews continued to enter Brazil in significant numbers. Although almost half of those entering between 1933 and 1936 were Poles, the numbers of Germans had grown substantially.[206] Another trend also became apparent; even though most Eastern European Jews entered through Santos, an overwhelming percentage of German Jews disembarked in Rio de Janeiro.[207] This shows the force of the 1930 immigration laws, which made immigration difficult for nonfarmers who had no relatives in Brazil. Many Eastern European Jews had settled in São Paulo before 1930 and later called their relatives to that state. German Jews, on the other hand, began arriving after 1930 and often had no resident family. They entered through the traditional port for unaffiliated immigrants who knew nothing of Brazil except the name of its capital.

The relatively high number of Jewish entrances after 1934 is surprising given Brazil's increasingly restrictive policies. These laws, however, were often loosely interpreted, and sometimes ignored altogether. One month after the restrictions took effect in 1934, for example, three hundred Jews, the majority of them refugees in Holland, Belgium, and

France, were allowed to enter Brazil under old immigration laws.[208] Isaiah Raffalovich secured visas for three hundred others whose "unhindered debarkation is authorized by the Government as a favor." He also convinced the Brazilian government to extend by six months the old immigration rules for Jewish refugees still in Europe.[209]

The exceptions made for Jews caused confusion throughout the governmental infrastructure. The consul general in Amsterdam, for example, refused to issue visas without specific orders from Rio de Janeiro, while his counterpart in Antwerp would issue them with authorization from Luis Martins de Souza Dantas, the Brazilian ambassador in Paris.[210] Souza Dantas, a diplomat educated in Rio de Janeiro's Faculty of Juridical and Social Sciences who had spent most of his career in Europe, had been appointed ambassador to France in 1922 and gave special treatment to Jews even as restrictions were tightened. In both 1924 and 1926 he had served as Brazil's representative to the League of Nations, and his humanitarian approach to refugee issues was well-known to Jewish groups.[211] Yet lower-level diplomats were often confused by the contradictions between policy, rhetoric, and practice. Inconsistency also reinforced a bureaucratic problem: immigration policy-making was in the hands of the Ministry of Labor, while implementation was under the control of both the Colonization Department (which reported to the Ministry of Labor) and Itamaraty.

The complexity of the issue became clear in 1934 when Souza Dantas met with James McDonald and Louis Oungre to discuss a request to bring six hundred German Jewish immigrants per month, for six months, to Brazil. These immigrants were not eligible to enter under the quota system, and McDonald fell back on stereotypes of Jewish wealth to make his case. Jewish refugees, he promised, "bring a considerable amount of capital, [and are] destined to run commercial, industrial and agricultural firms of enormous capacity that will be capable of furnishing work for the immigrants and [Brazilian] workers."[212] A simple yes or no answer was expected to the request. Souza Dantas, however, sent the request to Rio, where the director general of the Colonization Department, although unclear regarding the exact policy, expressed his conviction that requests to bring large groups of Jews into Brazil had to be approved by Labor. If the "Minister of Labor [did] not find the introduction of these workers into Brazil inconvenient," it was then necessary to get the approval of the Ministry of Foreign Affairs before any visas could actually be distributed.[213] When the request arrived at Itamaraty it moved up the chain of command and was dismissed. Before it reached the foreign minister himself, Itamaraty bureaucrats underlined certain critical words so that their superiors would instantly know where to place the document. These words were, in order, *Jewish Colonization Association, immigrants,* and *Jews.* It is no surprise that the request was never approved.

As Jewish entry increased in the early 1930s, Brazilian nativists increasingly focused their anger. Even so, the negative images tended to be based on stereotypes of Eastern European Jewry. As attacks on Jewish entry became commonplace, and even attracted the notice of foreign observers, a new wave of Central European Jewry began to enter Brazil.[214] Policymakers were confused by this new group, who seemed not to fit the traditional image of Jews. Even so, the old image still predominated and there were growing indications that the Vargas regime was going to satisfy nativist sentiment by enacting a specific anti-Jewish immigration policy. Thus the debate over the "Jewish Question" shifted into the realm of policy as Brazil followed the restrictionist path that other American republics had embarked on a decade earlier. The movement to restrict immigration to those judged racially assimilable made it clear that the undesirables were no longer welcome in Brazil.

Colonists in the Jewish Colonization Association's "Colony Philipson" (Rio Grande do Sul, 1922). Courtesy of the Archives of the Instituto Cultural Judaico Marc Chagall, Porto Alegre.

Abraham Slavutsky, a Ukrainian Jewish Immigrant, with children and employees in his Porto Alegre furniture shop. (Porto Alegre, 1928–1929.) Courtesy of
the Archives of the Instituto Cultural Judaico Marc Chagall, Porto Alegre.

Directors and students in the "Renascença" Jewish School of São Paulo (São
Paulo, 1933).

The Jouchelevich family in front of their home on the Jewish Colonization Association's "Colony Baronesa Clara" (Rio Grande do Sul, 1938). Courtesy of the Archives of the Instituto Cultural Judaico Marc Chagall, Porto Alegre.

A Yiddish theater production in São Paulo's Municipal Theater (São Paulo, 1940s).

A Jewish religious holiday celebration. (São Paulo, 1940s.)

CHAPTER THREE

Brazil Responds to the "Jewish Question"

By 1935 the Jewish Question had become the Jewish Problem.[1] Anti-Semitism mixed with xenophobia, according to Robert Levine, "particularly among members of the intellectual elite increasingly disconcerted by the specter of Marxist-influenced internationalism."[2] As the Brazilian Communist movement reached its peak in the mid-1930s, politicians and intellectuals emphasized the presumed ties between Jews and Communism, and press reports in state capitals on the arrests of foreign Party militants Olga Benário Prestes and Arthur Ewert (Harry Berger) played up the Jewish backgrounds of the two.[3] Attacks on Jews and Jewish immigration in the respectable press mirrored an increasing desire to limit or end entrances.[4] Vargas appointees to Itamaraty (the Brazilian foreign ministry) began designing a restrictive immigration policy, with the support of many federal bureaucrats, and in 1937 stringent rules barred all Jews, including tourists and those coming for business purposes, from entering Brazil. Brazilian nativism had been transformed into anti-Jewish policy.

The alleged connection between Judaism and communism linked Brazilian intellectuals and politicians in new ways. Gustavo Barroso, the widely read Integralist and former federal deputy, used the preface to the Catholic priest J. Cabral's aggressively anti-Semitic *A questão judaica* to remark that the Jewish Question was a "racial problem" because of "Jewish messianic racism."[5] Barroso also regularly used the veneer of academic-double talk to make traditional anti-Semitic allegations of a Jewish-communist conspiracy appear indisputable.[6] One of

Rio's better-known weeklies, *Século XX,* concurred, claiming that a movement existed to "transform Brazil into a slave of Russia where the secret forces of international Judaism [would] predominate."[7] Francisco José Oliveira Vianna, the extremely influential social and political commentator who was closely tied to the Vargas regime, judged "the Jewish group [to be] infusible" (that is, did not melt into the pot) and argued that Aryans were non-Communist by nature.[8] The obvious corollary was that non-Aryans—Jews—were Communists. Similar sentiments were echoed by Labienne Salgado dos Santos, a diplomat in Bucharest and later chief of Brazil's Passport Division. He clearly distinguished between Christians, "who never participate in political disturbances," and the "Jewish business people . . . who frequently express subversive ideas . . . [and] sadly make up the majority of the Romanian immigrants to Brazil."[9] Even Oswaldo Aranha, considered a moderate by many in and outside of Brazil, argued that Communism, which he believed was harming the United States that he admired so much, was the result of "the Judaism which created and maintains this ambience, capable of sending this civilization into an abyss."[10]

The linkage between Judaism and political upheaval helped propel proposals for a policy to restrict Jewish immigration through the bureaucracy. Support could be found throughout the upper echelons of the government, in the overseas diplomatic corps, among intellectuals, and of course among Integralists and others who found their ideas appealing. Jorge Latour, commercial attaché in Warsaw, proposed that "special rules" be written "for the prohibition, or restriction, at least, of the entrance of Jews."[11] Letters from the public came in; one of them, which linked economic nationalism (the search for petroleum) with a desire to restrict the "evil Jewish immigration [that was] a million times a thousand worse than Japanese immigration," not only received a careful reading in President Vargas's office, but was then sent on to the National Department of Mineral Production in the Ministry of Agriculture.[12] Others used the language of war in their fight against Jewish immigration, claiming that "waves" of "undesirable and harmful Jews" were "infiltrating" the borders "without interruption."[13] Integralists demanded immigration restrictions with complaints to the influential Federal Police Chief Filinto Müller that they were "victim[s] of Jews."[14] Müller himself opposed Jewish immigration, and his stance was so obvious that Karl Loewenstein, an Amherst College political scientist whose on-the-spot study of the Estado Novo was generally apologetic, pointed it out.[15]

The solidification of anti-Jewish sentiment among office holders collided with two issues certain to challenge nativist and anti-Jewish positions. First, in the mid-1930s, Jews increasingly sought to flee Europe,
and relief organizations that had previously discouraged immigration
to Brazil now began to direct refugees there.[16] Furthermore, both the
U.S. and British governments asked that the regime treat the "Jewish
Question" in a less heavy-handed manner. Restrictions on Jewish immigration, even if they were politically expedient at home, placed Brazil
in a tenuous position abroad. That Jewish refugees could help Brazil
cement its alliance with the United States became especially apparent
after Oswaldo Aranha became foreign minister in 1938. Just a year
after the creation of an immigration policy that reduced Jewish immigration to its lowest point in over a decade, a new relationship with the
United States and shifting stereotypes about Jews helped pry open Brazil's doors. Jewish refugees were no longer simply and exclusively seen
in a negative light; they had become tools in a game of international
and domestic politics.

THE COLONY AT REZENDE

Brazil's official anti-Jewish policy became apparent in 1936. Ironically,
this occurred when the Jewish Colonization Association decided to offer the Brazilian government the immigrants it wanted—farmers.[17] No
immigration plan was more carefully constructed than the one to create
an agricultural colony in Rezende, about 190 kilometers west of Rio de
Janeiro. In July 1936 the ICA purchased a two-thousand-hectare plot,
equipped the entire colony, and even found real farmers to settle it.[18]
The project was carried out in consultation with the minister of agriculture, who was invited to inspect the area. The ICA planned to recruit
refugees who might "obtain admission into the country . . . [within] the
Brazilian immigration restrictions."[19] By depositing a bond in a Rio
bank, the ICA guaranteed that none of the 137 proposed families would
become public charges; the immigrants even managed to secure certificates of morality and capability from the Nazi government.[20] The minister of agriculture's blessing led the Department of Immigration to authorize visas, which, much to everyone's surprise, never arrived.
Apparently, when the Department of Immigration informed the foreign
minister, José Carlos de Macedo Soares, about the plans, he requested
more information. Assuming that the foreign minister's request was a
veiled sign of opposition, the Immigration Department referred the mat-

ter to the Ministry of Labor, which canceled the authorization without informing the ICA.[21]

Opposition to the organized settlement of Jews at Rezende could be found throughout the government. Labienne Salgado dos Santos did not "believe in either the sincerity of the organization [the ICA] or in the durability of the colony if it remains in the hands of Jews."[22] Filinto Müller opposed all ICA plans, especially after intercepting a letter from an ICA employee to the organization's Paris headquarters indicating that the ICA was regularly bribing immigration officials to let refugee Jews with tourist visas enter Brazil.[23] Oliveira Vianna, then a consultant to the Ministry of Labor, pointed to the few colonists who remained in the ICA's Quatro Irmãos colony as an argument for rejecting the visas.[24] Dulphe Pinheiro Machado, director general of the Departamento Nacional de Povoamento (DNP; the National Population Department), the Ministry of Labor's agency in charge of colonization, complained of "Jews . . . and other parasitical elements that constitute ethnic minorities and that upset the tranquillity of the nations where they live."[25]

In December, Agamemnon Magalhães finally informed the Jewish Colonization Association that "the immigration of Jews to the property acquired . . . at Rezende would not be permitted."[26] No official reason was given, as the policy was kept hidden for fear of negative diplomatic repercussions. Relief groups were not fooled. Complaints of "anti-Semitic fascism" led the British ambassador, Sir Hugh Gurney, to broach the subject with Getúlio Vargas, who "fully recognizes the desirability of admitting agriculturists, particularly those with capital."[27] Even so the visas were not granted. Others soon began putting pressure on Brazil. The diplomat Leo S. Rowe, director of the Pan-American Union (which became the permanent secretariat of the Organization of American States in 1948), pleaded with Oswaldo Aranha to do "a very great service which will be greatly appreciated."[28] The U.S. government entered the fray after determining that the new colony might provide a legal residence for Jews who had overstayed their visas.[29] The diplomatic attempts were fruitless. Visas for Jews, according to the foreign minister, simply "were not in accord with the present interests of the country."[30]

After more than two years of pressure from British and U.S. diplomats, the government relented. In early April 1938 a different Rezende colony than the one envisioned finally opened. The settlers were already resident naturalized Brazilians and not new immigrants as originally planned. Thus the opening of the colony was played up as an example of how, with hard work on the land, foreign farmers could become "good" Brazilians. Ernani do Amaral Peixoto, Rio de Janeiro's federal interventor, visited the colony, and what he seemed to find "very agreeable" was that there were few Jews actually living there.[31] The non-Jewish residents of the city of Rezende agreed, and held a mass in honor of the colonists.[32] An official press release on the opening of the colony focused on the humanitarian aspects of permitting the "purely Brazilian project" to open. No Brazilian tax money, the government emphasized, had been invested, and although "the colony is for thirty families . . . for now there are only fifteen."[33] The original plan to locate 137 families in the colony went unmentioned, as did the fact that houses had already been built for eighty families.

Amaral Peixoto's visit to Rezende was fairly big news: it was reported in most of Rio de Janeiro's newspapers and even made the front page of O Carioca and the Correio da Manhã.[34] Yet if the interventor's visit was a mild propaganda opportunity for the regime, the arrival of Getúlio Vargas himself in May 1938 provided the Brazilian government, the Jewish Colonization Association, and the Brazilian Jewish community with a chance to toot their own horns.[35] The weekly Yiddish Idische Presse (Jewish Press) dedicated an entire issue to the story, while the Diário de Notícias headlined its story "The Jew Returns to the Land."[36] While the president's expected visits to the fields, a colonist's home, and a school were uneventful, his brief, perhaps apocryphal, meeting with a young boy was significant. Demonstrating both a hope for assimilation and a distrust of the foreign, Vargas, for no apparent reason, asked the young boy, "Are you Hungarian?" "No, sir," responded the boy, "I am Brazilian."[37]

Confused images of Jews abounded in the press reports on the opening of the colony. In most cases, however, the reports reflected a vision of "the Jews" as both positive for development and negative for Brazilian society. A picture of one colonist in the Diário de Notícias that was labeled inaccurately "son of a Berlin banker" led readers simultaneously toward traditional anti-Semitic associations of Jews with wealth and toward a hope that such wealth might find its way into Brazil.[38] Rio's A Noite called the colony "a small homeland for those without a homeland," suggesting that Jews could never become Brazilian and that Rezende was a state within a state.[39] This suggestion was reinforced by constant references to the "Fazenda dos Judeus" (the plantation of the Jews). Those in government shared these views, and no refugees were actually given visas to settle in Rezende. When the ICA sent a group to

examine the colony in 1939, a visitor commented: "It is sad and significant to see the new houses fully furnished, on small vegetable, dairy and
fruit farms, fenced and equipped, standing empty and deteriorating."[40]
In late 1942 Oswaldo Aranha even attempted to purchase five hundred
hectares of the land as a horse-breeding farm.[41]

The Jewish Colonization Association's attempt to play by the rules
and regain governmental favor was a failure, but the refusal of the Vargas regime to grant visas to Jewish farmers suggests a number of points
worth elucidating. A set of deep-seated preconceived notions led many
policymakers to reject the idea that Jews could be farmers. At the same
time even those who believed in the efficacy of the agricultural training
of the refugees saw the admittance of the group as both politically and
culturally dangerous. Jewish immigrants, even if they were farmers,
were viewed not as acceptable tillers of the soil but as undesirable Jews.

A MOVEMENT TAKES SHAPE

The guarantees of electoral democracy promised in the constitution of
1934 did not prevent the Brazilian political system from moving toward
the extremes, with Communists representing the left and Integralists the
right. It was a claimed fear of communism, however, that most frequently motivated members of the Vargas regime in their decisions, a
position reinforced by Vargas, who put Brazil under national emergency status six separate times (for three months each time) beginning
in December 1935. At the same time, the Integralists seemed to be
growing in power, supported by such regime insiders as Police Chief
Müller and General Newton Cavalcanti. The move toward the right
was frequently justified by pointing to the dangers of Jewish immigration, a position reinforced by the growing political influence of Germany and the intellectual influence of Nazi thinkers. Even foreign observers noted that "the infection [of anti-Semitism] has begun to spread
to some official quarters."[42]

The fear of Jews was a regular theme in mid-1930s political correspondence. Federal deputy Figueiredo Rodrigues labeled Jews "a danger" and claimed that one hundred thousand were already in Brazil, a
gross exaggeration.[43] Filinto Müller was told by a correspondent from
Bahia that "to improve the campaign [against communism] it would be
a good practice never to separate the idea of COMMUNISM from that
of JEW." In order to best do this, Müller was asked to order "the press
throughout the country [to] designate as JEWS all the criminals of true

Israelite origin: the pimps, the *contrabandistas,* [and those who have] biblical names. . . . "[44] Such notions hit a sympathetic chord with Müller; in early 1938 he prepared a thirty-page report for the Justice Ministry stating that Jews "of the lowest possible level" were coming to Brazil to transform it into "a giant Jewish encampment."[45] The industrialist Euvaldo Lodi (who would be president of the Confederação Nacional da Indústria from 1938 to 1954), one of the revolutionaries of 1930 and second vice president of the Federal House of Deputies, pressed for an immigration quota system that would impose the "restrictions necessary to guarantee the ethnic integration and physical and civil capacity of immigrants."[46] He wanted to reject all visa applications from stateless persons, pointing out that this would effectively block Jewish immigration. Playing on traditional notions of Jews as dirty and disease-ridden, the chief of Brazil's commercial office in Poland, Pedro M. da Rocha, complained that lax immigration laws had given the governments of Eastern Europe an "excellent opportunity to clean their ghettos."[47] According to da Rocha, between five hundred and one thousand Polish Jews, five to ten times the actual number, disembarked each month in Santos, the majority with forged *cartas de chamada* accepted by "venal authorities of the State of São Paulo."[48] Others conjured up ideas of insidious Jewish political power, blaming the supposed rise in immigration on "Jewish elements who are well connected in certain Brazilian political, military or social circles."[49] Edgardo Barbedo and Jorge Latour, two Brazilian diplomats in Poland, fused all the ideas together when they complained that Jewish entry created an "invasion of degenerate elements, parasitic and unassimilable, against whom only [we] are fighting."[50]

The anti-Jewish movement in Brazil appeared large and expanding in 1936 and early 1937, supported by everyone from intellectuals to government officials to Catholic authorities.[51] Memos aimed at stopping Jewish immigration regularly passed through the bureaucracy, giving the appearance of a well-organized and generally agreed upon anti-Jewish immigration stance. This, however, was not exactly the case. Those committed to ending Jewish entry manipulated information to give the movement a universal appearance. Anti-Semitic diplomats in Warsaw and Bucharest, for example, cited each other regularly. Higher-ranking diplomats and those in Rio would then quote seemingly well-documented and impartial diplomatic reports that claimed Eastern European Jews could never be farmers, that they were the "worst possible" immigrants, and that "there is a Jewish population of over a million and they are the only ones who go to Brazil." [52] Those opposed to Jewish entry also looked to Felix Pacheco's *Jornal do Comércio,* which published articles free of charge for the Society of the Friends of Alberto Torres, for ammunition. Scurrilous charges thus had an appearance of journalistic objectivity. Comments by "Friends" also found their way into governmental reports, giving an air of independent confirmation to the *Jornal do Comércio's* charges. The information in the articles and anti-Semitic diplomatic reports was then recycled and passed again through the Estado Novo bureaucracy, expanding the paper and the apparent strength of the movement. [53] The Foreign Ministry's huge files on Jewish immigration, it turns out, were all filled with the same misinformation from the same sources.

Brazil's diplomats in Europe often seemed to echo Nazi rhetoric about Jews, denouncing them as communists and rich capitalists simultaneously. Nazi foreign minister Joachim von Ribbentrop, for example, commented to a member of the U.S. diplomatic corps—who then passed it on to Joseph Kennedy, the U.S. ambassador in London—that "the Jews in Germany without exception were pickpockets, murderers and thieves. The property they possessed had been acquired illegally." [54] Compare this with an often-cited report titled "The Inconveniences of Semitic Emigration," prepared by Labienne Salgado dos Santos: "In Romania . . . [it is the] dishonesty of the businesspeople and the habit of the Jews to garner positions, favors, and privileges corruptly by distributing money both secretly and openly." [55]

Anti-Semitic discourse in Brazil was extremely derivative. Even the caricatures and anti-Semitic jokes contained little that made them "Brazilian." [56] All the usual accusations were repeated, focusing on alleged Jewish bolshevism, a claimed Jewish relationship to capitalism, and a presumed Jewish inability to assimilate, usually citing the false *Protocols of the Elders of Zion* and the also unoriginal writings of Henry Ford. Ironically, Brazilian anti-Semitic comments were also placed within a context of a supposed lack of prejudice. This gave nativists the opportunity to promote the idea that a specific Brazilian "race" existed that was uniquely generous and open, which Jews were not, while castigating the Brazilian government for allowing this open attitude to be reflected in lax immigration policies. This argument allowed these nativists to claim that Jewish immigration restrictions could not be anti-Semitic since "there do not exist in Brazil by natural disposition or law racial or religious prejudices." [57] Yet even this "Brazilian" formulation of anti-Semitism was not particularly original. Indeed, Wilhelm Mar's

1879 pamphlet *The Victory of Judaism over Germanism,* the first anti-Semitic best-seller, suggested that Jews had conquered Germany "through the fault of the Germans themselves."[58]

These assertions were part of the many hidden mechanisms constructed to legitimate bigotry. Even those favoring some Jewish immigration used the language of anti-Semitism. One proposal for a law to regulate immigration referred to Jews as both a nationality and a race.[59] Since Jews were often legally stateless, this implied a racial nationality—in other words, one that could not be modified by a legal process like naturalization. Mário Moreira da Silva, the consul general in Budapest who believed the ban on Jewish entry "should never be revoked," argued along these lines.[60] Jewish "individuals are, in general, unassimilable, continuing eternally as Jews, without any love or concern for the land that receives them and gives them shelter."[61]

Only the Portuguese language gave anti-Semitism a peculiarly Brazilian tinge. Take, for example, the often-made references to Jews as "individuals" ("individuals of the Jewish race," "individuals of the Jewish nationality"). The term *individuo,* according to the anthropologist Roberto da Matta, implies that its referent is not a "person" in the Brazilian context—in other words, not part of collective Brazilian society. In this view, the in-group is exempt from many of the strictures created by society to control social deviants, or in this case *"individuos."* If "laws . . . are applied only to individuals," the wording of anti-Semitic expressions takes on a meaning far more complex than the words suggest.[62] Consider, then, comments on Poland's Jewish population of "5 million individuals" or proposals to curb the entry of "individuals of Semitic origin." In both cases the terminology implies that Jews were unable, because of a character presumably inherited at birth, to become part of the Brazilian milieu. The term *individuo,* however, was rarely used in correspondence regarding, for example, Portuguese immigrants.

Although Jews bore the brunt of the attacks on immigrants considered unassimilable, and thus undesirable, other groups found themselves placed in the same position. One proposal that arrived on Agamemnon Magalhães's desk in September 1937 came from an Indian prince who wished to create a colony with his followers, all Hindu farmers. As in the Rezende case, the group fit Brazil's expressed developmental and legal goals. The potential immigrants were all experienced farmers, were willing to settle in underpopulated rural areas, and had a sponsor willing to guarantee their success financially. Even so, the proposal was rejected. As a Foreign Ministry consultant on immigration insisted, "it would establish in our country a serious problem of castes and religious myths, two things non-existent in our midst." [63]

JEWS NOT ALLOWED

Anti-Jewish sentiment dominated immigration policy-making. In January 1937 "Israelitas" began to be counted in São Paulo state entrance and exit statistics, supplanting the previous "Catholic" and "non-Catholic" categories.[64] On June 7, 1937, five months before the coup d'état that established the Estado Novo, Secret Circular 1,127 was issued by the Ministry of Foreign Relations and authorized personally by Getúlio Vargas.[65] This circular prohibited the concession of visas to persons of "Semitic origin," thereby causing a 75 percent drop in Jewish immigration over the next year.[66] Strict application of the few clauses that would permit Jews to enter further reduced the numbers. Visas, for example, were not to be refused to "Semites already living in the country, who are married to a Brazilian, have Brazilian children, or have real estate in Brazil." [67] A memo of clarification, however, granted resident status only to those who had been in Brazil for at least five years.[68] Those who were married to Brazilians or had Brazilian children but had no land or fixed goods were to be issued visas only in exceptional cases. Some visas could be granted by special permission to "well-known Jewish cultural, political or social figures," Jewish artists contracted to exhibit in Brazil, and those Jewish tourists visiting Brazil on cruises or package tours.[69] Despite these few loopholes, immigration officials regularly turned away Jewish tourists and businesspeople without fear of punishment.

Why was the term *Semite* used in Secret Circular 1,127 rather than *Jew?* There are a number of related answers. First, excluding "Semites" not only kept Jews out of Brazil, but kept out Arabs as well. This was an important consideration given the uproar a few years earlier when the Assyrian community had tried to enter Brazil from Iraq in large numbers (see chapter 2). Indeed, the linkage of Arabs and Jews by intellectuals and politicians has continued from the 1920s through today.[70] A popular joke told among politicians in the 1950s by Aziz Maron—leader of Bahia's Partido Trabalhista Brasileiro, a federal deputy from 1951 to 1959, and a Brazilian of Syrian/Lebanese descent—has come down to us with the title "Getúlio e os dois semitas" (Getúlio and the Two Semites).[71] According to Aziz, he and a journalist met Getúlio Vargas one day in 1954 in the press room of the Palácio Tiradentes. During the conversation the journalist, who went unnamed, asked Vargas if he had been wise to have Ricardo Jafet, a Paulista of Lebanese descent and president of the Banco do Brasil, and Horacio Lafer, the son of European Jewish immigrants and minister of the Interior (Fazenda), working together in two related and critical positions.[72]

> What was it, Getúlio asked, that the person found so strange about Jafet and Lafer working together? The man responded, "But, Your Excellency, an Arab and a Jew. They will be warring with each other constantly. You will have a real Palestine in your government."
> "Don't get scared," counseled Getúlio. "In the end it's all the same. Both are Semites, Lafer and Jafet. Arabs and Jews fight for the largest booty and after that they understand each other." Getúlio then pointed at Aziz Maron and said to the journalist, "And I would like to introduce you to Deputy Maron, who also has Arab blood and understands the race well."[73]

The use of the term *Semite* in Secret Circular 1,127 did more than link Jews and Arabs. The word itself was used commonly in Europe in the last two decades of the nineteenth century to suggest that Jews were a race, not a religion. By 1848 European racists such as Ernest Renan and Christoph Lassen had posited that the Semitic race (which obviously included Jews) lacked any positive qualities while a distinct Aryan race was "endowed with boundless natural gifts."[74] Such notions strongly influenced everyone from Gobineau to Chamberlain to Hitler and were accepted by many in the Vargas regime who wanted to construct an immigration policy that was specifically inclusive (that is, one that specified who could come in) while being generally exclusive (everyone else was kept out).[75] Secret Circular 1,127's prohibition of "Semites," then, was meant to emphasize that Jews were a problematic "racial group" both because of who they were and because of who they were not (Aryans). The language of Secret Circular 1,127 thus reflected both the anti-Jewish position and the pro–Northern European and Christian ideal as well. The depth and complexity of the nativism that led to the prohibition of "Semitic" entry are revealed in an article that Oliveira Vianna, undoubtedly involved in the construction of Secret Circular 1,127, wrote for the Vargas government's official *Revista de Imigração e Colonização:* "Os imigrantes semíticos e mongóis e sua caraterização antropológica" (Semitic and Mongol immigrants and their anthropological character) linked all the groups whose entry Vianna, education secretary and regime ideologue (and soon to be justice minister) Francisco Campos, Federal Police Chief Müller, and many others opposed by suggesting that Jews and Arabs were both Semites and "Asiatic," thus putting Jews (Semites) and Japanese (Asians) in the same troubling anthropological category.[76]

Given the intent behind Secret Circular 1,127, it comes as little surprise that the application of it effectively reduced Jewish entry. What made the circular particularly tragic was that it went into effect just as emigration from Nazi-occupied areas reached a peak. The new emigratory flow provided an important justification for those who feared a "voluminous current of Jewish immigration that threatened to rise to enormous proportions."[77] Anti-Semitic diplomats, especially those in Eastern Europe, now had a legal mechanism for curtailing what they believed was a huge wave of undesirable immigrants from entering Brazil. Consul General Barbedo, using an image of Jews as subversives who could take over a country without anyone realizing it until it was too late, claimed that "all of [Poland's] 4 million Jews . . . are finding ways to sneak around the immigration laws of our country" and immediately stopped giving visas to Jews. Only 13 of the 283 Polish Jews Barbedo officially permitted to immigrate to Brazil in 1937 received their visas after June.[78]

Why was Circular 1,127 kept a secret? The obvious answer is that members of Vargas's inner circle feared a negative international reaction. Yet secrecy had a more devious purpose: it produced an image of power critical to the regime. By labeling the circular secret, and then telling selected people about it, the Vargas government implied that Brazil was engaged in a struggle against a dangerous unnamed and unseen enemy, presumably an insidious Jewish capitalist-communist conspiracy that was out to sabotage the country. By suggesting that powerful forces dominant in the hemisphere but still weak in Brazil were knocking at the door, it appealed to nationalism. Circular 1,127's secret label also gave the regime room to maneuver by multiplying options for policy enforcement. As a "secret" it existed only by rumor and innuendo. Knowledge of the secret gave status to lower-echelon members of the regime who might exaggerate its virtues to nativists. By admitting, off the record, to the existence of the circular, increasingly vocal complaints about Jews entering Brazil could be defused. Anti-Semitism, the regime had discovered, was a useful tool in securing power.

Although the secret circular officially took effect on its date of emission, some Jews, especially those who already had visas, continued to enter Brazil as the immigration bureaucracy adjusted.[79] It took almost five months for new visa forms with a question on "ethnic origin" to arrive in New York, and queries on how applicants should fill in the section immediately arose. Should immigrants be classified by "the big divisions such as white, black, Asian etc." when the "sub-divisions of each race . . . are considerable?" What should be done, diplomats wondered, with those who "are part of a nation that is not a state like Jews?"[80] Although the questions were complex, the answers were simple. Jews were not to be given visas. A Viennese doctor and his wife wrote directly to Vargas requesting a visa after having been turned down repeatedly over the course of a year. The personal approach did not work: the pair were refused entry on the basis of the circular.[81] Those who "professed Catholicism or any religion that demands a baptism" had to produce a certificate in order to enter.[82] Others claiming to be Christian but bearing names that consular officials supposed were Jewish were also to be refused visas, although this often led to confusion when officials were (quite rightly) unable to decide if names like Braumann or Meland were "Jewish" or not.[83] An Italian with the "Jewish name" of Weinberg repeatedly applied for visas in both Hamburg and Genoa. He promised Vargas that "it is my great desire to become a useful Brazilian citizen, and to accept the Brazilian culture and nation," but never received a visa.[84] In 1937 fewer Jews legally immigrated to Brazil than in any year since 1924. Most Jews, then, could no longer get visas or enter Brazil. The Jewish Problem, so it appeared, had been solved quietly and efficiently.

Members of the U.S. diplomatic corps knew of the secret circular soon after it became operative.[85] So did international relief organizations, often because of the indiscretion of Brazilian diplomats. The Jewish Central Emigration Association of Poland was told outright by the consul general in Warsaw that "due to the instruction received today from Brazilian authorities, I will not persue [sic] any more cartas de chamada. Each passport must be separately considered and referred to the Ministry of Foreign Affairs. All the matters favorably considered up to date which you are keeping in your office remain for the time being invalid."[86]

With Jews no longer officially allowed to enter Brazil, those immigrants already resident in the country began to fear for their future. In 1937 the number of refugees in Brazil with expired tourist visas was so high that a representative of a relief group worried that "if the police authorities rigorously apply the laws against immigrants arriving in the country illegally as tourists, there will be a virtual pogrom."[87] Relief groups thus concentrated much of their energy on finding ways to get

legal residence documents for Jews. When James G. McDonald suggested that Oswaldo Aranha entertained a liberal attitude toward refugee admission, the Brazilian was approached by relief groups. Playing
on Aranha's belief in Jewish influence in the United States, they argued
that "a bad impression was created by the anti-Semitic moves and [that]
there was danger of a cessation of coffee imports on the part of Jewish
importers in New York in retaliation."[88] Within Brazil, refugees with
expiring visas discovered that they would be reclassified as capitalists
eligible for permanent resident status by the Ministry of Justice if they
deposited at least thirty thousand milreis (eighteen hundred U.S. dollars) in a Brazilian bank, registered a business, or bought property. Relief groups developed a plan with the help of the Banco Holandês that
deposited money in the accounts of refugees seeking registration as capitalists. Once the registration was complete, the amount was, according
to a secret memo, "withdrawn and redeposited on the behalf of another
person and so on and so forth."[89] The purchase of a small plot of land
could also achieve reclassification, and regular and rapid sales between
refugees were the rule.

A SECRET IS DISCOVERED

Getúlio Vargas's four-year term was scheduled to end in 1938. Those
who wished to replace him as the presidential campaign began in 1937
included Armando de Oliveira Sales of the newly created Constitution-
alist Party and José Américo de Almeida, considered by most to be the
candidate that Vargas supported. In midyear the Integralist Plínio Salgado also entered the fray, and soon violence and radical pronounce-
ments led many to wonder if a unity candidate might be found if elections were postponed.[90] This sentiment was encouraged by a group of
authoritarian nationalists that included Army Chief of Staff Góis Monteiro, Minister of War Eurico Dutra, pro-Nazi police chief Filinto
Müller, and Francisco Campos, the chief ideologue of nondemocratic
rule.[91] The national mood was exploited by Vargas, who seemed intent
on remaining in power by simultaneously encouraging the Integralists
while playing up the specter of communism.[92]
    Latent anti-Semitism was one of the keys toward justifying the move-
ment to authoritarianism. In late September 1937, the "Cohen Plan,"
an Integralist forgery that alleged plans for a violent Communist over-
throw of the government that specifically included the burning of
churches, was "discovered."[93] The plan, which was widely accepted by

the press as legitimate, was authored by Olympio Mourão Filho, a captain in the Brazilian Army and head of the AIB's propaganda section, and then passed on to General Góis Monteiro.[94] Both the title—"The Cohen Plan"—and the means by which it was arrived at suggest a linkage of Judaism and communism. According to Olympio Mourão Filho, he originally signed the document with the name of the Hungarian communist Bela Kun as a joke. Later, "I remembered that one of our leaders always referred to Kun as Cohen [so I] crossed out the surname Kun and wrote Cohen."[95] The forgery, when released, thus appeared to be authored by the nonexistent Cohen, presumably a Jew.

The fictitious "Cohen Plan" was made public on September 29 when War Minister Dutra urgently requested a renewal of previous national emergency decrees on the *Hora do Brasil* radio program broadcast throughout the country. The request was overwhelmingly approved by Congress, and an executive decree suspended many of the personal rights granted by the 1934 constitution. A public campaign against communism began as everyone from reactionary military officers to high church officials began seeing red. Among the groups most satisfied with the changes were the Integralists, whose close ties to Francisco Campos led them to believe they would be important components in any new government. In early November Plínio Salgado marched thousands of Integralists in front of the presidential palace, where they were reviewed by Vargas and his anti-Semitic confidant General Newton Cavalcanti, one of Salgado's most powerful military allies.[96]

By the end of the first week of November all the parts were in place to create a new regime. The false "Cohen Plan" gave the state a means of squashing dissent simply by labeling it "communist." On November 8 the only moderate left in Vargas's cabinet, Justice Minister Macedo Soares, resigned; his place was taken by Francisco Campos, who had already written a new corporatist constitution. That constitution had received the approval of the entire Vargas cabinet with the exception of the minister of agriculture, Odilón Braga, who was immediately replaced. Early in the morning of November 10 the anticipated *auto-golpe* took place as the cavalry surrounded the presidential palace and copies of the constitution were distributed. The Estado Novo, with Vargas as its head, had been created.

Less than a month after the coup, on December 2, Vargas banned all political parties from operating in Brazil.[97] On that same day the maritime police were ordered to enforce Circular 1,127 in such a way that no Jews would be allowed into Brazil for any reason, even if they possessed legitimately issued visas.[98] This gave port authorities, under the direction of Filinto Müller, new power, and Jewish tourists and businesspeople were immediately denied entry.[99] When minor Brazilian officials admitted the circular's existence to annoyed shipping companies whose passengers were not allowed to disembark, this information was passed on to the passengers. They, in turn, began to complain to their congresspeople and members of parliament, spreading knowledge of the circular's existence into more public spheres.

Both governments acted rapidly on the complaints from American and British Jewish travelers—and voters. U.S. diplomats in Rio were incensed when they discovered that Jews who were U.S. citizens were to be admitted to Brazil only with special permission from the minister of labor. David Kamisar's case was typical. An importer of Brazilian products to the United States, a U.S. citizen, and, according to the U.S. diplomat in charge of the case, a "member of the Jewish race," Kamisar often visited Brazil. In December 1937 he was, much to his shock, denied entrance. Kamisar's son and partner, a U.S. citizen legally resident in Brazil, tried to persuade immigration officers to admit his father but was "advised specifically that the immigration service had received oral instructions to prevent the entrance of Jews."[100] Only after obtaining a release from the minister of labor through a personal connection was David Kamisar's entry permitted. In December, the U.S. embassy dealt with six cases of American Jews denied entrance on the basis of their religion. Each was resolved only after the consul general issued a letter to the Department of Colonization stating the people in question would not overstay their visas.[101]

At first U.S. and British concerns about Circular 1,127 were related to tourists and businesspeople, and a confidential report written by Consul General William C. Burdett, titled "Anti-Semitic Influence in Brazilian Immigration Service," ignored the fact that the orders would also keep Jewish refugees out of Brazil.[102] This focus, however, would soon change as it became clear that Brazil, which the United States hoped would accept Jewish refugees and relieve pressure on the United States and England, was refusing to do so. U.S. and British protests now tied the refugee issue to complaints about how their citizens were treated in this "new phase which is distinctly prejudicial [not only] against Jewish immigrants from Europe but to temporary visitors of the Jewish religion from the United States as well."[103] Robert M. Scotten, counselor for the American embassy, was sent to speak with the ambassador to the United States, Aranha, in Brazil at the time, to "point out that during the tourist season, which is about to commence, a fairly large percentage of visitors from the United States are liable to be Jews. I urged the Brazilian Government to make sure that any American citizens whose travel documents are in order should be permitted to land without hindrance. . . . I pointed out that a continuance of the anti-Jewish policy on the part of the Brazilian Government could not fail to have a deplorable effect upon public opinion in the United States."[104] The discussion distressed the ambassador, who feared that the denial of entry to American Jews provided "a favorable argument to the campaign that Brazil is linked to Germany, something we are fighting here [in the United States]."[105]

Scotten's meeting with Aranha produced two different results. The first was a formal admission that Jewish immigration was "in general undesirable."[106] Second, it confirmed to Aranha, "an ardent champion of the special relationship" between Brazil and the United States, that the refugee issue could be used to improve relations between the two nations.[107] Informally meeting with U.S. Ambassador Jefferson Caffery, Aranha agreed that "it is a grave mistake to continue anti-Jewish activities here . . . [and promised to] talk to President Vargas along those lines."[108] He then promised that temporary visitors would no longer be hindered and that the Brazilian consul general in London would be given permission "to use his discretion in granting tourist visas to British subjects of the Jewish race."[109] Aranha also vowed that "immigration authorities shall in the future place no hindrance of any kind in the way of tourists arriving in Brazil, irrespective of race or religion."[110]

Aranha's pledge did not improve the situation immediately: the following week four American citizens were detained and permitted to enter only after a letter was dispatched from the U.S. embassy. Of all the members of a British tour group wishing to spend a week on Copacabana Beach, only five—the Jewish members—were denied visas.[111] Montague Meyer, a British citizen traveling for health reasons, had his four-day visa refused by the Brazilian consul general in London. His nurse, whose surname was Brown, was given her visa on the spot. Meyer, whose "family has been in England for at least one and a half centuries" and who was a member of the Church of England, complained that the consul general had "come to the conclusion that my surname being 'Meyer' he assumes that I am a Jew and/or a Communist and am likely to be of some danger to the Government of Brazil."[112] His complaint led Sir Hugh Gurney, British ambassador in Rio, to take up the case. Gurney was told that "general instructions had been issued to Brazilian consular officers to refuse visas for Jews [since] they were regarded as an undesirable element and that the Brazilian Government wished to avoid the creation of a Jewish Question in the country."[113] Of course the Jewish Question already existed, and the Brazilian government had responded in a resounding way with Circular 1,127.

By the end of January 1938, things had changed. Brazilian immigration authorities were no longer making apparent efforts "to segregate any [American] Jewish passengers or to prevent the disembarkations of persons of that race [sic]."[114] Jewish travelers with legitimate business interests now entered with ease, although the government continued to deny permanent visas to Jews. International pressure had worked to prevent the most extreme reading of Circular 1,127.

ILLEGALLY IN THE NEW STATE

The advent of the Estado Novo left Jews in Brazil in a precarious position. Discussions of a comprehensive anti-Jewish policy were led by Francisco Campos, the new minister of justice, a founder of the fascist-inspired Legião Liberal Mineira and an aggressive proponent of authoritarianism who sought to remake Brazil along Italian fascist lines.[115] Campos, labeled by Jewish groups "a notorious Integralist and fascist," ordered that all visa applications be accompanied by a baptismal certificate, a rule the U.S. embassy noted "is only enforced in the case of Jews who apply for visas."[116] He also ordered that three-month temporary visas, previously extendable for a second three months, could not be renewed.[117] This simple change increased the number of Jews who would become illegal immigrants on January 1, 1938.[118] Of the forty-four hundred German Jews who had entered with tourist visas between 1933 and 1937, as many as two thousand were, by 1938, illegally in Brazil. By mid-November 1937, between six hundred and eleven hundred German Jews, perhaps 10 to 15 percent of those in Brazil, had been served notice that they were to be deported on December 15.[119]

News of the projected deportations caused great concern among Jewish groups and the U.S. government, both of which realized that expelled Jews "will probably be seized by German authorities and placed in concentration camps."[120] If the Brazilian government embarked upon its deportation plan, the United States would have little choice but to modify or terminate its warming relationship with Brazil in the face of international outrage. This gave Jewish leaders the edge they needed in forcing the United States to take action. In early December 1937, representatives from the Refugee Economic Corporation (REC) and the American Jewish Joint Distribution Committee (AJJDC) met with Laurence Duggan, chief of the U.S. State Department's Division of American Republics, to inform him that a newspaper in New York knew of the deportation orders but, for the time being, "agreed to suspend publication of the news." [121] The blackout, however, would not last forever. If the news became public there would be "severe attacks upon Brazil for the treatment it is according to these Jews," something the U.S. government wanted to avoid. [122]

Duggan promised to mention in a "personal and informal way to the Brazilian Ambassador [Oswaldo Aranha] what the groups have in mind." [123] Jewish relief groups were not so confident, however, and decided to dispatch their own representative to Brazil. Alfred Houston, a lawyer for the Guggenheim family who liked to point out that he was not Jewish and his interests were "wholly philanthropic," was to meet with members of the Brazilian government. By offering to post bonds for all Jews to be deported, Houston hoped to get six-month visa extensions and a promise that no one would be deported to Germany. [124] The AJJDC and the REC would even open visa negotiations with other countries for the to-be-deported refugees.

Alfred Houston's call to the State Department to explain that he was leaving immediately for Brazil led to a meeting with Ambassador Aranha in Washington. Aranha seemed attentive and sympathetic, claiming the situation "could not be as serious as had been portrayed" since "the Brazilian Government would not engage in wholesale deportations." [125] Aranha was leaving for Rio on December 11 and asked Houston to postpone his trip until he investigated the situation personally. A few days later it appeared that Aranha's promises had been accurate: Brazil's chargé d'affaires informed the Department of State that "there are no grounds for the rumor that the Government intend to expel Jews residing in São Paulo and Rio de Janeiro, numbering approximately one thousand. [The] [i]ntention is only to compel return of a few Israelites who entered the national territory illegally and each case will be treated individually with no steps of a general nature in view." [126] Deportation notices had been sent out, explained the chargé, but the Brazilian government had changed its policy. Those illegally in Brazil (that is, those who had overstayed their visas) had no worries, although those who had entered Brazil illegally (that is, with false visas) would be deported.

Washington dismissed the deportation orders as false rumors, but those in Brazil heard a different story. Jewish organizations reported that the Brazilian Government was only willing to "reconsider favorably the situation of Jewish residents, provided moral guarantees as to their behavior and material guarantees that they would not become public charges, could be furnished."[127] The U.S. embassy found that the Brazilian government was enforcing its immigration rules on temporary visas "principally against the large numbers of Jews, mostly of German nationality."[128] The British reached the same conclusion, and Ambassador Gurney complained that the discovery of a cache of forged visas and *cartas de chamada* by the Federal District Police was simply an excuse to apply entry controls "with a special stringency to Jews."[129] Aranha's promise that there would not be general deportations of Jews seemed inaccurate: "the threats to deport, as well as actual deportations, have gone on as in the past."[130]

The twists and turns that were a regular part of Brazil's policies toward Jewish refugees convinced Alfred Houston that he should make another appointment to see Oswaldo Aranha, also now in Brazil. The ambassador suggested that they see President Getúlio Vargas together. Why would a foreign lawyer command an immediate audience with the president of a large nation over the question of the admissions of a refugee group generally deemed undesirable? The answer has little to do with humanitarian issues. Rather, Brazil's relationship with the United States and erroneous notions of Jewish influence gave the issue high priority. If, as Aranha mistakenly believed, the American Jewish community was extraordinarily influential in U.S. political and economic spheres, representatives of Jewish "interests" had to be treated as high-level diplomats. The U.S. embassy, perhaps unwittingly, played on such beliefs. It had pointed out "in an entirely informal and friendly manner the fact that this new policy of the Brazilian Government, if carried very far, could not fail to produce a most unfortunate impression upon public opinion in the United States."[131]

On January 3, 1938, Alfred Houston walked through the arched entry of the Catête Palace, the presidential residence in Rio de Janeiro, to meet with the president and the ambassador. The meeting was a telling one. Vargas declared that "whatever action the Government had taken as regards foreign residents it was not aimed at Jewish ones in particular because in Brazil there is no hatred against, or persecution of Jews."[132] Even so, the president claimed incorrectly that "the great majority of Jewish foreign residents . . . had entered the country on tourist visas which had already expired and were, therefore, subject to deportation."[133] In spite of earlier statements, Vargas himself confirmed that the deportations had been ordered.

Getúlio Vargas was right: Jews with expired tourist visas had broken Brazilian law and were subject to deportation. Perhaps, wondered Alfred Houston, an economic approach might convince the president to see things in a different light. What better residents could Vargas ask for than Jewish refugees who had "secured remunerative employment, have become established in business, and have devoted themselves to agricultural pursuits, thus becoming a source of national wealth."[134] Vargas was interested. Might Houston provide financial assurances that the refugees would not become public charges? queried the president. Houston said that he could, and Vargas agreed to suspend all deportations for sixty days and set up a committee to investigate the matter.

Why did Vargas rescind, at least temporarily, the deportation orders? He tried to give the impression that it was for humanitarian reasons, but this was not the case. Vargas, however, was deeply concerned "about the publicity given, particularly in the United States, to incidents dealing with the entry and permanence of Jews in Brazil."[135] By suspending the deportation orders, Vargas gave himself the time to reconsider the position of Jewish refugees. Furthermore, Houston was now in the president's debt. The quid pro quo was not long in coming: as Houston left the President's office, Aranha took him aside and asked that he and his clients "refrain from all publicity on the subject and . . . discourage such publicity."[136] Houston kept his promise and wired his contacts in relief organizations that they were not to take Brazil to task publicly for its anti-Jewish policies.

A few days later Brazil's Jewish immigration policies were favorably discussed in the *New York Times*. According to correspondent Turner Catledge, the Brazilian government had suspended deportation orders and granted legal status to many refugees. Since most of the deportations were to have been to Germany, the press played the story exactly as both the U.S. and Brazilian governments would have wanted, as "a move dictated by both humanitarian considerations and a desire to strip the 'unitarian' Vargas Government of every possible appearance of nazism and fascism."[137] Vargas also appears to have kept his part of the bargain: less than two weeks after Vargas's meeting with Houston, the minister of justice began "to endeavor to find means to allow . . . Jews to remain in Brazil even though, under the law, they are subject to deportation."[138]

If Jews illegally in Brazil were to be allowed to stay, the nondeportations had to be framed in a way palatable to nativists. Thus the government always implied that it was strictly enforcing immigration legislation. At the same time, it created nondescript categories to include refugees who had overstayed their tourist visas. Brazil, according to Filinto Müller, who never really was able to hide his distaste for Jews, had no desire "to persecute the sons of other lands," and refugees would be allowed to legalize their status if they were married to a Brazilian, had relatives in Brazil, were able to transfer at least fifty contos (twenty-nine hundred U.S. dollars) to a Brazilian bank, or were in Brazil for artistic or scientific purposes.[139] To nativists whose stereotypes of Jews were based on Eastern European models, the categories appeared extremely exclusive. This was not so. The new orders included virtually every refugee in Brazil. Both the United States and Brazilian nativists appear to have been satisfied with the resolution.

U.S. pressure on Brazil had more than a short-term effect. When the sixty-day visa extension expired, thirty more days were added.[140] By early May 1938, all the deportation orders had been canceled and all refugees were given a chance to regularize their status.[141] This action resonated favorably in the U.S. press, which reported Vargas's policy on the front pages. By limiting its concessions to Jews already in Brazil, the Vargas government also relieved pressure to let in new refugees. Minister of Justice Francisco Campos asserted to foreign reporters "that the purpose of the Vargas regime was to do everything possible to prove to the world and the United States particularly that the corporative state [in Brazil] is motivated by no Nazi or Fascist spirit and will countenance no such ideologies as are expressed in racial and religious oppressions."[142] This, of course, contradicted statements Campos had made just a few months earlier.[143] While domestic elites considered Circular 1,127 evidence of the Estado Novo's nationalist spirit, the United States saw Brazil as amenable to pressure on the refugee issue.

Brazil acceded to U.S. pressure, and throughout 1938 Vargas strengthened his ties to the United States and Great Britain. Oswaldo Aranha's excellent relationship with Jefferson Caffery made diplomatic pressure even more effective when the Brazilian was appointed foreign minister in March. Almost immediately Caffery let the new Itamaraty chief know that the United States took interest in "the matter of Jewish immigrants in Brazil, with special reference to . . . the matter of the efforts now being made by outside Jewish agencies to persuade the Brazilian government to allow at least some of the Jewish immigrants illegally in the country to remain."[144] The intimation was important.

The U.S. government expected Brazil to accord special treatment to Jews.

ANTI-FOREIGNER LEGISLATION AND THE JEWISH COMMUNITY'S RESPONSE

Government fears of ethnic separatism, especially in southern Brazil, where many of German descent were concentrated, motivated many of Brazil's policies toward those considered foreigners, often including Brazilian citizens. René Gertz has convincingly shown that such fears were basically paranoid, but even so the Nazis did regularly call on the so-called Teuto-Brazilians (Brazilians of German descent) for support, and Nazi-sponsored activism and propaganda were widespread in Brazil.[145] These laws were applied as strictly to refugee Jews, the overwhelming majority coming from Germany, Italy, or Axis-controlled countries, as to others from those areas. In April 1938, two new laws limited the rights of foreigners and were enforced regularly against Jews. The first gave the government the right to "expel foreigners who for any motive compromise national security, the structure of institutions, or political tranquillity."[146] A second law denied foreigners the right to engage in political activity, join organizations of a political character, or maintain political contact with countries of origin.[147]

Germany's friendly relations with Brazil deteriorated because of the new legislation, as Vargas was accused of acceding to "the increasing domination of Brazil by the United States."[148] Eventually each of the two countries declared the other's ambassador persona non grata.[149] Whatever relief this brought to Brazil's Jewish community, however, must have been tempered when Zionism was banned as indicative of allegiance to a foreign government. Although the Zionist Federation of Brazil tried electing an entirely Brazilian-born board of directors, the Justice Ministry declared the organization illegal since it "must and would remain an essentially foreign organization and since its aims were also clearly political in that its avowed objectives were to collaborate in the creation in Palestine of a home for the Jews."[150] Using the Vargas regime's definition, then, Brazilian citizens could be "foreign." Non-Brazilian relief officials were now allowed to engage in public meetings only if they were conducted entirely in Portuguese. The *pushke* of the Jewish National Fund (KKL)—a simple metal collection box about four inches high, for contributions for the creation of Israel—was declared "illegal and dangerous."[151]

The ban on Zionism created conflicts between Central and Eastern European Jews resident in Brazil, especially in São Paulo, where the majority of refugees were settling and relief problems were most complex. In one case, the Eastern European Centro Hebreu Brasileiro (Brazilian Jewish Center) officially complied with new regulations on political activity while still participating secretly in Zionist activity.[152] The public acceptance of the anti-Zionist regulation, however, gave a small but growing Zionist faction in the German-dominated and generally anti-Zionist Congregação Israelita Paulista a chance to solidify its own position and garner the support of other Central European Jews. The pro-Zionists were led by a group of Italian Jews, the most important of whom was Vittorio Camerini, once known affectionately as "Kamerinsky" because of his attempts to form an alliance with Eastern European Zionists. Following his election as first secretary of the executive committee of the CIP, Camerini realized that he might use Central European Jewish prejudices about Eastern European Jews to help convince German Jews to support Zionism.[153] He thus pointed to the new Brazilian "nationalist" line that the Centro Hebreu Brasileiro took as required by law and claimed that while Eastern European Jews were not true Zionists, Central European Jews "in spite of all pre-Hitler assimilative tendencies never lost their Jewish consciousness . . . and only a very few lost their feeling of *Kol Israel haverim* [All Israel is one]." [154] Camerini's analysis of the situation was far from accurate. Every Eastern European Jewish group in Brazil clandestinely supported Zionist organizations such as the *Keren Hayesod* (Palestine Foundation Fund).[155] The policies of the Estado Novo, however, and the willingness of the Eastern European group to go along with them on paper, gave Camerini's Zionist faction an opportunity to seize power.

The splits between Central and Eastern European Jews were exacerbated as each group felt pressure to provide growing amounts of relief funds while maintaining cultural autonomy. The Jewish Telegraphic Agency, for example, reported that

> [a refugee] relief committee, in which the so-called "East-European Jews" who have been residing in Brazil for many years are not given any representation, has stimulated antagonistic feeling within the Jewish community. In fact, it has split the Jewish community in Brazil into two separate camps, one representing the "Ost-Juden" who are the bulk of the population, and the other representing the newcomers from Germany.[156]

One stimulus for these antagonistic feelings was the creation by German Jewish immigrants of religiously Liberal *einheitzgemeinde* (unified community) synagogues in Brazil's three major centers of Jewish concentration—São Paulo, Rio de Janeiro, and Porto Alegre. In each case, newly arriving German Jews rejected established Eastern European communal institutions, instead creating anti-Zionist organizations that encouraged social integration by teaching of Portuguese and providing refugee relief.[157] From the perspective of the Eastern European Jews who formed the majority of Brazil's Jewish population, however, the creation of these institutions posed a challenge for leadership of Brazil's Jewish community.

The Congregação Israelita Paulista, under the leadership of the stridently anti-Zionist Dr. Ludwig Lorch, was the earliest and most powerful of these Central European Jewish institutions.[158] The gauntlet of challenge presented by the CIP to the Centro Hebreu Brasileiro, a loose confederation of Eastern European organizations, quickly divided São Paulo's Jewish community. Given the increasing effort that Jewish relief organizations had to spend on getting visas for Jews to come to Brazil, this conflict diverted energy away from refugee relief, probably the most critical issue of the moment. In June 1939 a report for the American Jewish Joint Distribution Committee expressed concern over the formation of the CIP exactly on these grounds: "forming a religious congregation . . . conducted in a very beautiful manner by an ordained rabbi . . . may segregate the German Jewish group from the . . . East-European Jews," thus preventing the maximization of community efforts toward refugee relief.[159] Implied is that the "beautiful" services of the CIP would be viewed by many in the Eastern European community as "assimilationist" and therefore anti-Jewish.

The tense atmosphere for minorities living in Estado Novo Brazil, and the conflicts it emphasized within the Jewish community, even spilled over into the realm of language. Rejected by German Jewry after emancipation in 1848 as *zhargon,* Yiddish had remained the language of Eastern European Jewry. In the early twentieth century, however, Central European Zionists believed, as did the Austrian "father of Zionism," Theodore Herzl, that Hebrew, and not Yiddish, should be the language of Zionism. These assumptions were mirrored in Brazil by Jacob Schneider, the Bessarabian-born president of the Brazilian Zionist Organization.[160] He expressed a widely held belief that the far-reaching changes brought on by the *Haskalah,* the artistic and cultural Jewish enlightenment of Eastern Europe, had led to a dismissal of political Zionism by Eastern European Jewry on the grounds that a Jewish homeland was unneeded by those living Jewish lives in segregated areas.

Schneider even claimed that among anti-Zionists *the most active are the Yiddishists* . . . coming from the Ukraine."[161] Eastern European Jewish leaders in Brazil (and elsewhere), however, claimed that true Zionists spoke Yiddish, while Central Europeans resented "being classed as assimilationists 'for the sole reason we cannot speak Yiddish.' "[162] It was in fact Yiddish, not Hebrew, that was the de facto language of Zionism in Brazil through the 1940s, indicating that the power in the Jewish community lay with the Eastern European group, which had migrated earlier, was numerically larger, and set the agenda for conflict. Eastern Europeans saw German- and Italian-speaking Jews, secularized to the point of no longer using a specific Jewish language, as unconcerned with a "return to Zion."

Tensions between Jews of different national origins and the nationalist rhetoric of the Brazilian government did not always prevent the Jewish community from working together to help refugees and fight the new policies. The Society of Jews of Polish Origin continued to operate in spite of being targeted by the Secção de Ordem Social as "a true cell of denationalization."[163] The Jewish Benevolent and Immigrants Protection Society remained in existence by placing a majority of Brazilians on its board and dropping the words "and Immigrants Protection" from its title. When it was discovered that Filinto Müller was censoring mail arriving in Brazil for Jewish groups, organizations started to send their mail by hand via the ever friendly directorate of the Chargeurs Réunis shipping company.[164] Jewish groups were permitted to display the Zionist flag and sing the *Hatikvah* (Zionist national anthem) after convincing officials that they were "symbols of religious significance."[165] A Zionist Boy Scout troop in São Paulo masked its political orientation by changing its name to *Avanhandava*, a Tupi word that is said, among other things, to mean "people of all races."[166] In one strange case a Yiddish-speaking Jewish police censor permitted a lecture on the life of Theodore Herzl when the speaker promised to avoid the word *Zionism*, instead referring to it as "a certain idea, well known to all, which Herzl helped to establish."[167]

If the April 1938 decrees forced Jewish relief work and activism underground, a May 4 decree seemed to solidify Brazil's anti-Jewish refugee position. Patterned on U.S. immigration law, it regulated the entrance of foreigners and reinforced the 2 percent nationality quota established under the 1934 constitution, although those with expired tourist visas were given the opportunity to legalize their status.[168] More troubling, however, the federal government now "reserved the right to

limit or suspend, for economic or social motives, the entrance of individuals of determined races or origins."[169] Without singling out any
particular group, the new law proclaimed Brazil's fears of its own social
experiments in miscegenation. Although Jews were not mentioned by
name, a U.S. military attaché in Brazil believed the law "a forehand
defense against a possible avalanche of undesired Semites fleeing from
Nazi persecution in Germany and Austria."[170] This would be carried
out by the always willing Police Chief Müller, and an American consul
complained that "an unfortunate degree of authority remains . . . in the
hands of the police, whose administration of alien control has been the
basis of severe criticism and the cause of extensive annoyance."[171]

The new decrees extended control over immigrants to a degree never
before felt. Foreign-language publications could not be printed without
official permission, and foreign-language instruction for children under
fourteen years of age was banned.[172] Yiddish newspapers, like all others
in foreign languages, were forced to print all pages with Portuguese
translation or go out of business. Foreign names for businesses and associations were banned.[173] Now that assimilation was a federal legal
issue, new agricultural colonies would have to admit a minimum 30
percent of Brazilian citizens and could admit no more than 25 percent
of a single nationality.[174] This ended the hope that new settlements
might be established exclusively for refugee Jews. Relief groups attempted to respond to the restrictions by asking Brazilian Jews with
social, economic, and political influence to contact friends in the press
so that favorable articles might be published. Others thought that the
federal government's desire to colonize and develop the Amazon might
be used to help refugees get visas.[175] Local Jewish groups immediately
devised plans for Amazonian Jewish colonies, but the Jewish Colonization Association chose not to pursue them.[176]

THE LANGUAGE AND POLITICS OF THE ANTI-JEWISH
IMMIGRANT MOVEMENT: EVIAN AND THE INTER-
GOVERNMENTAL COMMITTEE

Refugee admission held both symbolic and real political significance in
Brazil. Some well-known intellectuals, including Gilberto Freyre, whose
notion of a Brazilian ethnic, cultural, and racial democracy was seemingly at odds with many of the racial doctrines prevalent in European
thought, published essays that viewed Jews in a positive light.[177] Bernardo Schulman openly argued that the Jewish Problem was Brazilian

anti-Semitism.[178] Yet when ex–minister of labor Joaquim Pedro Salgado Filho complained about the rise of Brazilian nativism, he was attacked on the floor of the House of Representatives for "wanting to send 60,000 Assyrians to invade 11,000 kilometers of Brazilian land," a blatant untruth.[179]

Nationalist and anti-immigrant rhetoric abounded among those campaigning for federal and state offices.[180] Such sentiment made the "Jewish Question" a powerful magnet for attracting political debate. A federal committee on Jewish refugees was "designed to weed out undesirables such as 'white slavers, narcotics peddlers, professional gamblers, and anyone not engaged in an honest occupation," language later used in immigration legislation on the subject.[181] Others, like São Paulo State Legislative Assembly deputy Chiquinha Rodrigues, saw Jews simply as another immigrant group unwilling to assimilate rapidly.[182] Those linked to the Integralist movement regularly produced tracts that simply rehashed false charges against Jews and gave the appearance of objectivity by the regular citation of other anti-Semitic works produced in Brazil. Father J. Cabral's *A questão judaica*, one of the most ardent, and unoriginal, attacks on Jews, had a preface written by Gustavo Barroso. Anor Butler Maciel's *Nacionalismo: O problema judaico no mundo e no Brasil: O nacional-socialismo* (Nationalism: The Jewish problem in the world and in Brazil: national socialism), published in 1937 by the widely distributed and respected Livraria do Globo of Porto Alegre, began with a quote from Oliveira Vianna's *Raça e assimilação,* and cited Gustavo Barroso and Afonso Arinos's *Preparação ao nacionalismo* throughout. While Maciel devoted 4 of his 147 pages to an attack on Nazism, his intent was to promote immigration laws that would selectively target Jews. Such restriction was necessary since the "traditionally chivalrous and welcoming Brazilian people" had allowed tens of thousands of Jews, who were by his definition unassimilable, to settle.[183] Basing his arguments on discredited documents like *The Protocols of the Elders of Zion,* articles from Henry Ford's *Dearborn Independent,* and a pseudoscientific study by Oliveira Vianna that showed that Jews had a "fusibility index" of zero, Maciel demanded, "Let's react!!" Responses to the Jewish Question were easy to find in Estado Novo Brazil.[184]

The debate over refugees was mirrored in the highest echelons of the Vargas government, especially after the Conselho de Imigração e Colonização was established in May 1938 to supervise the colonization and admission of immigrants. In his first official declaration, the council's director, João Carlos Muniz, stated that "the Semitic problem [will] assume an essentially critical position."[185] Muniz's language in the three-page statement is revealing. Two groups were "threatened," according to the CIC director: Jews (by Nazis), and Brazil (by "the race of Israel," which "threatened to enter in voluminous proportions"). Claiming erroneously that two hundred thousand Jews had arrived between 1934 and 1937, Muniz stated that "Brazil should not open its doors to Jewish immigration," while at the same time arguing that absolute restriction was not acceptable, for "either economic or humanitarian motives."[186] Francisco Campos met with representatives of the Ministry of Foreign Relations to "examine and resolve the situation of certain foreign elements, especially those of Hebraic origin" who desired to immigrate to Brazil.[187] U.S. influence lent further legitimacy to the option of accepting refugees in significant numbers. When U.S. President Franklin Roosevelt organized an international conference to deal with the refugee crisis, Brazil found that it could no longer resolve the Jewish Question behind closed doors. Now Brazil would be forced to make public statements and deal with the consequences.

On July 6, 1938, the Hôtel Royal in Evian-les-Bains, France, was a center of world attention. Representatives of thirty-two nations, including Brazil, began a nine-day meeting that would examine the possibilities for the mass resettlement of refugees from Germany and Austria.[188] The solution to the crisis was potentially an easy one, as became clear at the Hôtel Royal: nations had to open their doors wide. Few, however, were willing to expand their quotas to allow the resettlement of the primarily Jewish refugees.

The best hope, according to those sponsoring the conference, was the large, underpopulated Latin American republics.[189] Representatives from the United States and Europe presupposed that the past acceptance of large numbers of immigrants, especially in Argentina and Brazil, meant a willingness to take in Jewish refugees. Those who had spent time with Latin American decision makers, on the other hand, knew this was not the case. Almost all the Latin American delegates at Evian opposed the acceptance of "non-Aryan" refugees, giving credence to the saying that there were two kinds of countries in the world, "the kind where Jews cannot live and the kind where Jews could not enter."[190] Brazil's sentiments were very much the norm. One high-ranking Itamaraty official noted that "all the South American Republics made it clear at Evian that they were repulsed by Jewish immigration [and would never] receive these subversive elements who bring social disorder."[191] Another blamed the victim, proposing that the acceptance of German Jewish refugees would propel German minorities into forming a fifth column.[192]

Brazil, more than any other nation represented at Evian, was targeted as the prime area of refugee resettlement.[193] The existence of a vociferous pro-Nazi movement and the many Estado Novo bureaucrats opposed to letting Jewish refugees enter was glossed over by the United States.[194] Hélio Lobo, Brazil's ebullient representative at the conference, encouraged this attitude, intertwining comments on the growing special relationship with the United States with others on the need to populate Brazil's vast interior. Lobo also enjoyed playing the humanitarian, saying "that as regards German and Austrian refugees, the question is urgent. [Brazil] is prepared to respond to the noble appeal of the American government and to make at this critical moment her contribution toward a favorable solution of the problems within the limits of her immigration policy."[195] Myron C. Taylor, former U.S. Steel chairperson and the U.S. representative at Evian, was charmed by Lobo and found "the delegate of Brazil . . . most extraordinarily helpful in bringing his Latin American colleagues to a reasonable point of view."[196] Lobo's status, his friendliness toward the United States, and his apparent willingness to help refugees made him a critical actor.[197]

The Intergovernmental Committee on Political Refugees (IGC) created at Evian met again in London less than a month after the conference ended.[198] Attention focused on Brazil, which was expected to play an important role in what the United States deemed a "major international undertaking." Why was Brazil seen in such a light when U.S. officials knew about the secret orders banning the entry of Jews? Two separate yet connected trends form the answer. One was U.S. confidence that "the similarity of outlook and traditional close collaboration" between the two nations would lead Brazil to follow U.S. suggestions, but not its lead, on refugees.[199] In other words, Brazil could be pushed on the refugee issue. The other was that Brazil increasingly saw itself on the threshold of becoming a major player in hemispheric, if not international, politics. Following the U.S. lead on the refugee issue would help advance that cause.

The desire for warm relations with the United States did not diminish Brazilian hesitancy about accepting Jewish refugees. Brazil reluctantly accepted a vice-chair's role on the IGC, which put it on a par with the United States, France, and the Netherlands. The IGC applied pressure on Brazil to appoint Lobo, but the importance that the United States attached to Brazil's role in the IGC went unmatched by the Brazilian government.[200] The Brazilian government instead offered a commercial attaché already in London. This rankled U.S. Secretary of State Cordell Hull, who ordered Robert Scotten to "take this matter up informally with Aranha." The foreign minister then promised that Brazil would send Lobo, while accepting the vice-chair's position without designating publicly a specific person to hold it.[201]

Two weeks after Brazil agreed to accept the vice-chair, no delegate had been appointed.[202] Soon a strange and convoluted story began emerging out of Itamaraty. According to a "very upset and chagrined" Oswaldo Aranha, Lobo had been ordered to London on August 4. This order had been countermanded when a United Press International dispatch appeared in the Brazilian press claiming that Argentina, originally designated for a vice-chairship on the IGC, had been asked to give it up and had refused. When the report was confirmed, Aranha directed that Brazilian officials "while doing nothing to actually embarrass the conference nevertheless [should] refrain from all part therein and under no conditions act as vice chairman."[203] According to Aranha, Brazil's lack of participation had nothing to do with refugees. Rather, as the foreign minister emphasized, "Brazil would in no case play second fiddle to Argentina." Scotten believed this was all a fit of pique. He suggested that a similar situation had taken place in 1935 when Brazil's Macedo Soares had refused to participate in a regional conference because Brazil's name was inadvertently left off a press release. Perhaps, thought the diplomat, the United States could "assuage Brazil's pride and bring her back into line."[204]

Hull's response to the problem was quick and direct. Ambassador Caffery was ordered to see Aranha and "make clear . . . that from the very inception [the IGC has] . . . been exceedingly anxious to have a representative from Brazil, particularly Lobo, serve as vice chair."[205] This gave Aranha a chance to up the stakes and preserve the regime's nationalist credentials. Whatever Lobo had implied, Aranha emphasized that Brazil was uninterested in helping refugees and had taken "part in the Evian meeting solely because [the United States] had asked."[206] Public opinion, furthermore, would never allow Brazil to appear subordinate to Argentina in the international sphere. Aranha proposed a solution: Brazil's representative to the IGC would be instructed to "cooperate fully with the United States . . . and to follow the policy pursued by Lobo at Evian" but would not "assume" the vice-chair's seat, in spite of the fact that Brazil had already accepted it.[207]

Hull was "greatly disappointed" at the small role Brazil wanted to play in solving the refugee crisis. Now he was also in the tricky position of convincing Aranha to instruct his delegate to assume the previously accepted vice-chairship. If, as appeared increasingly likely, Brazil would never really accept the position, there was nothing to lose by giving the spot to another country. Unfortunately Argentina, the most likely candidate, had also been slighted (in favor of Brazil) and would probably refuse on the same grounds as had Brazil. Moreover, Jefferson Caffery suggested that if the seat went to another country Brazil might withhold all cooperation.[208] Hull accepted Caffery's advice and decided to gamble on Aranha's nationalist pride and desire for international power. Citing Brazil's "eminent position" in the hemisphere, Hull claimed that the acceptance of a vice-chair in the IGC "could not but bring increased recognition of the prestige of Brazil on the part of other nations," a somewhat doubtful assertion.[209]

Throughout August the situation of the Jews of Europe worsened while Aranha and Hull tangled. Aranha remained willing to cancel his noncompliance orders and instruct his delegate to cooperate if he was not asked to "assume" the vice-presidency. At the same time Hull was under increasing pressure from his own diplomats to cement Brazil's role in the IGC, because a positive response might convince other Latin American nations to accept Jewish refugees.[210] U.S. diplomats in Poland, where many Germans and Austrians were stranded, were passing on unofficial reports that Brazil was willing to take "large numbers of Jewish refugees under certain conditions," and this further burdened the U.S. Secretary of State.[211] Another complication was a fear that international proposals for refugee relief might appear so generous as to "encourage persecution by other Governments aimed at forcing out unwanted sections of their populations and the dumping of these people onto the hand of international charity."[212] With the United States refusing to exceed its own quotas, the need for others to take refugees assumed even greater importance.

When the IGC director, George Rublee, an international lawyer from the United States, called the first official meeting on August 31, 1938, Brazil was not represented.[213] The "failure of American and British diplomatic representatives at Rio to dissuade the Brazilian Government from adopting a course which is causing the Committee embarrassment" led to yet another attempt to clarify whether, having accepted a vice-chair's position, Brazil would actually assume it. The Peruvian government was willing to take the post, and the British and

French hinted that they would take action to force Brazil to retire its post.[214] With Brazilian goodwill now the goal of official U.S. policy, however, the U.S. ambassador in London was ordered not to "create even more unfortunate circumstances in . . . active Brazilian ill-will."[215] For two long months no progress was made in convincing any Latin American republics to open their doors or the Brazilians to take a role in solving the refugee crisis. In early September the situation became more muddled. Newly created Italian "racial laws" meant that more refugees now looked to Brazil for salvation.[216] When newspapers throughout Europe incorrectly reported that Brazil would accept ten thousand Jewish refugees, the Brazilian diplomatic corps responded with a tizzy of inaction.[217]

A breakthrough occurred in late September when the Conselho de Imigração e Colonização decided to modify Brazil's immigration policy to make it "considerably more liberal as regards the entry of certain classes of Jewish refugees than was the case up to very recently."[218] Soon a new secret circular, number 1,249, "The Entrance of Jews [Is-raelitas] in National Territory," replaced the earlier one. By replacing Semitas with the more neutral and acceptable (at the time) Israelitas, even Circular 1,249's official heading suggested that Jews were no longer going to be considered as a uniformly unwelcome "race." Indeed, Circular 1,249 was anti-Jewish without prohibiting all Jews from entering. Rather, it created visa categories based on economic benefit. Now Jewish capitalists bearing a minimum five hundred thousand milreis (twenty-nine thousand U.S. dollars), technical experts, and scientists might enter Brazil. Brazil also emphasized its desire to accept Jewish artists and intellectuals of international renown.[219] As O Estado de São Paulo reported accurately in 1948, "The Estado Novo closed its doors to all poor Jews . . . [B]ut those who had some transferable capital could, with some ingenuity, enter the country."[220] Even so, those in the upper echelons of Itamaraty labeled the new position a secret to prevent a negative reaction from domestic observers who believed that no Jewish refugee had a place in Brazil.[221]

Circular 1,249 resolved a number of problems created by the first secret circular. Restrictions against Jews entering with chamadas were terminated as relatives through the second degree could now be "called" by foreign Jews residing legally on Brazilian territory. Jews with return tickets, as well as tourists and businesspeople whose status had been verified by the consular authority, now entered unhindered. Jews were granted tourist visas after submitting a letter from the gov-

ernment that issued their passport stating that there was no legal imped-
iment to their return.[222] Since German and Austrian Jews would presumably be unable to obtain the official letter, false tourism would end.
At the same time international complaints would diminish, because
British and American tourists could now continue to spend their money
at Rio's luxurious beaches.

The new circular had two components. One was to present Brazil as
anti-Nazi/Fascist by allowing British and U.S. citizens easy entry, regardless of their religion. This helped to soften Brazil's identity as
a dictatorship, since reports out of Germany that emphasized the in-
humanity of the Nazi regime had increased popular and press anti-
German sentiment in Brazil.[223] At the same time European Jewish refugees with either capital or skills deemed desirable might now become
eligible for visas. The economic and diplomatic aspects of the circular
were clear to Aranha, who even suggested that the unemployed in the
United States should emigrate to Brazil to help combat German and
Italian influence and strengthen ties between the two countries.[224]

Aranha's desire to keep relations between the United States and Brazil strong led him to promise that Hélio Lobo would represent Brazil at
the December meeting of the IGC and "take an effective part in that
meeting."[225] Aranha's words were carefully chosen. When Lobo did
appear he stated that he did so of his own initiative and without instructions. The optimism he had shown at Evian had also disappeared. Immigration regulations, emphasized Lobo, were made by Vargas, and no
changes would take place before the new year.[226] Three weeks later
Lobo still had not been instructed to take a vice-chair, and his conversations with other Latin American diplomats had shown them unwilling
to accept many refugees. More devastating, an off-the-record claim by
Lobo that Brazil would take five thousand "involuntary emigrants"
(rarely was the term *refugee* or *Jew* used in official conversation) a year
for three years was unfounded. Rather, Brazil was willing to take three
thousand Jews if "they are proven agriculturalists and possess the sum
of 500 pounds each plus fare and settlement expenses."[227]

The Intergovernmental Committee on Political Refugees accom-
plished little before it was eventually disbanded less than a decade after
its creation.[228] The main reason was the unwillingness of most nations,
including Brazil, to accept Jews. Anti-Jewish sentiment among many in
the regime and the nativist press had become an accepted part of the
political discourse on immigration. The desire to close Brazil's doors to
Jews, however, was always in conflict with the view that a relationship

with the United States needed to be cultivated. Orders banning Jews from entering Brazil were kept secret, and discussions of the refugee problem were encouraged. Yet the image of Jews in Brazil was not a static one. Indeed, within a year of the distribution of Secret Circular 1,127, new pressures, and new interpretations of old stereotypes about Jews, would lead decision makers to wonder if absolute bans of Jewish entry were wise. German, Austrian, and Italian refugees were beginning to be seen in a new light—as immigrants whose skills and capital would help Brazil's industrial development. In 1938 Brazil yet again began welcoming the undesirables.

CHAPTER FOUR

Anti-Semitism
and Philo-Semitism?

Few intragovernmental conflicts aroused as much passion, or focused as much attention, as did Jewish immigration during 1939. Over four thousand Jews entered Brazil in that year, more than in any year since 1929.[1] The marked increase should not suggest that prejudices against Jews and Jewish immigrants and refugees disappeared. Indeed, traditional images of Jews—urban based, nonfarming, financially oriented, and internationally powerful—that had been the basis for so much Jew hatred were, in late 1938 and early 1939, increasingly viewed as indicators of Jewish usefulness for Brazil's economic development.[2] In other words, stereotypes about Jews that had previously been judged as negative had come to be regarded by some important decision makers as positive attributes. The reasons for these changes were numerous. Jewish relief groups actively put positive twists on old stereotypes. The United States, itself unwilling to make a major commitment toward Jewish refugees, put pressures on other nations to do so. Furthermore, important federal politicians realized that Jewish refugees from Italy, Austria, and Germany did in fact have occupational experience needed in Brazil's industrializing economy and urbanizing society. The rejection of the absolute ban on Jewish entry thus did not signal so much a change in attitude as a change of interpretation. This reconceptualization of stereotypes gave almost ten thousand Jewish refugees a chance to survive.

From 1930 to 1937 Jewish stereotypes, when used by those making crucial decisions on immigration policy, worked to the disadvantage of

Jewish immigrants and refugees. In 1938, however, this situation had begun to change—a development directly related to the appointment of Oswaldo Aranha, Brazil's ambassador to the United States, as foreign minister. Aranha, it must be emphasized, adhered to many of the same anti-Jewish stereotypes held by other politicians in the Americas and elsewhere.[3] He often tied Jews to an alleged world communist conspiracy, and expressed the belief that Jews were "radically averse to agriculture" and that "en masse they would constitute an obvious danger to the future homogeneity of Brazil."[4] Aranha was not, however, a Judeophobe. There was an important philo-Semitic component found in his conceptions. Jews, in the view of the new foreign minister, were rich, skilled, and influential and thus useful for Brazil's economic development. Moreover, Aranha recognized that the resolution of the Jewish Question in Brazil would have an impact on relations with the United States, a country he admired greatly.[5] As early as 1937 he had worried, as ambassador to the United States, that Brazil's ban on Jewish entry had to avoid provoking "the immense and powerful [U.S.] Jewish colony."[6] The notion of Jewish world influence played an important part in Aranha's attempt to present Brazil in a more liberal international light.

A policy shift allowing Jews considered useful to enter Brazil seems, at first glance, simply rational. Since few Brazilians were trained industrial managers or skilled technicians, the undesirability of certain immigrants could be overlooked if they delivered needed economic or political benefits. Many German and Austrian Jewish refugees were in fact capitalists or industrialists, giving a factual basis to at least one stereotype.[7] Italian Jewish refugees, who often referred to themselves as the "colônia Mussolini," were almost universally administrators, academics, businesspeople, and members of liberal professions.[8] Ethnic prejudice seemed momentarily to take a secondary role to development, but the desire to keep out Jews—deemed unable to guard "what is most sacred to us, the basis of our institutions: Country, Religion, Family"— still remained.[9] Something, however, had changed. Starting in 1938 influential politicians began implying that certain Jews did not carry the stain of being Jewish. This view helps explain why so many Jews were allowed into Brazil even while anti-Semitic images remained so preponderant. Ideas about Jews never changed, only ideas about who fit the category.

THE IMAGE IS CHANGED

In 1938 just five hundred Jews immigrated legally to Brazil, the lowest number in years. The clandestine orders that prevented Jews from entering, however, had a number of unplanned effects. The negative international reaction enhanced the image of Brazil as a fascist dictatorship, and this had deleterious effects on relations with the United States. At the same time, the very effective ban did not take the Jewish Question off the domestic political agenda. Indeed, the press and nativist politicians continued to exaggerate the numbers of Jewish refugees entering Brazil. When reporting on a Conselho de Imigração e Colonização meeting in which Jewish immigration was only one minor issue among the many discussed, the *Correio da Manhã* used the headline "Entry of Jews into Brazil," although its report was simply a copy of the text released by the regime and printed in the *Diário Oficial da República* two weeks later.[10] Another *Correio da Manhã* article complained of a "Dangerous Immigration" and dredged up images of invasion and immorality in questioning the wisdom of permitting the entry of "certain foreigners . . . who seek shelter on American soil resulting from the fact that their countries of origin do not desire them."[11] The ban on Jews had been successful only in keeping Jews out of Brazil. But those who should have been pleased seemed not to know or care.

The realization that the bar on Jewish entry had not brought the intended domestic reaction, and had created an unintended international one, led Oswaldo Aranha to contemplate a new policy. Aranha was a critical figure, since it was the potential entry of refugees (considered an immigration issue to be handled by the Foreign Ministry), and not the existence of a Brazilian Jewish community, that defined Brazil's Jewish Problem. Yet the growing number of refugees knocking at Brazil's door was more than a question of bans or quotas; symbolic issues such as Jewish entry could generate political and economic capital and were a critical part of foreign relations. Within six months of assuming the foreign minister's position, Aranha began to test the waters. Soon Brazilians and foreigners who broached the subject of refugee admission discovered a surprising new flexibility. As early as November 1938, Oswaldo Aranha was publicly expressing a desire to cooperate with British/U.S. plans to help German Jews, commenting that "we welcome them [Jews] with open arms but reserve to ourselves, because of geographic and economic evolution, the right to locate them in accordance with our plan for the development of the country."[12]

The most important reason that the images of Jews began to change was related to the way in which Brazilian anti-Semitic stereotypes were conceived and discussed. By maintaining the traditional stereotypes and simply modifying the assessment of them, international relief organizations could turn accepted stereotypes to the advantage of refugees. One image of Jews, for example, involved money and economic success. Rich Jews could thus be seen as part of an international conspiracy to force national wealth to the exterior, or glorified for their ability to help domestic industrial development by injecting capital into Brazil. Influential Jews were hailed for the propaganda opportunities they represented, not the unassimilable foreign culture they had been accused of maintaining in the past. Negative stereotypes of "Jewish millionaires . . . [who] flee from their various European homelands, come to Brazil, and leave their capital in the United States or bring it to Argentina" were transformed into new ones of Jews as accountants, bookkeepers, and financial planners.[13] By promoting the existence of "Jewish" wealth and industriousness, past accusations of communist activity were dismissed. In a moment of crisis, Jews used anti-Semitic stereotypes against the anti-Semites. The haunting ghost of Theodore Herzl, who believed that he could count on anti-Semites to be rational in their desire to get rid of Jews and thus create a Jewish state, had arrived in Brazil.[14] Stereotypes of Jews helped refugees get visas.

Critical in convincing Brazilian leaders that some Jews were acceptable immigrants were both informal and formal United States influence. Old stereotypes took on new meanings when U.S. diplomats disingenuously overstated the leverage of Jews in their country's political, economic, and journalistic spheres. Notions of Jewish influence were encouraged when financial schemes that would benefit Brazil's economy were offered by relief officials in exchange for visas. In March 1939 Oswaldo Aranha arrived in the United States to negotiate a series of trade and loan agreements with the U.S. government. While attending a dinner at New York's Council of Foreign Relations, the foreign minister was politely asked by a director of the stock firm of Bendix, Luitweiler and Company if Brazil "was prepared to accept Jewish emigrants of a type and training to be readily assimilated and having sufficient financial resources."[15] Perhaps visas might be tied to reducing Brazil's debt. The foreign minister seemed interested and the following day was informed that an "American group interested in the problem of Jewish emigration from Germany" was prepared to accept a "substantial amount" of Brazilian currency as repayment for debt contracted in dollars. Deposits to a fund to help Jewish refugees would be accepted as payback for debt obligations, having "a most salutary effect upon the standing and credit of Brazil." The plan appears never to have been acted on. Even so, it highlighted to Brazilian authorities a stereotype that they already held: that international Jewish power and wealth existed and were committed to helping refugees. Anti-Semitic stereotypes were turned on their heads.

I have just outlined a framework in which negative images about Jews were reformulated as positive. At certain points, however, this conflicts with the available data. There are a number of instances of Jewish U.S. citizens (not refugees/immigrants) being denied entry rights by minor officials.[16] Along these same lines, Maria Luiza Tucci Carneiro has shown that some Jews were denied visas even if they were economically desirable scientists or engineers.[17] In one case, even the strong personal support of Luiza Aranha, the foreign minister's mother, did not result in a visa grant.[18] What is curious, however, is that approximately ten thousand visas were given to refugee Jews between 1939 and 1942. The question, then, is not whether most Estado Novo decision makers held anti-Semitic notions about Jews; they did. Rather, the challenging problem is to understand why some Jews were allowed into Brazil and others were not: why Stefan Zweig received a visa and Claude Lévi-Strauss did not; why U.S. influence sometimes led to visa grants and sometimes not.[19]

There are a number of possible responses to the question. Perhaps my assertion that refugee-relief officials, members of Brazil's Jewish community, and some Brazilian and foreign politicians changed the terms of debate is wrong, and the granting of visas simply represents ten thousand exceptions. Yet if those making and enforcing immigration policy held exclusively negative images of Jews, we might expect a continued decline in entry in the years after 1937, even in the face of U.S. pressure. This was not the case. A second possibility is that all visas issued to Jews were purchased in one form or another. This suggests that the apparent rampant anti-Semitism among Brazilian diplomats, and the belief that Jews were dangers to Brazilian society, was secondary to immediate profit. But numerous Jews in a position to purchase visas, especially in late 1937 and early 1938, were denied entry.

There is a logical answer to the apparent contradictions in policy and practice. If, as I suggested above, influential policymakers held static images of Jews that could be positive, negative, or even both, those with the power to grant visas could easily shift between conceptions of Jews as useful to Brazil's economic development and conceptions of them as harmful to its social development. Lindolfo Collor's published political diary *Europa 1939* shows one example of this dual image. In it he reports on the purge of Maxim Litvinov as people's commissar of the Soviet Foreign Ministry. What was "picturesque," notes Collor, is that Litvinov's brother, a rabbi in Lodz, reportedly complained "of the detestable activity of my brother." [20] The story may or may not have been true. Either way, Collor's vision of "the Jew" as a communist and "a human symbol," as good and bad, is clear.

The tension between traditional anti-Semitic images and new positive judgments of Jews led some policymakers to simultaneously favor and oppose Jewish immigration. On any given day immediate political pressure, be it domestic or international, affected the implementation of policy. Correspondence sent by Oswaldo Aranha to various European diplomatic posts indicates the swings. On August 9, 1939, Itamaraty ordered H. Pinheiro de Vasconcelos, consul general in London, to give permanent visas to a number of Polish Jewish refugees; [21] the visas were issued a few months later. In mid-October 1939, on the other hand, the following orders were received by Brazil's legation in Helsinki: "The legation should stamp visas in passports of refugees as long as they are not Jews." [22] Seemingly contradictory memos granting visas to some refugees and denying them to others had an internal logic based on the dual images of Jews in Brazil.

Politicians in Rio were not the only ones revising their estimations of Jews; requests for exceptions to the anti-Jewish orders also arrived from Brazil's consulates and embassies in Europe. A diplomat in Paris, although believing in principle that Jews should not be allowed permanently into Brazil, wondered if it "would be prudent to persevere on the path" of absolute bans.[23] French Jews, he claimed, made up 75 percent of all French commercial interests and applied for Brazilian tourist visas only for business purposes. Pedro Leão Veloso, who considered himself "one of the few in our country who is not a declared enemy of the Jews," pointed out that "the Banco do Brasil can inform you that, thanks to the entrance of 70 capitalist Jews, the national economy benefited by 35 million milreis [2 million U.S. dollars]. Imagine what [all the others] brought?"[24] Jewish refugees, according to Leão Veloso, brought far more capital to Brazil than Argentine tourists, who were allowed to enter without question, presumably as long as they were not Jews.

Others wondered if visas for renowned Jews might promote Brazil's international image and help the country progress. Giorgio Mortara, the Italian Jewish editor of the prestigious *Giornale degli Economisti e Rivista di Statistica,* was dismissed from his post in 1938. Almost immediately thereafter he was invited to Brazil by the director of the Brazilian Institute of Geography and Statistics (IBGE), former foreign minister José Carlos Macedo Soares. Soon after arriving in Rio in early 1939 with his wife and four children, Mortara was appointed coordinator of the 1940 census.[25] The French playwright Hénri-Leon (Henry) Bernstein, living as a refugee in the United States, was rumored to believe that an extended visit to Brazil would inspire a new theater piece. In spite of Bernstein's well-known condemnation of anti-Semitism in his play *Israël,* a diplomat asked in a letter, "What reasons could be invoked to refuse him a visa?" and expressed concern that "our nation will lose an extraordinary propaganda opportunity [if he is refused a visa]."[26] Although Bernstein never pursued his desire for tropical inspiration, the Austrian Jewish novelist Stefan Zweig did. The granting of a lifesaving visa to Zweig may well have influenced his decision to write the propagandistic *Brazil: Land of the Future.* Indeed, Zweig's presence in Brazil was used by the Department of Press and Propaganda to promote such unexpected areas as municipal government organization.[27] Zweig's claim that "wherever in our troubled times we find hope for a new future in new zones, it is our duty to point out this country and these possibilities" aroused the enmity of other intellectuals, who recognized that anti-Semitism and visa grants for some Jewish refugees were not incompatible.[28]

U.S. INFLUENCE AND FEARS OF A NEW WAVE OF JEWS

In 1939 the number of Jews entering Brazil with permanent and temporary visas, according to Jewish groups, was 4,601, and according to the Conselho de Imigração e Colonização, 4,223.[29] Jews received more than 60 percent of the permanent visas and almost 45 percent of the temporary visas given to Germans and Poles.[30] Almost 9 percent of those with permanent visas and more than 14 percent of those with temporary visas were Jews.[31] One reason for the high numbers was the pressure the United States put on friendly nations to allow Jewish refugees to enter, a regular topic of correspondence between the Brazilian and U.S governments. The United States desired to "take an increased part in the establishment and settlement of Jewish immigrants in the Latin American countries," and regularly played on stereotypes of Jews by portraying refugees as having capital and skills.[32] Jews were also a frequently, and vehemently, discussed topic in meetings of the Conselho de Imigração e Colonização, which tried to moderate between those who believed that some refugees should be allowed to enter if they would aid Brazil's economic development and others who viewed all Jews as social dangers and wanted the absolute ban reinstated.

The CIC assumed a public stance against the unrestricted immigration of those of "ethnic Jewish origin," and João Carlos Muniz often contended that "this country has done its share in receiving Jewish refugees."[33] The CIC's *Revista de Imigração e Colonização* even published separate statistics on Jewish immigration.[34] Oliveira Vianna's aforementioned article (chapter 3) on the anthropological "character" of "Semitic and Mongoloid" immigrants gave an intellectual underpinning to the attempt to distinguish between unwanted Eastern European Jews and the desired Central European Jewish immigrants.[35] According to Vianna, Jews did not have a single "anthropological type" but were divided into those from Poland and Russia, who had "clearly Slavic characters," and those from Germany, who were "more similar to [non-Jewish] Germans than they are to their compatriots from Palestine."[36] Some Jews, suggested Vianna, might even have the virtues of Central European non-Jews. Arthur Hehl Neiva, a member of the CIC and Rio de Janeiro's Civil Police and the son of a nativist member of the 1934 Constitutional Assembly, wrote in favor of Jewish immigration in 1939. Neiva was attacked for his position by those who claimed that he was "of Jewish origin [and that] his father is a great protector of Jews."[37] Neiva's long treatise on the benefits of Jewish entry was repressed for "obvious reasons" by the CIC until 1944.[38] Vianna's work, then, which could be used as intellectual justification for opposing or supporting Jewish entry, was far more acceptable than Neiva's clear statement.

There was an angry reaction to the increase in Jewish entry, especially among consular officers forced to follow a policy with which they disagreed. Dulphe Pinheiro Machado, director of the Ministry of Labor's Departamento Nacional de Imigração (DNI; the National Department of Immigration), repeatedly complained that refugees claimed to be tourists in order "to more easily infiltrate into national territory" and were hard to deport.[39] Justice Minister Campos agreed, recommending that no visas be given to "elements" whose repatriation might be difficult.[40] Some diplomats complained that "Jews of Semitic origin" would do anything to obtain a visa.[41] In Egypt a consul feared that

Mussolini's anti-Jewish comments would lead to huge numbers of visa requests.[42] The discovery in Havana that the Hamburg-American shipping line was involved in helping refugees buy visas, and thus passages on their ships out of Europe, led to renewed concerns about a "migration of undesirables."[43] An unsigned memo, suggesting that diplomats "refuse to place visas in the passports of these undesirable and parasitical elements," circulated through Itamaraty. Aranha had been warned for years about the problems of Jewish immigration, so claimed the anonymous author, and "the Embassy in Berlin, the Consulate in Amsterdam, some consulates in France, the Legation in Bucharest and the Legation and Consulate in Warsaw have repeatedly explained the facts and the inconveniences that would result."[44]

Members of the Estado Novo also attacked resident refugees. Justice Minister Campos, in a bizarre twist of reasoning, criticized the United States for forcing Brazil to take European Jewish refugees who he claimed were members of a fifth column and were "elated with the present German victories."[45] In early 1938 Oswaldo Aranha griped about a São Paulo military police auditor, described as a naturalized Austrian Jew "deficient in Portuguese," accused of helping family members disembark in Santos without visas from the consulate in Vienna.[46] Unsubstantiated charges that huge numbers of Jews were sneaking into Brazil rang through the halls of Itamaraty. In a few cases, like that of a naturalized Uruguayan from Syria, this was true, since lax enforcement and greed among Brazil's overseas consuls provided ample opportunities to save Jews while giving Brazilian diplomats easy access to extra cash.[47] In one strange case a Belgian Jew named Zimmerman publicly denounced an attaché to the Brazilian consulate in Paris who sold visas but had refused him one.[48] The attaché, so claimed Zimmerman, worked with a "naturalized Belgian Jew from Russia" who was "an agent of the Comintern."[49] In other cases, a few Jewish residents bribed landowners to apply for *chamadas* for fictitious agricultural workers. Others transferred property to refugees in Europe to qualify them as landowners.[50] While forged and bought visas did exist, attempts to rescue Jews in this manner were minimally successful.[51] In 1940 Aranha admitted to Vargas that only one visa had been given "irregularly" to a Jew—by someone in the consulate in Paso de los Libres on Brazil's border with Argentina.[52]

The discussion of the illegal entry of Jews into Brazil has two interesting components. One is the extent of the official reaction to the discovery of some Jews with Uruguayan, Argentine, and Paraguayan, but

no Brazilian, visas in their passports, which was very much out of proportion to the small numbers involved. Yet in spite of the regular accusations that Brazilian officials were helping refugees cross the border
for a price, and numerous investigations by Itamaraty officials, rarely
was any action taken. The denunciation of the consul in Paris had no
effect, since that office continued to issue large numbers of visas for
Jews, often against specific orders from Rio, until 1941. Official regulations stating that a round-trip ticket and an unspecified amount of funds
were needed to get a tourist visa were often skirted. German and Austrian Jews, usually able to leave with little of their savings, soon discovered they could purchase a one-way ticket, get a three-month tourist
visa, extend it for another three months, and then, unable to return to
Europe, stay on illegally. Diplomats had discovered that the *chamada*
system was "truly a business [and] lucrative for certain intermedi-
aries."[53]

Nothing illustrates the dual attitude toward Jewish refugees better
than Itamaraty's April 1939 investigation of charges that consuls and
border officials were involved in a conspiracy to sell false visas to refugees.[54] When the inquiry began, Brazil's consuls in Paraguay and Uruguay confirmed that Jews were indeed entering Brazil illegally, but re-
proached border authorities in Rio Grande do Sul for allowing it to take
place. The envoy in Paraguay, Lafayette de Carvalho e Silva, thought
passports were not being carefully checked, since "there would be no
other way to explain . . . the presence of clandestine Semites in our own
capital."[55] Francisco Mascarenhas, consul general in Montevideo, also
found fault with frontier officials. According to Mascarenhas, a police
inspector from Rio Grande do Sul named Ewaldo Walter Bergmann
appeared at his office claiming to be on a secret mission to discover how
Jews were entering Brazil clandestinely. Bergmann had stumbled on an
office in Montevideo that sold safe-conduct passes to Jews for five hundred Uruguayan pesos, although "if the Jews did not have that much
money the price would be lowered."[56] When groups of ten or twelve
Jews were assembled, so it seemed, they were brought to the border and
then sent into Brazil at different points.

Mascarenhas confirmed the story with a friend in the Uruguayan
Federal Police, who reported that the scheme was headed by two people
"both of whom look like Jews but say they are German."[57] Mascarenhas also sent a private consul, identified only as "Pery," to the border
town of Rivera to investigate further. Pery reported that a member of
the "German Nazi element" in Rivera told him the intrigue was well

known "in all its details." Pery also learned that one Luiz Rosenbaumm, accused of running the safe-conduct scheme in Montevideo,
had been in Rivera for two months trying to buy himself a Brazilian
tourist visa.[58] Mascarenhas and Pery decided to try to sell a visa to
Rosenbaumm for two hundred pesos and catch him in the act, although
this apparently never took place.[59] In April members of the police in
four Brazilian border towns were imprisoned for allowing Jews to enter
illegally, reducing the "intensity of the dangerous machinations of this
strange Jewish-Brazilian consortium."[60] Six months later Mascarenhas
again weakly suggested that he and his subordinates were uninvolved
in selling visas. Although "the quantity of Israelites who live here in an
undefined situation has not diminished," the consul claimed, "in the
last few months no visas have been requested by Israelites who in the
past came in large numbers."[61]

A number of oddities arise from this case, since it seems only barely
conceivable that any significant flow of refugees into Brazil could have
taken place without the knowledge of powerful officials in the diplomatic corps. The first is that the reports placing blame on border police
all arrived in Rio at roughly the same time. This indicates that the attempts to confirm the illegal entry of Jewish refugees were motivated
by Itamaraty complaints, not by concerns in the field. Yet Consul Mascarenhas submitted documents to Aranha alleging that the sale of safe-
conduct passes to Brazil was well known to both Jews and "German
Nazis" in Uruguay. The documents also suggest that the sale of tourist
visas was relatively common, since the private consul Pery pointed out,
presumably in his own defense, that Jewish refugees often tried to buy
visas from consuls in Uruguayan border towns. Finally, those state border police accused, charged, and imprisoned following the investigation
were at the absolute lowest rungs of Brazil's civil service, traditional
scapegoats in moments of bureaucratic turmoil.

Although official estimates put the number of Jewish refugees who
had entered Brazil illegally at about two thousand, many within the
bureaucracy regularly repeated unbelievably inflated numbers.[62] Passport Service director Vaz de Mello claimed that between 1934 and
1937, forty thousand Jews had entered Brazil as tourists and remained,
and that another forty thousand had traversed the borders with Uruguay, Paraguay, and Argentina clandestinely.[63] The police in the Federal District complained of a "conspicuous increase in the number of
European Jews [in Rio] . . . [and] are of the opinion that a considerable
portion of these Jews have entered Brazil illegally."[64] The supposed

increases were explained by allegations that officials around the world were selling Brazilian visas, and in response a Brazilian Bureau of Jewish Immigration was proposed to Vargas.[65] João Carlos Muniz argued for further curbs, claiming Jews were unwilling "to follow a pioneering life or settle on the land and [have] a tendency to congregate in what amounts to ghettos in the larger cities."[66] As late as August 1941, a CIC report claimed, without offering any proof, that fifteen thousand to twenty thousand Jews had entered Brazil illegally.[67]

Most Jewish refugees in Brazil had in fact come with legal documentation, the result of the significant increase in the number of visas granted by Itamaraty. Even so, Vargas received regular complaints throughout 1940 that refugees were "augmenting the already enormous Jewish population."[68] Someone on the staff of the Department of Immigration sent a panicky telegram to Aranha reporting a large-scale "clandestine Jewish immigration organized in Buenos Aires."[69] When a Hungarian couple were arrested for directing an organization that brought Jews illegally into Brazil, they "committed suicide at police headquarters while awaiting trial."[70] Even the press got into the act. In late 1940 Rio de Janeiro's German-subsidized *Meio-Dia* ran an article headlined: "400,000 Jews Live in Brazil; 150,000 Jews have entered in just the last six months."[71]

The fears of an increase in the number of Jews in Brazil collided head-on with both new positive interpretations of stereotypes and U.S. diplomatic pressure. This situation left an impression with some foreign diplomats that the Brazilian government, "while feeling sympathetic toward the plight of Jewish refugees, will continue to be extremely cautious about receiving additional numbers."[72] The situation also gave Itamaraty officials the latitude to interpret visa regulations in light of their own opinions on Jewish immigration. Some consular officers gave visas to Jews in large numbers. In most German, Austrian, and Eastern European consulates, however, visa applications were often rebuffed on the basis of the (now countermanded) first secret circular. Itamaraty sometimes approved visas directly from Rio de Janeiro while at other times rejecting them.[73] While almost forty-five hundred refugees legally entered Brazil in 1939, many others were turned away.[74]

Nothing illustrates the shifting interpretations of policy more than a situation involving the famed scientist Albert Einstein, who visited Brazil in 1925. The voyage had been arranged by the ICA's Rabbi Raffalovich, eager to "demonstrate to the people of Brazil that Jews are not only peddlers but that among them one may find world-famous scientists." [75] Raffalovich's plan was a success. Brazil's most noted scientists formed a welcoming committee, important members of the Jewish community courted Einstein, and journalists, including Francisco de Assis Chateaubriand, owner of the Diários Associados chain of newspapers, printed long interviews with the scientist. [76] In spite of the fact that Einstein's trip was arranged by the ICA, and that he spent a significant amount of time meeting with Brazil's most active Zionists, Thomas F. Glick has pointed out that the press rarely mentioned Einstein's religion. [77] Gilberto Freyre, at the time a young journalist, did. Echoing themes later found in his comments on prostitution in *Ordem e progresso* (see chapter 1), Freyre suggested that Einstein's universal message was a function of his "Jewish blood," and his lack of a homeland. [78]

More than a decade later, Einstein's fame in Brazil and his warm feelings for the country encouraged him to approach Brazilian officials for help in getting visas for refugee Jews. [79] In 1938 an old friend of Einstein's, Dr. Hans George Katz, a German Jew living in São Paulo with a permanent visa, contacted the scientist about his sister, Helene Fabian-Katz. Katz was desperately worried because Helene was in Nazi Berlin, frantic to leave and unable to get a visa. Einstein supported her application for a U.S. visa, but this was rejected. Finally the scientist suggested that Brazil might have visas available. [80] On January 23, 1939, Einstein wrote directly to Aranha, noting that there was "no risk of Mrs. Fabian Katz ever becoming a public charge" and requesting that her visa application be approved. [81]

Aranha apparently never received the letter. In early February Dr. Katz again wrote Einstein, complaining that no action had been taken by Itamaraty and that the situation in Germany was becoming increasingly difficult. [82] Katz, however, had discovered that Aranha would be in the United States and wondered if Einstein could somehow contact the foreign minister while he was in Washington. The suggestion was a good one. Einstein wrote to Aranha in care of the U.S. State Department and had a copy delivered in person to Itamaraty in Rio by Cecilia Razovsky, the executive director of the National Coordinating Committee for Aid to Refugees and Emigrants Coming from Germany. [83] The request was received, held for three months, and then sent to the Conselho de Imigração e Colonização. [84] The visa for Fabian-Katz was then apparently granted, because, some months later, Einstein again wrote to Aranha asking for a visa for another family friend, noting that "your kind assistance in a previous case encourages me." [85] Typed in the corner of the letter is a note from Einstein's secretary explaining that the "previous case" was that of Helene Fabian-Katz. Indeed she and the scientist were in correspondence, she in São Paulo and he in Princeton, as late as 1953.[86]

Immigration legislation put into effect after 1940 was more easily and strictly enforced because it was public. Einstein's early efforts on behalf of German Jewish refugees were successful because his fame encouraged the authors of the anti-Jewish orders to countermand them, something easily done since they were "secrets" that officially never existed. His later attempts, however, did not work, since Aranha could not risk ignoring published immigration laws. The varying success of Einstein's requests also hints at the dual nature of the Jewish Question within the Estado Novo. A perfect example came in 1938, when a new immigration decree stated that no visas would be granted above set quota limits.[87] At times this order was used to prevent the entry of "Jews, who in certain cases, because of their desperation, try to get around the regulations and instructions . . . by acts of bad faith."[88] In 1939, however, the Conselho de Imigração e Colonização exempted the Portuguese from the quota because of "their assimilation to social, political and economic institutions . . . [and] their religious identity, language and customs."[89] More baffling was the expansion of Germany's 1939 quota, by which eight hundred visas were put aside specifically for Jews.[90] Four months later the consul in Hamburg was authorized to grant "another 800 visas for Semites and non-Semites."[91] When the Polish quota was raised from 1,230 to 3,000, a Brazilian diplomat confidentially remarked to U.S. Consul General William Burdett that "Polish immigration is in complete harmony with the national interests in its ethnical, economic and cultural aspects," a remark Burdett found "of particular interest in view of the large proportion of Jews now desiring to emigrate from Poland."[92] Imagine the bewilderment among diplomats when Rio regularly overruled its own strict anti-immigrant policies.

The increasing entry of Jews started a small war within Itamaraty. On one side was Oswaldo Aranha, who believed it necessary to resolve "the most urgent and dramatic cases, that [are] precisely those of families whose members have been separated."[93] The Jewish Question could not be simply solved by exclusion but, according to Aranha, had become a "very complicated issue, with political, economic and social aspects."[94] Justice Minister Francisco Campos and Ciro Freitas Vale, the ambassador to Berlin and a relative of Aranha's, disagreed.[95] An anticommunist and a Judeophobe, Freitas Vale believed the granting of

visas to the relatives of Jews already in Brazil without an examination
of potential economic benefit was not only an error but a danger as
well. The ambassador pointed out that, of the 600 visas granted to Jews
leaving Germany in 1939, only 51 were for technical experts and 12 for
capitalists.[96] None of the others should have been allowed to enter,
because they were simply "the old relatives of furniture salesmen and
the in-laws of candy makers."[97]

Freitas Vale decided to take policy into his own hands in July 1939.
He proposed that Germans with "J" (for *Jew*) passports not be allowed
to enter under the German quota, thus blocking German Jewish entrances.[98] While awaiting a response Freitas Vale suspended approved
visa applications and ordered his consuls to follow his new "provisional
rule," leading to infuriated protests from the British.[99] In September
1939, the ambassador complained that "more than one Brazilian consul
has directed my attention to the bad quality of the Jews" being granted
visas from Rio.[100] His complaint was met with an angry note from Aranha—"It is strange that only now [the consuls] allege the bad quality of
the individuals"—and a curt instruction to drop the subject.[101]

Freitas Vale was not easily dissuaded. He wondered, "How should a
consul who has turned down a visa application for a Jew because he
appears inadequate for emigration [act] when the same [Jew] receives
a special authorization from the Foreign Minister?"[102] This frequently
occurred. Thirteen Jews, all of whom had been refused permanent visas
by the consuls in Paris, Budapest, and Berlin, were, under direct orders
from Vargas's office, given tourist visas.[103] In another case, Paul Rosenstein, a German medical researcher who had been invited to Brazil
by the government in 1935 and had applied for a permanent visa in
1939 when he was a lecturer at New York University, was turned down
in Berlin.[104] Getúlio Vargas intervened in his favor, and Rosenstein arrived in Brazil in April 1940. The promised visas for his wife and three
children, however, were held up without reason in Berlin. After Rosenstein discussed the issue personally with Oswaldo Aranha and had a
friend intercede in his favor, the case was resolved, prompting Rosenstein to write: "I consider it my duty to return hearty thanks for your
kindness [and] I hope I shall get the opportunity to be of service to
this wonderful and hospitable country with all my physical and mental
power."[105] Rosenstein's kind words did not soothe the outraged Freitas
Vale. No longer willing to attach his name to visas approved by Itamaraty, Freitas Vale began communicating approvals to subordinate consuls by attaching his signature only, "in the name of the Minister of
Foreign Affairs."[106]

Freitas Vale, who saw his position as "a mission, not a job," continued to press Aranha to bar all Jewish refugees from Brazil, always claiming, "I am not, and never was, against the Jews."[107] He also began to enlist the support of other diplomats. Labienne Salgado dos Santos, who had been sending anti-Semitic missives to Rio since 1935 and was now head of Brazil's Passport Division, prepared a long report entitled "The Entrance of Jews in Brazil," from which Freitas Vale quoted frequently.[108] Relying on the same myths about Jews that had formed the "factual" basis of his earlier reports, Salgado dos Santos complained that Jews formed unassimilable separate communities and had "implanted communism in Russia and other countries."[109] The report defended Germany's anti-Semitic policy and correctly predicted that continuing hostilities in Europe would result in an ever-growing number of Jews applying for visas.

In November, Freitas Vale sent a confidential letter to Aranha claiming that "there exist consortia [that included government officials] to introduce Jews into Brazil" that sold visas for 440 U.S. dollars, and that "the orders for visas continue to arrive [from Rio] for the most foolish cases."[110] When Aranha did not respond, Freitas Vale "for the first time in 25 years of service to The Nation, [decided] to criticize an action of the Government" by writing personally to President Getúlio Vargas.[111] Freitas Vale's complaint did have an effect, although not the intended one. Vargas ordered João Carlos Muniz, a loyal confidant of Aranha in spite of his opposition to Jewish entry, to investigate the claims. Muniz immediately contacted the foreign minister so that he could answer the "anonymous allegations" in order to "destroy any suspicions which might hover over Itamaraty."[112] Muniz claimed that stories of visa sales were false and had been created by European emigration companies in order to lure customers. He also assured Aranha of the CIC's support, noting that humanitarian, and economic and political, considerations made it "impossible to close Brazil completely to immigrants of this [Jewish] race."[113]

Oswaldo Aranha knew immediately who had made the allegations. He angrily demanded that Freitas Vale "document your information to the President of the Republic regarding irregular concessions of visas and abusive entrances of Jews in Brazil."[114] When he received no reply, Aranha sent a less than cordial ten-page letter to Berlin, making it clear that no more criticism of Itamaraty's "Semitic policy" would be tolerated, because "you are wrong when you affirm that Jews continue to enter Brazil in ever growing numbers."[115] The Jewish issue could "not be resolved in absolute terms but only in relative ones," and, as Aranha pointedly noted, "for criticism to be constructive . . . it needs to be based upon a perfect knowledge of the facts." Freitas Vale was then informed that the numbers of entering Jews had dropped from 9,263 in 1937 to 4,900 in 1938.[116] The foreign minister maintained that "the number of individuals of Semitic origin who entered Brazil in 1939 was 2,289," an apparently large reduction from the previous years.[117] This, however, was not the case. As has been previously demonstrated, the figures bandied about by Itamaraty and the CIC were often exaggerated. More accurate figures, on the other hand, come from the major Jewish relief organizations, all of which agree that Jewish immigration increased markedly between 1938 and 1939.[118]

The figures sent by Aranha to Freitas Vale are surprising. First, they suggest incorrectly that almost five thousand Jews entered Brazil in a period when a secret circular banning *all* Jews was in effect.[119] Second, the figures show the numbers of Jews arriving in Brazil decreasing between 1937 and 1939, when they in fact rose. Apparent increases in the number of Jews entering Brazil legitimated new restrictive laws, while supposed decreases were used to show the effectiveness of the regime in protecting national interests. In December 1940, for example, Itamaraty informed the French embassy in Rio that "the Brazilian government, in affirmation of humanitarian principles, has conceded 3,000 visas per year to Jewish immigrants and refugees since 1937," something that no Brazilian government statistic supported.[120] The DNI's Dulphe Pinheiro Machado claimed that 80 percent of the German quota was reserved each year for farmers, while the remaining 20 percent was completely filled by Jews, all parents or children of legal residents.[121] If this had been the case, only 954 German Jews would have received visas in 1939, since no Jews were granted agricultural visas. In fact, 2,357 German Jews received visas, over 50 percent of all Germans entering Brazil in that year.[122] Furthermore, Brazil never filled its German quota in 1939.

Aranha attempted to preserve his position among those opposing Jewish immigration by suggesting that special restrictions guaranteed careful control of Jewish entrances.[123] In 1939 a new order, designed to stop allegations that diplomats were "deliberately extorting additional sums from emigrant Jews," denied consuls the right to grant visas without Passport Division approval.[124] Aranha also claimed that the only Jews to whom Itamaraty granted tourist visas were from Northern and Western Europe and the United States, and that Itamaraty pursued this policy in order to stop the entrance of false tourists. This allegation is not confirmed by CIC statistics. In 1939 almost 20 percent of those with tourist visas held Eastern European passports, and others entered with Middle Eastern, Asian, or Latin American papers.[125] In 1940, more than 15 percent of those with tourist visas were Eastern European.[126] The lack of enforcement of the rule, however, did not mean that it went uninvoked. As late as 1945 a Czech Jew living in England was told that he was ineligible for a tourist visa because he held an Eastern European passport.[127]

NEW LEGISLATION, 1940–1942

Diminishing Jewish emigration and diminishing general immigrant entry in the Americas were worldwide phenomena after 1940. In Brazil, as in the United States, Argentina, and Palestine, 1939 represented the high-water mark for the entry of Jews; the numbers dwindled through the end of 1944. (See table 4.1.) The reductions represent a combination of factors: the increased difficulty anyone had in leaving Europe, the expansion of Nazi control into Eastern Europe and the concurrent impossibility for Jews of fleeing, and a pervasive lack of interest by most non-Axis powers, including the United States, Great Britain, and Canada, in making the salvation of refugees a priority.[128] This development demoralized Brazilian Jewish groups, and Marc Leitchik, director of a HICEM-funded organization in Rio de Janeiro, expressed his belief that the group "had finished its work in Brazil."[129]

Although there was a worldwide drop in the number of Jews leaving Europe, factors specific to Brazil were critical in the rapid decrease in Jewish entry after 1939. One important issue was that the expansion of Jewish immigration in 1939 prompted a flurry of new decrees between 1940 and 1942 that explained how the general immigration regulations were to be applied against Jews. Furthermore, the U.S. government decreased pressure on Brazil to take Jews now that the two countries seemed firmly allied. Opposition to continued Jewish entry in Brazil came from both the military and the Ministry of Justice, both headed by Vargas confidants. Minister of War Eurico Dutra argued that Jewish immigrants were the most dangerous of all foreign communities in Brazil.[130] Lieutenant Colonel Affonso de Carvalho, editor of *Nação Armada*, a semi-affiliated military journal that represented the General Staff Office position and was influenced by Nazi ideology, complained that Rio de Janeiro's "most beautiful neighborhoods" had become "ghettos," terming Copacabana "Copacabanovich" and "Jaco-

TABLE 4.1
JEWISH IMMIGRATION TO BRAZIL AND OTHER COUNTRIES, 1939–1947, INCLUDING PERCENTAGE OF GENERAL JEWISH MIGRATION

Year	Brazil	(%)	U.S.A.	(%)	Argentina	(%)	Canada	(%)	Palestine	(%)	Total
1939	4,601	(5.7)	43,450	(53.6)	4,300	(5.3)	890	(1.1)	27,561	(34.1)	80,802
1940	2,416	(4.7)	36,945	(72.0)	1,850	(3.6)	1,643	(3.2)	8,398	(16.3)	51,252
1941	1,500	(4.4)	23,737	(69.9)	2,200	(6.4)	626	(1.8)	5,886	(17.3)	33,949
1942	108	(0.6)	10,608	(65.6)	1,318	(8.1)	388	(2.4)	3,743	(23.1)	16,165
1943	11	(0)	4,705	(33.5)	524	(3.7)	270	(1.9)	8,507	(60.6)	14,017
1944	6	(0)	2,400	(13.7)	384	(2.1)	238	(1.3)	14,464	(82.6)	17,492
1945	120	(0.6)	4,160	(22.5)	728	(3.9)	347	(1.8)	13,121	(71.0)	18,476
1946	1,485	(3.9)	12,774	(33.7)	295	(0.7)	1,517	(4.0)	21,085	(55.6)	37,876
1947	2,637	(4.7)	29,274	(52.7)	126	(0.2)	1,866	(3.3)	21,542	(38.8)	55,455
Total	12,884	(3.9)	168,053	(51.6)	11,725	(3.6)	7,785	(2.3)	124,307	(38.1)	325,654

SOURCES Mark Wischnitzer, *To Dwell in Safety: The Story of Jewish Migration since 1800* (Philadelphia: Jewish Publication Society of America, 1948), p. 293, table 6. Leonard Dinnerstein and David M. Reimers, *Ethnic Americans: A History of Immigration and Assimilation*, 2d ed. (New York: Harper and Row, 1982), 163–65, table A.2. Figures do not include undocumented immigrants.

bacabana" and Leme "Jerusaleme."[131] Minister of Justice Francisco Campos fought against Jewish entry by insisting that the Justice Ministry be involved in the immigration question, a somewhat odd request since its duties officially revolved around the issue of foreigners resident in Brazil and not the question of immigration per se. By linking to immigration the question of those in Brazil with expired tourist visas, however, Campos was able to insert his ministry into a new area, while maintaining that his proposals had nothing to do with Jews. The justice minister thus attacked groups with large numbers of Jews (refugees, stateless persons, those unable to return to their countries of origin) in order to suggest that race, ethnicity, and religion were not really the issue. This sophisticated anti-Semitism fit into the new economic orientation of the Estado Novo and highlighted questions of economic value, not assimilation. Even so, the many new immigration laws put in place in 1940 and 1941 functioned to keep out Jews, and the decrease in Jewish immigration after 1939 was more significant to Brazil than it was to other American nations.

In 1940 Campos proposed that the inflow of "numerous foreigners without economic value who are taking advantage of the chaotic international situation" be stopped.[132] He hoped that Brazil would deny entry to all with temporary visas "except perhaps those with money and the authorization to return [to their countries of origin]," and refuse visas for all except rural laborers and illustrious foreigners. Not surprisingly, Campos believed that the Ministry of Justice, and not Itamaraty, should have the right to authorize the exceptions. Such a proposal should not sound unfamiliar, since it basically rehashed Secret Circular 1,127 without mentioning Jews. Even so, it was clear that Jews were the problem. João Carlos Muniz told Campos his proposal was unneeded since the CIC had "established conditions for the concession of visas to individuals of *that* racial origin."[133] Furthermore, argued Muniz, it was Brazil's diplomatic corps, and not the Ministry of Justice, who could best guarantee the application of the "assimilation" rule that informed current immigration law.[134]

In January 1941, Itamaraty ordered its consular officers to suspend the issuance of visas to all except Portuguese citizens, nationals of American countries, and experts, artists, and capitalists who could transfer more than four hundred contos (twenty thousand U.S. dollars) to the Banco do Brasil.[135] The intent, according to a report on a conversation between a U.S. diplomat and Ambassador to France Souza Dantas, was to "reduce immigration into Brazil to practically nothing"—sentiments echoed by German Ambassador Curt Max Prüfer.[136] A month later the CIC proposed that Jews not be given any more visas, a policy later formalized by Itamaraty circular.[137] In April a tightening of immigration laws, based on Campos's earlier plan, nearly ended the concession of visas to Europeans.[138] The Foreign Ministry had considered the Campos proposal "a dead issue until the new decree law appeared today," but Aranha, with U.S. encouragement, decided to try to get Vargas to revoke it.[139] A new police bureau, part of the Justice Ministry and free from Itamaraty and CIC control, was created in May to supervise the registration and activities of aliens. In its first act the office recommended that 129 refugees who had overstayed their temporary visas be deported.[140] This never took place, because there were no countries that would accept the potential deportees.

Although a total of almost four thousand Jewish refugees legally entered Brazil in 1940 and 1941, representing about 15 percent of all foreign entries, the increasingly stringent rules contributed to the virtual end of Jewish entry in 1942. (See appendix 5.) Temporary visas were granted only to applicants from the Americas and to those who could return to the countries from which they held a passport.[141] Only foreigners married to native-born Brazilians or with children born in Brazil received permanent visas, as did those few Jews the government invited.[142] When James McDonald, then chair of the U.S. President's Advisory Committee on Refugees, reported that Henry Ford was willing to make some of his properties in Brazil available to refugees, Aranha refused, claiming "they would never remain there [and] we would have endless difficulties with them."[143] Later that year, Getúlio Vargas canceled already-issued visas and decreed that his personal authorization was necessary for all future visas.[144] Even those in transit were refused entry.

The general restrictions on immigration made the secret circulars moot. A Jewish immigration policy was no longer needed, since the new limitations could be applied with the same result. Even so, the tightening of immigration rules appeared directed at Jews.[145] Three hundred Japanese emigrants ready to sail to Brazil were delayed because of "regulations in order to prevent the illegal entry of Jewish refugees."[146] Major Aristóteles de Lima Câmara, a member of the army general staff assigned as one of the CIC's military representatives, told journalists that Brazil needed to "check the influx of refugees, especially Jews from Europe."[147] In 1940, in one of his frequent contributions to the *Revista de Imigração e Colonização,* Câmara had argued that Jews were not a race but that Western European Jews were preferable to those from other regions since "they have the highest percentage [among Jews] of type A blood."[148] Eduardo Oungre, director of the HICEM, believed the legislation "in reality . . . is intended only for our co-religionists. For the past few years, in every decree and resolution, the meaning is the same, 'no Jews' although this has actually never been mentioned."[149] The S.S. *Alsina* left Marseilles on January 1, 1941, with 570 passengers, including many Jewish refugees as well as Alcalá Zamora, the ex-president of the Spanish Republic.[150] Some of the passengers had visas for the United States, but most had been issued Brazilian visas in France. The group was refused entry to Brazil and sailed on.[151] Only after being refused entry to a number of British territories was the group allowed to land in the United States. The *Alsina* case was not isolated. Ten Polish Jews with visas certified by the Brazilian consul in Glasgow were not allowed to board the S.S. *ZamZam* in Capetown.[152]

"THE TRUTH ABOUT THE *CABO DE HORNOS*"

The extreme restrictiveness of Brazil's immigration regulations opens up a problematic area of analysis: how should the refusal of entry to desperate Jewish refugees be judged? One argument is that Brazil had a humanitarian obligation to accept all refugees fleeing Nazism.[153] Of course, if it had done so, Brazil would have been unique in the Americas. Another argument is that Brazil's restrictions on immigration were part of a historical trend that began after World War I and were basically unrelated to Jews. One might point to Brazil's refusal to give visas to Mormon missionaries from the United States and Lutheran missionaries from Germany as support for this position.[154] Jews, it might be suggested, simply had the bad luck to flee Europe just as Brazil's doors were closing. The final possibility is that Brazil's virtual stoppage of immigration was related directly to the Jewish Question. In other words, general immigration law, without ever saying so, was really about Jews.

These propositions may be untangled by examining the case of the Spanish-registered S.S. *Cabo de Hornos*. The ship arrived in the Rio de Janeiro harbor in late 1941 carrying about ninety-five Jewish refugees, mainly from Poland and Czechoslovakia, many of whom had spent six months looking for refuge.[155] The story, however, began long before the Jewish refugees arrived in Brazil. Several months earlier the refugees, while waiting in Cadiz for transport out of Europe, realized that their entry visas to Brazil, issued in 1940 by Brazil's ambassador to Vichy France, Luis Martins de Souza Dantas, were about to expire. As the date neared, Souza Dantas ordered the consul in Cadiz to renew the expired visas.[156] What the refugees did not know was that the ambassador was at odds with Itamaraty over the high numbers of tourist visas he had granted to Jews since the early 1930s and, more importantly, because of "the significant numbers of diplomatic visas" he issued without authority.[157] Between the issuance of the original visas and the renewed ones, Souza Dantas had been reprimanded by Itamaraty and, according to J. Edgar Hoover, had lost his right to authorize Brazilian entry papers because "nearly all the visas granted were for persons of Jewish origin."[158]

Itamaraty's orders did not stop Souza Dantas, one of the few Brazilian diplomats who appear to have sincerely tried to help Jewish refugees, from ordering the visa renewals. The group on the *Cabo de Hornos* therefore sailed for Rio believing they would have little trouble disembarking. They were wrong. Brazilian authorities refused admission to the group on October 16, 1941. As the vessel proceeded to Buenos Aires, where entry would be denied because of a lack of visas, members of the American Jewish Joint Distribution Committee contacted John Simmons, U.S. embassy counselor in Rio de Janeiro. Simmons, along with diplomats from France and Italy, began to pressure Aranha and Ernani Reis, a Justice Ministry official, to allow the group to enter Brazil. The situation was desperate, with "the majority prefer[ing] suicide to the somber future awaiting them."[159] The Spanish ambassador begged Vargas to authorize the visas and insisted that the refugees embarked because of a conviction by Spanish officials that the visas were valid and "issued by career Consuls from Brazil."[160] Even Vargas's friend Cardinal Leme of Rio took up the case, asking the president's wife and daughter for help.[161]

As the *Cabo de Hornos* traveled south, negotiations began with members of the Paraguayan cabinet. In return for a large bribe, it appeared, the refugees would be saved.[162] All Brazil had to do was issue transit visas allowing the refugees to disembark when the boat stopped in Rio on its way back to Europe. Early on the morning of November 7 the *Cabo de Hornos* arrived. The boat was scheduled to stay only twelve hours, but when it was discovered that the Paraguayan visas had not been issued, the shipping agents were persuaded to postpone its departure until the following day. Officials in Brazil's Passport Division (run by the Judeophobe Salgado dos Santos) openly refused to admit the Jews, terming them "non-assimilable" refugees.[163] Other Brazilian authorities "expressed goodwill in principle but an unwillingness to take action" despite U.S. pressure and categorization of the *Cabo dos Hornos* situation as "triple priority."[164] U.S. Congressman Sol Bloom made a personal appeal to Carlos Martins Pereira e Souza, Brazilian ambassador to the United States, who telegrammed Vargas asking permission to grant visas.[165] Vargas refused, citing Brazilian law and telling U.S. officials that "the Brazilian Foreign Office was not responsible for visas issued against their orders."[166] As the passengers saw their hopes dashed, panic set in. Lustig Chazen telegrammed to Simmons as the *Cabo de Hornos* sailed for Europe, "Don't abandon us, please continue intervention to prevent return Europe . . . Save us."[167] Ten days later the Dutch colony of Curaçao accepted the refugees, pending transfer elsewhere.[168] Their lives, unlike so many others, were saved.

Brazil's refusal to allow the *Cabo de Hornos*'s passengers to disembark is to be expected given Itamaraty's reprimand of Souza Dantas and the fact that it considered his orders to renew visas illegal. Yet a closer reading shows an increased sophistication in the anti-Jewish politics of the Vargas regime. With only a single exception (a telegram from Pereira e Souza to Vargas), those on the boat were never referred to as Jews. The government and its supporters always claimed the refusal was based on published law and was not related to anti-Semitism, an important position given the alliance with the United States. Rio de Janeiro's *A Noite*, in an article titled "The Truth About the Cabo de Hornos," never used the term *Jew* as it argued that the denial of entry "was not inspired by precepts of race, of nationality, of religion, of origin" but that it was "an established universal rule that visas for entering a country are valid for a certain period, at the end of which the authorities again review the admissibility of the foreigner."[169] *A Noite* even labeled the Vargas regime benevolent because it had not "handed [the refugees] over to governments considered to be their enemies" and had permitted "thousands of false temporaries" to remain in Brazil.

The reference to the "false temporaries," of course, invoked old stereotypes of Jewish criminal insidiousness. The anti-Nazi *Diário da Noite* went even further, falsely claiming that thirty thousand refugees—each of whom was presumed to have deposited three hundred contos (fifteen thousand U.S. dollars) in the Banco do Brasil in order to qualify for a visa—had entered Rio between January 1941 and June 1942.[170] This was seen not as good for the economy but rather as having created "Jerusalem in Rio de Janeiro." While the terms *Jew* or *Jew-*

ish were never used, anti-Semitic clichés of Jewish wealth, usurious charging of interest, and social invasion were dredged up. The subheadline, "Copacabana and Ipanema Evacuated by Brazilians—A Partial Explanation of the Surprising Rise in Rents of Apartments and Houses—30,000 War Refugees Who Represent a Purchasing Power of 90,000 Contos [4.5 million U.S. dollars] Lease Whole Buildings in Order to Sub-let Them," needed no explanation then, nor does it now.

REFUGEES IN BRAZIL

In spite of its restrictions on Jewish immigration, Brazil established a relatively liberal attitude toward resident refugees. Domestic policies, however, were often couched in strong anti-immigrant rhetoric, in part because anti-Semitic attacks on Jewish residents and citizens were common, especially among German sympathizers.[171] A document produced by the Departamento Nacional de Povoamento complained that an "organization of Jewish merchants is dangerous to the security of our country and national interest."[172] A CIC memo opposed a Justice Ministry amnesty plan for those whose visas had expired as allowing "undesirable individuals to stay in Brazil, generally of Semitic origin."[173] Such sentiment, however, was far from unanimous, and the harsh decrees were often left unenforced or were quietly reformed. In 1939, for example, Vargas ordered that undocumented residents and all who had entered after January 1, 1939, be fined and deported or serve in agricultural work camps.[174] According to the Ministry of Justice the draconian legislation would affect fifteen thousand resident Jews. Yet no work camps were ever built, and the decree was not enforced. Francisco Campos even promised U.S. Ambassador Jefferson Caffery that "he would neither expel those German [Jewish] refugees nor place them in any sort of concentration camp; in other words he would leave them alone."[175]

On August 20, 1938, all Jews with expired tourist visas were given permanent status except "white slavers, narcotics peddlers, and professional gamblers"—language taken directly from an ad hoc committee on Jewish refugees that the regime had established.[176] In August 1939, fifty-four Germans with tourist visas, virtually all with the middle name Israel or Sara, as demanded by the Nazi regime, were reclassified as permanent residents following a request from São Paulo's Delegation of Political and Social Order.[177] Refugees not only stayed in Brazil, but often found jobs, in many cases working illegally in spite of government

knowledge of such activity.[178] Complaints about illegal employees, often hired by firms thrilled to have experienced managers and technicians
at bargain refugee salaries, were rarely followed up, since Jewish refugees played an increasingly important role in developing the economy.
Labienne Salgado dos Santos, whose Judeophobic communiqués from
Bucharest may have helped his promotion to head of Brazil's Passport
Division, complained repeatedly to Aranha about the illegal employment of refugees. He was particularly angry about a group of Italian
Jewish administrators and laboratory directors, "well paid, in places
that could be occupied by good Brazilians" in the firm of Indústrias
Reunidas F. Matarazzo.[179] Aranha ignored these charges, although he
cleverly passed Salgado dos Santos's letter of complaint on to Vargas as
evidence that Itamaraty was examining the charges.[180]

Most of the anti-immigrant laws were never applied. Even so, some
refugees legally in Brazil may have been disqualified for jobs because
they were Jewish. Camillo Kahn applied for a job at a General Electric
plant in Rio de Janeiro and alleged he was rejected "for the simple reason that I am a Jew."[181] A letter of complaint to Franklin Roosevelt
was passed on to the U.S. embassy in Rio, which expressed its belief that
"there is nothing [we] can do."[182] Lourival Fontes, a close presidential
adviser and Hitler admirer who headed the Department of Press and
Propaganda (DIP), the powerful state organ that controlled all public
communication in Brazil and reported directly to Vargas, promised,
however, that the government would not take action against Jewish
refugees.[183] The promise was an accurate one. In July 1941 all refugees
in Brazil with temporary or "irregular" status were given official permission to remain until the end of the war with the full privileges of
those with permanent visa status.[184]

The refusal to institutionalize anti-Semitism in domestic policy was
part of Brazil's continued desire to portray itself in a positive light to
the world. Refusing entry to Jews on the basis of immigration law was
much easier than attacking refugees already in Brazil. Furthermore, by
blaming general immigration law for the refusal of visas to Jews, important politicians could still claim a willingness to make exceptions. In
1940, for example, Vargas and Aranha met with a World Jewish Con-
gress/American Jewish Congress study group traveling through South
America.[185] The group also met with João Carlos Muniz, who, in spite
of his regular attacks on Jewish immigrants and immigration, "expressed himself as highly gratified with the valuable contribution the
Jewish community was making . . . [as] the refugees who had come in

recent years had . . . brought new industries, supplementing their limited financial capital with large technical and intellectual capital [and
providing] work opportunities for native Brazilians." [186] In late 1940 a
firm in Porto Alegre requested diamond cutters, and a group of French
Jewish refugees experienced in the trade were given visas as technical
experts. [187] The almost twenty-five hundred visas given to Jews in 1940
led refugee organizations to believe that "Brazil still continues to accept
a great many [Jewish] immigrants." [188]

In January 1942, Vargas severed relations with the Axis and Japan;
in August, Brazil entered the war on the side of the Allies. This gave
Jews an opportunity to be "good" citizens and residents of Brazil, show
solidarity with the plight of European Jewry, and battle anti-Semitism—
all at the same time. Later that year a group of Jews presented five
military training planes to Getúlio Vargas "as a gesture of solidarity in
the war." [189] A few days later a fast day was observed in protest against
the Nazi murders taking place in concentration camps. [190] Many young
Jews joined the Brazilian armed forces, including, to the surprise of a
journalist in Rio, a German Jew living in Belém do Pará. [191] Others contributed money to Brazilian relief organizations. [192]

With Brazil a member of the Allied camp, much of the antagonism
directed at Jewish refugees seemed to subside. This change was certainly
related to a drop in Nazi propaganda in the Brazilian press. Furthermore, the resignations of three of the most powerful nationalist authoritarians in the Vargas regime, Justice Minister Campos, Police Chief
Müller, and DIP head Fontes, the latter two open Axis supporters, lowered the priority given to discussion of Jews. Of course the fact that less
than 2,500 immigrants entered Brazil in 1942, only 108 of whom were
Jews, diminished the importance of the refugee debate. The press responded to the new rules, now glorifying the position of Jews in Brazil.
The *Correio da Manhã* reported with excitement that Brazilian Jews
and Jewish refugees attended a special religious service in Rio to "thank
President Getúlio Vargas for saving their children." [193] Historical memory suddenly returned to the press as journalists began portraying Jews
as successful farmers. A *Diário de Notícias* editorial complimented the
"splendidly organized" agricultural colony in Rezende and observed
that "the activities of the Jews are not limited exclusively to city trade.
Actually they are capable of engaging in other spheres of work that is
certainly more useful to the country that did not deny them shelter." [194]
Niterói's *Diário da Manhã* echoed the praise, reflecting that Jewish children in the colony of Quatro Irmãos (referred to incorrectly as Dois

Irmãos) spoke Portuguese "and are masters of the history, geography and economics of Brazil [unlike] Aryan races where thousands of Brazilians do not speak their own language." [195] *O Globo* reported that Brazil's treatment of "Jewish victims of Nazi-Fascism" had led "a huge group of Israelites . . . to believe in our glorious flag" and volunteer for military service; the article was even reprinted in *Nação Armada*, the military journal that had regularly attacked Jews since its inception in 1939.[196]

Both attitudes and policy changed between 1939 and 1942. The ups and downs of refugee admission, and the decision to legalize the status of refugees in Brazil, indicate the new dual image of Jews among policymakers. This complicated and contradictory image allowed some Jews to enter Brazil while still more were rejected. Jews were never acceptable socially, even if they occasionally were useful economically. Nothing indicates this more than the Brazilian reaction to the potential entry of a group of refugees considered Catholic by Jews and the Vatican, and Jews by the Nazis and the Brazilian government—the so-called Catholic non-Aryans. The refusal of visas to this group shows that in Vargas-era Brazil even Catholics could be Jews.

CHAPTER FIVE

The Pope, the Dictator, and the Refugees Who Never Came

Judaism, asserted many Brazilian intellectuals and politicians, was a racial category that brought with it a series of biological characteristics. Many of the eugenic theories espoused by Brazilians in the late 1920s had found their way into national legislation, and influential members of the government like Oliveira Vianna publicly admired European racists and described such Nazi favorites as Gobineau and Lapouge as "mighty geniuses."[1] The French count Arthur de Gobineau had been a diplomat in Brazil in the nineteenth century and had argued throughout his essay *The Inequality of Human Races* that religion was a racial category—a notion accepted among most intellectuals and politicians in predominantly Catholic Brazil.[2] The Nazis had transformed racialism to their own ends, and nativist intellectuals in Brazil were often attracted to such theories, which would help guarantee their place at the top of the Brazilian social hierarchy.

These conceptions were put to a strange and difficult test in 1939 when, without much warning, an odd set of international political forces coalesced to emphasize the often contradictory views that Brazilian policymakers had of Jews. The agreement that caused such a disturbance was a simple one: Getúlio Vargas, the dictator, told Pius XII, the pope, that he would set aside three thousand visas for a group of German Catholic non-Aryan refugees.[3] These Catholics, for the most part, had converted either as adults by choice or as children at the behest of their parents, or had been baptized at birth by converted parents. In spite of the religious affiliation of the Catholic non-Aryans, the Brazilian government considered them Jews and treated them as such. Like Gobineau a century earlier, the Brazilian government denied the efficacy of baptism, even a papal one. Judaism was defined as a racial category, not a religious one. Even the use of the term *non-Aryan* by the Vatican, the Nazis, and the Brazilian government showed an acceptance of pseudoscience and its nefarious objectives. The Catholic non-Aryan refugees, in spite of their special support from the pope, were never able to cleanse themselves of the Jewish taint.

The Vatican visa plan, and the reaction to it, symbolize more than the official Brazilian discourse regarding Jews. They also indicate the refinements made to Brazil's Jewish immigration policy since the promulgation of Secret Circular 1,127 two years earlier. That circular was domestically oriented and aimed at keeping all Jews out of Brazil. The Vatican visa plan, on the other hand, was oriented primarily toward influencing opinion. In other words, Vargas appears to have hoped that his public concession of visas to Catholic non-Aryans would be viewed as humanitarian and democratic, would strengthen his alliance with the United States, and would give the regime a papal stamp of approval.

These objectives, it was quickly discovered, could be achieved without actually distributing visas to refugees. Even as Vargas approved the visa plan, a series of obstacles was created by members of the Estado Novo bureaucracy that would prevent the entry of a group considered by both Nazis and the Brazilian government to be Jews. Previous policy had rejected Jews unless they could bring socioeconomic benefits to Brazil. These Catholic non-Aryans had already fled their homes, and had few possessions and little if any capital. All they could do was improve Brazil's international status. Jewish refugees—or in this case, those perceived as Jews—became pawns of the Vargas regime.

A PLAN IS HATCHED

In 1939 a surprising piece of news began making its way through diplomatic circles in Europe and the Americas. Brazil, in spite of its public refusal to open wide its doors for immigration and its secret, but well-known, orders banning Jewish entry, would permit three thousand Catholic non-Aryans into Brazil. The Vatican considered Catholic non-Aryans to be full members of the Church and invested considerable effort in trying to save them from the Nazis by sending them to Catholic countries around the globe.[4] Catholic non-Aryans were in a particularly difficult position because Jewish refugee organizations judged most who had converted to Catholicism apostates and ineligible for relief. Although both the Vatican and Jewish organizations regarded Catholic non-Aryans to be irrefutably Catholic, it was the Jewish "origins" of the group that made them so useful, and dangerous, to Vargas. Within Brazil Vargas portrayed the group as Catholics, while at the same time he hoped that his support of refugees would spotlight a seemingly humanitarian Estado Novo in the international arena. If the plan worked, Brazil would gain favor with the United States and Britain and garner the Vatican's public support, all without upsetting powerful nativist critics.

The idea of giving special visas to German Catholic non-Aryan refugees in transit and internment camps throughout Europe came from the archbishop of Munich, Michael Cardinal Faulhaber. Faulhaber was a German World War I hero who wore the Iron Cross First Class and had some influence in Nazi decision-making circles. He recognized the tenuous position of Catholics considered Jews by the Nazis and was concerned about the unwillingness of the United States and others to expand their quotas for refugees.[5] Furthermore, in the aftermath of the *Kristallnacht* and the Nazi formation of the Zentralstelle für Jüdische Auswanderung (Central Office for Jewish Emigration), both Jews and Catholic non-Aryans faced growing pressure to emigrate as the chances of deportation to the concentration camps increased.[6]

The problem, in the face of growing restrictions on refugee admission, was finding locations to place Catholic non-Aryan refugees.[7] Faulhaber believed Brazil and Argentina were realistic options for refugee relocation. They were primarily Catholic countries and had politicians who might be convinced, as the Vatican was, that Catholic non-Aryans were Catholics and not Jews. Both had immigration policies that appeared malleable to outside pressure. Brazil's diplomats, however, had a reputation for being more approachable than those from Argentina. With this in mind, Cardinal Faulhaber had Dom Odon, the duke of Württemberg, approach Hélio Lobo, Brazil's representative at the International Labor Organization in Geneva. A number of discussions took place between late October 1938 and January 1939. During each meeting Odon presented a list containing what would total some one thousand Catholic non-Aryan refugees needing visas. In late January 1939 Lobo sent the lists to Foreign Minister Aranha along with a letter of support suggesting that Catholic relief groups in Europe were better qualified than he to handle the selection of visa recipients.[8] Aranha appears not to have followed through on Lobo's suggestions, and in

March Cardinal Faulhaber sent the head of the Munich Raphaelsverein, a German charitable organization set up by the Vatican in order to find places of refuge for persecuted German Catholic non-Aryans, to approach Lobo again.

Hélio Lobo was not a surprising choice for a contact. He had attended the Evian Conference and had spoken consistently, if always unofficially, about the need to solve the refugee problem.[9] Moreover, Minister Lobo's ideas regarding immigration were rumored to carry a great deal of weight in Brazil. Meeting with the Raphaelsverein representative, Lobo implied that he had authority to give "visas to German and Austrian refugees as long as they were Catholic priests or members of a Catholic order," comments circulated by the Swiss press.[10] Lobo also seemed to believe, according to the Raphaelsverein representative, that he could convince President Vargas and Foreign Minister Aranha that three thousand special visas, beyond the national quota limits, should be allotted for Catholic non-Aryans. The number three thousand was not pulled out of the blue. Brazil gave each country sending immigrants a quota of three thousand visas, and it was at least arguable that the Vatican was an independent state whose citizens deserved visas. Furthermore, extensive rumors had circulated throughout the Vatican that three thousand visas had already been set aside by the Estado Novo, but never given out, for a group of Jewish farmers, probably those going to the Rezende colony.[11] Always optimistic in the presence of others, Lobo suggested that the three thousand visas might be available for distribution to Catholic non-Aryan refugees.

Believing that Lobo had the influence to garner the visas, Cardinal Faulhaber began investigating Brazilian immigration policy and politics. Faulhaber found out a great deal, and he detailed an approach to Getúlio Vargas in a letter to Pope Pius XII. The plan would work, wrote the Cardinal, only if it was personally approved by Vargas and was so specific that it could not get lost in the bureaucracy. Faulhaber therefore suggested that the three thousand special visas be given only to Catholic non-Aryans from Germany, Austria, or the Sudetenland (including those who had already fled to Holland or Switzerland and were stuck in transit camps) either by Hélio Lobo personally or by the Brazilian consul in Hamburg. The location of the two distribution points is suggestive. On the one hand, Lobo was *the* Brazilian diplomat in Europe charged with handling the refugee problem. The choice of Hamburg, on the other hand, was more elliptical. Certainly Hamburg was attractive because the Raphaelsverein was based there, but there was an added advantage. The Brazilian consul in Hamburg, the poet João Guimarães Rosa, who was imprisoned by the Nazis when Brazil entered the war on the Allied side, had helped Jewish victims of the Nazis in the past and was known to issue more than his share of immigrant visas.[12]

Cardinal Faulhaber had a number of other ideas that he believed might make Vargas more amenable to accepting Catholic non-Aryans. Hoping to dispel concern that some (or all) Catholic non-Aryans might be Jews baptized for convenience, he emphasized that Vargas should be assured that the Raphaelsverein would investigate all the applications carefully and that visas would be given to only "the most deserving people [from] well organized lists [from which] the less desperate cases could be separated."[13] Faulhaber, knowing something of the stated Brazilian preference for agricultural workers, emphasized that all Catholic non-Aryans given special visas to Brazil would be willing to work on the land. Finally, if Vargas was afraid that Germans might form a fifth column in Brazil, these Catholic non-Aryan refugees, so it was promised, "would show themselves thankful to the country which has taken them in through quiet work and loyalty."[14]

The early contacts between Luigi Cardinal Maglione, the Vatican secretary of state appointed for his pro-German stance, and Archbishop Aloisi Masella, the papal nuncio appointed to Brazil, were intended to create a way to convince Vargas to approve the plan.[15] The Vatican representative was primarily concerned with demonstrating the Catholic nature of the Catholic non-Aryans. Maglione never mentioned the term *Jew* and the Catholic non-Aryans were always presented as Catholic first, German second, and non-Aryans only by accident. Masella had to convince Vargas and his policymakers that Catholic non-Aryans "because of their nature and situation should not cause the same fears that the Mosaic Jews do."[16] Maglione emphasized that Nuncio Masella should concentrate on the "Christian" nature of the refugees, and on the fact that they were being helped by a German Catholic relief organization and were persecuted German refugees needing humanitarian aid from large Catholic countries like Brazil.[17]

Additional pressure was put directly on Itamaraty by Catholic relief groups in Europe. "For the love of Christ help us," begged one telegram from Holland's Catholic Committee for Victims of Religious Persecution, which had one thousand Catholic non-Aryans waiting for visas in a transit camp.[18] Nuncio Masella's assurance that there would be "favorable repercussions" if the visas were ceded interested Vargas.[19] Within weeks of receiving the formal request, Vargas ordered João Carlos Muniz and the Conselho de Imigração e Colonização to investigate the possibilities for the granting of the special visas.[20]

When the request left Vargas's office, a monumental shift in discourse took place. Suddenly, in spite of the Vatican's attempts to suggest otherwise, the Catholic non-Aryans became Jews. Up to that point the Vatican had controlled all correspondence and made sure that the Catholic non-Aryans were treated as a group of Catholic refugees. With the proposal in the hands of the CIC, the Vatican was no longer able to guarantee the terms that would be used to explain the plan. Now, as the CIC met to examine plans for the concession of the visas, the "Jewish" nature of the refugees became the critical issue. Unable to imagine that Catholic non-Aryans were anything but Jews, members of the CIC passed a resolution that transformed the group from acceptable "Germans" or "Christians" into unacceptable "Semites," "Israelites," and "Jews." The group, it seemed, had been incorrectly labeled as Catholics. The racial theory of religion had now become an instrument of policy: the refugees had become "Catholic immigrants, *but* of Semitic origin."[21] The Judaism of the Catholic non-Aryan refugees even penetrated into cold drawers of Itamaraty filing cabinets: official correspondence on the Catholic non-Aryan visa plan was filed under "Jewish Immigration." Thus, while other religious groups were categorized by their nationality, Jews, regardless of nationality or place of residence, were Jews first. They were separated from national immigration categories, which Itamaraty deemed, by their very nature, unable to include Jews.[22]

As soon as the discourse changed, the plan was doomed. Most members of the Conselho de Imigração e Colonização considered Catholic non-Aryans to be Jews with a different label and were outraged that the extra quota would almost double the number of Jews entering Brazil in 1939.[23] When news of the plan was leaked, influential politicians set out to sabotage it. Israel Pinheiro da Silva, Minas Gerais's minister of agriculture, made his distaste clear when he demanded that the Catholic non-Aryans: (1) be admitted only in one large group, (2) be Germans holding Catholic conversion documents, (3) be documented farmers, and (4) each bear a minimum of five hundred pounds in cash above and beyond the actual cost of the voyage to Brazil.[24] For the refugees to meet these requirements would, as Pinheiro da Silva well knew, be virtually impossible.

In spite of the CIC's opposition, Vargas ordered the visa grants. There are a number of reasons he may have done this. In spite of Vargas's own lack of religiosity, personal requests from Pope Pius XII, him-self being pressured heavily by the Raphaelsverein, were hard to ig-nore.[25] Indeed, Getúlio Vargas continued to encourage the Vatican throughout 1939 and 1940. Furthermore, agreeing to grant visas to refugees would bring a great deal of good publicity to Brazil and strengthen ties to the United States and the Vatican. Yet the fact that there was a formal agreement to take in the refugees does not imply that Vargas and those in the CIC actually were willing to admit them. Indeed, the members of the CIC made it clear that they would do every-thing possible to insure that three thousand refugees whom they consid-ered Jewish would not be admitted.

In early June, Cardinal Maglione requested confirmation of the Vati-can visa plan and received an optimistic response from Nuncio Masella, who had already met with Vargas.[26] In mid-June Foreign Minister Ara-nha announced that, in spite of the Conselho de Imigração e Coloniza-ção's intense opposition, he and the president had approved the plan out of respect for the pope. Aranha then told Masella that the only restriction on the Catholic non-Aryans would be that they follow cur-rent Brazilian immigration legislation.[27] Masella, knowing full well that conflicts and duplicity within the Vargas regime often led to rapid and extreme policy changes, asked Aranha to put the confirmation in writ-ing so that "all surprises would be avoided." Aranha said he would comply with the request, but a few days later the agreement remained unwritten. In a follow-up meeting Masella asked the foreign minister to write by hand, in his presence, that the Brazilian government was going to accept three thousand Catholic non-Aryan refugees: Aranha refused to comply with the request.[28] Even so, less than two weeks later the plans for the visa project seemed to be in full swing. Little did anyone in the Vatican know that the agreement to grant the visas would never lead to their actual issuance.

Cardinal Maglione was informed that Vargas had agreed to the plan on June 20, and three days later the Conselho de Imigração e Coloniza-ção formally approved the three thousand visas.[29] It had not been an easy decision to make. Complicated internal negotiations had taken place between Vargas and Aranha, who seemed in favor of the project, and CIC Director João Carlos Muniz, who opposed it. Muniz com-plained that he was under pressure to admit Jews who "are persecuted in their countries of origin, the same countries that push for their entry into Brazil."[30] Brazil, suggested the immigration chief, should either completely prohibit Jewish immigration (as it had done just two years earlier) or set rigid and well-enforced norms that would put all decision-making power into the hands of the Conselho de Imigração e Colonização. For Muniz the deciding factor seems to have been unrelated to the CIC's opposition to giving visas to Jews. Rather, the Catholic non-Aryan situation provided Muniz with an opportunity to enhance his own power because "the intervention of the CIC can only take place in cases of collective immigration, of which the proposal from the Vatican is the only example." [31]

Getúlio Vargas was an astute politician. Even as he encouraged the Vatican and gave no sign of accepting the CIC's opposition, he had found a way to have his plan and reject it too. By allowing the CIC to handle the actual distribution of the visas, barriers and new requirements would be set up to keep Jews out. For the next eighteen months the CIC would constantly add new requirements for entry that forced Catholic non-Aryans into an impossible dilemma. In addition to meeting all other requirements outlined in previously published Brazilian immigration legislation, the refugees had to be farmers or industrialists in families with a minimum of three people between the ages of ten and fifty, have all travel expenses paid personally or by a Catholic relief group, and disembark in Rio de Janeiro.[32] Later requirements included a substantial transfer of money to the Banco do Brasil and demands that the refugees be selected first by papal representatives and later by Brazilian officials. Finally, disregarding the difficulties for those considered Jews, the Brazilians decided to grant visas only in the Nazi capital of Berlin, and only to those with letters of recommendation from a papal nuncio and certificates of baptism dated before 1933. These requirements were almost impossible to meet.

ACCENTUATING THE POSITIVES

The opposition within the Vargas government to the entry of the Catholic non-Aryans did not prevent the regime from reaping the benefits that accrued when the plan was announced to the world press. Within days of the official approval of the visas, both the Vatican and the Brazilian Press Office began a publicity blitz. The *New York Times,* sharing the outlook of those in Brazil who continued to focus on the "Jewish" nature of the refugees, headlined its article "Brazil Will Admit German Refugees: Bars Lifted to Allow Prompt Entry of 3,000 Catholics of Jewish Ancestry" and viewed the move as "a humanitarian gesture" because the three thousand were "expected to leave Germany for Brazil immediately." [33] The Associated Press presented both the Vargas regime and the Vatican favorably. [34] Attempting to show Brazil's humanitarian side, Itamaraty publicized what appear to be a number of blatant untruths. One was that the states of Minas Gerais, Santa Catarina, and São Paulo were all bidding to receive the refugees. Another was that the majority of the three thousand refugees would go to Santa Catarina, where there was a concentration of German speakers and where the refugees "would be likely to counteract Nazi activities among New Germans who follow foreign ideologies"—exactly the opposite of the argument used at Evian to reject refugees. [35] Less than a week after the plan had been approved, Brazil had gotten the favorable publicity it wanted without granting a single visa.

The second benefit of the plan was of a familiar kind: the capital of fleeing refugees. The wealth-conscious Brazilian government demanded that Catholic non-Aryans, prior to receiving their visas, transfer at least twenty contos (one thousand U.S. dollars) per family for rural development to the Banco do Brasil. If Brazil was going to accept undesirables, they would have to pay. Catholic non-Aryans, so went the equation, were Jews, and Jews were rich. Such ideas were encouraged by none other than the secretary general of the Raphaelsverein, who claimed that "Catholics of non-Aryan descent have, like the Jews, rich parents and rich friends who live abroad." [36] If any particular Catholic non-Aryan family had enough money to save themselves, it was the Brazilian government, and not some local diplomat, who would have to be bribed for entry. The financial conditions, however, could also function as a deterrent. Few Catholic non-Aryan refugees had the forty thousand marks (one thousand U.S. dollars) needed to purchase a Brazilian visa, and the Nazi regime forced emigrants to exchange their marks at only 4 percent of their real value as a condition of leaving Germany. Since few Catholic non-Aryans could come up with the money, few visas would be forthcoming.

The wording of the visa agreement also reduced the chances that German Jews would have the legal right to immigrate. The three thousand special visas were to be authorized under the German nationality quota, itself only slightly more than three thousand, and almost 60 percent of those visas were already going to Jews. The new visas, then, would not increase the number of refugees entering Brazil. Rather, visas formerly given to Jews under the German quota would now be reserved for Catholic non-Aryans, most of whom would be unable to fulfill the stringent conditions demanded for entry.

Resolution 39, as the visa agreement was labeled, did more than create a series of impossible restrictions on the granting of visas to Catholic non-Aryans. It also created a bureaucratic maze that almost no one could maneuver through. Catholic non-Aryans who desired visas, for example, had to be selected by the chief of the Brazilian Propaganda Office in Berlin, making it difficult for those who had already fled Germany to be selected.[37] The designation of Berlin, the capital of Nazi Germany, as the visa distribution center was to become even more problematic in August 1939 with the appointment of Ciro de Freitas Vale as ambassador to Germany (see chapter 4). Freitas Vale was no friend of the Jews—or, for that matter, of the Catholic non-Aryans. With Freitas Vale having the power over visa distribution, it was clear that few visas would actually be granted.

Brazil, it seemed, had gotten away with murder. In early July the already impossible restrictions were tightened when refugees were told to include a recommendation from the papal nunciature in their respective countries with their applications. The Vatican, which had pinned its hopes on Brazilian goodwill, responded by issuing a formal statement of thanks from the pope.[38] Vatican Secretary of State Maglione termed Brazil a "noble nation" for its humanitarianism.[39]

If Vargas believed that the Vatican would never react to the severe restrictions placed on the three thousand visas, he was wrong. For the next eighteen months the Vatican would furiously try to convince Brazil to change its rules. One influential member of the Vatican hierarchy suggested that visas be placed exclusively in the hands of the Hamburg Raphaelsverein, while another expressed the belief that the Raphaelsverein should give instructions on the distribution of visas to the papal nuncio in Rio de Janeiro.[40] The response from Itamaraty was not encouraging: all visa applications from Catholic non-Aryans would be evaluated and then distributed through the Brazilian embassy in Berlin.

The bureaucratization of the visa project came just when centralization and efficiency were becoming increasingly necessary to save lives. Papal nuncios and Catholic relief organizations in Germany, the Netherlands, Belgium, and Switzerland all increased pressure on the Vatican to get Brazil to issue visas to Catholic non-Aryans in their transit camps. As the Vatican became frustrated, it began letting relief organizations and local papal offices know of the problems. These groups, unlike the Vatican diplomatic corps, had nothing invested in the plan, and their primary concern was to save lives. A representative of the archbishop of Utrecht went to Brazil's legation in the Hague with a letter claiming that Hélio Lobo had been given permission to give out three thousand visas. When confirmation was requested from Rio, the response was a clear: "this news . . . is not true."[41] Soon complaints were pouring in to Saint Peter's and Rio de Janeiro. The Brazilian consul general in Antwerp told the papal nuncio in Brussels, for example, that a recommendation from the Vatican was needed in order for a Catholic non-Aryan to receive a visa. What was the Belgian to do, however, with the many Catholic non-Aryans (or at least people claiming to be so) who did not have Vatican letters and were in Brussels with their German "J" (that is, Jewish) passports and promises from "a group of rich Americans" to pay their passage out of Europe if they could get visas?[42] Neither the Vatican nor the Brazilian diplomatic corps had a satisfactory answer.

The president of the Raphaelsverein, Archbishop Wilhelm Berning of Osnabrück, properly and publicly accused the Brazilians of specifically setting up conditions to limit the numbers of Catholic non-Aryans who might receive visas. The archbishop complained that the Brazilian demand that each family deposit twenty contos in the Banco do Brasil might be possible "for twenty or thirty of our emigrants, but not for 3,000."[43] Even more problematically, the condition that all Catholic non-Aryan families have at least three persons who were able to work in agriculture or industry was "practically unattainable" because "our percentage of factory and agricultural workers is minimal."[44]

The Vatican never gave up hope. Perhaps Vargas had approved the visas and then let others set up requirements "that were in practice [completely] restrictive," suggested Archbishop Berning.[45] If this was the case, there was still a chance. Rio's Nuncio Masella remained upbeat in an attempt to placate his Vatican superiors and intimated that Brazilian Archbishop Leme, a close friend of Vargas, believed the restrictions might be modified. Even so, the nuncio apparently felt a need to ensure that he would not be blamed for the lack of visa distribution. Masella accused the Brazilian diplomatic corps of using the three thousand visas to extort money from refugees. He even reported that Hélio Lobo, the same minister who had originally encouraged the plan, was telling refugees that they had to pay forty contos (two thousand U.S. dollars) to his office—double the twenty-conto requirement set out in Resolution 39—and presumably pocketing the difference.[46]

Unlike Lobo, most Brazilian diplomats seemed to have no idea that the visa plan had been formalized, and European Catholic relief organizations seemed to know more about the new policy than the foreign service. In mid-July 1939, the Brazilian delegation in Utrecht received a visa request from a Catholic refugee organization in charge of a transit camp that included "non-Aryans, but of the Catholic confession" and a number of "Aryan" German military and police officers who had married non-Aryans.[47] Claiming not to know of the special visas, the Brazilian delegate in charge of the Utrecht office, Ruy Ribeiro Costa, simply pushed what seemed a nonsensical request up the diplomatic ladder to Rio de Janeiro. While waiting to hear from Itamaraty, Costa apparently felt a need to respond to the question of whether Brazil was granting special visas to German non-Aryan Catholics. Unable to conceive of Catholic non-Aryans as different from Jews or of the possibility that anti-Semitism could exist in Brazil's social democracy, Costa explained that immigrants "without capital [or] without knowledge of rural life" would not be granted visas since Brazil wished to "avoid an influx of anti-social and anti-economic parasitic masses" into the urban areas.[48]

> It is perfectly comprehensible that Brazil should not give refuge to the trash from the German ghettos. Among the refugees of the Third Reich and Italy, however, there are studious men, those of the laboratory . . . mechanics, skilled workers and other useful manual laborers from whom the fact that they are Jews is not the contamination of an abominable addiction. Furthermore, the masses of German refugees contain a large number of non-Jews, at least according to our habitual Brazilian criterion [since] we do not apply racist standards [such as] the blood scales of the Third Reich. Many are "Jews" for Germany, in virtue of the mingling of Israelite blood in past generations; for us they are Germans as much as Chancellor Adolf Hitler.[49]

Costa phrased his public comments politely. Even so, they reflected the confusion among Brazilian diplomats who had been instructed to both keep out Jews and give visas to immigrants who would be useful for industrial development.

Ruy Ribeiro Costa was not the only Brazilian diplomat who claimed ignorance of the Catholic non-Aryan visas. In Hamburg consul general João Guimarães Rosa asserted that he was "absolutely ignorant" of the Vargas-Vatican scheme. The consul claimed to be shocked that refugees were demanding visas, and he noted that they "say they have been given authorization by the Brazilian Government, with special attention from the Pope, to enter into national territory with permanent visas."[50] Guimarães Rosa was an extremely concerned and helpful diplomat, but like virtually every member of the Vargas regime, he conceived of Catholic non-Aryans as racially and immutably "Semites of the Catholic religion" or "Jewish Catholics." What particularly surprised the consul was that among those applying for Catholic non-Aryan visas were a considerable number of German Catholic high clergy fleeing from the Nazis.

Guimarães Rosa was no fool, even if he knew how to play one. In spite of the diplomat's contention, he did know that negotiations were under way to give three thousand visas to Catholic non-Aryans. When Guimarães Rosa innocently asked Aranha about the plan, he attached a copy of a telegram from Cardinal Maglione to Cardinal Faulhaber about the Catholic non-Aryans, which "accidentally fell into my hands." Assuming for his own purposes that Aranha was also unaware of the plan (and knowing that Aranha had neglected to tell him and other diplomats about it), Guimarães Rosa proposed that the CIC give him a special quota of one thousand visas in order to deal with the new and unexpected requests from Catholic refugees.[51] This request, apparently, received no response.

If the Brazilian government had maintained the rules set out in its formal resolution, it is likely that few, if any, Catholic non-Aryans would have entered the country. Within a month of the issuance of Resolution 39, however, even further restrictions were imposed. Ambassador to Germany Freitas Vale created what would be just one of many "provisional rules" designed to stop what he believed was a tidal wave of Jewish refugees from going to Brazil. Without instructions from Rio de Janeiro, the ambassador decided that only those with German Aryan passports would be given immigrant visas, effectively cutting off all those stripped of their nationality or issued a "J" passport when Germany passed its racial laws.[52] These increasingly numerous restrictions concerned Vatican Secretary of State Maglione. By August he had privately written off the plan as not having very "high hopes of success."[53] Such pessimism was not unwarranted. One Catholic non-Aryan family in Prague who met all the conditions, and even had the Archiepiscopal Curia (chancery office of the archdiocese) send a letter of recommendation directly to Itamaraty, was told by the Brazilian Foreign Office that the only chance of their getting a visa was through the Raphaelsverein in Hamburg.[54]

Maglione's dejection at the failure of the plan did not stop others in the church hierarchy from trying to create ways "to mitigate the economic conditions [imposed by Resolution 39] that serve to work against the granting of the 3,000 visas."[55] Forcing the refugees to pay twenty contos up front in order to get a visa, suggested Papal Nuncio and Archbishop Cesare Orsenigo of Berlin, was ludicrous. Perhaps Catholic non-Aryans could be obligated to work a specified period of time in a place of the Estado Novo's choosing in Brazil. The visas could then be distributed and "would crown the many hopes brought about by [Vargas's] magnificent gesture that has been impeded bureaucratically."[56] Yet it was capital, not labor, that concerned the Vargas regime. Such ideas went nowhere, and bureaucratic roadblocks continued to be thrown up on a regular basis.

The Brazilian government had little desire to actually distribute visas to Catholic non-Aryans.[57] As 1939 drew to a close, an extremely frustrated Father Max Grösser, secretary general of the Raphaelsverein, wrote directly to Dulphe Pinheiro Machado, director of the Ministry of Labor's National Department of Immigration, to complain that the Raphaelsverein's "[happiness] was reduced greatly by the conditions [created] by the Conselho de Imigração e Colonização."[58] A full six months after the formal agreement to concede visas to Catholic non-Aryans had been reached, not a single visa had been issued from any Brazilian consulate in Germany. Ambassador Freitas Vale in Berlin, Consul General Guimarães Rosa in Hamburg, and Hélio Lobo in Geneva all claimed to "be ignorant of any information about the 3,000 visas."[59]

Father Grösser would aggressively criticize Brazil's inaction until the visa program formally ended. Unwilling to give up hope, he even tried to strike a chord in Brazilian hearts by portraying the potential visa recipients as women. The secretary general of the Raphaelsverein claimed he could "demonstrate that our Catholic non-Aryan women and the Jews to whom they are wed, are much different than Mosaic Jews."[60] This tactic had just the opposite of the desired effect: the Brazilian government had no desire to give Catholic non-Aryan visas to Jewish men married to Catholic women. In fact, Dulphe Pinheiro Machado's response to Grösser's suggestion was typical. After letting the letter sit for some time, he decided that, rather than dealing with the problem himself, he would simply send the letter up the chain of command to the Conselho de Imigração e Colonização. The CIC echoed Pinheiro Machado's clever inefficiency. It allowed the letter to sit for three more months before propelling the document upward into Itamaraty's bureaucratic black hole.[61]

THE BRAZILIAN RESPONSE

The Vatican, increasingly frustrated by the lack of action, pressured Brazil to accept at least some Catholic non-Aryan refugees. This forced the Vargas regime to explain the lack of visas in a way that was pro-Catholic, pro-refugee, and not openly anti-Semitic. One means of doing so was to divert attention from the issue at hand. When asked if Protestant non-Aryan refugees might be eligible for visas, Itamaraty refused to give a clear answer, arguing that Brazil was "not concerned about race, but religion."[62] Yet the Catholic non-Aryan visa problem was simply another component of the Jewish Question. The Foreign Ministry, for example, often justified its actions by accurately noting that many applicants had been baptized at the last minute in order to garner visas. But if, as the Raphaelsverein always maintained, even recently baptized Catholics "neither have a relationship with a Synagogue nor with Jews," why not grant the visas?[63] The answer, of course, was unrelated to the time that elapsed between baptism and visa application. Jews simply could not become real Catholics.

Filled with misinformation and outright lies, the continuing negotiations for the distribution of visas increasingly took on a life of their own, based primarily on the saving of face. Hélio Lobo had implied to Vatican officials that visas were available, so he put pressure on his friend Labienne Salgado dos Santos, chief of the Passport Division, to grant them.[64] Salgado dos Santos, however, had for years been openly and aggressively opposed to giving visas to those he considered Jews. Hoping other countries would press Itamaraty on the point, Lobo also began telling his colleagues in the Inter-Governmental Committee that Brazil had a large number of visas available for Jews and that none of the Catholic non-Aryan visas had been given out. The British government picked up the information and decided to use it in order to resolve its own Jewish refugee problem. The British ambassador in Rio de Janeiro suggested that Brazil should modify its immigration policy and take German refugees living in England in light of the "urgency of the situation and the humanitarian sentiments which have always inspired the attitude of the Brazilian government."[65] Lobo's interest may have had a further motivation. If he was indeed selling visas, as Nuncio Masella alleged, the visas needed to be distributed for the scam to function.

Lobo was not the only one concerned about the three thousand visas for personal reasons. The Vatican, Nuncio Masella, and Foreign Minister Aranha all feared appearing incompetent. Each thus put pressure and blame on the other. A claim in November 1939 by Aloisi Masella that Aranha had promised to instruct Berlin to issue visas to Catholic non-Aryans unable to pay the twenty-conto tax may as easily have been wishful thinking on the part of Masella as a deliberate attempt by Aranha to deflect criticism away from himself.[66] A month after Masella's meeting with Aranha, no such instructions had been issued to Berlin.[67]

DASHED HOPES

After approving the visa plan, Getúlio Vargas refused to make any decisions about the refugees, leaving his subordinates to try to guess how he wanted the policy implemented. This put Oswaldo Aranha in a dangerous, but potentially powerful, position. He asserted that he wanted to give the visas to Catholic non-Aryans, and soon both Masella in Rio and Maglione in the Vatican began to pressure him, not Vargas, for help. Even so, as far as the Vatican was concerned, the major obstacle to giving out the visas was the financial conditions outlined in Resolution 39. The negotiations, then, revolved around a reduction of the twenty-conto payment. In early 1940, Masella, already embarrassed once by a claim that the visa problem had been solved, again reported that Aranha had dispensed with the monetary requirements. Masella apparently believed that this would lead to an almost immediate granting of the visas, and he went so far as to tell Cardinal Maglione that "Brazil's government deserves praise" and presumably another public "thank-you."[68] Masella's communiqué must have been convincing. Soon afterward Vatican officials around Europe were advised that the financial conditions had been reduced and that Freitas Vale would facilitate the concession of visas for Catholic non-Aryans.[69] The Vatican believed the corner had been turned.

A new problem, however, soon arose. Many Catholic non-Aryans were recent converts, and even church officials were willing to concede privately that a large number may have converted only to escape the Nazis.[70] The Vatican, however, need not have wasted its time worrying about such matters. Regardless of the sincerity of the Catholic non-Aryans awaiting relief, the visas remained blocked. In January 1940, a group of thirty-five German Catholic non-Aryan families in Antwerp met all the conditions set out by Resolution 39, including the financial ones, and purchased passages to Brazil. They were not granted visas in spite of repeated telegrams sent to both Freitas Vale in Berlin and Hildebrando Accioly, Brazil's ambassador to the Vatican.[71] Three and a half months later these families were still awaiting visas.[72] Fifty refugees in Switzerland, with few resources but all the needed approvals and a personal commitment from Pope Pius XII to pay three thousand dollars toward their travel expenses between Europe and Brazil, were denied visas for financial reasons.[73]

Aranha's suggestion that the financial conditions attached to the Catholic non-Aryan visas would be reduced had never been approved by Vargas. Aranha did write to the president in early May requesting that the monetary requirements be removed, but the foreign minister's reasoning was careful, and he never expressed any approval of the plan (approval that might later have been used against him). Rather, Aranha suggested that the financial reductions were necessary because "the Ministry of Foreign Relations . . . is having serious difficulties executing Your Excellency's [wishes] for the entrance of the Catholic non-Aryans."[74] Vargas, however, seemed to have no more interest in the plan. A month later the most the Conselho de Imigração e Colonização could tell Itamaraty was that it should inform Nuncio Masella that it still had "not heard a response [from Vargas]."[75]

As Vargas phased himself out of the decision-making process, the CIC, against the plan from the beginning, started to gain influence. Whatever concerns the Brazilian government might have had about offending the Vatican were subordinated to a greater fear that Brazil might be forced into accepting some refugees. By continuing to insist on financial transfers as a condition of entry, even as the Vatican tried to have them dismissed, Estado Novo politicians maintained a facade of goodwill by insisting that, in spite of the rules, Vargas had approved the three thousand visas.[76] The regime, however, had little fear that it would look bad internationally because the Vatican, which had promoted the scheme from the start, would never admit publicly to its failure. In fact, after the flurry of press activity announcing the granting of the visas in June 1939, not another word about the plan was published in major newspapers in the United States. To the world Vargas seemed a humanitarian.

In early 1940, the conflicts within the CIC yet again complicated the plan as the two military representatives on the council continued to oppose even the highly restrictive Resolution 39 as being too lenient.[77] The resolution, however, had already been made public, and so Brazil's embassy at the Vatican, wishing to make "perfectly clear the Resolution that permits the entrance in Brazil of 3,000 Catholic non-Aryans," was ordered by Itamaraty to inform the Holy See that two-thirds of the visas would be distributed from the embassy in Berlin, while the other third would be granted to refugees from any European country exclusively through the Brazilian embassy at the Vatican.[78] Furthermore, all visa requests would need to be justified by either the Raphaelsverein in Hamburg or the papal nuncio in Berlin. The new rules stated that potential immigrants had to have their Catholic sentiments affirmed by ecclesiastical authorities and "guaranteed by a baptism certificate from before 1933."[79] These rules, however, were simply a smokescreen for the real intention: to keep out Jews.

The new restrictions were intended to make it virtually impossible for anyone to fulfill all the conditions needed for a visa while simultaneously overwhelming the system bureaucratically. Now those who held German passports but had fled to transit camps in Switzerland, Holland, or Belgium would have to return through war-ravaged Europe to an increasingly dangerous Germany in order to get the religious guarantees needed for a visa.[80] Those yet in Germany would still have to travel to Berlin, with papers from the Hamburg Raphaelsverein, for visas. Non-German Catholic non-Aryans would have access to the one thousand visas set aside for them only by going to Rome. Pleas sent directly to Oswaldo Aranha from Catholic relief agencies throughout Europe were all ignored.[81]

If any requirement was clearly intended to sabotage the Catholic non-Aryan visa plan, it was the demand that all Catholic non-Aryans be baptized before 1933. According to a very angry Hildebrando Pinto Accioly, the baptism requirements were enacted because the few "Hebrews who are arriving [as Catholic non-Aryans] are making a terrible impression [and because] many appear to have been baptized only in 1939."[82] By maintaining that the requirements were meant to guarantee that visa recipients were Catholic, attention was diverted from the refugee issue. The Brazilian government now had a simple way to deny visas to virtually all Catholic non-Aryans.[83]

The Vatican always asserted that converts were sincere. At the same time it furiously denied converting people only in order to get them visas.[84] Although both claims may have been true, many of those applying for the visas were in fact new converts. Cardinal Maglione received regular reports about Catholic non-Aryans that criticized the "improper conduct and alleged demands [that] have not corresponded to the concern which the Holy See has shown."[85] The Raphaelsverein also recommended new, and perhaps insincere, converts, but it also tried to dissuade the Vargas regime from enforcing the baptism provision by claiming to examine carefully the "sincerity of conversion" of the recently baptized.[86] In spite of their urgency, the pleas had little effect. Ambassador Ciro de Freitas Vale was irritated by constant requests for visas and complained to Aranha that "we have not had a moment of tranquillity in this Embassy."[87] Freitas Vale, who never used the socially acceptable terms *Jews, Israelites,* or *Hebrews,* referred to Catholic non-Aryans and Jews alike as "Semites." He even tried to present the group as Nazi sympathizers, claiming that "the United States of America has prohibited the emigration of Jewish Catholics because of [fears of the] fifth column."[88]

Free enterprise and human desperation played a role in Brazil's increasing vigilance over the distribution of visas. Diplomats in Rome, it was alleged, were selling the visas to a private agency that then resold them to non-Catholic and non-baptized Jews for two hundred dollars.[89] In spite of the vociferous denials by a Brazilian government loath to admit that its diplomats were selling visas, it is likely that the rumor was true.[90] Indeed, there was a general belief that "with money everything can be arranged in Brazil."[91] At the same time, European government officials with contacts among Brazil's diplomatic corps were also selling visas to refugees, a fact that Itamaraty was well aware of. In Prague an office supported by the Bohemian Ministry of Social Welfare was openly selling visas for entry to both Brazil and Palestine, but little attempt was made to close it down.[92]

A few of the special visas needed to be distributed, if only to reduce the number of communiqués from the Vatican that were bombarding Brazilian decision makers. In September 1940, Oswaldo Aranha created a set of rules just for the consulate in Hamburg that would open the restrictions enough so that a few Catholic non-Aryans might be given visas. Those who could transfer the twenty contos *or* had a guarantee from a Catholic organization in Brazil that they would have employment upon arrival were now eligible. In addition, the consul general in Hamburg was given the authority to issue as many as fifty visas a month (twenty-five from Raphaelsverein recommendations and twenty-five from the embassy at the Vatican) to Catholic non-Aryans who had direct authorization from the Passport Division in Rio de Janeiro.[93] Visas could now be given to those baptized before 1935 (if they were at least twenty-one years old), but with a preference for "individuals or family heads who were technicians specializing in agricultural or industrial work."[94] In a stroke of the pen Aranha's new plan could force families to send a father or older son to Brazil with a visa and no guarantee that the rest of the family would ever be permitted to join him.

One refugee who fell into this morass was Rudolph Max Neumann, an Austrian Catholic non-Aryan engineer. In July 1939 Neumann's brother-in-law, Frederico Safranek, the director of the Professional School of the State of São Paulo and a naturalized Brazilian, made a request for Neumann and his wife and child to enter Brazil.[95] According to Safranek, Neumann would either build a new machine factory or become a partner in an existing one. Useful for Brazil's industrial development, and with a Vatican reference in hand, Neumann received a permanent visa as a "Catholic technical specialist" in October 1940.[96] In November, Neumann made visa applications for his wife and fourteen-year-old son, both of whom held Austrian passports but were in a transit camp in Genoa, Italy. The applications were deferred by the consulate, and the two were told their visas could be issued only in Austria. Neumann's request to the Ministry of Foreign Relations for information brought no response, so he appealed directly to Getúlio Vargas. By this time Neumann was employed in a Rio de Janeiro firm, and his wife had returned to Vienna while his son had been sent to safety in London.[97] The president's office directed Neumann's plea back to Itamaraty, which responded negatively. A month later the final judgment was made; although "Neumann entered Brazil as one of the 3,000 Catholic non-Aryan refugees, [and although] his wife is also one of the 3,000 . . . they will be treated as Jews."[98] The visas were not granted, and there is no record of whether Neumann's wife and child survived the war.

The granting of a visa to Max Neumann and not to his family was typical of the varied messages passed to European diplomatic posts. Aranha, for instance, would give a set of instructions to one consul even as Itamaraty told another consul the opposite.[99] Finally, in September 1940 Ambassador Accioly called Cardinal Maglione at the Vatican to tell him that the concession of visas to Catholic non-Aryans under the special plan had been suspended.[100] In 1941, just preceding decisions by Portugal and Spain to deny transit visas to refugees who hoped to depart from those countries, Ambassador Accioly curtly informed Cardinal Maglione that Brazil had ended the Catholic non-Aryan visa plan. The Catholic Church acquiesced with hardly a murmur, accepting Accioly's comment that "if the world situation changes . . . my Government might revoke its decision."[101] This was not to be the case. In late July 1942, the Brazilian government again refused to modify its immigration policies to accept Catholic non-Aryan refugees.

The failure of the Vatican visa plan is one of the most telling Brazilian responses to the Jewish Question. A racial view of Judaism remained predominant, although it was occasionally ignored if a person was wealthy. Yet Catholic non-Aryans rarely had access to capital. Unable to work through Jewish relief groups who had learned to manipulate Nazi and Brazilian regulations, the Catholic non-Aryans were simply common people whose only support group was a distant Vatican.

Most Brazilian policymakers, whether or not they were in favor of giving visas to Catholic non-Aryan refugees, never accepted these people as Catholics and viewed them as members of a Jewish race. Oswaldo Aranha's concerns were primarily restrictive, not relief oriented, and the foreign minister always maintained that "the maximum vigilance should be exercised to avoid the entrance of undesirable elements."[102] Other diplomats, notably in Hamburg, Antwerp, and Brussels, did try to find ways to distribute the visas, but even their discourse showed that they were unable to conceive of Catholic non-Aryans as anything but Jews. This perception played on the anti-Semitic fears of those in power. Jews were simply the wrong race.

As 1940 came to a close, the human tragedy in Europe continued and the high hopes that the Vatican-Brazilian visa plan had engendered were dashed. In a futile attempt to salvage something of the plan the Vatican even suggested that the three thousand visas be given to Catholic Aryans, but this was also rejected.[103] For those desperately searching for a way out of Europe, these visas provided, at least for a moment, a chance. Yet in case after case the Brazilian government systematically refused to help the refugees. Jersy Sachs and his family applied for Catholic non-Aryan visas with the support of Brazil's Polish legation. Although none of the one thousand visas that were in Hildebrando Accioly's hands had yet been issued, he showed no sympathy and no interest in authorizing visas that would be distributed away from Rome. In spite of the fact that Sachs had the support of the Holy See, Accioly referred to the family as "those Israelites," and refused "the indication of the Vatican, with the recommendation of the high personalities of the Church and Diplomatic Corps here" simply because the family had been baptized after 1934.[104]

By making it virtually impossible for Catholic non-Aryans to garner a special visa, the number who actually entered Brazil was limited.[105]

Of the 3,000 visas that Getúlio Vargas originally approved, between 15 and 30 percent appear to have been issued, apparently only to those who met the capital requirements. In September 1940 Ambassador Freitas Vale stated that he had not given out any of the 2,000 visas allotted to the embassy in Berlin, and when the visa program was terminated, the ambassador had not issued a single visa.[106] Hildebrando Accioly authorized other consulates in Europe to give out 720 of the 1,000 visas allotted to the embassy at the Vatican, but most, apparently, were never issued.[107] In November 1940, Hildebrando Accioly informed Itamaraty that 959 visas had been issued to Catholic non-Aryans, but other sources suggest the number was lower.[108]

In April 1940, the U.S. embassy in Brazil reported that "the first batch of [forty-five] German and Austrian Catholic refugees of Semitic origin arrived," but later reports make no mention of other arrivals.[109] By October 1940 the Brazilian consulate in Antwerp had distributed 57 visas to Catholic non-Aryans, but in December of that same year Accioly had not yet issued any from the embassy in Rome.[110] A small batch of visas was issued outside of Germany. The Brazilian consul in Brussels, the consul general in Antwerp, the Raphaelsverein, the Dutch Catholic Committee for Victims of Religious Persecution, and Papal Nuncio Archbishop Clement Micara all worked together, for example, to get transit visas from the Belgian government and Catholic non-Aryan visas from Brazil for two hundred refugees who had been interned in camps in Germany and Holland.[111] Although many had been baptized at the last minute, Nuncio Micara of Brussels "continued to insist that the conversions are done as seriously as possible" and that the Catholic non-Aryans were "sincere [even though] neophytes."[112]

A report from the Conselho de Imigração e Colonização on forty-five Catholic non-Aryans arriving in Santos noted that "they are well educated; speak various languages; and among them are automobile and aviation mechanics, a technician in cooperative organizations, a specialist in sawmill machinery . . . professional men and factory experts, and two families of agriculturalists . . . destined for Rio Grande do Sul."[113] Those who did not meet the development requirements, however, rarely received visas. A Jewish barber resident in São Paulo tried to get visas for his wife and daughter in Romania after the two received baptismal certificates from the pope. His direct petition to Vargas, when passed on to the lower bureaucracy, was refused on the basis of Secret Circulars 1,127 and 1,249 because "in spite of [the two] saying they are Catholic, their surname reveals Semitic origin."[114] In spite of the government's supposed desire for rural labor, there is no evidence that any of the few Catholic non-Aryans who entered were farmers or even claimed to be. In spite of the demand that Catholic non-Aryans be baptized before 1933, most who received visas had not been, leading to regular charges that the visas were being sold. In spite of the evident urgency, the visas were distributed over a period of several years to minimize the appearance of a sudden flood of Jewish arrivals.[115]

The Vatican visa plan helped the Vargas regime to satisfy contradictory domestic and international forces. By initially agreeing to the quota the Vargas regime received international recognition for its humanitarian stance, put the Vatican in its debt, and strengthened its relations with the United States and England. By issuing only some of the promised visas it maintained the domestic position that Jews were undesirable. The agreement was held up as an example of Brazil's willingness to take refugees, yet most Catholic non-Aryans were rejected because they were considered Jews. By enforcing strict requirements of capital, it was presumed that those few entrances that were allowed would be somewhat more palatable to nativists.[116]

Fourteen months after Vargas agreed to grant visas to Catholic non-Aryans, the program was suspended following the Brazilian government's constant complaints that the Catholic non-Aryans were rarely true converts.[117] The cancellation only masked the fact that the Catholic non-Aryans were never seriously considered acceptable immigrants. Since religion and race were considered synonymous, Jews could never be Catholics. From the Brazilian standpoint the Vatican visa plan had been a success, and a bust of Pope Pius XII was unveiled at the presidential palace with much fanfare.[118] Vargas's claims of humanity were confirmed by an important collaborator, and Brazil had saved itself from the Catholic non-Aryan undesirables.

CHAPTER SIX

Epilogue: Brazilian Jews, Jewish Brazilians

Between 1942 and 1945 a *total* of 235 Jews legally entered Brazil as immigrants.[1] Yet Brazil's Jewish Question did not disappear. As general immigration levels dropped to their lowest levels in years, industrialists and large landowners in Rio de Janeiro and São Paulo began pushing for more labor and claimed that "Brazil will need an increase of twenty million [people in order to alleviate] the shortage of hands."[2] Even so, nativists continued to express concern about the mass entry of Jewish refugees and displaced persons. Indeed, the specter of waves of Jews entering Brazil hovered around most immigration policy decisions in the 1940s.

In 1943 the Conselho de Imigração e Colonização began to debate a future national immigration policy. The aim was to examine all existing immigration legislation and consolidate it into a single decree law. CIC members advanced four main options. Proposals for an open-door policy were based on the idea that the Brazilian melting-pot society would easily assimilate all immigrants. No member of the CIC openly supported this position. The other extreme was most vociferously represented by Ernani Reis, the secretary of the Ministry of Justice. Reis advocated closing Brazil to all but the Portuguese and "Mediterranean Latin" peoples, arguing that the existing population would have a large natural rate of increase and did not need many immigrants.[3] This position was a logical extension of existing Brazilian immigration policy. What made it different from the third position, which focused on tinkering with the immigration quotas set out in the 1934 constitution, was that it defined who was desirable, and thus eligible for immigration rights; all others would simply be banned from entering Brazil. While no CIC member actively supported the status quo, most supported a fourth position—a preferential open-door policy. Under this scheme Brazil would be open to those from the Americas and Portugal while banning Africans, Asians, and all who descended from them. Numerical quotas were unworkable, so went the argument, because they were indiscriminate and "restrict the entry of desirable races and favor races not wanted."[4] Who were the undesirable races? Africans and those of African descent topped the list, while the Japanese, accused of creating "pre-war headaches arising from haphazard immigration," were often mentioned by those not tied to the large landowners.[5] The CIC still focused on whitening Brazil racially, with some members even arguing that it was already "the only great white country in the tropical area."[6]

Not surprisingly, the other troubling "non-white race" was Jews. A U.S. State Department official in Brazil noted that the "sentiment for the exclusion of Jews is stronger than is generally thought."[7] CIC members complained that Jews did not assimilate and displaced Brazilian businesspeople. Although two members of the military on the CIC, Navy Captain Atila Monteiro Aché and Army Major Miguel Lage Saião, did not openly oppose Jewish immigration, they were most committed to the General Staff position that European refugees not be allowed into Brazil for security reasons. Only Arthur Hehl Neiva, a member of the CIC whose 1938 defense of a liberal Jewish immigration policy was censored and remained unpublished until 1944, spoke openly in favor of Jewish entry.[8]

Academic "research" continued to support restrictions on Jewish immigration by portraying Jews in stereotypical ways. An unsigned article titled "The Assimilation of the Foreign Element in São Paulo: Ethnological Notes on Israelites" made a clear distinction between "nationals, [that is,] legitimate Brazilians[,]" and Jews, who could presumably never be "legitimate."[9] Manuel Diégues, Jr., whose *Etnias e cultura no Brasil* was published in the 1950s and is still considered a standard work on the subject, claimed that "the great [Jewish] activity was, and is, commerce. It can be said that international commerce is in their hands."[10] Professor Everardo Backheuser, a technical consultant to the National Geographic Council associated with the movement to institute Catholic religious training in public classrooms, broached both the assimilation and occupational issues. He insisted, in the respected *Revista*

Brasileira de Geografia, that "the only desirable immigration is that of farmers" and that "the Jew, of all nationalities, is a peddler. [He is] squirmy, unctuous, a monopolizer, and invincible. He constitutes, from the social and political point of view, a real danger, because he is inscrutable, not only by robbing his customers but by disseminating subversive ideas. He has been named one of the best agents of Bolshevism."[11] The widely published and respected Osório Lopes's ideas were equally pedestrian: he suggested in 1942 that the solution to "The Jewish Problem" (the title of his book) was to convert all Jews to Catholicism.[12]

In April 1943, the *New York Times* quoted a Brazilian diplomat as saying that "[we are] not eager to receive refugees in our cities as traders," and in August the CIC drafted a plan that would abolish the old quota system and would limit entry to Europeans, with an emphasis on farmers and technical specialists.[13] The draft, however, was never formalized into policy, and few immigrants or refugees entered Brazil between 1943 and 1945. In early 1944, the War Refugee Board approached the Brazilian ambassador in London, who doubled as the representative on the Intergovernmental Committee on Refugees, with a plan to send a group of Jewish children from France to Brazil.[14] Fifteen months later, when the Brazilian government finally agreed to accept the children after much debate, the situation had already been resolved. The debates on immigration policy continued through 1945. A new decree law that ostensibly "facilitate[d] European immigration" was in fact concerned with limiting it.[15]

In 1946, a total of 1,486 Jews entered Brazil, a number that doubled the following year.[16] This figure represents more than 10 percent of all immigrants to the country. Complaints about "the ghettos of the city" again began to appear, even in the prestigious *Jornal do Brasil.*[17] In 1947, a Jewish federal deputy from Rio de Janeiro, Maurício Grabois (Communist Party of Brazil, PC do B), spoke against the "illegal prohibition of the entry of Jews in the country," and, according to Elias Lipiner, Secret Circular 1,249 was not officially canceled until February 1951, even though it had not been enforced in years.[18] The renewal of Jewish immigration testifies to the ways that refugees and displaced persons managed to manipulate Brazil's immigration system. For example, the Brazilian government insisted that all ships list their passengers by religion, and it appears that the category labeled "Orthodox," and meant to include Greek and Russian Orthodox immigrants, often "included many 'Orthodox' and not-so-Orthodox Jews."[19]

Negative images of Jews did not disappear after the war. A 1950 survey of two thousand São Paulo university students found that most would not want Jews in "close kinship by marriage."[20] In 1957 Arthur Hehl Neiva and Manuel Diégues, Jr., completed a UNESCO study titled "The Cultural Assimilation of Immigrants in Brazil."[21] In spite of the claim that immigrants easily assimilated in Brazil, Jews and Hindus were referred to as members not of religions but of nationalities, placing a question of dual loyalties on the two groups. In spite of such notions, Jews continued to find Brazil a nation of social, political, and economic mobility.

The character of Brazil's Jewish community changed markedly after Israel was established in 1948. Yet Zionism, although important in postwar Brazilian Jewish life, never played the same role that it did in other communities in Latin America. A preparatory kibbutz (agricultural community) was founded in 1948 for those thinking of making *aliyah* (a "returning" to Israel). This late date, and the general lack of participation of the Brazilian Jewish community in the agricultural Zionist movement, led one Jewish leader to complain that because "the economic situation of Brazilian Jewry is fantastic . . . one finds [the group] in the process of complete assimilation."[22] Between 1948 and 1977, 6,268 Brazilian Jews made *aliyah*.[23] A small group committed to agriculture emigrated in 1950, and among Israelis, the kibbutz begun by that group, Kibbutz Bror Chail, is called "the Brazilian kibbutz."

Following the Suez crisis and the rise of Arab nationalism in the 1950s, about five thousand Jews from Egypt and other Arab countries immigrated to Brazil. The established Syrian and Lebanese community "facilitated their penetration into channels of trade and even into politics of the small towns, many of which had Arab mayors."[24] The Sephardic newcomers initially had little contact with the established Ashkenazic community, but this has changed. Intermarriage between the groups is high, and it is significant that the former German congregations in Rio de Janeiro and São Paulo have recently elected Sephardic presidents.

The establishment of a military regime in Brazil in 1964 brought new challenges to the Jewish community. Although many Jews were prominent members of the opposition, others supported the twenty-one-year military regime (1964–85) and "as allies and supporters of the ruling oligarchies . . . tend[ed] to remain aloof from the incipient movements aimed at renovating Brazil's social and political system."[25] State suppression of all political movements ensured that the level of anti-Semitism would remain low, an additional motive for Jewish support. With the suppression of the left, many Jews believed the new military government had made a commitment to the continuation of Brazilian Jewry. This was not the case. Brazil's authoritarian regime never provided the expected protection for minority groups, and political violence against dissenters led many Jews to relocate to Israel, where the Brazilian-born population doubled between 1977 and 1982 to about 11 percent of Israel's 109,865 Jews of Latin American origin.[26] The Brazilian military's foreign policy also made many Jews uncomfortable. In 1975 Brazil voted in favor of the United Nations resolution equating Zionism with racism, and soon afterward the military decided to base its foreign policy on a "responsible pragmatism" that included a heavy dose of pro-Arab rhetoric.[27]

While it is unclear exactly how many Jews live in Brazil today, in part because there is no exact definition of who is a Jew, the figure is between 100,000 and 150,000.[28] The Jewish Congregation of São Paulo is the largest synagogue in South America, boasting a membership of over two thousand families. Conservative and Orthodox synagogues are found in all of Brazil's major cities, and the Reform movement has recently established itself in São Paulo.[29] Jewish parents continue to have the option of sending their children to Jewish or secular schools, and about one-third of the community is educated in Jewish schools.[30] Brazilian Jews are widely integrated into the political system at its highest levels. The 1988 presidential elections saw Brazil's most famous television personality, Senor Abravanel (known to all by his stage name, Silvio Santos), the son of Sephardic Jews from Greece, briefly enter the race. His public acknowledgement, but nonpractice, of Judaism appears not to have hurt his base of support among the poor and urban working classes, who generally seem unaware that Brazil has a Jewish population. Jews have also been promoted to the higher ranks of the Brazilian armed forces, and in 1988 a Jew became military commander of one of Brazil's largest states. Even so, a 1977 confidential report by the army's Division of Security and Information, written at the height of the controversy over Brazil's proposed nuclear agreement with West Germany, claimed that Jews opposed to the agreement were Zionists.[31] While the Jewish Question may no longer be asked, questions about "Jewish issues" still exist.

The integration of Jews into Brazil's political and economic system has not diminished the fear of anti-Semitism. Many Jews believe that Brazilian Jewish life is precarious and that only unity will allow the community to maintain its status. Such notions, of course, are reinforced by concerns about losing wealth and power in a society in which the overwhelming majority have little. With recent and growing criticism of the State of Israel, this position has hardened, most notably as the Jewish community has taken divergent paths on appropriate responses to criticism of Israeli policy. Such concerns about the future are understandable as the Brazilian press and some political leaders continue to question Jewish loyalty.

In the economic sphere, Brazil's large arms-manufacturing export firms Engesa and Avibras, both competitors with Israel's armament industries for a share of the Third World market, have boomed because of contracts with many Arab nations. A weapons manufacturer that sells armored cars to Libya, Engenheiros Especializados, is reported to refuse "to employ Brazilians of Jewish origin to avoid offending Arab customers."[32] The report went on to claim that "although such discrimination is illegal, it is also practiced to a much lesser extent by Petrobrás [the government-owned petroleum corporation] in dealings with its Arab suppliers."

In 1989 the Brazilian people chose Fernando Collor de Mello as president in a free election. The return to democracy, however, has also led to a limited rise in anti-Semitism among some members of the urban middle class. During the campaign, the publication in Rio Grande do Sul of literature denying the existence of the Holocaust became a "Jewish issue" of sorts. Politicians, however, did not actively support requests by the Rio Grande do Sul Jewish Federation that such books be outlawed in accordance with the 1988 Brazilian constitution, which makes the public expression of religious or racial prejudice a crime.[33] A skinhead movement began in the late 1980s and a revived Integralist Party has gained notoriety and national fame even though the levels of actual participation remain extremely low.[34]

How do we judge Brazil, a country that appears to have simultaneously restricted and promoted Jewish immigration? Clearly, it was a nation whose intellectuals and political leaders were beset by stereotypes to such an extent that they were unconcerned with the essence of individuals and groups. They cared only about labels. Yet the stereotypes were often fluid and could be interpreted in both positive and negative ways. This challenged the status quo and upset the system even while conventional clichés about Jews remained remarkably consistent in Brazil throughout the first half of the twentieth century. What changed over the course of the 1930s was that stereotypes that had been previously interpreted in a negative way were viewed positively by some influential Brazilian policymakers. The result was that positions on Jewish immigration were always in flux. Jews were deemed nonwhite and antithetical to Brazil's racial whitening policy while simultaneously being viewed as crucial to Brazil's economic development. In 1939, in spite of secret orders restricting Jewish entry, more Jews entered Brazil than had done so at any time in the previous ten years.

The existence of a "Jewish policy" in a nation with only a small population of Jews might suggest that the Vargas regime leaned more toward the German model of anti-Semitism than the American one. The close alliance between the regime and the Nazis in the mid-1930s and the existence and encouragement of the Integralists, whose funding partially came from the German embassy, gives further credence to such a view. Even so, inconsistency and selective enforcement of Jewish immigration policy were the rule. As some Jews were turned away, others arrived. In this sense, Vargas's Brazil had a "Jewish policy" much like that of Franco's Spain.[35]

These contradictions force us to reject the question as to whether the Brazilian government was "for" or "against" Jewish immigration. Indeed, such a query may lead us to focus on the refusal of the Brazilian government to let a group of Vatican-supported Catholics, albeit non-Aryans, enter as somehow part of a different policy from the one that permitted significant numbers of Jewish refugees to enter Brazil legally in the five years after their entry was banned by secret diplomatic circular. Yet *neither* of these discrete pieces of information signals the pattern. Rather, by taking both together, and understanding that Jews were seen as a race whose characteristics were difficult to judge with any absolute finality, we see that acceptance and denial were both part of the ideology of Brazilian policymakers.

What does this seemingly contradictory policy mean when placed in the context of Brazilian ethnic relations? It shows that race was not, at least in the first half of the twentieth century, simply an issue of skin color. Indeed, my analysis challenges a number of general assumptions about race in Brazil. Most certainly it shows that the "racial" question includes ethnicity, language, nationality, and religion. The study of the Jewish Question in Brazil pulls together several themes that have in the past been considered as separate. In twentieth-century Brazil, race, ethnicity, and nationality were so closely linked that it became virtually impossible to distinguish between them. Brazil's racial democracy, as I have shown, was never about democracy; rather, it was about a concept of race that easily pointed to "the other." In spite of their "Caucasian" racial background and European nationality, Jews were deemed by many politicians and intellectuals as nonwhite and non-European—a dangerous "other" to whom immigration rights should be denied.

Not only did Jews challenge stereotypes of what "white" and "European" meant; they also challenged stereotypes of themselves. This helps explain why, in spite of the vociferous and effective anti-Jewish movement among intellectuals and politicians, those Jews who did settle in Brazil not only survived, but prospered in the same ways that many other white, European groups did. It appears that the reaction against Jewish immigration was a reaction against an unknown, fearsome image for which little real evaluative information existed. Once Jewish immigrants actually arrived in Brazil they were to a large extent accepted, in part because their ethnic background was not always self-evident. Some Jews discovered ways to keep entering Brazil even after the anti-Jewish immigration movement seemed to have won its battle over policy. Others devised ways to help thousands of refugees in Brazil with expired visas stay on and lead productive lives. Jewish refugees, in spite of the horror from which they had fled, and the lack of concern that they faced, were never simply victims. If there are any heroes in this sad story, they are to be found among the refugees and immigrants themselves.

The nature of Brazil's Jewish Question can also be seen by the powerful (but sporadic) effects of international diplomacy on Brazilian refugee policy. The Jewish refugee issue was one important element of U.S.-Brazilian economic and political relations. Those in Itamaraty, especially the actively pro-Yankee Foreign Minister Aranha, realized that concessions on the refugee issue could improve relations with the United States, improve Brazil's international status, and bring in economically desirable newcomers. Yet whatever influence the United States may have had in encouraging Brazil to accept Jews ended after August 1942 with the Brazilian declaration of war against Germany and Italy and the consequential unwillingness among U.S. diplomats to criticize Brazilian policy.[36]

Manipulation of immigrants has been a constant in Brazilian history. With judgments about Jewish stereotypes always in flux, however, absolute policies never functioned as well as relative ones. In this sense Jews were tools of the elites, pawns of state and federal regimes that looked upon all immigrants as components in the building of a white, elite-dominated, economically and militarily secure Brazil. Yet the policies were not made in an ideological vacuum. Ideology was, in fact, a particular concern of the Vargas regime, which sought to create justifications for all positions. The active support that both the press and intellectuals gave to the anti-Jewish immigration regulations is striking. Indeed, few were willing to speak openly in favor of humanitarian policies. The Jewish Question in Brazil had many answers, usually contradictory and generally given at the same time. Yet the question, although asked by a small group of nativists, politicians, journalists, and intellectuals, had an effect on real people trying to save themselves at a particularly tragic moment in the modern era. The story has both triumphant and tragic aspects. In spite of the power of anti-Semitic politicians and intellectuals, Jews did make an exodus to Brazil, the land of the future. There, they were welcomed as undesirables.

A number of different organizations kept statistics on Jewish immigration to Brazil. While there is a general, and occasionally exact, agreement on totals, discrepancies can be attributed to different sources.

APPENDIX 1
THE JEWISH POPULATION OF BRAZIL

States with Largest Jewish Populations	1872	1890	1900	1920	1940	1950
São Paulo	—	—	226	—	20,379	26,443
Rio de Janeiro	—	—	25	—	1,920	2,209
Federal District	—	—	0	—	19,473	25,222
Rio Grande do Sul	—	—	54	—	6,619	8,048
Bahia	—	—	17	—	955	1,076
Paraná	—	—	17	—	1,033	1,340
Minas Gerais	—	—	37	—	1,431	1,528
Total Jewish population of Brazil (all states)	—	—	300	—	55,666	69,957

NOTE Jews were not counted in the 1920 census.
SOURCE Brazil, Fundação Instituto Brasileiro de Geografia e Estatística, Conselho Nacional de Estatística, Serviço Nacional de Recenseamento, *Recenseamento geral do Brasil, 1950* (Rio de Janeiro: Imprensa Nacional, 1954); state totals from Regional Series, *População presente na data dos recenseamentos gerais, segundo algumas das principais características individuais*, São Paulo (vol. 25, pt. 1), Rio de Janeiro (vol. 23), Federal District (vol. 24, pt. 1), Rio Grande do Sul (vol. 28, pt. 1), Bahia (vol. 20), Paraná (vol. 26), Minas Gerais (vol. 21, pt. 1); national totals from National Series, *População presente na data dos recenseamentos gerais, segundo algumas das principais características individuais*, vol. 1, pt. 1.

APPENDIX 2
JEWISH AND GENERAL IMMIGRATION TO BRAZIL, 1881–1942

Years	Overall Immig. to Brazil	Jewish Immig. to Brazil	%	As % of World Jewish Mig.
1881–1900	1,654,101	1,000	0.06	0.1
1901–1914	1,252,678	8,750	0.07	0.5
1915–1920	189,417	2,000	1.0	2.2
1921–1925	386,631	7,139	1.8	1.7
1926–1930	453,584	22,296	4.9	12.9
1931–1935	180,652	13,075	7.2	5.5
1936–1942	120,318	14,576	12.1	3.6

SOURCE Maria Stella Ferreira Levy, "O papel da migração internacional na evolução da população brasileira (1872–1972)," *Revista de Saúde Pública,* supp. 8 (1974), 72; Jacob Lestschinsky, "Jewish Migrations, 1840–1956," in *The Jews: Their History, Culture and Religion,* 3d ed., ed. Louis Finkelstein (New York: Harper and Brothers, 1960), 2:1554.

APPENDIX 3
PORT OF JEWISH ARRIVALS IN BRAZIL, 1925–1930

Year	Rio	Santos	Pernambuco	Bahia
1925	1,804	820	not listed	not listed
1926	2,785	1,121	not listed	not listed
1927	2,940	1,227	not listed	not listed
1928	2,080	1,257	105	60
1929	3,486	1,995	96	23
1930	2,274	1,231	33	30
Total	15,369	7,651	234	113

SOURCE Jewish Colonization Association, *Rapport de l'administration centrale au conseil d'administration* (Paris: Imprimerie R. Veneziani, 1925–1930).

APPENDIX 4
JEWISH IMMIGRATION TO BRAZIL, 1925–1935

Country	1925	1926	1927	1928	1929	1930	1931	1932	1933	1934	1935
Poland	802	1,009	1,095	1,290	2,765	1,168	753	931	1,920	1,746	1,130
Germany	0	0	0	0	0	0	0	0	363	835	357
Russia	225	283	286	315	0	0	0	0	0	0	0
Lithuania	0	0	0	151	60	7	0	0	0	0	0
Romania	220	283	571	43	58	0	135	0	210	292	127
Other	0	0	0	0	0	0	0	0	824	921	144
Total	1,690	3,154	3,175	3,167	4,874	3,558	1,985	2,049	3,317	3,794	1,758

SOURCES Figures on Eastern European immigration from SCA, 1925–1933, JCA-L. Figures on German immigration from "Les juifs dans l'histoire du Brésil," *Rapport d'activité pendant la période 1933–43*, HIAS-Brazil, folder 1, YIVO-NY. Totals from "Discriminação por nacionalidade dos imigrantes entrando no Brasil no período 1924–1933 e 1934–1939," *RIC* 1:3 (July 1940), 633–38.

JEWISH AND GENERAL IMMIGRATION TO BRAZIL, 1925–1947

Year	General	% Change	Jewish	% Change
1925	82,547	—	1,690	—
1926	118,686	44	3,154	+87
1927	97,974	−17	3,175	0
1928	78,128	−19	3,167	0
1929	96,186	23	4,874	+54
1930	62,610	−35	3,558	−27
1931	27,465	−56	1,985	−44
1932	31,494	14	2,049	+3
1933	46,081	48	3,317	+61
1934	46,027	00	3,794	+14
1935	29,585	−36	1,758	−54
1936	12,773	−57	3,418	+94
1937	34,677	270	2,003	−41
1938	19,388	−45	530	−73
1939	22,668	117	4,601	+768
1940	18,449	−19	2,416	−47
1941	9,938	−47	1,500	−38
1942	2,425	−76	108	−93
1943	1,308	−46	11	−90
1944	1,593	121	6	−46
1945	3,168	198	120	+1,900
1946	13,039	411	1,485	+1,137
1947	18,753	143	2,637	+78

SOURCES "Discriminação por nacionalidade dos imigrantes entrando no Brasil no período 1924–1933 e 1934–1939," *RIC* 1:3 (July 1940), 633–38.SCA, 1926–1935, JCA-L. *Rapport d'activité pendant la période 1933–1934*, HIAS-Brazil, folder 1, YIVO-NY. Mark Wischnitzer, *To Dwell In Safety: The Story of Jewish Migration since 1800* (Philadelphia: The Jewish Publication Society of America, 1948), p. 293, table 6.

APPENDIX 6
JEWISH IMMIGRATION TO BRAZIL, BY COUNTRY OF ORIGIN, 1933–1942

Year	Poland	Germany	Romania	Other	Total
1933	1,920	363	210	824	3,317
1934	1,746	835	292	921	3,794
1935	1,130	357	127	144	1,758
1936	1,147	1,172	177	322	3,418
1937	405	1,315	85	186	2,003
1938	22	445	7	56	530
1939	845	2,899	107	750	4,601
1940	455	1,033	68	860	2,416
1941	333	406	—	759	1,500
1942	15	4	—	89	108
Total	8,018	9,431	1,085	5,019	23,445

SOURCE "Les juifs dans l'histoire du Brésil," *Rapport d'activité pendant la période 1933–1943*, HIAS-Brazil, folder 1, YIVO-NY.

JEWISH EMIGRATION FROM GERMANY AND JEWISH
IMMIGRATION TO BRAZIL, 1933–1941

Year	Total Jewish Emigr. from Germany	German-Jewish Immig. to Brazil	As % of Total Jewish Emigr.	As % of World Jewish Mig. from Germany
1933	37,000	363	1.0	10.9
1934	23,000	835	3.6	22.0
1935	21,000	357	1.7	20.0
1936	25,000	1,772	7.1	51.8
1937	23,000	1,315	5.7	65.6
1938	40,000	445	1.1	83.9
1939	78,000	2,899	3.7	63.0
1940	15,000	1,033	6.9	27.2
1941	8,000	408	5.1	3.7
Total	270,000	9,427	3.5	40.3

SOURCES Werner Rosenstock, "Exodus 1933–1939: A Survey of Jewish Emigration from Germany," *Leo Baeck Institute Yearbook* 1 (1956), 377. Herbert A. Strauss, "Jewish Emigration from Germany: Nazi Policies and Jewish Responses (I)," *Leo Baeck Institute Yearbook* 25 (1980), 326. "Les juifs dans l'histoire du Brésil," *Rapport d'activité pendant la période 1933–1943*, HIAS-Brazil, folder 1, YIVO-NY.

APPENDIX 8
JEWISH IMMIGRANTS AS A PERCENTAGE OF ALL
IMMIGRANTS TO BRAZIL AND OTHER COUNTRIES, 1933–1947

Year	Brazil	U.S.A.	Canada	Argentina
1933	7.2	10.3	5.3	6.5
1934	8.2	14.0	7.5	6.6
1935	5.9	13.8	7.8	7.7
1936	26.7	17.2	7.5	11.9
1937	5.7	22.6	4.0	10.0
1938	2.7	29.0	3.3	2.7
1939	20.2	52.3	5.2	29.6
1940	13.1	52.2	14.5	29.7
1941	15.0	45.8	6.7	47.0
1942	4.4	36.9	5.1	71.2
1943	0.8	19.8	2.7	65.1
1944	0.3	8.4	1.8	50.7
1945	3.7	10.9	1.5	73.6
1946	11.3	11.8	2.1	6.6
1947	14.0	19.9	2.9	0.3

SOURCES Mark Wischnitzer, *To Dwell in Safety: the Story of Jewish Migration since 1800* (Philadelphia: Jewish Publication Society of America, 1948), 289–93, tables 3, 4 and 6. Leonard Dinnerstein and David M. Reimers, *Ethnic Americans: A History of Immigration and Assimilation,* 2d ed. (New York: Harper and Row, 1982), 163–65, table A.2. Maria Stella Ferreira Levy, "O papel da migração internacional na evolução da população brasileira (1872–1972)," *Revista de Saúde Pública,* supp. 8 (1974), 72. Warren E. Kalbach and Wayne W. McVey, *The Demographic Bases of Canadian Society* (Toronto: McGraw-Hill, 1971), 33, table 2.1. Haim Avni, *Argentina y la historia de la inmigracíon judía, 1810–1950* (Jerusalem: Editorial Universitaria Magnes, 1983), 542–44. International Labour Office, *Yearbook of Labour Statistics, 1940* (Geneva: International Labour Office, 1940), 160, table 22. International Labour Office, *Yearbook of Labour Statistics, 1949–1950* (Geneva: International Labour Office, 1951), 400, table 39.

Notes

INTRODUCTION: BRAZIL AND THE JEWS

1. Jacob Robinson, *Palestine and the United Nations: Prelude to Solution* (Washington, D.C.: Public Affairs Press, 1947), 145; Edward B. Glick, *Latin America and the Palestine Problem* (New York: Theodore Herzl Foundation, 1958); Ignacio Klich, "Latin America, the United States and the Birth of Israel: The Case of Somoza's Nicaragua," *Journal of Latin American Studies* 20:2 (November 1988), 389–432; Jorge García-Granados, *The Birth of Israel: The Drama As I Saw It* (New York: Alfred A. Knopf, 1949), 247.

2. Cited in Ignacio Klich, "The Roots of Argentine Abstentionism in the Palestine Question, 1946" (unpublished manuscript used by permission of the author).

3. From 1900 to 1945, between 90 and 95 percent of the Jewish immigrants arriving in Brazil were from Europe. The others came from Turkey, Morocco, Palestine, and other parts of the Ottoman Empire.

4. Jeremy Cohen has expressed such a notion, perhaps anachronistically, in his *The Friars and the Jews: The Evolution of Medieval Anti-Judaism* (Ithaca, N.Y.: Cornell University Press, 1982), 254.

5. In Europe anti-Semites began commenting on "the Jewish Question" in the early nineteenth century to suggest that the cultural and economic success of Jews meant that they would never adequately fit into the majority cultures in which they resided. By the late nineteenth century, however, European Jews and Gentiles used the phrase as a shorthand for how the national political elite and intelligentsia viewed the Jewish populations who lived within their national boundaries. See Isaac Landman, "Jewish Question," in *The Universal Jewish Encyclopedia* (New York: Universal Jewish Encyclopedia, 1939–43), 6:140–41. As early as 1933 the term was used in Brazil in José Pérez's *Questão judaica, questão social* (São Paulo: Empresa Grafica da "Revista dos Tribunaes," 1933). See also J. Cabral, *A questão judaica* (Porto Alegre: Livraria do Globo, 1937);

187

Anor Butler Maciel, *Nacionalismo: O problema judaico no mundo e no Brasil: O nacional-socialismo* (Porto Alegre: Livraria do Globo, 1937); Osório Lopes, *O problema judaico* (Petrópolis: Vozes, 1942).

6. Cohen, *The Friars and the Jews,* 242.

7. W. Darrel Overdyke, *The Know-Nothing Party in the South* (Baton Rouge: Louisiana State University Press, 1950), 2.

8. Lyle N. McAlister, *Spain and Portugal in the New World, 1492–1700* (Minneapolis: University of Minnesota Press, 1984), 53.

9. Benedict Anderson, *Imagined Communities: Reflections on the Origin and Spread of Nationalism,* 2d ed. (London: Verso, 1991), 50.

10. I have used the term *elites* throughout this text to refer to the intellectuals and politicians affiliated directly with the Vargas regime, including those in the diplomatic corps or its related international economic organs. It also includes state politicians who represented urban working- and middle-class constituencies. "Elite" should not be read as referring to traditional members of Brazil's elite classes such as rural oligarchs, or *coronéis.*

11. Thomas E. Skidmore, *Fact and Myth: Discovering a Racial Problem in Brazil,* Helen Kellog Institute for International Studies Working Paper no. 173 (Notre Dame, Ind.: University of Notre Dame, 1992); George Reid Andrews, *Blacks and Whites in São Paulo, Brazil, 1888–1988* (Madison: University of Wisconsin Press, 1991); Jan Fiola, *Race Relations in Brazil: A Reassessment of the "Racial Democracy" Thesis,* Program in Latin American Studies Occasional Paper Series, no. 24 (Amherst: University of Massachusetts at Amherst, 1990); Pierre-Michel Fontaine, ed., *Race, Class and Power in Brazil* (Los Angeles: Center for Afro-American Studies, 1985); Thomas E. Skidmore, *Black into White: Race and Nationality in Brazilian Thought* (New York: Oxford University Press, 1974); Anani Dzdidzienyo, *The Position of Blacks in Brazilian Society* (London: Minority Rights Group, 1971); Florestan Fernandes, "Immigration and Race Relations in São Paulo," in Magnus Mörner, ed., *Race and Class in Latin America* (New York: Columbia University Press, 1970), 122–42.

12. "Manifesto dos intelectuais brasileiros contra o preconceito racial" of October 1935, reprinted in Arthur Ramos, *Guerra e relações de raça* (Rio de Janeiro: Departamento Editorial da União Nacional dos Estudantes, 1943), 171–74; Skidmore, *Black into White,* 207. In a later essay, Skidmore acknowledged Brazil's anti-Semitic visa policy during the Vargas era but continued to argue that "no significant number [of Brazilians] wanted to apply political racism in Brazil"; see "Racial Ideas and Social Policy in Brazil, 1870–1940," in Richard Graham, ed., *The Idea of Race in Latin America, 1870–1940* (Austin: University of Texas Press, 1990), 26.

13. Anita Novinsky, *Cristãos novos na Bahia, 1624–1654* (São Paulo: Editora Perspectiva, 1972); Arnold Wiznitzer, *Jews in Colonial Brazil* (New York: Columbia University Press, 1960).

14. Eva Alterman Blay, "Inquisição, inquisições: Aspectos da participação dos judeus na vida sócio-política brasileira nos anos 30," *Tempo Social* 1:1 (1989), 105–30.

15. Jacob X. Cohen, *Jewish Life in South America: A Survey Study for the American Jewish Congress* (New York: Bloch Publishing, 1941), 30; Maria Lu-

iza Tucci Carneiro, "Os novos-cristãos do século XX," in *O anti-semitismo na era Vargas: Fantasmas de uma geração (1930–1945)* (São Paulo: Brasiliense, 1988), 234–46.

16. Yosef Hayim Yerushalmi, *Assimilation and Racial Anti-Semitism: The Iberian and the German Models,* Leo Baeck Memorial Lecture no. 26 (New York: Leo Baeck Institute, 1982), 5.

17. Andrews, *Blacks and Whites,* 151. Jeffrey D. Needell, *A Tropical Belle Epoque: Elite Culture and Society in Turn-of-the-Century Rio de Janeiro* (Cambridge: Cambridge University Press, 1987).

18. Steven Topik, "Middle Class Brazilian Nationalism, 1889–1930: From Radicalism to Reaction," *Social Science Quarterly* 59:1 (June 1978), 101–2.

19. Daphne Patai, "Minority Status and the Stigma of 'Surplus Visibility,' " *Chronicle of Higher Education* 38:10 (October 30, 1991), A52.

20. Decree law 528 (28 June 1890), art. 1.

21. Flávio V. Luizetto, "Os constituintes em face da imigração: Estudo sobre o preconceito e a discriminação racial e étnica na constituinte de 1934" (master's thesis, Department of History, University of São Paulo, 1975); Robert M. Levine, *The Vargas Regime: The Critical Years, 1934–1938* (New York: Columbia University Press, 1970), 24.

22. Readers should not expect to find a community history of Jews in Brazil here. Those looking for a discussion of the formation of Brazil's modern Jewish community should see Egon Wolff and Frieda Wolff, *Os judeus no Brasil imperial* (São Paulo: Centro de Estudos Judaicos, 1975) and *Os judeus nos primórdios do Brasil-República, visto especialmente pela documentação no Rio de Janeiro* (Rio de Janeiro: Biblioteca Israelita H. N. Bialik, 1979); Raphael Copstein, "O trabalho estrangeiro no município do Rio Grande," in *Boletim Gaúcho de Geografia,* Série geografia, no. 4 (Porto Alegre: n.p., 1975); Bruno Basseches, *Bibliografia dos livros, folhetos e artigos referente a história dos judeus no Brasil, incluindo as obras sobre judaismo publicadas no Brasil* (Rio de Janeiro: n.p., 1961); Salomão Serebrenick and Elias Lipiner, *Breve história dos judeus no Brasil* (Rio de Janeiro: Edições Biblos, 1962); Kurt Loewenstamm, *Vultos judaicos no Brasil,* vol. 2, *Império 1822–1899* (Rio de Janeiro: Editora A Noite, 1956); Samuel Malamud, "Contribucíon judía al desarollo del Brasil en las 150 años de la independência," in *Comunidades judías de Latinoamérica* (Buenos Aires: Oficina Subamerica del Comité Judía Americano, 1971–1972), 330–39; Samuel Malamud, *Do arquivo e da memória: Fatos, personagems e reflexões sobre o sionismo brasileiro e mundial* (Rio de Janeiro: Bloch Editores, 1983); Anita Novinsky, "Os israelitas em São Paulo," in *São Paulo: espírito, povo, instituições,* ed. J. V. Freitas Marcondes and Osmar Pimentel (São Paulo: Livraria Pioneira Editora, 1968), 107–26; Nachman Falbel, *Estudos sobre a comunidade judaica no Brasil* (São Paulo: Federação Israelita de São Paulo, 1984); Alice Irene Hirschberg, *Desafio e resposta: A história da congregação israelita paulista* (São Paulo: Congregação Israelita Paulista, 1976); Henrique Rattner, *Tradição e mudança: A comunidade judaica em São Paulo* (São Paulo: Editora Ática, 1977); Jeffrey Lesser, "Pawns of the Powerful: Jewish Immigration to Brazil, 1904–1945" (Ph.D. diss., New York University, 1989).

23. The terms *refugee* and *immigrant* are used interchangeably here. Although they theoretically have distinguishable meanings, in this case they do not. While most European Jews who migrated to Brazil may not have left their countries of origin by choice (thus making them refugees), their inability to return to their homelands often led them to be treated, both hypothetically and practically, as immigrants. Jews entering Brazil with tourist visas often intended to remain permanently, exactly as authorities assumed they would. Furthermore, as open anti-Semitism in public policy became less acceptable to the pro-Allied international community that Brazil strived to be part of, policymakers discovered that general anti-immigrant legislation could easily be applied to Jewish refugees.

24. Carneiro, *O anti-semitismo;* Júlio José Chiavenato, *O inimigo eleito: Os judeus, o poder e o anti-semitismo* (Porto Alegre: Mercado Aberto, 1985); Alcir Lenharo, *Sacralização da política* (Campinas: Papiras, 1986); Marcos Chor Maio, *Nem Rotschild nem Trotsky: O pensamento anti-semita de Gustavo Barroso* (Rio de Janeiro: Imago, 1992); Roney Cytrynowicz, "Integralismo e anti-semitismo nos textos de Gustavo Barroso na década de 30" (master's thesis, Department of History, University of São Paulo, 1991).

25. Roberto Schwarz, "Brazilian Culture: Nationalism by Elimination," *New Left Review* 167 (January/February 1988), 77–90. This essay has appeared in Portuguese in Schwarz's *Que horas são* (São Paulo: Companhia das Letras, 1987), 29–48.

26. Getúlio Vargas, *A nova política do Brasil,* vol. 6, *Realizações do Estado Novo, 1 de agôsto de 1938 a 7 de setembro de 1939* (Rio de Janeiro: José Olympio Editora, 1940), 88.

27. It is important to remember that immigrants destined for rural areas were not always given the right to enter Brazil. A mid-nineteenth-century attempt to bring in Chinese rural labor was rejected by Brazil's Congress, and, as late as the 1920s, attempts by North American blacks to form colonies in Matto Grosso were rejected by the Brazilian government. See Teresa Meade and Gregory Alonso Pirio, "In Search of the Afro-American 'Eldorado': Attempts by North American Blacks to Enter Brazil in the 1920s," *Luso-Brazilian Review* 25 (1988), 85–109; and Jeffrey Lesser, "Are African-Americans African or American? Brazilian Immigration Policy in the 1920s," *Review of Latin American Studies* 4:1 (1991), 115–37.

28. Brazilian constitution of 25 March 1824, pt. 1, art. 5; Geraldo Fernandes, "A religião nas constituicões republicanas do Brasil," *Revista Eclesiástica Brasileira* 8:4 (December 1948), 830–57.

29. George P. Browne, "Government Immigration Policy in Imperial Brazil, 1822–1870" (Ph.D. diss., Catholic University of America, 1972), 301; Brazilian constitution of 25 March 1824, pt. 1, art. 5; Joseph Love, *Rio Grande do Sul and Brazilian Regionalism, 1882–1930* (Stanford, Calif.: Stanford University Press, 1971), 24.

30. Browne, "Government Immigration Policy," 301; Brazilian Constitution of 25 March 1824, pt. 1, art. 5.

31. Michael M. Hall, "The Origins of Mass Immigration to Brazil, 1871–1914" (Ph.D. diss., Columbia University, 1969).

32. Anthony H. Richmond, *Immigration and Ethnic Conflict* (New York: St. Martin's Press, 1988), 9.

33. The plans to encourage European entry were helped by the surprisingly small price differential between domestic and international transportation and the growing expulsion of poor Italian farmers from their plots. See Douglas H. Graham and Sérgio Buarque Hollanda Filho, *Migration, Regional and Urban Growth, and Development in Brazil: A Selective Analysis of the Historical Record, 1872–1979* (São Paulo: Instituto de Pesquisas Econômicas   Universidade de São Paulo, 1971).

34. Maria Stella Ferreira Levy, "O papel da migração internacional na evolução da população brasileira (1872–1972)," *Revista de Saúde Pública* (São Paulo), supp. 8 (1974), 71–72. In 1903, based on regular reports of the poor treatment of immigrants, Italy promulgated the so-called Prinetti decree, prohibiting Italian citizens from accepting free transportation to Brazil.

35. Richmond, *Immigration and Ethnic Conflict*, 9.

36. José Sebastião Witter, "A política imigratória no Brasil," in *Inmigración y politica inmigrante en el cono sur de America*, ed. Hernán Asdrúbal Silva (Washington, D.C.: CPDP-CAS-PAIGH, 1990), 3:253–60.

37. Seymour B. Liebman, *New World Jewry, 1493–1825: Requiem for the Forgotten* (New York: KTAV Publishing House, 1982), especially pp. 131–68.

38. Novinsky, *Cristãos novos na Bahia*, 67.

39. Jacob Lestschinsky, "Jewish Migrations, 1840–1956," in *The Jews: Their History, Culture and Religion*, 3d ed., ed. Louis Finkelstein (New York: Harper and Brothers, 1960), 2:1554; Wolff and Wolff, *Os judeus nos primórdios do Brasil-República*.

40. Between 1840 and 1900 the United States received about 875,000 Jews and Argentina about 27,000. See Lestschinsky, "Jewish Migrations, 1840–1956," 2:1554; and Mark Wischnitzer, *To Dwell in Safety: The Story of Jewish Migration since 1800* (Philadelphia: Jewish Publication Society of America, 1948), 295.

41. Loewenstamm, *Vultos judaicos no Brasil*, 2:25.

42. Cited in Allan Peskin and Donald Ramos, "An Ohio Yankee at Dom Pedro's Court: Notes on Brazilian Life in the 1850s by an American Diplomat, Robert C. Schenk." *Americas* 38:4 (April 1982), 511.

43. *American Israelite* (Cincinnati), 18 March 1881, 300.

44. *Encyclopedia Judaica* (Jerusalem, Keter Publishing House, 1971), 4B:1, 326.

45. Nachman Falbel, "Oswaldo Boxer e o projeto de colonização de judeus no Brasil," *Jornal do Imigrante* 10 (December 1987/January 1988), 18.

46. Leon Kellner, *Theodore Herzl's Lehrjahre, 1860–1895* (Vienna and Berlin: R. Loewit Verlag, 1920), 142–44.

47. *Encyclopedia Judaica*, 4B:1,326. Sarah Bernhardt, who first visited Brazil in 1886, complains in her correspondence of yellow fever in Rio de Janeiro and that "rats and mice [are] everywhere"; cited in Arthur Gold and Robert Fizdale, *The Divine Sarah: A Life of Sarah Bernhardt* (New York: Alfred A. Knopf, 1991), 225.

48. Brazil, Fundação Instituto Brasileiro de Geografia e Estatística, Con-

selho Nacional de Estatística, Serviço Nacional de Recenseamento, *Recenseamento geral do Brasil, 1950,* National Series, *População presente na data dos recenseamentos gerais, segundo algumas das principais características individuais* (Rio de Janeiro: Imprensa Nacional, 1954), vol. 1, pt. 1.

49. Wolff and Wolff, *Os judeus no Brasil imperial,* xxi; Harry S. Linfield, "Statistics of the Jews," in *American Jewish Yearbook—5683* (Philadelphia: Jewish Publication Society of America, 1922), 22:301. See also Leib Hersch, "Jewish Migrations during the Last Hundred Years," in Central Yiddish Culture Organization, *The Jewish People: Past and Present* (New York: Jewish Encyclopedic Handbooks, 1946), 1: 407–30. Statistics on Jewish immigration to Brazil tend to vary greatly. All information prior to 1937 comes from various volumes of the *American Jewish Yearbook,* which itself notes that its statistics on Jewish immigration to Brazil are somewhat unreliable. Jacob Lestschinsky's statistics are the most generally accepted, but in the case of Brazil his information appears as unreliable as other, less scholarly sources. See Lestschinsky, *De lage fun yidn in lateyn-amerikaner lender* (The situation of Jews in Latin America) (New York: World Congress for Jewish Affairs, 1948), and "Jewish Migrations, 1840–1956," 1536–96.

50. Barbara Weinstein, *The Amazon Rubber Boom, 1850–1920* (Stanford, Calif.: Stanford University Press, 1983), 50–51, 259–60; Serebrenick and Lipiner, *Breve história dos judeus no Brasil,* 95. Haquitia is a dialect that mixes Spanish, Hebrew and Arabic and is principally spoken by Jews in Morocco. Ladino combines Spanish and Hebrew and is spoken by many other Sephardic Jews.

51. Isaiah Raffalovich (New York) to ICA Head Office (Paris), 8 July 1930, Séance du Conseil d'Administration (27 September 1930), 2:57, Archives of the Jewish Colonization Association, London.

52. Eulália Maria Lahmeyer Lobo, *História do Rio de Janeiro: Do capital ao capital industrial e financeiro* (Rio de Janeiro: IBMEC, 1978), 443–71.

53. Moritz von Hirsch was born in 1831. His grandfather Jacob had been granted the title of nobility in 1818 because of banking skills that had aided Bavaria's reigning family. See Maurice de Hirsch, "My Views on Philanthropy," *North American Review* 153 (July 1889), 2. See also S. Adler-Rudel, "Moritz Baron Hirsch," *Leo Baeck Institute Yearbook* 8 (1963), 45; and Howard Morley Sachar, *The Course of Modern Jewish History,* 2d ed. (New York: Dell Publishing Company, 1977), 510–18.

54. Theodore Norman, *An Outstretched Arm: A History of the Jewish Colonization Association* (London: Routledge and Kegan Paul, 1985), 21. The word *Jewish* in popular Eastern European Yiddish was pronounced "idisheh" and was often transliterated as *Idische.* Thus the popular acronym for the Jewish Colonization Association was ICA.

55. Jewish Colonization Association, *Jewish Colonization Association: Su obra en la república Argentina, 1891–1941* (Buenos Aires: ICA, 1941). See also Mark Freeman's documentary film *The Yidishe Gauchos* (Berkeley, Calif.: Fine Line Productions, 1989); and Jewish Colonization Association, *Rapport de l'administration centrale au conseil d'adminstration pour l'année 1901* (Paris: Imprimerie R. Veneziani, 1902), Arquivo Histórico Judaico Brasileiro, São Paulo.

56. Jewish Colonization Association, *Le baron Maurice de Hirsch et la Jewish Colonization Association (à l'occasion du centenaire de la naissance du Baron de Hirsch* (Paris: Imprimerie R. Veneziani, 1931), 14.

57. Ernesto A. Lassance Cunha, *O Rio Grande do Sul: Contribuição para o estudo de suas condições econômicas* (Rio de Janeiro: Imprensa Nacional, 1908), 253; Brazilian constitution of 24 February 1891, art. 72, no. 3.

58. Luiza H. Schmitz Kliemann, "A ferrovia gaúcha e as diretrizes de 'Ordem e progresso,' 1905–1920," *Estudos Íbero-Americanos* (Porto Alegre) 3:2 (December 1977), 189.

59. "Constituição política de 11 de julho de 1891 do estado de Rio Grande do Sul," part 4, "Garantias gerais de ordem e progresso no estado," art. 71, no. 7. See also Zilah C. Didonet, *O positivismo e a constituição rio-grandense de 14 de julho de 1891* (Santa Catarina: Imprensa Universitária, 1977); and Ivan Lins Lima, *História do positivismo no Brasil* (São Paulo: Editora Nacional, 1967).

60. For a full discussion of these colonies see Jeffrey Lesser, *Jewish Colonization in Rio Grande do Sul, 1904–1925* (São Paulo: Centro de Estudos de Demografia Histórica de América Latina, Universidade de São Paulo, 1991); Isabel Rosa Gritti, "A imigração judaica para o Rio Grande do Sul: A Jewish Colonization Association e a colonização de Quatro Irmãos" (master's thesis, Department of History, Pontifícia Universidade Católica do Rio Grande do Sul, 1992); Leon Back, "Imigração judaica no Rio Grande do Sul," *Enciclopédia rio-grandense* (Canoas: Editora Regional, 1958) 5:273; Marlene Kulkes, ed., *Histórias de vida: Imigração judaica no Rio Grande do Sul* (Porto Alegre: Instituto Cultural Judaico Marc Chagall, 1989); and Moacyr Scliar, *Caminhos da esperança: A presença judaica no Rio Grande do Sul* (Porto Alegre: Riocell, 1990). A number of former colonists have also written about their experiences: Jacques Schweidson, *Judeus de Bombachas e Chimarrão* (Rio de Janeiro: José Olympio Editora, 1985); Martha Pargendler Faermann, *A promessa cumprida* (Porto Alegre: Metrópole, 1990); Eva Nicolaiewsky, *Israelitas no Rio Grande do Sul* (Porto Alegre: Editora Garatuja, 1975); and Frida Alexandr, *Filipson: Memórias da primeira colônia judaica no Rio Grande do Sul* (São Paulo: Editora Fulgor, 1967).

61. Love, *Rio Grande do Sul*, 18.

62. Eugenio Dahne, ed., *Descriptive Memorial of the State of Rio Grande do Sul, Brazil* (Porto Alegre: Commercial Library, 1904), 29.

63. J. F. Camargo, *Crescimento da população no estado de São Paulo e seus aspectos econômicos* (São Paulo: University of São Paulo, 1952), 228.

64. Camargo, *Crescimento da população*, 228.

65. Camargo, *Crescimento da população*, 228.

66. Jean Roche, *A colonização alemã e o Rio Grande do Sul* (Porto Alegre: Editora Globo, 1969); Lucy Maffei Hutter, *Imigração italiana em São Paulo, 1880–1889* (São Paulo: Instituto de Estudos Brasileiros, 1972).

67. On the Japanese in Brazil, see, among others, Arlinda Rocha Nogueira, *A imigração japonesa para a lavoura cafeeira paulista, 1908–1922* (São Paulo: Instituto de Estudos Brasileiros, 1973); and Patrick N. Fukunaga, "The Brazilian Experience: The Japanese Immigrants during the Period of the Vargas Re-

gime and Its Immediate Aftermath" (Ph.D. diss., University of California at Santa Barbara, 1983).

68. For more on the anti-Asian movements, see Alexander Saxton, *The Indispensable Enemy: Labor and the Anti-Chinese Movement in California* (Berkeley: University of California Press, 1971); Roger Daniels, *The Politics of Prejudice: The Anti-Japanese Movement and the Struggle for Japanese Exclusion* (Berkeley: University of California Press, 1962); and Evelyn Hu-DeHart, "Racism and Anti-Chinese Persecution in Sonora, Mexico, 1876–1932," *Amerasia Journal* 9:2 (fall/winter 1982), 1–28.

69. Levy, "O papel da migração internacional," 72.

70. John Higham, *Strangers in the Land: Patterns of American Nativism, 1860–1925* (New Brunswick, N.J.: Rutgers University Press, 1955), 310.

71. *Revista de Imigração e Colonização* 1:4 (October 1940), 641–42. This figure does not include Russian immigration, which, as a result of the Russian Revolution, was restricted by the Soviet government. Between 1914 and 1923 Eastern European immigration to Brazil was less than 2 percent of the total.

72. Extract of report of HM Consul, São Paulo, to British Foreign Office, February 1927, FO 371/11,196 A2,074/2,074/6, p. 181, British Public Record Office, London.

73. Sir T. Vaughan (British consul, Kovno, Lithuania) to Sir Austen Chamberlain, 29 December 1927, FO 371/13,270 W70/70/59, p. 183, PRO-L.

74. The historiography on Eastern Europeans in Brazil uniformly ignores the large numbers of Jewish immigrants. See, for example, Paul H. Price, "The Polish Immigrant in Brazil: A Study of Immigration, Assimilation and Acculturation" (Ph.D. diss., Vanderbilt University, 1950); Edmundo Gardolinski, *Escolas da colonização polonesa no Rio Grande do Sul* (Porto Alegre: Escola Superior de Teologia São Lourenço de Brindes, 1976); Alberto Victor Stawinski, *Primórdios da imigração polonesa no Rio Grande do Sul (1875–1975)* (Porto Alegre: Escola Superior de Teologia São Lourenço de Brindes, 1976).

75. Samuel L. Baily, "Chain Migration of Italians to Argentina: Case Studies of the Agnonesi and Sirolesi," *Studi Emigrazione* 19 (March 1982), 73; John S. MacDonald and Leatrice D. MacDonald, "Chain Migration, Ethnic Neighborhood Formation and Social Networks," *Milbank Memorial Fund Quarterly* 13:42 (1964), 82–95.

76. Cecilia Razovsky, "The Jew Re-Discovers America: Jewish Immigration to Latin American Countries," *Jewish Social Service Quarterly* 5:2–3 (December 1928–March 1929), 127.

77. This was one result of the coming of age of the children of the earlier immigrant generation. See Michael M. Hall, "New Approaches to Immigration History," in *New Approaches to Latin American History,* ed. Richard Graham and Peter H. Smith (Austin: University of Texas Press, 1974).

78. The Japanese immigrant, however, was to fit into global power politics in a way that other immigrant groups did not, enjoying the protection and moral support of a powerful regime that saw each Japanese immigrant success story as an example of Japanese national superiority.

79. A sophisticated and full literature has emerged on the role of Germany in Brazil's foreign policy. Outstanding examples include Stanley Hilton's *Brazil*

and the Great Powers, 1930–1939: The Politics of Trade Rivalry (Austin: University of Texas Press, 1975); Gerson Moura's *Autonomia na dependência* (Rio de Janeiro: Nova Fronteira, 1980); and Ricardo Seitenfus's *O Brasil de Getúlio Vargas e a formação dos blocos: 1930–1942* (São Paulo: Companhia Editora Nacional, 1985).

80. Roberto Gambini, *O duplo jogo de Getúlio Vargas: Influência americana e alemã no Estado Novo* (São Paulo: Editora Símbolo, 1977).

1. THE "OTHER" ARRIVES

1. Levy, "O papel da migração internacional," 49–90; "Les juifs dans l'histoire du Brésil," *Rapport d'activité pendant la période 1933–43*, HIAS-Brazil, folder 1, YIVO-NY; Linfield, "Statistics of the Jews," 301.

2. On South African Jewry, see Stephen Cohen, "Historical Background," in *South African Jewry: A Contemporary Survey*, ed. Marcus Arkin (Capetown: Oxford University Press, 1984), 1–22.

3. "Summary of Jewish Immigration to Canada, 1901–1939," in *AJYB-5701* (1940), 42:624, table 25.

4. Lucien Wolf, "Report to the Directors of the Jewish Colonization Association (London, 2 September 1923)," SCA (15 December 1923), 3:181, JCA-L; Haim Avni, "Argentine Jewry: Its Socio-Political Status and Organizational Patterns," *Dispersion and Unity*, vol. 12 (1971).

5. Isaiah Raffalovich, "The Condition of Jewry and Judaism in South America," in *Central Conference of American Rabbis Yearbook* (New York, Central Conference of American Rabbis, 1930), 11:5–6.

6. Marcos Pereira (Rio de Janeiro) to ICA (Paris), 23 June 1921, SCA (21 September 1921), 4:161, JCA-L.

7. Decree law 4,247 (6 January 1921); Brazil, Ministério da Justiça e Negócios Interiores, *Estrangeiros: Legislação, 1808–1939* (Rio de Janeiro: Serviço de Documentação, 1950), 1:152–53 (hereafter *Estrangeiros*).

8. Arnold Rushton (Liverpool Town Hall) to Isaiah Raffalovich (on board the S.S. *Araguaya*), 10 December 1923, SCA (8 March 1924), 3:239, JCA-L.

9. Raffalovich (Rio de Janeiro) to ICA (Paris), 11 July 1924, SCA (11 October 1924), 4:1, JCA-L.

10. Raffalovich (on board the S.S. *Araguaya*) to ICA (Paris), 18 December 1923, SCA (8 March 1924), 3:237, JCA-L.

11. Raffalovich to ICA, 18 December 1923, SCA, 3:241.

12. Members of the Haas family were involved in industry and exporting throughout Brazil. See Egon and Frieda Wolff, *Dicionário biográfico*, vol. 2, *Judeus no Brasil: Século XIX* (Rio de Janeiro: Egon and Frieda Wolff, 1987), 157–62.

13. Raffalovich to ICA, 11 July 1924, SCA, 4:1.

14. "Annual Report, 1924," SCA (17 October 1925), 2:45, JCA-L.

15. Decree law 16,761 (31 December 1924), art. 4.

16. Decree law 16,761 (31 December 1924).

17. Decree law 16,761 (31 December 1924), art. 7.

18. "Notes sur les questions inscrites à l'ordre du jour," SCA (13 May 1922), 1:25–26, JCA-L.

19. Raffalovich to ICA, 11 July 1924, SCA, 4:3.

20. Raffalovich to ICA, 11 July 1924, SCA, 4:4.

21. Raffalovich to ICA, 11 July 1924, SCA, 4:4.

22. Raffalovich to ICA, 11 July 1924, SCA, 4:4.

23. Isaiah Raffalovich, "Report for the Year 1926," SCA (2 July 1927), 1:130, JCA-L; Stanley Hilton, *Brazil and the Soviet Challenge, 1917–1947* (Austin: University of Texas Press, 1991), 16.

24. Lestschinsky, "Migrations of the Jews"; SCA 1927–1931, JCA-L.

25. Pereira to ICA, 23 June 1921, SCA,4:162.

26. Pereira to ICA, 23 June 1921, SCA,4:162.

27. United Evacuation Committee Report of 18 October 1925, annex 5, SCA (8 January 1927), 3:121, JCA-L.

28. Lucien Wolf, "Report to the Directors of the Jewish Colonization Association [London]," 2 September 1923, SCA (15 December 1923) 3:162, JCA-L.

29. Isaiah Raffalovich, *Brazilye: A tsukunftsland far idisher emigratsye* (Brazil: The land of the future for the Jewish Emigrant) (Berlin: HIAS-ICA-EMIGDIRECT, 1928).

30. Thomas W. Merrick and Douglas H. Graham, *Population and Economic Development in Brazil, 1800 to present* (Baltimore, Md.: Johns Hopkins Press, 1979), 38.

31. Warren Dean, "Economy," in *Brazil: Empire and Republic, 1822–1930*, ed. Leslie Bethell (Cambridge: Cambridge University Press, 1989), 237.

32. June E. Hahner, *Poverty and Politics: The Urban Poor in Brazil, 1870–1920* (Albuquerque: University of New Mexico Press, 1986), 261.

33. By 1940 more than 80 percent of all Brazil's Jews lived in São Paulo, Rio de Janeiro, or Porto Alegre, where they concentrated in the districts of Bom Retiro, Praça Onze, and Bom Fim, and were engaged in urban trades that ranged from peddling to small industry. See Leon Back, "Imigração judaica no Rio Grande do Sul," in *Enciclopédia Rio-Grandense* (Canoas, 1958), 5:271–82. See also Luiza H. Schmitz Kliemann, *História da questão agrária* (Porto Alegre: Mercado Aberto, 1986); and Judith L. Elkin, *Jews of the Latin American Republics* (Chapel Hill, N.C.: University of North Carolina Press, 1980).

34. Oliveira Vianna's comments to the Chamber of Deputies, 27 December 1923. Cited in Fidelis Reis and João de Faria, *O problema immigratorio e seus aspectos ethnicos: Na camara e fóra de câmara* (Rio de Janeiro: Typ. "Revista dos Tribunaes," 1924), 57.

35. Wilson Martins, *História da inteligência brasileira*, vol. 6, *1915–1933* (São Paulo: Cultrix, 1978), 323–24.

36. Raffalovich to ICA, 11 July 1924, SCA, 4:94; Nelson Werneck Sodré in *História da imprensa no Brasil* (Rio de Janeiro: Editora Civilização Brasileira, 1966). Unfortunately neither Brazil's National Archives nor National Library has an extant copy of this issue of *O Brasil*.

37. Fundação Instituto Brasileiro de Geografia e Estatística-IBGE, *Estatísticas Históricas do Brasil: Séries Econômicas, Demográficas e Sociais de 1550 a*

1985 (Rio de Janeiro: IBGE, 1986), 32, table 1.7; Lestschinsky, "Jewish Migrations, 1840–1956"; "O projeto Fidelis Reis" (October 22, 1923) in Reis and Faria, *O Problema immigratorio,* 12; John D. Wirth, *Minas Gerais in the Brazilian Federation, 1889–1937* (Stanford, Calif.: Stanford University Press, 1977), 87–88.

38. Carlos S. Bakota, "Crisis and the Middle Classes: The Ascendency of Brazilian Nationalism, 1914–1922" (Ph.D. diss., University of California at Los Angeles, 1973), 144–45.

39. This is similar to a pattern found throughout South America. See, for example, Carl Solberg's discussion in *Immigration and Nationalism: Argentina and Chile, 1890–1914* (Austin: University of Texas Press, 1970).

40. Jacob Lestschinsky, "The Industrial and Social Structure of the Jewish Population of Interbellum Poland," YIVO *Annual of Jewish Social Science* 11 (1957), 246, table 1.

41. Raffalovich (Rio de Janeiro) to ICA (Paris), 27 March 1926, SCA (3 July 1926), 2:103, JCA-L.

42. Register of Sociedade Israelita de Beneficência e Proteção ao Imigrantes "EZRA" (São Paulo), "Jewish Immigrants Entering Port of Santos, 1928–1932," AHJB-SP.

43. Pereira (on board the S.S. *Flandria*) to ICA (Paris), 3 August 1923, SCA (6 October 1923), 4:229, JCA-L.

44. Jose Carlos G. Durand, "Formação do pequeno empresariado têxtil em São Paulo (1880–1950)," in *Pequena empresa: O comportamento empresarial na acumulação e na luta pela sobrevivência,* ed. Henrique Rattner (São Paulo: Brasiliense, 1985), 1:112.

45. On the earliest peddlers in Brazil, see José Alipio Goulart, *O mascate no Brasil* (Rio de Janeiro: Editora Conquista, Coleção Terra dos Papagaios, 1967), especially pp. 165–89.

46. On Syrian and Lebanese peddlers in Brazil, see Claude Fahd Hajjar, *Imigração árabe: 100 anos de reflexão* (São Paulo: Editora Cone, 1985); Clark Knowlton, *Sírios e libaneses* (São Paulo: Editora Anhembi, 1960); Jorge S. Safady, "A imigração árabe no Brasil" (Ph.D. diss., Department of History, University of São Paulo, 1972); Manoelito de Ornellas, *Gaúchos e beduínos: A origem étnica e a formação do Rio Grande do Sul* (Rio de Janeiro: Editora José Olympio, 1948); and Jamil Safady, *O café e o mascate* (São Paulo: Editora Comercial Safady, 1973).

47. Fahd Hajjar, *Imigração árabe,* 89. On the similar images of Arab and Jewish immigrants held by members of the Brazilian elite, see Jeffrey Lesser, "From Pedlars to Proprietors: Lebanese, Syrian and Jewish Immigrants in Brazil," in *The Lebanese in the World: A Century of Emigration,* ed. Albert Hourani and Nadim Shehadi (London and New York: I. B. Tauris and St. Martin's Press, 1992), 393–410.

48. Pierre Deffontaines, "Mascates," *Geografia* 2:1 (1936), 28.

49. Evaristo de Moraes, "*Judeus sem dinheiro* taes como eu vejo," in *Os judeus na história do Brasil,* ed. Afrânio Peixoto (Rio de Janeiro: Uri Zwerling, 1936), 105.

50. Guilherme de Almeida, "Cosmópolis: O 'Ghetto,'" *O Estado de São Paulo,* 31 March 1929; de Moraes, "*Judeus sem Dinheiro,*" 106.

51. Data from "Estatística Industrial" da Secretaria da Agricultura, published in Oscar Egídio de Araújo, "Enquistamentos étnicos," *Revista do Arquivo Municipal de São Paulo* 6:65 (March 1940): 241.

52. *Idische Folkszeitung* (Jewish Gazette) (Rio de Janeiro), 1 August 1941.

53. Isaiah Raffalovich, "Report of Tour in North of Brazil," SCA (5 September 1931), 2:87, JCA-L; *RACCA* 1923, p. 300, AHJB-SP; Pereira (São Paulo) to ICA (Paris), 20 July 1923, SCA (6 October 1923), 4:214, JCA-L.

54. Saúl Givelder, interview by Avram Milgram and Janette Engellaum, Rio de Janeiro, 31 November 1985, interview no. 13, American Jewish Archives, Cincinnati.

55. Givelder, interview, AJA-C.

56. "Minutes of an Interview with Mr. Jacob Schneider, President of the Zionist Organization in Brazil, London, 2nd November 1924," ZU/2350, p. 1, Central Zionist Archives, Jerusalem.

57. Raffalovich to ICA, 11 July 1924, SCA, 4:94.

58. Almeida's use of the term *ghetto* should not be confused with the more recent use of the word to signify any area that has a high concentration of one or more minority groups. See Peter I. Rose, "Ghetto," in *Academic American Encyclopedia* (Darien, Conn.: Grolier, 1986), 9:167.

59. Almeida, "Cosmópolis: O 'Ghetto.' " The entire collection of articles was republished as *Cosmópolis: São Paulo/29* (São Paulo: Companhia Editora Nacional, 1962).

60. Paul Appleton, *La traite des blanches* (Paris: Librairie Nouvelle de Droit et de Jurisprudence, 1903), 34.

61. International Emigration Commission, *Report of the Commission, August 1921* (Geneva: International Labour Office, 1921), 107.

62. League of Nations, *Report of the Special Body of Experts on Traffic in Women and Children* (Geneva: League of Nations, 1927); Louis Layrac, *La traite des blanches et l'excitation à la débauche* (Paris: V. Girard et F. Briere, 1904); George Rylel Scott, *A History of Prostitution from Antiquity to the Present Day* (London: T. Werner Laurie, 1936).

63. Guido Fonseca, *História da prostituição em São Paulo.* (São Paulo: Editora Resenha Universitária, 1982), 140.

64. Fonseca, *História da prostituição,* 141.

65. Needel, *A Tropical Belle Epoque,* 172.

66. J. R. Pires de Almeida, *Hygiene moral* (Rio de Janeiro: Laemmert, 1906); Needel, *A Tropical Belle Epoque,* 172.

67. Francisco Ferreira da Rosa, *O lupanar: Estudo sobre o caftanismo e a prostituição no Rio de Janeiro* (Rio de Janeiro: n.p., 1896), 8.

68. Ferreira da Rosa, *O lupanar,* 45–46. Emphasis in original.

69. Ferreira da Rosa, *O lupanar,* 13–16.

70. Fonseca, *História da prostituição,* 140–44; Margareth Rago, *Os prazeres da noite: Prostituição e códigos da sexualidade feminina em São Paulo (1890–1930)* (Rio de Janeiro: Paz e Terra, 1991), 285–309.

71. Edward J. Bristow, *Prostitution and Prejudice: The Jewish Fight against the White Slave Trade* (New York: Schocken Books, 1974), 13; Needel, *A Tropical Belle Epoque,* 172; Samuel Malamud, *Recordando a Praça Onze* (Rio de

Janeiro: Editora Kosmos, 1988), 81; Konrad Wrzos, *Yerba Mate* (Warsaw: Rój, 1937), 47.

72. Sander Gilman, *The Jew's Body* (New York: Routledge, Chapman and Hall, 1991), 122.

73. Gilberto Freyre, *Ordem e progresso* (Rio de Janeiro: José Olympio Editora, 1959), 2:95–96.

74. Freyre, *Ordem e progresso,* 2:95; Ferreira da Rosa, *O lupanar,* 46.

75. "O mysterio da Rua dos Arcos: Frida Mystal, a estrangulada," *Vida Policial* vol. 1, no. 1 (14 March 1925). While *Vida Policial* often focused on the "Jewish race" of prostitutes, it was more attuned, as Sueann Caulfield has shown, toward portraying all "modern women" in a poor light; see "Getting into Trouble: Dishonest Women, Modern Girls and Women-Men in the Conceptual Language of *Vida Policial,* 1925–1927," *Signs* 19:1 (fall 1993).

76. There is some debate as to what "Zwi Migdal" means. One explanations is that the crime ring was founded by a man named Zwi, who named the groups Zwi's Tower (Hebrew: migdal), an appropriately phallic reference. Another explanation is that the founders of the group were two brothers named Migdal and thus *zwei* (Yiddish: two) Migdal.

77. Robert Weisbrot, *The Jews of Argentina: From the Inquisition to Perón* (Philadelphia: Jewish Publication Society of America, 1979), 60. Weisbrot arrives at this figure by counting "Jewish" last names, a far from perfect method for discovering who is Jewish and who is not. See also Victor A. Mirelman, *Jewish Buenos Aires, 1890–1930: In Search of an Identity* (Detroit, Mich.: Wayne State University Press, 1990), 197–220.

78. Bristow, *Prostitution and Prejudice,* 141.

79. On the Zwi Migdal in Rio, see Samuel Malamud, "T'meim: Os judeus impuros," in *Shalom* 13:260 (May 1988), 29–30.

80. Rago, *Os prazeres da noite,* 301–2. Moacyr Scliar's novel *O ciclo das águas* (Porto Alegre: Editora Globo, 1977) deals extensively with the theme of the Jewish white slave trade in Brazil.

81. *Livro de Atas de "Sociedade Religiosa e Beneficente Israelita," São Paulo,* meetings of 30 June 1924, p. 1, and 22 June 1925, p. 6, Archives of the Lar dos Velhos, São Paulo. The reports of meetings in this book are often incomplete. It is unclear if all the funds for the organization came from membership dues, or if the pimps themselves contributed.

82. Abe Shulman, "Unclean Burial Place in Brazil," *Jewish Week* 8 (June 1980).

83. *SRBI,* meeting of 18 December 1924, p. 3, ALV-SP.

84. *SRBI,* meeting of 15 April 1927, p. 16, ALV-SP.

85. In 1927 a battle for power took place that began with a police raid following a telephone tip that members were "drunk and had among them unaccompanied minors." See SRBI, meeting of 4 May 1928, p. 33, ALV-SP.

86. *RACCA* 1925, p. 296, AHJB-SP.

87. Bristow, *Prostitution and Prejudice,* 113, n. 8.

88. Malamud, *Recordando a Praça Onze,* 82.

89. Rachel Geiger, interview by Janette Engellaum, Rio de Janeiro, September 1985, AJA-C.

90. "Annual Report, 1930," SCA (27 September 1930), 2:115, JCA-L.

91. Donna J. Guy, "White Slavery, Public Health, and the Socialist Position on Legalized Prostitution in Argentina, 1913–1936," *Latin American Research Review* 23:3 (1988), 74.

92. Jewish Colonization Association, Bureau de Rio de Janeiro Affilié à la HIAS-JCA-EMIGDIRECT, "Report for the year 1932," SCA (16 March 1933), 252, JCA-L.

93. Raffalovich, "Report for the Year 1926," SCA (2 July 1927), 1:134, JCA-L.

94. Raffalovich, "Report for the Year 1926," SCA, 1:134.

95. Raffalovich, "Report for the Year 1926," SCA, 1:137–8.

96. Guy, "White Slavery, Public Health," 74; Bristow, *Prostitution and Prejudice*, 319.

97. SRBI, meeting of 11 November, 1939, p. 84, ALV-SP.

98. SRBI, meeting of 14 June 1956, p. 111, ALV-SP.

99. SRBI, meeting of 31 July 1968, p. 192, ALV-SP.

100. See Gilman, *The Jew's Body*, 120–27.

101. Cezar Magalhaens, *Pela brazilidade: Discursos e Conferências* (Rio de Janeiro: Typ. A. Pernambucana Hermes Poffes, 1925), 42.

102. Fonseca, *História da prostituição*, 209–26; Bristow, *Prostitution and Prejudice*, 111–45.

103. Adolfo Coelho, *Ópio, cocaína e escravatura branca* (Lisbon: Livraria Clássica Editora, 1931), 244.

104. Anésio Frota Aguiar, *O lenocínio como problema social no Brasil* (Rio de Janeiro: n.p., 1940), 21.

105. Aguiar, *O lenocínio*, 17–20.

106. Aguiar, *O lenocínio*, 15.

107. This phenomenon has continued to this day. Guido Fonseca's contemporary historical study of prostitution in São Paulo, for example, demonstrates that the majority of prostitutes in São Paulo were Brazilian and that, of the non-Brazilians, the majority were not Eastern European. He gives no indication that all, or even a significant percentage, of Eastern European prostitutes were Jewish. Yet his discussion is illustrated with a distraught letter written in 1931 to a São Paulo police delegation in which a mother complained that "my daughter, against my wishes, married a Polish Jew" who then took her to Buenos Aires for illicit purposes. See Fonseca, *História da prostituição*, 144.

108. Moraes, *"Judeus sem dinheiro,"* 107.

109. Raffalovich, "Report for the Year 1926," SCA, 1:128.

110. Esther Regina Largman and Robert M. Levine, "Jews in the Tropics: Bahian Jews in the Early Twentieth Century," *Americas* 18 (October 1986), 161.

111. Pereira to ICA, 3 August 1923, SCA, 4:227.

112. Pereira to ICA, 3 August 1923, SCA, 4:227.

113. On Jewish education, see Falbel, *Estudos*, 118–30; and Rattner, *Tradição e mudança*, especially pp. 61–69.

114. *RACCA* 1930, p. 61, AHJB-SP.

115. Raffalovich to ICA, 27 March 1926, no. 44, SCA 2:100.

116. On the Jewish press in Brazil, see Isaac Z. Raizman, *A fertl yorhundert yiddishe prese in Brazil* (A quarter century of Jewish press in Brazil) (Tzfat: Museum le-Omanut ha-Dfus, 1968); Sergio Robert Margulies, "História da imprensa judaica no Brasil," in Small Collection, American Jewish Archives, Cincinnatti; and Falbel, *Estudos*, 155–60.

117. Pereira (on board the *Flandria*) to ICA (Paris), 3 August 1923, SCA (6 October 1923) 4:222, JCA-L.

118. Nachman Falbel, "Early Zionism in Brazil: The Founding Years, 1913–1922," *American Jewish Archives* 38:2 (1986), 128.

119. A fine survey of Brazilian Zionism by one of its leaders can be found in Malamud, *Do arquivo e da memória*, 21–110.

120. *Dos Idische Vochenblatt* (The Jewish Weekly) (Rio de Janeiro), 23 November 1923, 1. Microfilm in newspaper holdings of the Hebrew Union College/Jewish Institute of Religion Library, Cincinnati, Ohio.

121. *Dos Idische Vochenblatt*, 22 February 1924, 9, HUC/JIR-C.

122. Eliezer Levy to Chaim Weizmann, 20 November 1919, ZU/2350, CZA-J.

123. Falbel, *Estudos*, 134–39.

124. Pereira (on board the *Flandria*) to ICA (Paris), 3 August 1923, SCA (6 October 1923) 4:222, JCA-L.

125. *Dos Idische Vochenblatt*, 14 and 21 August 1925, 1, HUC/JIR-C.

126. Raffalovich, "Report for the Year 1926," SCA, 1:138.

127. Raffalovich, "Report for the Year 1926," SCA, 1:131, JCA-L.

128. Raffalovich, "Report for the Year 1926," SCA, 1:132, JCA-L.

129. "Annual Report, 1927," SCA (15 October 1928), 1:271, JCA-L.

130. Raffalovich, *Brazilye*, 1.

131. Raffalovich (Rio) to ICA (Paris), 30 April 1929, no. 110, SCA (6 July 1929) 1:188, JCA-L; "Rapport sur l'activité de la HIAS-JCA-EMIGDIRECT, 1 avril 1927 à 31 décembre 1928," SCA (6 July 1929) 2:118, JCA-L; Falbel, *Estudos*, 129.

132. Raffalovich, "Report for the Year 1926," SCA, 1:136.

133. "L'Activite de la HIAS-JCA-EMIGDIRECT," SCA, 2:117.

134. "Annual Report, 1927," SCA, 1:273.

135. "Report of the United Evacuation Committee (Paris) 4 July 1926," SCA (9 October 1926), 3:235, JCA-L.

136. "Annual Report, 1930," SCA (27 September 1930), 2:104, JCA-L.

137. Rosaura Street (Serviço de Colocação de Imigrantes Dirigidos) to Director of INIC, 2 May 1957, Processo 11.007, Fundo: Hospedaria dos Imigrantes, Secção: Documentação Administrativo, Archive of the Secretaria de Estado da Promoção Social-Centro Histórico do Imigrante, São Paulo.

138. Raffalovich to ICA, 30 April 1929, no. 110, SCA, 1:188.

139. Draft copy of Raffalovich speech to Central Conference of American Rabbis, SCA (27 September 1930), 2:63, JCA-L; Jewish Colonization Association, "Report for the Year 1932," SCA, 250.

140. Jewish Colonization Association, "Report for the Year 1932," SCA, 247.

2. NATIONALISM, NATIVISM, AND RESTRICTION

1. Boris Fausto, "Society and Politics," in *Brazil: Empire and Republic, 1822–1930*, ed. Leslie Bethell (Cambridge: Cambridge University Press, 1989), 300, 305; Thomas Skidmore, *Politics in Brazil, 1930–1964: An Experiment in Democracy* (New York: Oxford University Press, 1967), 13.

2. Joseph L. Love, *São Paulo in the Brazilian Federation, 1889–1937* (Stanford, Calif.: Stanford University Press, 1980), 48–50.

3. Political surveys of this period may be found in Skidmore, *Politics in Brazil*, 3–21; and Jordan M. Young, *The Brazilian Revolution of 1930 and the Aftermath* (New Brunswick, N.J.: Rutgers University Press, 1967), 30–54.

4. Boris Fausto, *A revolução de 1930: Historiografia e história* (São Paulo: Brasiliense, 1986), 29. See also Wilson Suzigan, *Indústria brasileira: Origem e desenvolvimento* (São Paulo: Brasiliense, 1986), 74–115.

5. Decree law 19,482 (12 December 1930), *Collecção das leis da República dos Estados Unidos do Brasil de 1930*, vol. 2, *Actos da junta governativa provisória e do governo provisório (outubro a dezembro)* (Rio de Janeiro: Imprensa Nacional, 1931), 82.

6. Skidmore, *Black into White*, 38.

7. Alcir Lenharo, for example, has correctly pointed out that "the characteristic that marked anti-Jewish racial [sic] prejudice [was] to hide racism under apparently non-biological stereotypes"; see Lenharo, *Sacralização da política*, 114.

8. Francisco José Oliveira Vianna, *Populações meridonais do Brasil*, 5th ed. (Rio de Janeiro: José Olympio, 1952), 1:429.

9. Vianna, *Populações meridonais*, 1:13; Francisco José Oliveira Vianna, *Raça e assimilação* (São Paulo: Companhia Editora Nacional, 1932), 93–126; Skidmore, *Black into White*, 64.

10. Vianna, *Raça e assimilação*, 97; Nancy Leys Stepan, *"The Hour of Eugenics": Race, Gender and Nation in Latin America* (Ithaca, N.Y.: Cornell University Press, 1991), 156.

11. Vianna, *Raça e assimilação*, 109; Bessie Bloom Wessel, "Ethnic Factors in the Population of New London, CT," parts 1 and 2, *American Journal of Sociology* (July 1929), 18–34, 263–70.

12. Stepan, *"The Hour of Eugenics,"* 157–58.

13. Hiroshi Saito, *O japonês no Brasil* (São Paulo: Editora Sociologia e Política, 1962), 23.

14. Jacob Lestschinsky, "National Groups in Polish Emigration," *Jewish Social Studies* 5:2 (April 1943), 110–11; C. R. Cameron, "Immigration into São Paulo," parts 2 and 3, 14 April 1931, 832.55/78, NARC-W.

15. Decree law 19,482, art. 1a.

16. Decree law 19,482, arts. 1a, 1b, 1c.

17. Péricles de Mello Carvalho, "A legislação imigratória do Brasil e sua evolução," *RIC* 1:4 (October 1940), 725.

18. Decree law 19,482, art. 2; Philip P. Williams (vice-consul, U.S. consulate, Rio de Janeiro), "Brazilian Immigration," 22 May 1939, 832.55/174, NARC-W; Eduardo Oungre (HIAS-ICA-Emigdirect-Paris) to Jewish Coloniza-

tion Association (Paris), 15 December 1930, SCA (27 January 1931), 1:49, JCA-L.

19. Jewish Colonization Association, Bureau de Rio de Janeiro affilié à la HIAS-JCA-Emigdirect, "Report for the year 1932," SCA (16 March 1933), 243–44, JCA-L.

20. "Discriminação por nacionalidade dos imigrantes entrando no Brasil no período 1924–1933 e 1934–1939," *RIC* 1:3 (July 1940), 633–38; SCA 1926–1935, JCA-L.

21. A *despachante* is a person who is paid to help a member of the public negotiate the immense and confusing Brazilian bureaucracy in order to get some kind of governmental approval.

22. Raffalovich, "Report of Tour in North of Brazil," SCA (5 September 1931), 2:83, JCA-L.

23. Telegram EM/4/2/31, 4 February 1931, Maço 9,993 (680), AHI-R.

24. Jewish Colonization Association, "Report for 1932," SCA, 247.

25. Raffalovich, "Tour in North of Brazil," SCA, 2:83.

26. Raffalovich, "Tour in North of Brazil," SCA, 2:85.

27. Jewish Colonization Association, "Report for 1932," SCA, 244.

28. Sociedade Israelita de Beneficência e Proteção aos Imigrantes "EZRA" (São Paulo), "Livro de Cartas de Chamadas, 1932," AHJB-SP.

29. Jewish Colonization Association, "Report for 1932," 245.

30. Flávio Mendes de Oliveira Castro, *História da organização do ministério das relações exteriores* (Brasília: Editora da Universidade de Brasília, 1983), 286.

31. Brasil, Ministério das Relações Exteriores, *Almanaque do pessoal* (Rio de Janeiro: Imprensa Nacional, 1945).

32. Vianna, *Populações meridonais*, 13.

33. The growing fear of communism is explored in Skidmore, *Politics in Brazil*, 10; and Hilton, *Brazil and the Soviet Challenge*, especially pp. 22–52.

34. *O comunismo e sua nefasta propaganda* (São Paulo: Typ. Zaegreb, 1931), 7; Secção de Arquivos Particulares, Pedro Aurélio de Góis Monteiro, AP 51 (12), 1:"Comunismo," AN-R. Although claims that most communists were Jews were common in Brazil, no evidence exists to suggest that this was the case. See John W. F. Dulles, *Anarchists and Communists in Brazil, 1900–1935* (Austin: University of Texas Press, 1973); and *Brazilian Communism, 1935–1945: Repression during World Upheaval* (Austin: University of Texas Press, 1983).

35. The anti-Zionist Jewish Socialist Movement, the Bund (General Jewish Workers' Union), was founded in 1897 in Lithuania, Poland, and Russia. Its separation from general radical social democratic parties is evidence, as David Vital points out, of the "remarkable . . . isolation of the Jews within the national working class"; see *The Origins of Zionism* (Oxford: Oxford University Press, 1975), 312–13. See also Walter Laquer, *A History of Zionism* (New York: Schocken Books, 1972).

36. Nabuco Gouvêa to Itamaraty, 1934 (n.d.), NC/63/324.19 (239), 1934 anexo. A photocopy of this document was kindly given to the author by Maria Luiza Tucci Carneiro.

37. Commercial Attaché (Alexandria) to Octavio Mangabeira (foreign minister, Rio de Janeiro), 17 April 1930,
38. Commercial Attaché to Mangabeira, 17 April 1930. This was representative of comments made in justifying restrictive immigration policies throughout the Americas. See, for example, Hu-DeHart, "Racism and Anti-Chinese Persecution," 1–28.
39. Bhagwan Singh (manager, Indo-Brazilian Association) to Vicente Avelina (Brazilian consul general, Calcutta), 2 August 1930, Maço 29.625/29 (1,291), AHI-R.
40. Avelina to Singh, 5 August 1930, Maço 29.625/29 (1,291), AHI-R.
41. Decree law 16,761 (31 December 1924), art. 4.
42. Octavio Pacheco to Cavalcante de Lacerda, 10 March 1932, Maço 29.625/29 (1,291), AHI-R.
43. Murillo M. de Souza (Brazilian consul, Calcutta) to Bhagwan Singh, 29 March 1932, Maço 29.625/29 (1,291), AHI-R.
44. *Indian Daily Mail*, 25 February 1932.
45. de Souza to Manoel A. de Heredia (Brazilian consul general, Bombay), 5 March 1932, Maço 29.625/29 (1,291), AHI-R. *Advance* (Calcutta), 24 March 1932; *Indian Daily Mail*, 10 March 1932.
46. de Souza to Singh, 29 March 1932.
47. de Souza to Sir Evelyn Howell, 28 March 1932, Maço 29.625/29 (1,291), AHI-R.
48. Telegram EM/20/10/30, 20 November 1930, Maço 29.625/29 (1,291), AHI-R.
49. Alberto Torres, *A organização nacional* (São Paulo: Companhia Editorial Nacional, 1938). Torres rejected concepts of racial superiority. See also Douglas McLain Jr., "Alberto Torres, Ad Hoc Nationalist," *Luso-Brazilian Review* 4:4 (December 1967), 17–34; and Adalberto Marson, *A ideologia nacionalista em Alberto Torres* (São Paulo: Duas Cidades, 1979).
50. Bakota, "Crisis and the Middle Classes," 149.
51. Samuel Guy Inman to Committee on Cooperation in Latin America (New York), 15 April 1935, James G. McDonald Papers, "Inman, S. G., Interviews, 1935," D356-H16 in Herbert H. Lehman Papers, Columbia University, New York.
52. Nicolau Debané, "Algumas considerações sobre o problema da imigração no Brasil," *Jornal do Comércio*, 3 June 1934; Martins, *História da inteligência brasileira*, vol. 6, *1915–1933*, 78, 191.
53. Inman to Committee on Cooperation in Latin America, 15 April 1935, McDonald Papers.
54. Morris Melvin Wagner (Sacramento, Calif.) to Getúlio Vargas, 12 October 1933, AN-R; Departamento Nacional do Povoamento Memo [signature illegible], 28 November 1933, Fundo Secretaria da Presidência da República, Ministério do Trabalho, Indústria e Comércio, lata 103 (27,569), AN-R. Documents courtesy of Cliff Welch.
55. Cytrynowicz, "Integralismo e anti-semitismo," 192.
56. Edgard Carone, *A segunda república (1930–1937)* (São Paulo: Corpo e Alma do Brasil-Difusão Européia do Livro, 1973), 315.

57. Ação Integralista Brasileira, "Manifesto de outubro," reprinted in Hélgio Trindade, *Integralismo: O fascismo brasileiro na década de 30*, 2d ed. (São Paulo: Difel, 1979), 90–91; Galeazzo Ciano, *Ciano's Hidden Diary, 1937–1938* (New York: E. P. Dutton and Co., 1953), 30; Levine, *The Vargas Regime*, 81–99. Carone, *A segunda república*, 309–15.

58. For a discussion of the basis and development of Integralist ideology, see Ricardo Benzaquen de Araújo, *Totalitarismo e revolução: O integralismo de Plínio Salgado* (Rio de Janeiro: Jorge Zahar Editor, 1987); and Gilberto Vasconcellos, *Ideologia curupira: Análise do discurso integralista* (São Paulo: Brasiliense, 1979).

59. René Gertz, *O fascismo no sul do Brasil: Germanismo, nazismo, integralismo* (Porto Alegre: Mercado Aberto, 1987), 113; Levine, *The Vargas Regime*, 83.

60. Trindade, *Integralismo*, 154, table 25.

61. Gustavo Barroso, *Judaismo, maçonaria e comunismo* (Rio de Janeiro: Civilização Brasileira, 1937); Trindade, *Integralismo*, 226–28.

62. Miguel Reale, *O capitalismo internacional: Introdução à economia nova* (Rio de Janeiro: José Olympio, 1935) and *ABC do integralismo* (Rio de Janeiro: José Olympio, 1935); "Anti-Semitism in Brazil and the Argentine," no author, n.d., South America section, folder 2, c/11/12/4, Archives of the Board of Deputies of British Jews, London.

63. Reale, *O capitalismo internacional*, 7, 30.

64. Cytrynowicz, "Integralismo e anti-semitismo," 8.

65. Martins, *História da inteligência brasileira*, vol. 7, *1933–1960*, 20–22.

66. *Os protocolos dos sábios de Sião: O imperialismo de Israel, o plano dos judeus para a conquista do mundo, o código do Anti-Cristo, provas de autenticidade, documentos, notas e comentários*, translated, organized, and annotated by Gustavo Barroso (São Paulo: Editora Agência Minerva, 1936).

67. Gustavo Barroso, *A sinagoga paulista*, 2d ed. (Rio de Janeiro: Empresa Editora ABC, 1937), especially pp. 1–13. São Paulo state deputy A. Vicente de Azevedo attacked *A sinagoga paulista* soon after it was published; see *Diário Oficial—Estado de São Paulo* 178 (10 August 1937).

68. Robert Levine, "Brazil's Jews during the Vargas Era and After," *Luso-Brazilian Review* 5:1 (June 1968), 50.

69. Levine, *The Vargas Regime*, 83. Gustavo Barroso, *Brasil, colônia de banqueiros* (Rio de Janeiro: Civilização Brasileira, 1934); Stanley E. Hilton, "Ação Integralista Brasileira: Fascism in Brazil, 1932–1938," *Luso-Brazilian Review* 9:2 (December 1972), 15; Renato Lemos and Joana Angélica Melo, "Meira de Vasconcelos," in *Dicionário histórico-biográfico brasileiro, 1930–1983*, ed. Israel Beloch and Alzira Alves de Abreu (Rio de Janeiro: Editora Forense-Universitária, 1984), 4:3, 517.

70. Morris Davidson, "Anti-Semitism in South America," n.d., South American section, folder E3/509, 1, BODBJ-L.

71. João Alberto Lins de Barros to Luís Carlos Prestes, 8 June 1937, cited in Levine, "Brazil's Jews," 53, and Moniz Bandeira, *Presença dos Estados Unidos no Brasil: Dois séculos de história* (Rio de Janeiro: Civilização Brasileira, 1978), 247.

72. Levine, "Brazil's Jews," 48.

73. Moises Rabinovitch, *Die Iceh fartretersheft in Brazil un ireh zahrgn toyves-hakla'l* (The ICA representative in Brazil and the public trust) (Rio de Janeiro: n.p., 1933); Raffalovich to Francisco Antunes Maciel (minister of justice), 19 April 1933, Ministério da Justiça e Negócios Interiores, IJJ, caixa 75, 1933, AN-R.

74. Müller to Antunes Maciel, 2 May 1933, Ministério da Justiça e Negócios Interiores, IJJ, caixa 75, 1933, AN-R.

75. Levine, *The Vargas Regime*, 3, 56.

76. Levine, *The Vargas Regime*, 139.

77. Stanley Hilton, *Hitler's Secret War in South America, 1939–1945: German Military Espionage and Allied Counterespionage in Brazil* (Baton Rouge: Louisiana State University Press, 1981), 189.

78. Affonso Henrique de Miranda, Special Delegate of Political and Social Security, to Müller, 25 April 1933, Ministério da Justiça e Negócios Interiores, IJJ, caixa 75, 1933, AN-R.

79. Raffalovich (Rio de Janeiro) to ICA (Paris), 4 August 1933, SCA (16 September 1933), 170, JCA-L.

80. Raffalovich (Rio de Janeiro) to ICA (Paris), 25 October 1934, O.M. no. 202, SCA (15 December 1934), 109–10, JCA-L; Ludwig Lauerhass, Jr., "Getúlio Vargas and the Triumph of Brazilian Nationalism: A Study on the Rise of the Nationalist Generation of 1930" (Ph.D. diss., University of California at Los Angeles, 1972), 189.

81. Raffalovich to ICA, 25 October 1934, SCA, 109–10.

82. James G. McDonald, "Confidential Draft of an Interim Report on the Mission to South and Central America of Dr. Samuel Guy Inman and the High Commissioner, March–June, 1935," 40, JCA-L.

83. John W. F. Dulles, *Carlos Lacerda, Brazilian Crusader*, vol. 1, *The Years 1914–1960* (Austin: University of Texas Press, 1991), 28.

84. Antônio Baptista Pereira, *O Brasil e o anti-semitismo* (Rio de Janeiro: Editora Guanabara, 1934); Azevedo Amaral, Review of *O Brasil e o anti-semitismo* in *Revista Brasileira* 2 (August 1934), 77–80. Wainer's parents were Romanian Jewish immigrants to Brazil. For more information on Samuel Wainer, see his *Minha razão de viver: Memórias de um repórter* (Rio de Janeiro: Record, 1987).

85. José Pérez, *Questão judaica, questão social* (São Paulo: Empresa Gráfica da "Revista dos Tribunaes," 1933), 13.

86. *Por que ser anti-semita?: Um inquérito entre intellectuaes brasileiros* (Rio de Janeiro: Civilização Brasileira, 1933).

87. *Por que ser anti-semita?*, 8.

88. Gilberto Amado, "Momentos de vibração," in *Por que ser anti-semita?*, 93. For a fuller discussion of this and other essays, see Carneiro, *O anti-semitismo*, 468–82.

89. Herbert V. Levy, *Problemas actuaes da economia brasileira* (São Paulo: Empresa Gráfica da "Revista dos Tribunaes," 1934), 104. When Levy was asked if ethnic solidarity might be a reason for his support of the entry of German Jews, and his desire to prohibit Arab immigration, he replied that "neither

[I] nor my close ancestors are Jewish." Herbert V. Levy, "A propósito de uma carta aberta ao Dr. José Maria Whitaker," in Júnior Amarilio, *As vantagens da immigração syria no Brasil (em torno de uma polêmica entre os Snrs. Herbert V. Levy e Salomão Jorge, no "Diário de São Paulo")* (Rio de Janeiro: Off. Gr. da S.A. A Noite, 1935), 46.

90. Fritz Pinkuss, interview by author, São Paulo, 1 September 1986.

91. Jeffrey Lesser, "Diferencias regionales en el desarrollo histórico de las comunidades judeo-brasilcñas contemporáneas: San Pablo y Porto Alegre," *Estudios Migratorios Latinoamericanos* 4:11 (April 1989), 71–84.

92. Bernhard Wolff, interview by author, Porto Alegre, 21 July 1986; Herbert Caro, "SIBRA 50 anos," in *Sociedade Israelita Brasileira de Cultura e Beneficência, 1936–1986* (Porto Alegre: SIBRA, 1986), 48. Léons de Poncins, *As forças secretas da revolução: Maçonaria e judaismo* (Porto Alegre: Editora do Globo, 1931). A discussion of both European and Brazilian anti-Semitic literature published in Brazil can be found in Carneiro, *O anti-semitismo*, 351–417; and Chiavenato, *O inimigo eleito*, 229–78.

93. Oscar Messias Cardoso, "A emigração israelita através do mundo," *Correio da Manhã* (Rio de Janeiro), 27 August 1933. Cardoso apparently was unaware that the Jewish Colonization Association was unable to find many Jewish farmers in Germany.

94. "Who's Who" (unsigned and undated diplomatic note), Hugh Gibson Collection, box 99, folder Diplomatic Posts, Brazil (Rio de Janeiro) General, Hoover Institution Archives, Stanford, Calif.; Ildefonso Falcão to Afrânio de Mello Franco, 27 June 1933, EC/191/558/Reservado/1935/Anexo, Maço 10.561 (741), AHI-R.

95. Falcão to Mello Franco, 27 June 1933.

96. Falcão to Mello Franco, 27 June 1933.

97. Mello Franco to Joaquim Pedro Salgado Filho, 21 August 1933, EC/191/558, Maço 10.561 (741), AHI-R.

98. Cavalcanti de Lacerda (in name of A. de Mello Franco) to Jan Wagner (provisional director of Brazilian business relations with Poland), 29 September 1933, Sp/52/558.(72), Maço 9,650(622), AHI-R.

99. "Rapport sur les possibilités actuelles d'émigration," 23 October 1933, no author, pamphlets box A 95 RAP, Mocatta Library, Pamphlets Collection, University College, London.

100. Cavalcanti de Lacerda to Wagner, 29 September 1933, AHI-R.

101. Raffalovich (Rio de Janeiro) to ICA (Paris), 17 December 1933, SCA (17 March 1934), 2:287, JCA-L.

102. Raffalovich to ICA, 17 December 1933, SCA, 2:288.

103. Higham, *Strangers in the Land*, 310.

104. "Emendas ao projeto da constituição apresentadas à Assembléia Nacional Constituinte—Emenda n. 1,164," 22 December 1933, in Xavier de Oliveira, *O problema imigratório*, 74.

105. Jorge Americano, "Sangue puro," in *São Paulo nesse tempo (1915–1935)* (São Paulo: Edições Melhoramentos, 1962), 282–86. Americano made a similar point in his *São Paulo atual (1935–1962)* (São Paulo: Edições Melhoramentos, 1963), 322.

106. Pedro Aurélio de Góis Monteiro, "Discurso à assembléia constituinte de 1934," Secção de Arquivos Particulares, Pedro Aurélio de Góis Monteiro, AP 51 (12), "Comunismo, 1930–1936," AN-R.

107. Morais Andrade, 55th session, 22 January 1934, in Brazil, Assembléia Nacional Constituinte, *Annaes da assembléia nacional constituinte organizados pela redação dos annaes e documentos parlamentares* (Rio de Janeiro: Imprensa Nacional, 1935), 6:348.

108. Xavier de Oliveira, 58th Session, 25 January 1934, in Brazil, Assembléia Nacional Constituinte, *Annaes da assembléia nacional*, 6:451.

109. Ângela Maria de Castro Gomes, ed., *Regionalismo e centralização política: Partidos e constituinte nos anos 30* (Rio de Janeiro: Nova Fronteira, 1980).

110. Afonso Arinos de Mello Franco, *Preparação ao nacionalismo: Cartas aos que têm vinte anos* (Rio de Janeiro: Civilização Brasileira, 1934). Vera Calicchio and César Benjamin, "Arinos, Afonso," in Beloch and Alves de Abreu, *Dicionário histórico-biográfico brasileiro*, 1:203–9.

111. Arinos de Mello Franco, *Preparação ao nacionalismo*, 53–88.

112. Arinos de Mello Franco, *Preparação ao nacionalismo*, 91.

113. Arinos de Mello Franco, *Preparação ao nacionalismo*, 104–51; Solidônio Leite, "O concurso dos judeus na civilização brasileira," in *Por que ser anti-semita?*, 179–91.

114. Fidelis Reis, "A imigração e a raça," *Correio da Manhã*, 6 February 1934.

115. *A Nação* (Rio de Janeiro), 9 March 1935.

116. *Correio da Manhã*, 6 February 1934. "Zegwill" was probably the well-know essayist and novelist Israel Zangwill (1864–1926).

117. Maço 11.487/88 (809), AHI-R.

118. Ângela Maria de Castro Gomes, "A representação de classes na constituinte de 1934," in Gomes, ed., *Regionalismo e centralização política*, 427–91.

119. Hélio Silva, *1934: A Constituinte* (Rio de Janeiro: Editora Civilização Brasileira, 1969), 209–17.

120. Brazilian constitution of 16 July 1934, art. 121, par. 6.

121. Brazilian constitution of 16 July 1934, art. 5, par. 19g, and art. 121, par. 6.

122. Brazilian constitution of 16 July 1934, art. 133 and art. 136, par. a.

123. Brazilian constitution of 16 July 1934, art. 133.

124. "Interview of Samuel Guy Inman with Dr. Francisco Campos," 1 April 1935, JM-Inman, HL-NY.

125. Skidmore, *Politics in Brazil*, 30.

126. Júlio de Revorêdo, *Immigração* (São Paulo: Empresa Gráfica da "Revista dos Tribunaes," 1934), 228.

127. Vianna, *Raça e assimilação*, 150–51.

128. Arnoldo Carlos Hans Kuhn to Pedro Aurélio de Góis Monteiro, 20 September 1930, Secção de Arquivos Particulares, Pedro Aurélio de Góis Monteiro, AP 51 (12), "Comunismo, 1930–1936," AN-R.

129. The High Commission that McDonald headed was made up of repre-

sentatives of all the countries adjacent to Germany and Austria as well as Great Britain, Sweden, the United States, and Uruguay. Its charge was to "negotiate and direct the international collaboration necessary to solve the economic, financial, and social problems of refugees." See S. Adler-Rudel, "The Evian Conference on the Refugee Question," *Leo Baeck Institute Yearbook* 13 (1968), 235.

130. Phebe Marr, *The Modern History of Iraq* (Boulder, Colo.: Westview Press, 1985), 57–59; Khaldun S. Husry, "The Assyrian Affair of 1933," parts 1 and 2, *International Journal of Middle East Affairs* 5:2 (1974), 161–76; 5:3 (1974), 348–52.

131. A discussion of the linkage of Jews and Arabs among Brazilian intellectuals can be found in Lesser, "From Pedlars to Proprietors," 393–410.

132. Costa Rego, "Amabilidade de inglezes," *Correio da Manhã,* 27 February 1935.

133. "Disrespecting the Constitution with Regard to Immigration: An Appeal by the Society of the Friends of Alberto Torres to the President of the Republic," *Jornal do Comércio,* 1 November 1934.

134. George A. Gordon (interim chargé d'affaires, Rio de Janeiro) to Secretary of State, 5 April 1935, Correspondence, U.S. Embassy, Rio de Janeiro, 1935, vol. 19, 855-Immigration, NARC-W; Hugh Gibson (Rio de Janeiro) to Secretary of State, 1 November 1934, Correspondence, U.S. Embassy, Rio de Janeiro, 1934, vol. 18, 855-Immigration, NARC-W.

135. *Folha da Manhã* (Rio de Janeiro), 7 March 1935.

136. *Diário da Tarde* (Rio de Janeiro), 23 January 1935.

137. "Aide-Mémoire on the Meeting at Paris at the House of Baron Robert de Rothschild on Saturday, May 12, 1934," SCA (16 June 1934), 2:227, JCA-L.

138. "Aide-Mémoire," SCA, 2:227.

139. Samuel Guy Inman to Committee on Cooperation in Latin America (New York), 15 April 1935, JM-Inman, HL-NY.

140. *Diário de Notícias* (Rio de Janeiro), 23 February 1935; *Diário da Manhã* (Recife), 24 January 1935.

141. McDonald, "Confidential Draft," 37, JCA-L.

142. "Quotas provisórias da entrada de imigrantes, para vigorarem durante o ano de 1936," Presidência da República—Fundo Conselho Nacional de Economia, Série Intercâmbio Comercial, lata 174-no. 468-1936, p. 70, Arquivo Nacional, Rio de Janeiro.

143. "Memo on visits of S. G. Inman to Porto Alegre, Montevideo, Buenos Aires, April 12–14, 1935," JM-Inman, HL-NY.

144. About ten thousand of the refugees were in France, four thousand in the Netherlands, and twenty-five hundred in Great Britain. See "Estimate of the Distribution of Refugees as of June 15, 1935," League of Nations Office of the High Commissioner for Refugees Coming from Germany, *Fourth Meeting of the Governing Body of the High Commissioner for Refugees (Jewish and Other) Coming from Germany, July 17, 1935 (including the opening remarks of the Chairman, The Rt. Hon. Viscount Cecil of Chelwood, and the Report of*

the High Commissioner, Mr. James G. McDonald (London: Office of the High Commissioner, 1935), 10.

145. McDonald (Rio de Janeiro) to Sir Osmond E. D'Avigdor-Goldsmid (London), 15 March 1935, James G. McDonald Papers, "Sir Osmond E. D'Avigdor-Goldsmid—D356 H14," in Herbert H. Lehman Papers, Columbia University, New York; Papers of Samuel Guy Inman, MS 77–94c, Archives of the Case Memorial Library of the Hartford Seminary Foundation (Hartford, Conn.).

146. Inman papers, MS 77–94c.

147. Inman to Aranha, 4 February 1935, OA 35.02.04/5, CPDOC-R.

148. Inman to Aranha, 4 February 1935.

149. *Diário de Notícias,* 23 February 1935.

150. McDonald, "Confidential Draft," 2–3, JCA-L.

151. McDonald (Rio) to the R. Hon. The Viscount Cecil of Chelwood (London), 12 April 1935, SCA (4 May 1935), 295, JCA-L.

152. "Interview of Dr. Inman and Mr. McDonald with Dr. Vaz de Mello of the Foreign Office in Rio," 29 March 1935, JM-Inman, HL-NY.

153. "Memo on Dr. Inman's Visit to São Paulo, March 21–24, 1935. Re. Employment Refugee Professors," JM-Inman, HL-NY.

154. "Interview of Dr. Inman and Mr. McDonald," 29 March 1935, JM-Inman, HL-NY.

155. Levine, *The Vargas Regime,* 28.

156. McDonald to D'Avigdor-Goldsmid, 15 March 1935, JM-Goldsmid, HL-NY.

157. McDonald, "Confidential Draft," 52–53, JCA-L.

158. McDonald to D'Avigdor-Goldsmid, 15 March 1935, JM-Goldsmid, HL-NY.

159. Sir W. Seeds (Rio) to Sir John Simon, Secretary of Foreign Affairs (London), 14 March 1935, FO 371/18,861 C3,040/232/18, 140–1, PRO-L.

160. Seeds to Simon, 14 March 1935.

161. McDonald, "Confidential Draft," 42, JCA-L.

162. McDonald (Rio de Janeiro) to D'Avigdor-Goldsmid (London), 21 March 1935, JM-Goldsmid, HL-NY.

163. McDonald to D'Avigdor-Goldsmid, 15 March 1935, JM-Goldsmid.

164. Bandeira, *Presença dos Estados Unidos,* 242.

165. McDonald, "Confidential Draft," 43, JCA-L.

166. Viscount Cecil to Orme Sargent, 19 March 1935, FO 371/18,861 C2,289/232/18, PRO-L.

167. Bernard Wasserstein, *Britain and the Jews of Europe, 1939–1945* (New York: Oxford University Press, 1979).

168. Internal memo [names illegible], 25 March 1935, FO 371/18,861 C2,464/107,337, PRO-L.

169. McDonald, "Confidential Draft," 44, JCA-L.

170. "Memo on Dr. Inman's Visit," JM-Inman, HL-NY.

171. McDonald to the Viscount Cecil of Chelwood, 12 April 1935, 296.

172. McDonald, "Confidential Draft," 44, JCA-L. Magalhães was not paranoid. As will be seen in chapter 4, federal decision makers were regularly

attacked by nativists in the House of Representatives for allowing undesirable immigrants to enter.

173. Voluntary Report of Vice-Consul Harold B. Minor, "Some Notes on Brazilian Immigration Problems Including Statistics for 1934," 20 September 1935, Correspondence, U.S. Embassy, Rio de Janeiro, 1935, vol. 19, 855-Immigration, NARC-W.

174. *Jornal do Comércio*, 4 June 1935.

175. Translation of letter of Raúl de Paula attached to George A. Gordon (interim chargé d'affaires, Rio de Janeiro) to Secretary of State, 5 April 1935, Correspondence, U.S. Embassy, Rio de Janeiro, 1935, vol. 19, 855-Immigration, NARC-W.

176. "Memo on Dr. Inman's Visit," JM-Inman, HL-NY.

177. "Aide-Mémoire for His Excellency, the Minister of Foreign Affairs, from the High Commissioner for Refugees (Jewish and Other) Coming from Germany," in McDonald, "Confidential Draft," annex C, JCA-L.

178. McDonald, "Confidential Draft," 46, JCA-L.

179. [signature illegible] (Bucharest) to José Carlos de Macedo Soares, 2 December 1935, Maço 29.644 (1,291), AHI-R.

180. [signature illegible] (London) to José Carlos de Macedo Soares, 27 March 1935, Maço 9.599 (612), AHI-R.

181. "Interview of Dr. Inman and Mr. McDonald with Dr. Vaz de Mello of the Foreign Office in Rio," 29 March 1935, JM-Inman, HL-NY.

182. "Interview of Dr. Inman and Mr. McDonald," 29 March 1935, JM-Inman, HL-NY.

183. McDonald, "Confidential Draft," 49, JCA-L.

184. ICA (Paris) to Raffalovich, 15 May 1934, Box 14-A-19, Rezende Dossier, AHJB-SP.

185. Dr. Moses Rabinovitch (Associação Israelita Brasileira, Rio de Janeiro), "Apelo e advertência aos senhores diretores da Associação Israelita de Colonização," 28 March 1935, file 16.152, 1935, Archive of *O Estado de São Paulo*.

186. "Centro pró lavoura israelita no Brasil," *A Vanguarda* (São Paulo), 7 June 1935, n.p, file 16.152, 1935, AESP.

187. "Memo on Dr. Inman's Visit," JM-Inman, HL-NY.

188. "Memo on Dr. Inman's Visit," JM-Inman, HL-NY.

189. "Record of Interview with Dr. Odilon Duarte Braga, Minister of Agriculture," 29 March 1935, JM-Inman, HL-NY.

190. "Summary of Situation re: Refugee Professors and Specialists in Research on Departure of Samuel Guy Inman on April 10, 1935," in McDonald, "Confidential Draft," annex E, 15–21, JCA-L.

191. McDonald (Hotel Glória, Rio de Janeiro) to Sir Osmond D'Avigdor-Goldsmid, Bart. (London), 5 April 1935, SCA (4 May 1935), 291, JCA-L; "Who's Who" (unsigned and undated diplomatic note), Hugh Gibson Collection, box 99, folder Diplomatic Posts, Brazil (Rio de Janeiro) General, Hoover Institution Archives, Stanford, Calif.; Afrânio Peixoto, "O pequenino grande povo" in *Por que ser anti-semita?*, 53–56.

192. Julio de Mesquita Filho, *Política e cultura* (São Paulo: Livraria Mar-

tins, 1969), 192; Simon Schwartzman, *A Space for Science: The Development of the Scientific Community in Brazil* (University Park: Pennsylvania State University Press, 1991), 132.

193. Inaugural speech of Campos as secretary of education of the Federal District in *Correio da Manhã*, 25 December 1935, 2.

194. Support for the Campos plan can be found in the AIB's *A Ofensiva* (Rio), 28 December 1935, 1.

195. "Letter of Resignation of James G. McDonald to the Secretary General of the League of Nations," 27 December 1935, JM—pamphlets Q 4, HL-NY; Haim Avni, "Latin America and the Jewish Refugees," 56–57.

196. Samuel Guy Inman, "Refugee Settlement in Latin America," *Annals of the American Academy of Political and Social Science* (May 1939), 183.

197. Haim Avni, "Patterns of Jewish Leadership in Latin America during the Holocaust," in *Jewish Leadership during the Nazi Era: Patterns of Behavior in the Free World*, ed. Randolph L. Braham (New York: Columbia University Press, 1985), 89.

198. *Jüdische Rundschau*, nos. 7, 11, 12, 13, and 15, published between 24 January and 21 February 1936; *Jewish Chronicle*, supplement of April 1936, pp. iv-vi; Arthur Ruppin, *Los judíos de America del Sur* (Buenos Aires, 1938).

199. *Jewish Chronicle*, supplement of April 1936, vi.

200. *Jewish Chronicle*, supplement of April 1936, v.

201. RACCA 1935, p. 197, AHJB-SP.

202. Alfred Hirschberg, "The Economic Adjustment of Jewish Refugees in São Paulo," *Jewish Social Studies* 7 (January 1945), 37.

203. Hirschberg, *Desafio e resposta*, 17. Complete collections of the *Crônica Israelita* can be found in the Biblioteca Alfred Hirschberg of the Congregação Israelita Paulista (São Paulo) and in microfilm at the American Jewish Archives (Cincinnati).

204. *Jewish Chronicle*, supplement of April 1936, vi.

205. On Rolândia's Jews, see Ethel Volfzon Kosminsky, *Rolândia, a terra prometida: Judeus refugiados do nazismo no norte do Paraná* (São Paulo: Faculdade de Filosofia, Letras, e Ciências Humanas/Centro de Estudos Judaicos-USP, 1985); and Max Hermann Maier, *Um advogado de Frankfurt se torna cafeicultor na selva brasileira: Relato de um imigrante (1938–1975)* (mimeographed).

206. "Annual Report 1934," SCA (26 October 1935), 2:168, JCA-L. A total of 3,794 Jews entered Brazil in 1934; 835 of them (22 percent) were German.

207. "Annual Report 1934," SCA, 168.

208. Edouard Oungre (HICEM), Strictly Confidential Hicem Circular no. 136, 11 July 1934, HIAS-Brazil, folder 4, YIVO-NY.

209. Raffalovich (Rio de Janeiro) to Hicem, quoted in Oungre, Strictly Confidential Circular, HIAS-Brazil.

210. Reserved note of A. Bandeira de Mello, 21 September 1934, DNT 20.568-934, Maço 10.561 (741), AHI-R.

211. Oungre, Strictly Confidential Circular, HIAS-Brazil.
212. Reserved note of de Mello, 21 September 1934, AHI-R.
213. Reserved note of de Mello, 21 September 1934, AHI-R.
214. Samuel Putnam, "Brazilian Culture under Vargas," *Science and Society* 6:1 (winter 1942), 52.

3. BRAZIL RESPONDS TO THE "JEWISH QUESTION"

1. Cabral, *A questão judaica* (1937); Maciel, *Nacionalismo: O problema judaico* (1937); Lopes, *O problema judaico* (1942).
2. Levine, *The Vargas Regime*, 21.
3. Fernando Morais, *Olga: A vida de Olga Benário Prestes, judia comunista entregue a Hitler pelo governo Vargas* (São Paulo: Alfa-Ômega, 1986); José Joffily, *Harry Berger* (Rio de Janeiro: Paz e Terra, 1987).
4. Barroso, *Brasil, colônia de banqueiros*; Levine, "Brazil's Jews," 52.
5. Gustavo Barroso, preface to Cabral, *A questão judaica.*
6. A devastating attack on Barroso can be found in Bernardo Schulman, *Em legítima defesa: A voz de um judeu brasileiro*, 2d ed. (Curitiba: n.p., 1937), 55–69.
7. *Século XX* (Rio de Janeiro), 21 April 1936.
8. Vianna, *Raça e assimilação*, 107–10; "Os imigrantes germânicos e slavos e sua caracterização antropológica," *RIC* 1:1 (January 1940), 23–32.
9. Labienne Salgado dos Santos to José Carlos de Macedo Soares, 2 December 1935, Maço 29,644 (1,291), AHI-R.
10. Aranha (Washington, D.C.) to Vargas, 19 May 1937, OA 37.05.19, CPDOC-R; Theodore Michael Berson, "A Political Biography of Dr. Oswaldo Aranha of Brazil, 1930–1937" (Ph.D. diss., New York University, 1971), 265.
11. Jorge Latour (Warsaw), 8 November 1936, Maço 9,650 (622), AHI-R.
12. Valentim da Silva Alvim (Belo Horizonte) to Vargas, 22 August 1937, National Department of Mineral Production in the Ministry of Agriculture Memo no. 2,947, 21 September 1937, Fundo Secretaria da Presidência da República, 2,947/39-Série Ministério da Agricultura, lata 103 (27,569), AN-R. Documents courtesy of Cliff Welch.
13. Valentim Gentil (secretary of agriculture) to Hildebrando Accioly, 11 March 1937, N.S. 1,611 558.(72), Maço 29,630 (1,291), AHI-R; J. R. de Barros e Pimental to Macedo Soares, 30 September 1936, Maço 9,650 (622), AHI-R; Pimental Brandão to Luiz de Toledo Piza Sobrinho (São Paulo state secretary of agriculture), 5 November 1936, Maço 9,650 (622), AHI-R; Carneiro, *O anti-semitismo*, 155–64.
14. J. Vieira da Piosa to Filinto Müller, 27 November 1937, FM 35.07.15 chp/ad, CPDOC-R; Darcy Duque Viriato Catão to Müller, 16 October 1937, 35.02.21 chp/ad 1,129–77, CPDOC-R. See also Cytrynowicz, "Integralismo e anti-semitismo," 160–61.
15. "Brazil and German Refugees," Department of State, Memorandum of Conversation, 15 February 1939, 832.55 J/1, NARC-W; Kurt Loewenstein, *Brazil under Vargas* (New York: Macmillan, 1942), 180.

16. Herbert Frankenstein, *Brasilien: Als Aufnahmeland der jüdischen Auswanderung aus Deutschland* (Berlin: Joseph Jastrow Verlagsbuchhandlung, 1936).

17. Although entry quotas demanded that 80 percent of all immigrants to Brazil be farmers or rural workers, 1937 statistics published by the Brazilian Institute of Geography and Statistics (which was part of the Ministry of Foreign Affairs) show that only 22 percent actually were. See Brazil, Instituto Brasileiro de Geografia e Estatística, *Brazil 1938: A New Survey of Brazilian Life* (Rio de Janeiro: Serviço Gráfico do Instituto Brasileiro de Geografia e Estatística, 1939), 43–45.

18. For more on the birth and death of Rezende, see Avraham Milgram, "A colonização agrícola a refugiados judeus no Brasil, 1936–1939," *Proceedings of the Tenth World Congress of Jewish Studies* (Jerusalem: World Union of Jewish Studies, 1990), 583–93.

19. *RACCA* 1937, p. 66, AHJB-SP.

20. "Rapport sur l'activité de la JCA" (December 1936–January 1937), SCA (30 February 1937), 1:131, JCA-L; Sir Osmond D'Avigdor-Goldsmid (London) to Under Secretary of State (London), 29 April 1937, SCA (29 June 1937), 1:113, JCA-L.

21. Mr. Coote (Rio de Janeiro) to British Foreign Office (London), 23 September 1937, FO 371/2,060 A 6,925/78/6, PRO-L.

22. Labienne Salgado dos Santos, "Inconvenientes da emigração semita," attached to Ciro de Freitas Vale (Bucharest) to Aranha, 12 September 1938, Maço 10.561 (741), AHI-R.

23. Müller to Campos, 5 February 1938, Maço 10.561 (741), AHI-R.

24. Milgram, "A colonização agrícola," 585.

25. Dulphe Pinheiro Machado, 9 January 1937, PRCNE-Série Intercâmbio Comercial, lata 174, no. 468-1936, AN-R.

26. Hugh Gurney (British Embassy, Rio de Janeiro) to Anthony Eden (Principal Secretary of State, London), 31 December 1936, FO 371/20,604 A78/78/6, pp. 15–17, PRO-L.

27. Gurney (Rio de Janeiro) to Mr. Troutbeck (London), 1 April 1937, FO 371/20,604 A2,910/78/6, PRO-L; R. G. Gahagon (Foreign Office, London) to Sir Osmond D'Avigdor-Goldsmid (London), 27 April 1937, FO 371/20,604 A2,910/78/6, PRO-L.

28. Leo S. Rowe (Washington, D.C.) to Aranha (Rio de Janeiro), 5 April 1937, OA 37.04.05, CPDOC-R.

29. Department of State Memorandum of Conversation between Alfred Houston, Laurence Duggan, and Mr. Manning (Division of American Republics), 16 February 1938, 832.52 Germans/10 LH, NARC-W.

30. Coote (Rio) to British Foreign Office (London), 23 September 1937, FO 371/2,060 A 6,925/78/6, PRO-L.

31. *Diário Oficial—Estado do Rio de Janeiro*, 6 April 1938.

32. Heinz Lewinsky, interview by Denise Simanke, Oral History Archives of the Instituto Cultural Judaico Marc Chagall, Porto Alegre.

33. *Diário Oficial—Estado do Rio de Janeiro*, 6 April 1938.

34. *O Carioca* (Rio de Janeiro), 6 April 1938; *Correio da Manhã*, 6 April 1938; *A Opinião* (Rezende), 9 April 1938; *A Lyra* (Rezende), 7 April 1938.

35. "Exposição das demarches feitas pela JEWISH COLONIZATION AS-SOCIATION junto ao Governo Brasileiro, com o propósito de trazer imigrantes agricultores para sua Fazenda de Rezende, Estado do Rio," PRRE, box 27.586, document 185,660–1938, AN-R.

36. *Idische Presse* (Rio de Janeiro), 8 July 1938; *Diário de Notícias*, 19 October 1938.

37. *A Noite* (Rio de Janeiro), 30 June 1938.

38. *Diário de Notícias*, 19 October 1938.

39. *A Noite*, 30 June 1938.

40. "Report of Mr. Tracy Phillips, 13 January 1939," SCA (6 May 1939), vol. 2, JCA-L.

41. ICA (Rio de Janeiro) to Louis Oungre (ICA, New York), 9 December 1942, fundo ICA, box 14 (Diverse Correspondence re: Rezende, 1936–1944), AHJB-SP.

42. Loewenstein, *Brazil under Vargas*, 180; Foreign Office Minutes, 5 March 1937, FO 371/20,604 A1,830/78/6, 20–22, PRO-L.

43. Figueiredo Rodrigues, "Contra a revogação dos 6 e 7 do artigo 121 da constituição: Discurso pronunciado na sessão de 3 de março de 1937," in Xavier de Oliveira, *O problema imigratório*, 119.

44. Darcy Duque Viriato Catão to Filinto Müller, 16 November 1937, FM 33.02.21 chp/ad II 29–77, CPDOC-R.

45. Müller to Campos, 5 February 1938, p. 20, Maço 10.561 (741), AHI-R.

46. "Imigração: Parecer do Dr. Euvaldo Lodi," 7 December 1936, p. 1, attached to letter of Sebastião Sampaio, "O problema da imigração," to Getúlio Vargas, 10 December 1936, PRCNE-Série Intercâmbio Comercial, lata 174, no. 468-1936, AN-R. While Lodi's antirefugee position was typical, he was frequently at odds with other regime insiders, notably Filinto Müller and Francisco Campos, on other matters.

47. Pedro M. da Rocha, "Tópico da comunicação do chefe do escritório comercial do ministério do trabalho na Polônia que a requerimento do conselheiro Raul Leite, deve ser remetido ao chefe de polícia, ao ministério do trabalho e a câmara dos deputados em carácter confidencial," n.d., PRCNE-Série Intercâmbio Comercial, lata 174, no. 468-1936, AN-R. For a treatment of how Jews, and other minority groups, came to be seen as "unclean," see Carneiro, *O anti-semitismo*, 98–121 and 155–214.

48. Jorge Latour to Pimentel Brandão, 19 April 1937, Maço 9,650 (622), AHI-R.

49. C. Alves de Souza, 20 August 1938, Maço 9,601 (612), AHI-R.

50. da Rocha, "Tópico da comunicação," PRCNE-Serie Intercâmbio Comercial, AN-R.

51. Martins, *História da inteligência brasileira*, vol. 7, *1933–1960*, 93–96; Cabral, *A questão judaica*; Maciel, *Nacionalismo: O problema judaico*.

52. Müller to Campos, 5 February 1938, p. 21, Maço 10.561 (741), AHI-R.

53. Freitas Vale, for example, circulated Salgado dos Santos's "small study . . . on the inconveniences of Semitic emigration." See Ciro de Freitas Vale (Bucharest) to Aranha, 12 September 1938, Maço 10.561 (741), AHI-R.

54. Kennedy to Hull, 8 December 1938, 840.48 Refugees/1,072, in United States, Department of State, *Foreign Relations of the United States, Diplomatic Papers*, vol. 1, *1938* (Washington, D.C.: Government Printing Office, 1955), 862.

55. dos Santos, "Inconvenientes da Emigração Semita," Maço 10.561 (741), AHI-R.

56. See, for example, the covers of the weekly *Careta* (Rio de Janeiro) for 9 April 1938, 17 September 1938, and 10 October 1938. Also see Carneiro, *O anti-semitismo*, 418–58.

57. da Rocha, "Tópico da comunicação," PRCNE-Serie Intercâmbio Comercial, AN-R.

58. Jacob Katz, *From Prejudice to Destruction: Anti-Semitism, 1700–1933* (Cambridge: Harvard University Press, 1980), 260.

59. "Projecto de Decreto-Lei: Regulada a entrada de indivíduos de nacionalidade judaica, no território nacional," 558.(99), Maço 10.561 (741), AHI-R.

60. Mário Moreira da Silva to Aranha, 4 April 1938, Maço 558 (770), AHI-R.

61. Secret memo no. 115 of Mário Moreira da Silva to Aranha, 10 September 1938, Maço 10.561 (741), AHI-R.

62. Roberto da Matta, *Carnivals, Rogues, and Heroes: An Interpretation of the Brazilian Dilemma* (Notre Dame, Ind.: University of Notre Dame Press, 1991), 183–89.

63. Conselho Federal de Comércio Exterior, "Imigração indiana no Brasil," 13 September 1937, PRCNE-Série Intercâmbio Comercial, lata 174, no. 468, v. 4., 1937, AN-R.

64. "Estatísticas do movimento pelo porto de Santos durante ano 1937," Secretaria da Agricultura, Indústria, e Comércio, Inspetor de Imigração (Santos), 24 February 1937, no. 1,749, series 3,845, box 0100, Fundo: Hospedaria dos Imigrantes, Secção: Documentação Administrativa, Série 2, Processos, Archives of the Secretaria de Estado da Promoção Social-Centro Histórico do Imigrante (São Paulo). From the early nineteenth century onward, the term *Jew* was considered pejorative and thus the use of words like *Israelite* and *Hebrew* were considered polite neutral euphemisms by Jews and non-Jews alike. Of course, such terms could easily be used in a derogatory way by anti-Semites.

65. Secret Circular 1,127, "Entrada de estrangeiros no território nacional," art. 3c., Maço 29.653–29.655 (1,292), AHI-R; "Discourse of João Carlos Muniz on the Inauguration of the CIC," n.d., Secretaria da Presidência da República, Conselho de Imigração e Colonização, p. 3, CIC-PR/SC 3,117–2,197, AN-R.

66. On Secret Circular 1,127, see Alberto Dines, *Morte no paraíso: A tra-*

gédia de Stefan Zweig no país do futuro (Rio de Janeiro: Nova Fronteira, 1981), 281; Falbel, *Estudos,* 52–53; and Carneiro, *O anti-semitismo,* 166–77.

67. Secret Circular 1,127, art. 3f, AHI-R.

68. Secret memo of Conde de Ouro Preto to Ciro de Freitas Vale, 13 December 1937, NP/28, Maço 29,656/57 (1,292), AHI-R.

69. Secret circular 1,127, arts. 3h and 3i.

70. Almeida, *Cosmópolis;* Rollie E. Poppino, *Brazil: The Land and People* (New York: Oxford University Press, 1973), 194; Richard B. Morse, *From Community to Metropolis: A Biography of São Paulo, Brazil* (Gainesville: University of Florida Press, 1958), 175; R. A., "A assimilação do elemento estrangeiro em São Paulo: Notas etnológicas sobre os israelitas," *Planalto* 1:3 (15 June 1941); Manuel Diégues, Jr., *Etnias e cultura no Brasil,* 5th ed. (São Paulo: Círculo do Livro, 1976), 147; Eva Alterman Blay, "As duas memórias: Pequena história da imigração judaica," *Shalom* 19:223 (August 1984), 7; Lesser, "From Pedlars to Proprietors," 393–410.

71. Aziz Maron was only one in a long list of Syrian/Lebanese politicians who began attaining office in the late 1930s. The Partido Trabalhista Brasileiro was formed in 1945 during the period of redemocratization following eight years of near dictatorial rule by Getúlio Vargas. The PTB, however, was created with Vargas's open encouragement by those who hoped he would continue his political influence in democratic Brazil.

72. Jafet was one of the leading members of the 350,000-strong Lebanese community in Brazil. Lafer was of equal standing among the approximately 100,000 Jews in the country. See Elie Safa, *L'émigration libanaise* (Beirut: Université Saint-Joseph, 1960), 54–68; and Malamud, *Do arquivo e da memória.*

73. José Queiroz, *222 anedotas de Getúlio Vargas: Anedotário popular, irreverente e pitoresco. Getúlio no Inferno. Getúlio no Céu.* (Rio de Janeiro: Companhia Brasileira de Artes Gráficas, 1955), 179.

74. Katz, *From Prejudice to Destruction,* 136.

75. George L. Mosse, *Toward the Final Solution: A History of European Racism* (New York: Howard Fertig, 1978), 205.

76. Oliveira Vianna, "Os imigrantes semíticos e mongóis e sua caraterização antropológica," *RIC* 1:4 (October 1940), 610–16.

77. "Discourse of João Carlos Muniz on the Inauguration of the CIC," n.d., Secretaria da Presidência da República, Conselho de Imigração e Colonização, CIC-PR/SC 3,117-2,197, AN-R.

78. Edgardo Barbedo to Pimentel Brandão, 30 December 1937, Maço 9,650 (622), AHI-R.

79. Dulphe Pinheiro Machado to Hildebrando Accioly, 20 November 1937, DNP 4,941/37, Maço 9,600 (612), AHI-R.

80. Consulate General (New York) to Mario de Pimentel Brandão, 5 November 1937, Maço 9,600 (612), AHI-R.

81. Ella Pfeffer (Vienna) to Vargas, 30 March 1938, PRRE, box 27.586, document 8,155, AN-R.

82. Secret Circular 1,127, art. 3d., Maço 29.653–29.655 (1,292), AHI-R.

83. The widow Braumann and her daughter Theodora Meland were in fact Catholics and were considered "good racial elements and useful to society." See

Conde de Ouro Preto to Filinto Müller, 24 November 1937, SP/162/558, Maço 9,600 (612), AHI-R.

84. Harry Weinberg (Milan) to Vargas, 1 April 1938, PRRE, box 27.586, document 8,136, AN-R.

85. Elizabeth Cancelli, "O Mundo da violência: Repressão e estado policial na era Vargas (1930–1945)" (Ph.D. diss., Department of History, University of Campinas, 1991), 254–55.

86. Edgardo Barbedo to Jewish Central Emigration Association of Poland, 21 July 1937, trans. from Polish by the HICEM, HIAS-Brazil, folder 4, YIVO-NY.

87. Marc Leitchik, "Memorandum se rapportant aux différents problèmes migratoires en corrélation avec la situation politique actuelle au Brésil, présenté à la direction de la HIAS-JCA EMIGRATION ASSOCIATION," 10 January 1937, SCA (20 March 1937), p. 127, JCA-L.

88. Aronstein (Washington, D.C.) to HICEM (Paris), n.d., HIAS-Brazil, folder 4, YIVO-NY.

89. Aronstein to HICEM, n.d., HIAS-Brazil, folder 4, YIVO-NY; "Procedure to Follow for the Legalization of the Status of Tourists," HIAS-Brazil, folder 5, YIVO-NY.

90. Ronald M. Schneider, *"Order and Progress": A Political History of Brazil* (Boulder, Colo.: Westview Press, 1991), 136.

91. Levine, *The Vargas Regime,* 138.

92. Eli Diniz, "O Estado Novo: Estrutura de poder, relações de classes," in *O Brasil republicano: Sociedade e política (1930–1964),* ed. Boris Fausto (São Paulo: Difel, 1985), 3:3, 107.

93. Hélio Silva with Maria Cecília Carneiro and José Augusto Drummond, *A ameaça vermelha: O plano Cohen* (Porto Alegre: L and PM Editores, 1980); Levine, *The Vargas Regime,* 145; Carlos Lacerda, *A missão da imprensa* (Rio de Janeiro: Livraria AGIR Editora, 1950), 61.

94. Edgard Carone, *A terceira república (1937–1945)* (Sao Paulo: Difel/Difusão Editorial, 1976), 7–8.

95. Olympio Mourão Filho, "Minha defesa," in Silva et al., *A ameaça vermelha,* 142. In an interview with the magazine *Manchete,* Olympio Mourão Filho commented that the leader he had referred to was Gustavo Barroso. See *Manchete,* 11 November 1958.

96. Cytrynowicz, "Integralismo e anti-semitismo," 216.

97. Carone, *A terceira república,* 26–28.

98. Consul General William C. Burdett to Hull, 31 December 1937, 832.55/131, NARC-W.

99. Edward Coote (Rio de Janeiro) to A. Holman (Foreign Office, London), 28 December 1937, FO 372/3,276 107,337 T 1,231/479/378, PRO-L.

100. Burdett to Hull, "Anti-Semitic Influence in Brazilian Immigration Service," 21 December 1937, 832.55/128, NARC-W.

101. Burdett to Caffery, 31 December 1937, 832.55/131, NARC-W.

102. Burdett to Hull, "Anti-Semitic Influence."

103. Scotten to Hull, "Jewish Visitors to Brazil," 31 December 1937, 832.55/130, NARC-W.

104. Scotten to Hull, "Jewish Visitors to Brazil."

105. Aranha to Pimental Brandão, 2 December 1937, EM/1/2/XII/37, Maço 9,600 (612), AHI-R.

106. Scotten to Hull, "Jewish Visitors to Brazil."

107. Stanley E. Hilton, "The United States and Argentina in Brazil's Wartime Foreign Policy, 1939–1945," in *Argentina between the Great Powers, 1939–1946*, ed. Guido di Tella and D. Cameron Watt (Pittsburgh, Pa.: University of Pittsburgh Press, 1990), 158–80; Levine, *The Vargas Regime*, 154.

108. Caffery to Sec. of State, 4 January 1938, 832.55 German/6, NARC-W.

109. British Foreign Office to J. Teller, 28 March 1938, C11/12/4, folder 3, BODBJ-L.

110. Scotten to Hull, 4 January 1938, 832.55/132, NARC-W.

111. Anthony Eden to Gurney (Rio de Janeiro), 26 January 1938, FO 372/3,276 107,337 T 479/479/378, PRO-L.

112. Montague Meyer to Foreign Office, 11 February 1938, FO372/3,276 107,337 T2,038/479/378, PRO-L.

113. Gurney to Anthony Eden, 18 February 1938, FO 372/3,276 107,337 T 262/479/378, PRO-L.

114. Burdett to Hull, 14 January 1938, 832.55/135, NARC-W.

115. Francisco Campos, "A técnica do estado totalitário a serviço da democracia," in *O estado nacional: Sua estructura, seu conteúdo ideológico* (Rio de Janeiro: José Olympio Editora, 1941).

116. "La situation politique au Brésil," 20 November 1937, no author, C11/12/4 folder 2, BODBJ-L; Marc Leitchik to HIAS, 2 December 1937, HIAS-Brazil, folder 4, YIVO-NY; Scotten to Hull, "Immigration into Brazil," 17 December 1937, SP 832.55/127, NARC-W.

117. "La situation politique au Brésil."

118. Scotten to Hull, "Immigration into Brazil."

119. Laurence Duggan, Department of State Memorandum of Conversation, 3 December 1937, 832.52 German/2, NARC-W.

120. Duggan memorandum, German/2.

121. Duggan memorandum, German/2.

122. Duggan memorandum, German/2.

123. Duggan memorandum, German/2.

124. Duggan memorandum, German/2.

125. Laurence Duggan, Department of State Memorandum of Conversation, 8 December 1937, 832.52 German/4 LH, NARC-W.

126. Duggan memorandum, German/4 LH.

127. "Memorandum of Audience Granted by Dr. Getúlio Vargas, President of Brazil, to Sr. Oswaldo Aranha, Ambassador of Brazil to the U.S.A. and to Mr. Alfred Houston of New York, at the Palácio Catête on January 3, 1938," attached to Scotten to Hull, 7 January 1938, 832.52 German/7 L/H1, NARC-W.

128. Scotten to Hull, "Immigration into Brazil."

129. Gurney to British Foreign Office, 16 December 1937, FO371/20,604 A9,186/78/6, PRO-L.

130. "Memorandum of Audience," attached to Scotten to Hull, 7 January 1938.

131. Scotten to Hull, "Immigration into Brazil."

132. "Memorandum of Audience," attached to Scotten to Hull, 7 January 1938.

133. "Memorandum of Audience," attached to Scotten to Hull, 7 January 1938.

134. "Memorandum of Audience," attached to Scotten to Hull, 7 January 1938.

135. "Memorandum of Audience," attached to Scotten to Hull, 7 January 1938.

136. "Memorandum of Audience," attached to Scotten to Hull, 7 January 1938.

137. Turner Catledge (Rio de Janeiro), "Brazil Repudiates Any Fascist Aims; Pleads for Amity," *New York Times,* 12 January 1938.

138. Caffery to Hull, 12 January 1938, 832.52 German/7–1/2 L/JPS, NARC-W.

139. Department of State Memorandum of Conversation between Alfred Houston, Laurence Duggan, and Mr. Manning (Division of American Republics), 16 February 1938, 832.52 Germans/10 LH, NARC-W.; Scotten to Hull, 10 February 1938, 832.52 Germans/9 LH, NARC-W.

140. Department of State Memorandum of Conversation between Alfred Houston and Mr. Manning (Division of American Republics), 19 April 1938, 832.52 Germans/13 LH, NARC-W.

141. Caffery to Hull, 12 May 1938, 832.55/146, NARC-W.

142. Catledge, "Brazil Repudiates Any Fascist Aims."

143. *Correio da Manhã,* 28 November 1938; *New York Times,* 29 November 1938.

144. Caffery to Hull, "Jewish Residents in Brazil," 8 March 1938, 832.55/138, NARC-W.

145. René Gertz, *O perigo alemão* (Porto Alegre: Editora da Universidade Federal do Rio Grande do Sul, 1991); Levine, *The Vargas Regime,* 27.

146. Carone, *A terceira república,* 161.

147. Decree law N. 383; *Diário Oficial da República* (Rio de Janeiro), 19 April 1938, 7,357–59.

148. Bandeira, *Presença dos Estados Unidos,* 261.

149. Ricardo Silva Seitenfus, "Ideology and Diplomacy: Italian Fascism and Brazil (1935–38)," *Hispanic American Historical Review* 64:3 (August 1984), 528.

150. Gurney to Viscount Halifax, 9 August 1938, FO 371/21,427 A 6,671/527/6, 373, PRO-L; *O Estado de São Paulo,* 5 August 1938.

151. Cohen, *Jewish Life in South America,* 26.

152. In Europe, as in Brazil, groups were divided over what the proper conception of Zionism should be. See Vital, *Origins of Zionism.*

153. Ludwig Lorch resigned from the executive board of the CIP in 1945 after clashing with Italian Zionists in the congregation. See "Interview of Dr. Walter Rehfeld by Rabbi Clifford Kulwin," July 1982, tape C-470, side a, AJA-C.

154. Veit and Camerini to President of Zionist Organization (London), 24 December 1945, CZA-J, ZU/10,229, p. 2.

155. The *Keren Hayesod* was founded in 1920 as the financial arm of the World Zionist Organization.

156. Memorandum of unnamed Brazilian correspondent of the Jewish Telegraphic Agency (JTA) to Jacob Landau, sent by Landau to Joseph C. Hyman of the American Jewish Joint Distribution Committee, 22 April 1938, Archives of the American Jewish Joint Distribution Committee, New York City, file 1,092.

157. Fritz Pinkuss, interview by author, São Paulo, 1 September 1986. Fritz Pinkuss was the first rabbi of the Congregação Israelita Paulista.

158. According to Alfred Hirschberg, "two thirds of [the German Jews in São Paulo] are registered with the . . . Congregação Israelita Paulista." See Hirschberg, "The Economic Adjustment," 31.

159. "Report of Friedrich Borchardt and David Glick," 27 June 1939, Rhodes Collection, box 2,249, AJA-C.

160. Malamud, *Do arquivo e da memória,* 25, n. 5.

161. Minutes of report on interview with Jacob Schneider, 2 November 1924, CZA-J, ZU/2,350, p. 2. Emphasis in original.

162. Bruno and Lena Castelnuove to Rachelle S. Yarden, 14 June 1945, CZA-J, s5/779, no. 244.

163. Secção de Ordem Social, *Relatório do ano de 1941: Sociedades estrangeiras,* 14, Arquivo Municipal de Rio Claro.

164. Leitchik, "Memorandum se rapportant aux différents problèmes migratoires," 10 January 1937, SCA (20 March 1937), 138, JCA-L.

165. Cohen, *Jewish Life,* 26.

166. *Avanhandava* is also understood to mean "waterfall." It is the name of a number of neighborhoods in the city of São Paulo as well as a city in the interior of the state. See Alfredo Moreira Pinto, *Apontamentos para o dicionário geográfico do Brasil* (Rio de Janeiro: Imprensa Nacional, 1894), 173; A. Gonzales Dias, *Dicionário da língua Tupy: Chamada língua geral dos indígenas do Brasil* (Leipzig: Brockhaus, 1858), 3; João Barbosa Rodrigues, *Vocabulário indígena com a orthographia correcta (complemento da poranduba amazonense)* (Rio de Janeiro: Typ. de G. Leuzinger & Filhos, 1893), 1. I would like to thank the members of the Brasnet computer network for their prompt responses to my queries on this subject.

167. Cohen, *Jewish Life,* 27.

168. Decree law 406 (4 May 1938), art. 92; Caffery to Hull, "New Brazilian Immigration Law," 9 May 1938, 832.55/145, NARC-W.

169. Decree law 406, art. 2; Caffery to Hull, 13 May 1938, 832.55/144, NARC-W.

170. Major Lawrence C. Mitchell (U.S. military attaché in Brazil), "Home Environment and Living Conditions—Immigration Law of 1938," 4 June 1938, p. 6., 832.55/151, NARC-W.

171. Stafford to Hull, "Deportation of Aliens from Brazil," 10 May 1938, 832.55/148. NARC-W.

172. Decree law 406, arts. 95 and 93.

173. Decree law 406, art. 42.

174. Decree law 406, arts. 39 and 40.

175. Decree law 406, art. 91; Mitchell, "Home Environment."

176. "Report of Mr. Tracy Phillips, 13 January 1939," SCA (6 May 1939) 2:5, JCA-L.

177. Jorge de Lima, *Os judeus* (Rio de Janeiro: n.p., 1938); Afrânio Piexoto, ed., *Os judeus na história do Brasil*; Dario Vellozo and Pahphilo D'Assumpção, introduction to Schulman, *Em legítima defeza*.

178. Schulman, *Em legítima defeza*, 25. Some information on Schulman may be found in Falbel, *Estudos*, 161–86.

179. "Contra a revogação dos 6 e 7 do artigo 121 da constituição: Discurso pronunciado na sessão de 3 de março de 1937," in Xavier de Oliveira, *O problema imigratório*, 119.

180. Loewenstein, *Brazil under Vargas*, 179; Lauerhass, "Getúlio Vargas," 147.

181. Robert F. Woodward to Mr. Butler and Mr. Duggan, Department of State, Division of Latin American Affairs Memorandum, 8 August 1938, 832.55/152, NARC-W; decree law 639 (20 August 1938), art. 1, par. b; Department of State-Division of Latin American Affairs Memorandum, 8 August 1938, 832.55/152, NARC-W.

182. Francisca Pereira Rodrigues, *O braço estrangeiro* (São Paulo: Imprensa Oficial do Estado, 1938), 145.

183. Maciel, *Nacionalismo: O problema judaico*, especially pp. 45–67, 99–104, and 131–42.

184. A short overview of Brazilian anti-Semitic literature can be found in Martins, *História da inteligência brasileira*, 7:93–96.

185. "Discourse of João Carlos Muniz on the Inauguration of the CIC," n.d., Secretaria da Presidência da República, Conselho de Imigração e Colonização, p. 1, CIC-PR/SC 3,117–2,197, AN-R; Artur Hehl Neiva, "Estudos sobre a imigração semita no Brasil," *RIC* 5:2 (June 1944), 215; decree law 406 (4 May 1938) and decree law 3.010 (20 August 1938); Jorge Emilio de Souza Freitas, "Primeiro ano de trabalhos do conselho de imigração e colonização," *RIC* 1:1 (January 1940), 5.

186. U.S. Department of State Memo of Conversation with João Carlos Muniz, 15 February 1939, 832.55 J/1, NARC-W; "Discourse of João Carlos Muniz," p. 3.

187. C. Alves de Souza to Aranha, 29 July 1938, Maço 9,601 (612), AHI-R.

188. Eric Estorick, "The Evian Conference and the Intergovernmental Committee," *Annals of the American Academy of Political and Social Science* 203 (May 1939), 136–41.

189. Henry L. Feingold, *The Politics of Rescue: The Roosevelt Administration and the Holocaust, 1938–1945* (New Brunswick, N.J.: Rutgers University Press, 1970), 31; Saul S. Friedman, *No Haven for the Oppressed: United States Policy toward Jewish Refugees 1938–1945* (Detroit, Mich.: Wayne State University Press, 1973), 61.

190. Friedman, *No Haven for the Oppressed*, 56.

191. C. Alves de Souza, 20 August 1938, Maço 9601 (612), AHI-R.

192. Feingold, *The Politics of Rescue*, 101.

193. Henry Feingold, "Roosevelt and the Resettlement Question," in *Res-*

cue Attempts during the Holocaust: Proceedings of the Second Yad Vashem International Historical Conference, ed. Yisrael Gutman and Efraim Zuroff (Jerusalem: Yad Vashem, 1977), 137.

194. Samuel Guy Inman, "Refugee Settlement in Latin America," *Annals of the American Academy of Political and Social Science* 203 (May 1939), 185; secret memo of Mário Moreira da Silva to Aranha, 4 April 1938, Maço 558 (99), AHI-R.

195. "Proceedings of the Intergovernmental Committee, Evian, July 6th to 15th, 1938: Record of the Plenary Meetings of the Committee, Resolutions and Reports (London, 1938)," in *Documents on the Holocaust: Selected Sources on the Destruction of the Jews of Germany and Austria, Poland, and the Soviet Union,* ed. Yitzhak Arad, Yisrael Gutman, and Abraham Margaliot (Jerusalem: Yad Vashem and KTAV Publishing, 1981), 17–18.

196. Telegram of Myron Taylor (Evian) to Secretary of State Hull, 14 July 1938, 840.48 Refugees/513, in *FRUS-1938,* 1:754.

197. As will be seen in chapter 6, Lobo was instrumental in both the birth and death of a plan to bring a group of three thousand so-called Catholic non-Aryans to Brazil.

198. "Proceedings of the Intergovernmental Committee," in Arad, Gutman, and Margaliot, *Documents on the Holocaust,* 95–98.

199. Hull to Caffery, 22 August 1938, 840.48 Refugees/677 CDG, NARC-W.

200. Hull to Scotten, 3 August 1938, 840.48 Refugees/611b, in *FRUS-1938,* 1:758–59.

201. Scotten to Hull, 17 August 1938, 840.48 Refugees/670, NARC-W; Hull to Scotten, 3 August 1938, *FRUS-1938,* 1:759.

202. Johnson (chargé in the U.K.) to Hull, 16 August 1938, 840.48 Refugees/663, in *FRUS, 1938* I, 767; Leonardo Senkman, "Argentina's Immigration Policy during the Holocaust (1938–1945)," *Yad Vashem Studies* 21 (1991), 155–88.

203. Scottten to Hull, 17 August 1938, p. 2.

204. Scottten to Hull, 17 August 1938, p. 3.

205. Hull to Caffery, 18 August 1938, 840.48 Refugees/670, NARC-W.

206. Caffery to Hull, 25 August 1938, p. 2, 840.48 Refugees/693, NARC-W; Caffery to Hull, 19 August 1938, 840.48 Refugees/677, NARC-W.

207. Caffery to Hull, 19 August 1938, p. 2.

208. Caffery to Taylor and Rublee (London), 22 August 1938, 840.48 Refugees/691, NARC-W.

209. Hull to Caffery, 22 August 1938, p. 2, 840.48 Refugees/677 CDG, NARC-W.

210. Johnson (chargé in the U.K.) to Hull, 25 August 1938, 840.48 Refugees/694, NARC-W.

211. Francis Biddle (U.S. ambassador to Poland) to Hull, 30 August 1938, 840.48 Refugees/707, In *FRUS, 1938* I, 778.

212. Hull to Biddle, 1 September 1938, 840.48 Refugees/707, in *FRUS, 1938* I, 783.

213. Joseph P. Kennedy (U.S. ambassador to the U.K.) to Hull, 1 September 1938, 840.48 Refugees/711, in *FRUS, 1938* I, 781.

214. Kennedy to Hull, 1 September 1938.

215. Hull to Kennedy, 2 September 1938, 840.48 Refugees/711, in *FRUS, 1938* I, 785.

216. Secret telegram EM/21/21/IX/38, 21 September 1938, Maço 9,652 (622), AHI-R; Susan Zuccotti, *The Italians and the Holocaust: Persecution, Rescue and Survival* (New York: Basic Books, 1987), 28–51.

217. *Pester Lloyd* (Budapest), 1 September 1938.

218. Scotten to Hull, 23 November 1938, 840.48 Refugees/963 G/HC, NARC-W.

219. "Secret Circular 1,249: The Entrance of Jews in National Territory," 27 September 1938, Secretaria da Presidência da República, Conselho de Imigração e Colonização, CIC-PR/SC 3,117–2,197, AN-R.

220. "A batalha contra a imigração: Anti-semitismo e xenofobia," *O Estado de São Paulo*, 14 November 1948, 2.

221. Letter of D. Bourke-Borrowes in the *Times* (London), 4 November 1938; Brazilian Embassy to Aranha, 4 November 1938, 638 558.(99), Maço 10.561 (741), AHI-R.

222. On the use of visas by refugees, see Nathan Eck, "The Rescue of Jews with Aid of Passports and Citizenship Papers of the Latin American States," in *Yad Vashem Studies on the European Jewish Catastrophe and Resistance,* ed. Benzion Dinur and Shaul Esh (Jerusalem: Yad Vashem, 1957), 125–52.

223. Scotten to Hull, 9 December 1938, 832.00/1,241 LH, NARC-W.

224. *Daily Telegraph* (London), 16 June 1938; *Times Picayune* (New Orleans), 7 March 1939.

225. Scotten to Hull, 23 November 1938, 840.48 Refugees/963 G/HC, NARC-W.

226. Kennedy to Hull, 3 December 1938, 840.48 Refugees/103, in *FRUS, 1938*, I, 852.

227. Johnson to Hull, 22 December 1938, 840.48 Refugees/1,169, in *FRUS, 1938*, I, 881.

228. David S. Wyman, *Paper Walls: America and the Refugee Crisis 1938–1941* (Amherst: University of Massachusetts Press, 1968), 51; Michael R. Marrus, *The Unwanted: European Refugees in the Twentieth Century* (New York: Oxford University Press, 1985), 166–76.

4. ANTI-SEMITISM AND PHILO-SEMITISM?

1. Except where noted, all figures regarding the number of Jewish immigrants to Brazil discussed in this chapter are based on the number of legal visas granted to Jews and accepted by Brazilian authorities.

2. Such stereotypes flowed directly from those that began in Europe in the mid-nineteenth century. See Robert M. Seltzer, *Jewish People, Jewish Thought: The Jewish Experience in History* (New York: Macmillan, 1980), 627–34; and Lucy S. Dawidowicz, *The War against the Jews, 1933–1945* (Toronto: Bantam Books, 1976), 29–62.

3. David S. Wyman, *The Abandonment of the Jews: America and the Holo-*

caust, 1941–1945 (New York: Pantheon Books, 1984), 178–92; Irving Abella and Harold Troper, *None Is Too Many: Canada and the Jews of Europe, 1933–1948* (New York: Random House, 1982), 101–26; Michael Blakeney, *Australia and the Jewish Refugees, 1933–1948* (Sydney: Croom Helm Australia, 1985), 101–21; Wasserstein, *Britain and the Jews of Europe*, 1–39.

4. Aranha to Adhemar de Barros, 20 October 1938, Maço 9,601 (612), AHI-R. The anti-Semitic component to Aranha's thought has been examined briefly by Theodore Michael Berson, "A Political Biography of Dr. Oswaldo Aranha of Brazil, 1930–1937" (Ph.D. diss., New York University, 1971), 265; and more carefully by Carneiro, *O anti-semitismo*, 258–95.

5. Aranha, for example, proposed that a U.S. public-relations firm be hired and that journalists be paid for image-enhancing stories. See Aranha to Vargas, 19 May, 4 June, 24 September, and 27 November 1937, OA 37.19. 5, OA 37.4.6, OA 37.24.9, OA 37.11.27, CPDOC-R.

6. Aranha to Vargas, 30 November 1937, EM/30/30/XI/37, Maço 9,857 (660), AHI-R.

7. Hirschberg, "The Economic Adjustment," 37.

8. Angelo Trento, *Do outro lado do Atlântico: Um século de imigração italiana no Brasil* (São Paulo: Nobel, 1989), 383–84.

9. Getúlio Vargas, 11 April 1939, attached to Scotten to Hull, 14 April 1939, 832.00/1,253, NARC-W.

10. *Correio da Manhã*, 10 November 1940; *Diário Oficial da República*, 27 November 1940.

11. *Correio da Manhã*, 2 September 1939.

12. *Christian Science Monitor*, 17 November 1938.

13. Rosalina Coelho Lisboa to Vargas, n.d., GV 40.09.00/4, CPDOC-R.

14. Herzl was wrong. Most nineteenth-century national political leaders were unwilling to invest time, money, or land in the creation of a Jewish state. See Amos Elon, *Herzl* (New York: Holt, Rinehart and Winston, 1975), 195–212.

15. [illegible] to Aranha, 8 March 1939, Maço 10,561 (741), AHI-R.

16. Philip Williams, "Brazilian Immigration," 22 May 1939, 832.55/174, NARC-W.

17. Carneiro, *O anti-semitismo*, 277–82.

18. Cora Meyer to Luiza Aranha, 15 December 1942, GV 42.01.05/2, CPDOC-R; O. Aranha to L. Aranha, 17 December 1941, GV 42.01.05/2, CPDOC-R.

19. The story of the visa refusal in 1941 is recounted in Claude Lévi-Strauss, *A World on the Wane* (New York: Criterion Books, 1961), 24.

20. Lindolfo Collor, *Europa 1939* (Rio de Janeiro: EMIEL Editora, 1939), 161.

21. Itamaraty to Embassy in London 511.14 (547)/324, 9 November 1939, Maço 29.630 (1,291), AHI-R; 511.14 (547)/326, 13 November 1939, Maço 29.630 (1,291), AHI-R.

22. Itamaraty to Legation in Helsinki, 13 October 1939, 558.(72), 511.14 (457), Maço 29.630 (1,291), AHI-R.

23. Consul General (Paris) to Aranha, 13 June 1939, Maço 10,561 (741), AHI-R.

24. Pedro Leão Veloso to Aranha, 26 January 1940, OA 40.02.01/1, p. 3, CPDOC-R.

25. Trento, *Do outro lado*, 385.

26. Consul general (Paris) to Aranha, 13 June 1939, Maço 10,561 (741), AHI-R.

27. Cândido Duarte, *A organização municipal no governo Getúlio Vargas* (Rio de Janeiro: Departamento de Imprensa e Propaganda, 1942), 213.

28. Stefan Zweig, *Brazil: Land of the Future* (New York: Viking Press, 1942), 13; Dines, *Morte no paraíso*; Leo Spitzer, *Lives In Between: Assimilation and Marginality in Austria, Brazil, West Africa, 1780–1945* (Cambridge: Cambridge University Press, 1989), 170–71.

29. Figures from "Rapport d'activité pendant la période 1933–1942," HIAS, folder 1, YIVO-NY. CIC figures from *Diário Oficial da República*, 27 November 1940, 22,135; and *RIC* 3:1 (April 1942), 184–94.

30. *RIC* 1:3 (October 1940), 123–24 (misprinted).

31. *RIC* 1:3 (October 1940), 123–24 (misprinted).

32. Morris C. Troper (American Jewish Joint Distribution Committee) to HIAS-JCA Emigration Association, 11 January 1939, SCA (10–11 February 1939), 2: 136, JCA-L; Achilles to Robert Pell, 20 March 1939, 832.55 J/3, NARC-W; Achilles to Briggs, 13 March 1939, 832.55 J/2, NARC-W.

33. Scotten (Rio de Janeiro) to Welles, 10 March 1939, 832.55 J/3, p. 2, NARC-W.

34. "Entrada de semitas no Brasil em 1939," *RIC* 2:1 (January 1941), pp. 193–94.

35. Vianna, "Os imigrantes semíticos e mongóis," 610–14.

36. Vianna, "Os imigrantes semíticos e mongóis," 611.

37. Francisco Souza to Filinto Müller, 27 January 1938, FM 33.04.26 chp/ad III 13–10, CPDOC-R.

38. Neiva, "Estudos sobre a imigração semita," 215.

39. Pinheiro Machado to Aranha, 1 August 1939, Maço 29,656/57 (1,292), AHI-R.

40. Campos to Aranha, 22 September 1939, GS/289 Maço 9,857 (660), AHI-R.

41. Osório Dutra to Aranha, 30 July 1940, Maço 558 (740), AHI-R.

42. Secret telegram, 21 September 1938, EM/21/21/IX/38, Maço 9,652 (622), AHI-R.

43. L. Teixeira Leite Filho to Aranha, 28 March 1939, Maço 9,652 (622), AHI-R.

44. no signature, n.d., Maço 9,652 (622), AHI-R.

45. Randolph Harrison, Jr., to Hull, 31 May 1940, 832.00 N/124, NARC-W.

46. Aranha to Adhemar de Barros, 20 October 1938, Maço 9,601 (612), AHI-R.

47. Case of Pedro Cohen, Rio Branco Consulate to Oswaldo Correia (consul general, Montevideo), 6 December 1937, 226/12/12/937/anexo, Maço 9,600 (612), AHI-R.

48. Memorandum to the Chief of Political Services from the Secretary of State of Exterior Relations, 22 March 1938, PRRE, box 27.586, 1938, AN-R.

49. Zimmerman (Antwerp) to Minister of Foreign Relations, n.d., PRRE, box 27.586, 1938, AN-R.

50. "Report by Mr. Benjamin Mellibovsky, Special Delegate of HICEM for South America on His Mission to Brazil," n.d., annex 4, "Confidential Procedures to Obtain 'Llamadas,' " HIAS-Brazil, folder 5, YIVO-NY.

51. Eck, "The Rescue of Jews," 125.

52. Aranha to Vargas, 30 September 1940, 658.(41) (42)/558.(41)/511.16, Maço 29,656/57 (1,292), AHI-R.

53. Luís Pereira Ferreira de Faro, Jr., to Aranha, 9 August 1937, OA 37.08.09/3, p. 3, CPDOC-J.

54. Aranha to Eurico Dutra, 18 May 1939, SP/202/558, Maço 9,857 (660), AHI-R.

55. Cyro de Freitas Vale to Lafayette de Carvalho e Silva, 3 April 1939, SP/ 12/558, Maço 9,652 (622), AHI-R; Carvalho e Silva to Aranha, 21 April 1939, SP/SN/558/1939/anexo único, Maço 9,652 (622), AHI-R; Carvalho e Silva to Aranha, 21 April 1939, reservado/54, Maço 9,652 (622), AHI-R.

56. Carvalho e Silva to Aranha, 21 April 1939, reservado/54, AHI-R.

57. [unsigned] to Commissioner of Police in Montevideo, 17 April 1939, SP/84/558/1939/anexo 3, Maço 9,857 (660), AHI-R.

58. Pery to Mascarenhas, 15 April 1939, SP/84/558/1939/anexo 2, Maço 9,652 (622), AHI-R.

59. Pery to Mascarenhas, 22 April 1939, SP/84/558/1939/anexo 6, Maço 9,652 (622), AHI-R.

60. Telegram, Pery to Mascarenhas, 22 April 1939, SP/84/558/1939/anexo 4, Maço 9,652 (622). AHI-R; Pery to Mascarenhas, 22 April 1939, AHI-R.

61. Mascarenhas to Aranha, 27 November 1939, 289.558, Maço 29,656/ 57 (1,292), AHI-R.

62. Scotten to Welles, 10 March 1939, 832.55 J/3, p. 2, NARC-W.

63. Scotten to Welles, 10 March 1939, p. 2.

64. Burdett to Hull, 1 April 1940, 840.48 Refugees/2,117, NARC-W.

65. [illegible] to Vargas, 13 February 1939, PRRE, box 27.586, no. 29.298, AN-R.

66. "Brazil and German Refugees," Department of State, Memorandum of Conversation, 15 February 1939, 832.55 J/1, NARC-W.

67. Randolph Harrison, Jr., to Hull, 13 August 1941, 832.55J/15, NARC-W.

68. Memo [signature illegible] to Vargas, 2 December 1940, PRRE-1938–41, 27.604/40, box 27.741–1940, lata 275, AN-R.

69. Ministry of Foreign Relations [unsigned] to Aranha, 26 January 1940, OA 40.01.26, CPDOC-R.

70. Burdett to Hull, 1 April 1940, 840.48 Refugees/2,117, NARC-W.

71. Meio-Dia (Rio de Janeiro), 28 December 1940; Frank D. McCann, Jr., The Brazilian American Alliance, 1937–1945 (Princeton, N.J.: Princeton University Press, 1973), 199.

72. Scotten to Welles, 10 March 1939, p. 4.

73. Raphael Fernandes to Aranha, 13 April 1939, OA 39.05.15/2, CPDOC-R; Aranha to Fernandes, 15 May 1939, OA 39.05.15/2, CPDOC-R.

74. Department of State, Division of European Affairs, Memorandum, 13

March 1939, 832.55 J/2, NARC-W. In March 1939, for example, the steamship *San Martín*, carrying twenty-one Jewish refugees from Germany and Italy, requested permission to disembark at Recife after being refused at Montevideo. Telegrams of support from around the world were of no help since Itamaraty claimed, untruthfully, not to have received any visa requests until four days after the ship had left Recife in search of another port. See Passport Division to Secretary of the President of the Republic, 24 March 1939, PRRE, box 27.586, documents 7,241 and 7,341, AN-R; and Alfred Rothschild to Vargas, 15 April 1939, PRRE, box 27.586, document 9,768, AN-R.

75. Isaiah Raffalovich, *Tsiyunim ve-tamrurim be-shiv'im shenot nedudim: Otobayografiya* (Landmarks and milestones during seventy years of wanderings: An autobiography) (Tel Aviv: Defus Sho-Shani, 1952), 200–203.

76. *A Noite*, 21 March 1925; *O Jornal* (Rio de Janeiro), 22 March 1925.

77. Thomas F. Glick, "Between Science and Zionism: Einstein in Brazil," 12–14 (unpublished manuscript used with permission of the author); Nachman Falbel, "A visita de Albert Einstein à comunidade judaica do Rio de Janeiro," in *Estudos*, 134–39; Roberto Vergara Caffarelli, "Einstein e o Brasil," *Ciência e Cultura* 31 (1979), 1,436–55.

78. *Diário de Pernambuco* (Recife), 4 May 1925 (reprinted as "Einstein, regionalista," in Gilberto Freyre, *Tempo de aprendiz* [São Paulo: Instituição Brasileira de Difusão Cultural, 1979], 2:140).

79. Carneiro examined only Einstein's last effort, in 1941. The unfulfilled request to Foreign Minister Aranha for a visa for a friend led to the erroneous conclusion that even the great scientist "was not sufficient to defeat the rigid Brazilian legislation." See Carneiro, *O anti-semitismo*, 283.

80. Einstein to Katz, 12 December 1938, and Katz to Einstein, 24 December 1938, Einstein Duplicate Archive, 53,602, 53,604, Seeley G. Mudd Manuscript Library, Princeton University Archives, Princeton, N.J.; Falbel, *Estudos*, 134–39.

81. Einstein to Aranha, 23 January 1939, Einstein Duplicate Archive, 53,607, SMML-NJ.

82. Katz to Einstein, 4 February 1939, Einstein Duplicate Archive, 53,608, SMML-NJ.

83. Einstein to Aranha, 14 February 1939, Einstein to Katz, 14 February 1939, Einstein Duplicate Archive, 53,609, 53,610, SMML-NJ; Einstein to Aranha, 24 February 1939, SP/SN/558/anexo único, Maço 9,857 (660), AHI-R.

84. Itamaraty memo to CIC, 11 May 1939, Maço 9,857 (660), AHI-R; Labienne Salgado dos Santos to Einstein, 11 May 1939, Maço 9,857 (660), AHI-R; Salgado dos Santos to Razovsky, 11 May 1939, Maço 9,857 (660), AHI-R.

85. Einstein to Aranha, 3 December 1940, Einstein Duplicate Archive, 54,769, SMML-NJ.

86. Fabian-Katz to Einstein, 18 September 1953, Einstein to Fabian-Katz, 25 September 1953, Einstein Duplicate Archive, 59,627, 59,629, SMML-NJ.

87. Decree law 3.010 (20 August 1938), art. 16.

88. Consul general in London to Aranha, 9 January 1940, Maço 29.625/29 (1,291), AHI-R.

89. Resolution no. 34, 22 April 1939, SP/SN/558/1939/anexo único, Maço 10,558 (740), AHI-R.

90. Resolution no. 30, Conselho de Imigração e Colonização, 3 April 1939, EM/8/4/39, Maço 10,453 (729), AHI-R; Itamaraty to consulate in Hamburg, 8 April 1939, EM/8/4/39, Maço 10,453 (729), AHI-R.

91. Itamaraty to consulate in Hamburg, 14 August 1939, EM/14/VIII/39, Maço 10,453 (729), AHI-R.

92. Burdett to Hull, 25 August 1939, 832.5560 c/7, NARC-W.

93. Aranha to Freitas Vale, 5 January 1940, OA 40.01.05/1, p. 6, CPDOC-R.

94. Aranha to Freitas Vale, 5 January 1940, p. 5.

95. Stanley Hilton, *Hitler's Secret War*, 20.

96. Unsigned internal memo to Aranha, 3 January 1939, PRRE-1940a, PR-69, box 27.667, lata 201, AN-R.

97. Freitas Vale to Aranha, 20 December 1939, OA 39.12.20, CPDOC-R.

98. Alfred Simonsohn (Rio de Janeiro) to A. de Camargo Neves (Berlin), 26 July 1939, FO 371/24,086 W 12,290/962/48, PRO-L.

99. Hélio Lobo (Brazilian delegate to Intergovernmental Committee) to Reilly (British Foreign Office), 31 August 1939, FO 371/24,086 W 13,616/962/48, PRO-L.

100. Freitas Vale to Itamaraty, 23 September 1939, telegram no. EM 23, PRRE-1940a, PR-69, box 27.667, lata 201, AN-R.

101. Itamaraty to Brazilian Embassy (Berlin), 23 September 1939, PRRE-1940a, PR-69, box 27.667, lata 201, AN-R.

102. Freitas Vale to Aranha, 9 October 1939, no. 324, PRRE-1940a, PR-69, box 27.667, lata 201, AN-R.

103. Secretaria de Estado das Relações Exteriores to Chief of Passport Division, 20 June 1939, PRRE-1940a, PR-69, box 27.667, lata 201, AN-R.

104. Paul Rosenstein to Aranha, 1 June 1940, OA 39.12.08/3, document 15, CPDOC-R.

105. Rosenstein to Aranha, 3 October 1940, OA 39.12.08/3, document 15, CPDOC-R. Interestingly, regardless of Freitas Vale's virulent dislike of Jews, numerous members of the community today have recounted to the author that it was through the intervention of the ambassador that they received visas.

106. See for example, tourist visa approval of Mr. and Mrs. Berthold Juttner, in Freitas Vale to Adolpho de Camargo Neves (Brazilian consul, Berlin) 30 June 1939, SP/16/511.114, "Vistos em passaportes," PRRE-1940a, PR-69, box 27.667, lata 201, AN-R.

107. Freitas Vale to Vargas, 5 November 1939, PRRE-1940a, PR-69, box 27.667, lata 201, AN-R; Freitas Vale to Aranha, 2 November 1939, no. 351, PRRE-1940a, PR-69, box 27.667, lata 201, AN-R.

108. Salgado dos Santos, "Entrada de semitas no Brasil," PRRE-1940a, PR-69, box 27.667, lata 201, AN-R.

109. Salgado dos Santos, "Entrada de semitas no Brasil, pp. 4–5.

110. Freitas Vale to Aranha, 2 November 1939, no. 351, PRRE-1940a, PR-69, box 27.667, lata 201, AN-R, p. 2.

111. Freitas Vale to Vargas, 5 November 1939, PRRE-1940a, PR-69, box 27.667, lata 201, AN-R, p. 3.

112. Muniz to Aranha, 19 December 1939, PRRE-1940a, PR-69, box 27.667, lata 201, AN-R.

113. Muniz to Aranha, 19 December 1939.

114. Aranha to Freitas Vale, 19 December 1939, PRRE-1940a, PR-69, box 27.667, lata 201, AN-R.

115. Aranha to Freitas Vale, 5 January 1940, OA 40.01.05/1, p. 9, CPDOC-RJ.

116. These figures have been accepted by some scholars as a sign of Circular 1,127's effectiveness. See Avni, "Latin America and the Jewish Refugees"; and Carneiro, O anti-semitismo.

117. Aranha to Freitas Vale, 5 January 1940, OA 40.01.05/1, CPDOC-RJ.

118. Arthur Hehl Neiva, "Getúlio Vargas e o problema da imigração e da colonização," RIC 3:1 (April 1942), 34. It is important to note here that Jewish relief groups kept independent statistics on the numbers of Jews being issued Brazilian visas. These statistics correspond extremely closely to the statistics published by the Brazilian government on Jewish entry. The numbers are further confirmed by synagogues and relief groups in Brazil, which also kept statistics on the number of Jews entering the country.

119. Aranha to Freitas Vale, 5 January 1940, CPDOC-RJ.

120. Itamaraty to Embassy in Paris SP/77/558.(99), 30 December 1940, Maço 10.561 (741), AHI-R.

121. Scotten (Rio de Janeiro) to Welles, 10 March 1939, 832.55 J/3, p. 3, NARC-W; Theodore C. Achilles (Rio de Janeiro) to Robert Pell (Intergovernmental Committee, London), 20 March 1939, 832.55 J/5, NARC-W.

122. RIC 1:3 (October 1940), 123–24 (misprinted) and 127–28 (misprinted); RIC 3:1 (April 1942), 185–95.

123. "Autorizações dadas pela secretaria geral, Cyro de Freitas Valle, recusados ou não satisfeitos pelo consulado do Brasil em Berlim," PRRE-1940a, PR-69, box 27.667, lata 201, AN-R.

124. Aranha to Freitas Vale, 5 January 1940, OA 40.01.05/1, p. 9, CPDOC-R.

125. RIC 1:3 (October 1940), pp. 131–32.

126. RIC 2:2–3 (April/June, 1941), 949. Note: The table is erroneously labeled as showing entrances with permanent visas.

127. Case of Egon Eisner, documents FO 371/44,851 AS2,336/AS2,447/AS2,677/AS2,803/2,331/6, April–May 1945, PRO-L.

128. See Abella and Troper, None Is Too Many, 67–100; Wyman, The Abandonment of the Jews, 61–103; Wasserstein, Britain and the Jews, 81–133; Marrus, The Unwanted, 219–33.

129. Oungre (Buenos Aires) to Gottschalk (HIAS), 28 November 1941, HIAS/NY, folder 10, p. 5., YIVO-NY.

130. Hilton, Hitler's Secret War, 190.

131. Francisco Ruas Santos, Coleção bibliográfica militar (Rio de Janeiro: Biblioteca do Exército, 1960), 408–9; Nação Armada (Rio de Janeiro) 24 (November 1941), 158; Nação Armada 26 (January 1942), 150.

132. Muniz to Campos, 24 December 1940, Maço 35,059 (1,639), AHI-R.

133. Muniz to Campos, 24 December 1940. My italics.

134. Decree law 3,010 (20 August 1938), art. 1; Muniz to Aranha, 20 March 1941, Maço 35,501 (1,722), AHI-R.

135. Burdett to Hull, 1 February 1941, 832.5594/119, NARC-W; decree law 3,175, art. 2, par. 5.

136. Memo of Robert McClintock, 9 September 1941, 832.111/193, NARC-W; Curt Max Prüfer, Latin American Diaries (Tagebücher), January 1941, Collection Curt Max Prüfer, folder 97,035–8.24, Hoover Institution Archives, California; "Report about the Activity of the Office in Rio de Janeiro in 1941," HIAS/NY, folder 15, p. 5., YIVO-NY; unsigned telegram of British Foreign Office, 21 July 1941, FO 371/29,220 W 8,930/570/48, PRO-L.

137. Circular no. 1,499, "Rules for the Entry of Aliens into Brazil," art. 3, 20 February 1941, SP/511.12, attached to Burdett to Hull, 21 February 1941, 8,322.55/196, NARC-W.

138. Decree law 3,175 (7 April 1941), in Estrangeiros 2:511–13.

139. Caffery to Hull, 20 March 1941, 832.55/199, NARC-W.

140. New York Times, 24 May 1941.

141. Decree law 3,175, art. 1.

142. "Rapport sur l'activité du bureau de Rio pendant des mois de novembre et decembre, 1941," HIAS-Brazil, folder 6, p. 5., YIVO-NY; Aryeh Tartakower and Kurt R. Grossman, The Jewish Refugee (New York: Institute of Jewish Affairs of the World Jewish Congress and American Jewish Congress, 1944), 316.

143. Caffery to Aranha, 9 April 1941, 558.(00), Maço 35,059 (1,639), AHI-R; Aranha, quoted in Caffery to Hull, 19 April 1941, 840.48 Refugees/2,543 PS/FLR, NARC-W.

144. Leon Alter to HICEM, 25 May 1942, "The Situation of Immigration in Brazil and the Activity of Our Organization in This Country," HIAS/NY, folder 21, YIVO-NY.

145. There are some few instances—for example, the case of the Portuguese steamer Servapinto—of refugees being permitted to land in Brazil, apparently without proper documentation. See New York Times, 14 August 1941.

146. New York Times, 27 May 1941.

147. Japan Chronicle (Tokyo), 29 January 1941.

148. Aristóteles de Lima Câmara, "Incompatibilidade étnica?" RIC 1:4 (October 1940), 665.

149. Oungre to Gottschalk (HIAS), 28 November 1941, HIAS/NY, folder 10, p. 1., YIVO-NY.

150. Wasserstein, Britain and the Jews, 141.

151. José Shercliffe, Daily Herald (London), 1 July 1941, in FO 371/29,220 W 8,189/570/48, PRO-L.

152. Ministry of War Transport to Foreign Office, 17 October 1941, FO 371/29,220 W 8,197/570/48, PRO-L.

153. Carneiro, O anti-semitismo, 213–15.

154. Hull to U.S. Embassy (Rio de Janeiro), 16 August 1941, 832.111/183, NARC-W; Paul Daniels to Welles, 22 October 1941, 832.111/195, NARC-W; Norman Armour to Hull, 27 July 1940, 832.55 J/12, NARC-W.

155. Although Brazilian and U.S. government documents put the number at ninety-five, the *New York Times* reported the number as eighty-six (9 November 1941).

156. John Simmons to Hull, 10 November 1941, 840.48 Refugees/2,672, NARC-W.

157. Souza Dantas to Aranha, 22 November 1940, Maço 558 (740), AHI-R. In October 1940, Souza Dantas's "right-hand man," a Mr. Lindberg, was accused of selling visas; see memo of Robert McClintock, 9 September 1941, 832.111/193, NARC-W.

158. J. Edgar Hoover to Adolf Berle, 7 March 1941, 832.55/197, NARC-W.

159. Captain Lanz Mayro quoted in the *New York Times,* 9 November 1941.

160. José Júlio de Morais to Chief of Passport Division, 6 November 1941, Maço 35,059 (1,639), AHI-R.

161. Laurita Pessôa Raja Gabaglia's *O Cardeal Leme (1882–1942)* (Rio de Janeiro: José Olympio Editora, 1962) makes no mention of the case.

162. Hull to Caffery, 8 November 1941, 840.48 Refugees/2,752, NARC-W.

163. Morais to Chief of Passport Division, 6 November 1941.

164. Caffery to Hull, 8 November 1941, 840.48 Refugees/2,753, NARC-W.

165. Hull to Caffery, 8 November 1941, 840.48 Refugees/2,752, NARC-W.

166. Carlos Martins Pereira e Souza to Vargas, 11 November 1941, GV 41.11.07, CPDOC-R; Vargas to Pereira e Souza, n.d., GV 41.11.07, CPDOC-R; Caffery to Hull, 8 November 1941, 840.48 Refugees/2,753, NARC-W; John Simmons to Hull, 10 November 1941, 840.48 Refugees/2,672, NARC-W.

167. Chazen to Simmons, quoted in Simmons to Hull, 10 November 1941, NARC-W.

168. *New York Times,* 18 November 1941; Haim Genizi, *American Apathy: The Plight of Christian Refugees from Nazism* (Ramat Gan, Israel: Bar-Ilan University Press, 1983), 265.

169. *A Noite,* 10 November 1941.

170. *Diário da Noite,* 22 June 1942.

171. Caffery to Hull, 18 July 1941, 840.48 Refugees/2,647, NARC-W.

172. [illegible] to José Bannwart, 11 February 1938, DNP 007/38, Maço 9,652 (622), AHI-R.

173. Muniz to Campos, 24 December 1940, Maço 35,059 (1,639), AHI-R.

174. Decree law 1,532 (23 August 1939), in *Estrangeiros,* 463; William C. Burdett to Cordell Hull, 30 August 1939, 832.55 J/7, NARC-W.

175. Caffery to Hull, 26 August 1939, 832.55 J/5, NARC-W.

176. Decree law 639 (20 August 1938), art. 1, par. b, in *Estrangeiros,* 343–47; Department of State, Division of Latin American Affairs Memorandum, 8 August 1938, 832.55/152, NARC-W. Elizabeth Cancelli finds Jews being accused of pimping as late as 1939; see Cancelli, "O mundo da violência," 255–56.

177. [illegible] to J. A. de Souza Ribeiro, 22 August 1939, SP/171/558 (81), Maço 10,453 (729), AHI-R.

178. "Report by Mr. Benjamin Mellibovsky, Special Delegate of HICEM for South America, on His Mission to Brazil," n.d., p. 11, HIAS-Brazil, folder 5, YIVO-NY.

179. Complaint of Salgado dos Santos, attached to Aranha to Vargas, 26 October 1939, Maço 9,857, AHI-R.

180. Aranha to Vargas, 16 January 1940, Maço 9,857 (660), AHI-R.

181. Camillo Kahn to Roosevelt, 3 May 1941, 832.4016 (1940–44), NARC-W.

182. Handwritten memo attached to Kahn to Roosevelt, 3 May 1941.

183. Caffery to Hull, 18 July 1941, 840.48 Refugees/2,647, NARC-W; Levine, *Vargas Regime*, 152, 167.

184. Governmental order 4,941 (24 July 1941), *Estrangeiros* 2:521–22; *New York Times*, 27 July 1941; Oungre to Gottschalk (HIAS), 28 November 1941, HIAS/NY, folder 10, p. 2, YIVO-NY; Caffery to Hull, 30 July 1941, 832.111/182, NARC-W.

185. Cohen, *Jewish Life*, 3. In all the other nations the study group visited, it gained access only to low-level officials.

186. Cohen, *Jewish Life*, 12.

187. Dr. A. d'Esaguy (HICEM) to Mr. Baumgold (NY), 18 December 1940, HIAS/NY, folder 37, YIVO-NY.

188. Oungre to Gottschalk (HIAS), 28 November 1941, HIAS/NY, folder 10, p. 2, YIVO-NY.

189. *New York Times*, 24 December 1942.

190. *New York Times*, 29 December 1942.

191. *Diário de Notícias*, 27 October 1942.

192. Memorandum of D. Bloomingdale, attached to Duggan to James W. Wise, 26 October 1942, 840.48 Refugees/3,421, NARC-W.

193. *Correio da Manhã*, 5 September 1942.

194. *Diário de Notícias*, 27 October 1942.

195. *Diário da Manhã* (Niterói), 24 November 1943.

196. *O Globo* (Rio de Janeiro), 18 September 1942; *Nação Armada* 35 (October 1942), 143–44.

5. THE POPE, THE DICTATOR, AND THE REFUGEES WHO NEVER CAME

1. Stepan, *"The Hour of Eugenics,"* 168; Vianna, *Populações meridionais,* 13.

2. Arthur de Gobineau, *The Inequality of Human Races* (Los Angeles: Noontide Press, 1966), 3, 122; Georges Raeders, *O inimigo cordial do Brasil: O conde de Gobineau no Brasil* (São Paulo: Paz e Terra, 1988); George L. Mosse, *Toward the Final Solution: A History of European Racism* (New York: Howard Fertig, 1978), 55.

3. The term *Catholic non-Aryan* appears to have been first used by the Vatican in early 1939; see "Introduction: 1. L'aide aux non-aryens," in Vatican,

Secrétairie d'État de Sa Sainteté, *Actes et documents du Saint Siège relatifs à la seconde guerre mondiale,* ed. Pierre Blet et al., 6:12–25. An excellent examination of the Vatican-Vargas visa deal can be found in Avraham Milgram, "O Brasil e a questão dos refugiados judeus durante a segunda guerra mundial: A tentativa de salvação de católicos não arianos da Alemanha ao Brasil através do Vaticano 1939–1942" (master's thesis, Hebrew University of Jerusalem, 1989). Lutz-Eugen Reutter competently analyzes the Vatican documentation (but no Itamaraty files) in his *Katholishe Kirche als Fluchthelfer im Dritten Reich: Die Betreuung von Auswanderern durch den St. Raphaels-Verein* (Recklinghausen-Hamburg: Paulus Verlag, 1971), 141–80. See also John F. Morley, *Vatican Diplomacy and the Jews during the Holocaust, 1939–1943* (New York: KTAV Publishing House, 1980), 18–22; Carneiro, *O anti-semitismo,* 234–47; and Genizi, *American Apathy,* 164–65.

4. Marrus, *The Unwanted,* 266; *ADSS* 6:12.

5. Cardinal Faulhaber, Archbishop of Munich, to Pope Pius XII, 31 March 1939, *ADSS* 6:63–64. Cardinal Faulhaber was instrumental in forcing the Nazis to modify medical testing on Aryan Germans (not Jews) who might propagate so-called congenitally diseased progeny. See J. P. Stern, *Hitler: The Führer and the People* (Berkeley: University of California Press, 1988), 214–15.

6. Dawidowicz, *War against the Jews,* 139–40.

7. According to the Vatican there were two hundred thousand Catholic non-Aryan refugees in Europe in 1939.

8. Lobo to Aranha, 28 January 1939, NP/SN/640.16 (99)/anexo 1, Maço 9,697, AHI-R.

9. Feingold, "Roosevelt and the Resettlement Question," 137.

10. Faulhaber to Pope Pius XII, 31 March 1939, *ADSS* 6:64; copy of an article from the *Neue Züricher Zeitung* in Maço 12,213 (833), 558 (99), 1/40/ 1939 anexo, AHI-R.

11. Faulhaber to Pope Pius XII, 31 March 1939, *ADSS* 6:64.

12. Itamaraty to Consulate in Hamburg, 8 April 1939, EM/8/4/39, Maço 10,453 (729), AHI-R; Itamaraty to Consulate in Hamburg, 14 August 1939, EM/14/VIII/39, Maço 10,453 (729), AHI-R.

13. Faulhaber to Pope Pius XII, 31 March 1939; *ADSS* 6:65.

14. Faulhaber to Pope Pius XII, 31 March 1939; *ADSS* 6:65.

15. Saul Friedländer, *Pius XII and the Third Reich: A Documentation* (New York: Alfred A. Knopf, 1966), 11.

16. Archbishop of Osnabrück to Pope Pius XII, 31 March 1939, *ADSS* 6:67.

17. Aloisi Masella (nuncio of Rio de Janeiro) to Getúlio Vargas, 14 April 1939, Fundo Secretaria da Presidência da República, Série Conselho de Imigração e Colonização, CIC-PR/SC 3,117–21,797, no. 9,404/39, AN-R.

18. Maço 12,213 (833), 558 (99), AHI-R.

19. Masella to Vargas, 14 April 1939, AN-R.

20. João Carlos Muniz to Vargas, 8 May 1939, Fundo Secretaria da Presidência da República, Série Conselho de Imigração e Colonização, CIC-PR/SC 3,117–21,797, no. 45/9, AN-R.

21. While the quoted sentence was not underlined in the original typed version of the resolution, it was heavily highlighted prior to its distribution to

various members of the CIC. See Conselho de Imigração e Colonização, Resolution no. 39, 23 June 1939, SP/23/558 (99)/1939/anexo único, Maço 12,213 (833), AHI-R; Verbal note SP/10/558, Itamaraty to Papal Nuncio (Rio de Janeiro), 24 June 1939, *ADSS* 6:101.

22. Lenharo, *Sacralização da política,* 107–38; Carneiro, *O anti-semitismo,* 237–46.

23. João Carlos Muniz to Oswaldo Aranha, 19 December 1939, PRRE-Relações Exteriores-1940a, PR-69, box 27.667, lata 201, AN-R; Aloisi Masella (nuncio of Rio de Janeiro) to Cardinal Maglione (Vatican), 28 June 1939, *ADSS* 6:99.

24. Israel Pinheiro da Silva (minister of agriculture, Minas Gerais) to Oswaldo Aranha, 25 May 1939, OA 39.05.26/2, CPDOC-R.

25. Secretary General of Raphaelsverein to Pope Pius XII, 5 June 1939, *ADSS* 6:91.

26. Maglione to Masella, 6 June 1939, *ADSS* 6:95.

27. Masella to Maglione, 31 July 1939, *ADSS* 6:118.

28. Masella to Maglione, 31 July 1939, *ADSS* 6:118.

29. Masella to Maglione, 20 June 1939, *ADSS* 6:98; Conselho de Imigração e Colonização, Decision no. 39, *ADSS* 6:98; Maglione to Faulhaber (Munich), 23 June 1939, *ADSS* 6:98.

30. Muniz to Aranha, 3 January 1939, PRRE-Relações Exteriores-1940a, PR-69, box 27.667, lata 201, AN-R.

31. Muniz to Aranha, 3 January 1939.

32. Conselho de Imigração e Colonização, Resolution no. 39, 23 June 1939, SP/23/558 (99)/1939/anexo único, Maço 12,213 (833), AHI-R.

33. Special cable to the *New York Times,* 25 June 1939, 22.

34. Associated Press story in the *New York Times,* 25 June 1939, 22.

35. Special cable to the *New York Times,* 25 June 1939, 22.

36. Max Grösser, Secretary General of the Raphaelsverein (Hamburg), to Papal Nuncio Cesare Orsenigo (Berlin), 1 September 1939, *ADSS* 6:132.

37. Conselho de Imigração e Colonização, Resolution no. 39, 23 June 1939.

38. Papal Nuncio Clement Micara (Brussels) to Maglione, 8 July 1939, *ADSS* 6:102; document no. 77, 5 July 1939, in SP/32/558.(99), Maço 12,213 (833), AHI-R.

39. Maglione to Masella, 11 July 1939, *ADSS* 6:103.

40. Father Hecht to Monsignor Dell'Acqua, 13 July 1939, *ADSS* 6:105; Hecht to Maglione, 17 July 1939, *ADSS* 6:106; Maglione to Masella, 16 July 1939, *ADSS* 6:106, n. 3.

41. Pedro de Moraes Barros (Itamaraty) to Legation in the Hague, 3 September 1939, EM/3/9/II/39, Maço 9,697, AHI-R.

42. Papal Nuncio Micara (Brussels) to Maglione, 8 July 1939, *ADSS* 6:102.

43. Archbishop Berning (Osnabrück) to Maglione, 20 July 1939, *ADSS* 6:108.

44. Berning to Maglione, 20 July 1939, *ADSS* 6:109.

45. Berning to Maglione, 20 July 1939. *ADSS* 6:109.

46. Maglione to Masella, 29 July 1939, *ADSS* 6:117; Maglione to Nuncio Orsenigo (Berlin), 30 August 1939, *ADSS* 6:124; Masella to Maglione, 31 July

1939, *ADSS* 6:119. Almost twenty years earlier Lobo had suggested a secret immigration policy that would have banned African Americans from immigrating to Brazil, without causing an international uproar; see Lesser, "Are African-Americans African or American?"
47. Ruy Ribeiro Costa (Utrecht) to Oswaldo Aranha, 14 July 1939, 640.16 (99), 588 (99), Maço 12,213 (833), AHI-R.
48. Costa to Aranha, 14 July 1939.
49. Costa to Aranha, 14 July 1939.
50. João Guimarães Rosa (Hamburg) to Aranha, 25 July 1939, 558.(99), Maço 12,213 (833), AHI-R.
51. Rosa to Aranha, 25 July 1939.
52. Max Grösser to Dulphe Pinheiro Machado, 4 December 1939, Maço 12,213 (833), AHI-R; Nuncio Micara (Brussels) to Maglione, 8 July 1939, *ADSS* 6:102.
53. Maglione to Nuncio Cesare Orsenigo (Berlin), 30 August 1939, *ADSS* 6:124.
54. Maglione to Orsenigo, 30 August 1939, *ADSS* 6:124.
55. Orsenigo to Maglione, 2 September 1939, *ADSS* 6:129; Maglione to Masella, 21 October 1939, *ADSS* 6:171.
56. Cesare Orsenigo to Maglione, 2 September 1939, *ADSS* 6:129.
57. Maglione to French Nuncio Valeri, 28 October 1939, *ADSS* 6:172.
58. Grösser to Machado, 4 December 1939, p. 1, AHI-R.
59. Grösser to Machado, 4 December 1939, p. 1.
60. Grösser to Machado, 4 December 1939, p. 3.
61. Reserved note no. 2, "Entrada no Brasil de católicos não arianos que se encontram na Alemanha," 26 March 1940, Maço 12,213 (833), AHI-R.
62. Notes of Monsignor Tardini (Vatican), 4 March 1940, *ADSS* 6:252; notes of the Vatican Secretary of State, 27 February 1940, *ADSS* 6:249.
63. Grösser to Nuncio Orsenigo (Berlin), 1 September 1939, *ADSS* 6:130 .
64. Hélio Lobo (Geneva) to Labienne Salgado dos Santos (Rio), 25 February 1940, Maço 10,561(741), AHI-R.
65. Verbal note no. 27 from British Embassy (Petrópolis) to Ministry of Foreign Affairs, 20 February 1940, Maço 10,561(741), AHI-R.
66. Masella to Maglione, 13 November 1939, *ADSS* 6:187.
67 Vatican Secretary of State to Hildebrando Accioly, 14 December 1939, *ADSS* 6:205.
68. Masella to Maglione, 6 January 1940, *ADSS* 6:217.
69. Maglione to Nuncio Micara, 14 January 1940, *ADSS* 6:221.
70. Maglione to Micara, 14 January 1940, *ADSS* 6:221; Meir Michaels, *Mussolini and the Jews: German-Italian Relations and the Jewish Question in Italy, 1922–1945* (Oxford: Clarendon Press, 1978), 238–49.
71. Maglione to Hildebrando Pinto Accioly, 10 February 1940, *ADSS* 6:234.
72. Notes of the Secretary of State, 21 May 1940, *ADSS* 6:314.
73. Nuncio Bernardini (Bern) to Maglione, 12 February 1940, *ADSS* 6:148; Maglione to Ambassador Accioly, 30 March 1940, *ADSS* 6:277.
74. Aranha to Vargas, 3 May 1940, SP/558.(99), Maço 12,213 (833), AHI-R.

75. Memo from Passport Division Chief to Itamaraty, 3 June 1940, 558.(99), Maço 12,213 (833), AHI-R.

76. Maglione to Masella, 19 September 1939, *ADSS* 6:148.

77. Itamaraty memo of 26 April 1940, Maço 12,213 (833), AHI-R.

78. Nemesio Dutra (Brazilian embassy, Rome) to the Vatican, 4 March 1940, 42/1940/anexo 3, 558.(99), Maço 12,213 (833), AHI-R.

79. Hildebrando Accioly to Maglione, 4 March 1940, *ADSS* 6:253.

80. Daniel Bourgeois, "La porte se ferme: La Suisse et le problème de l'immigration juive en 1938," *Relations Internationales* 54 (summer 1988), 181–204.

81. Dom Odon Duc de Württemberg to Aranha, 15 September 1939, Maço 9,857 (660), AHI-R.

82. Note of Cardinal Maglione in notes of Monsignor Tardini, 20 May 1940, *ADSS* 6:313.

83. Only fifty-seven visas were granted in the first two months of 1940. See Maurício Nabuco (Antwerp) to Hildebrando Accioly, 30 October 1940, SP/22/ 558 (99), Maço 12,213 (833), AHI-R.

84. Masella to Aranha, 29 July 1940, 23,225, 558.(99), Maço 12,213 (833), AHI-R; notes of the Secretary of State, 21 May 1940, *ADSS* 6:314.

85. Maglione to Archbishop Berning (Osnabrück), 27 December 1941, *ADSS* 8:398.

86. Alexander Menningen (Raphaelsverein), "A associação de S. Rafael: Sua organização e seu método de trabalho," Brazilian Embassy at the Holy See/ 107/1940/anexo único, Maço 12,213 (833), AHI-R.

87. Ciro de Freitas Vale to Itamaraty, 2 September 1940, EM/2/2/IX/40, 558.(99), Maço 12,213 (833), AHI-R.

88. Nuncio Orsenigo (Berlin) to Maglione, 6 April 1940, *ADSS* 6:284. Freitas Vale to Itamaraty, 2 September 1940.

89. Father Hecht (Rome) to Maglione, 22 May 1940, *ADSS* 6:318.

90. Notes of Monsignor Dell'Acqua, 30 May 1940, *ADSS* 6:325.

91. Affonso Henriques, *Ascensão e queda de Getúlio Vargas: O Estado Novo* (Rio de Janeiro: Distribuidora Record, 1966), 44.

92. Theodor Cabral (vice-consul, Prague) to Aranha, 7 July 1939, 16, 558, Maço 9,857 (660), AHI-R.

93. Aranha to Joaquim Antônio de Sousa Ribeiro, 12 September 1940, SP/ 31/5, 558.(99), Maço 12,213 (833), AHI-R.

94. Aranha to Ribeiro, 12 September 1940,

95. Request to Ministério do Exterior, Chief of the Passport Section, 21 July 1939, 558, Maço 9,857 (660), AHI-R.

96. File of Rudolph Max Neumann, no. 15.148, 20 November 1940, PRRE-1941, document 5.674/41, box 27.741, lata 275, AN-R.

97. Max Neumman to Vargas, 17 February 1941, PRRE-1941, document 5.674/198, box 27.741, lata 275, AN-R.

98. Itamaraty [signature illegible] to Vargas, 5 March 1941, PRRE-1941, document 5.674/41, box 27.741, lata 275, AN-R.

99. Maurício Nabuco (Itamaraty) to Hildebrando Accioly, 4 November 1940, SP/30/558.(99), Maço 12,213 (833), AHI-R.

100. Notes of the Secretary of State, 3 September 1940, *ADSS* 6:404.

101. Accioly to Maglione, 20 November 1941, *ADSS* 8:351; Morley, *Vatican Diplomacy,* 20–21.

102. Aranha to Joaquim Antônio de Sousa Ribeiro, 12 September 1940, SP/31/5, 558.(99), Maço 12,213 (833), AHI-R.

103. Notes of the Secretary of State, 25 October 1940, *ADSS* 6:453.

104. Accioly to Aranha, 4 November 1940, 122, 558.(99), Maço 12,213 (833), AHI-R.

105. Theodore C. Achilles (U.S. embassy, Rio de Janeiro) to Robert Pell (Intergovernmental Committee, London), 20 March 1939, 832.55, NARC-W.

106. Accioly to Maglione, 20 November 1941, *ADSS* 8:351, n. 2.

107. Accioly to Aranha, 2 September 1940, Maço 12,213 (833), AHI-R.

108. Accioly to Itamaraty, 10 November 1941, cited in Milgram, "O Brasil," 138, 145; *New York Times,* 14 March 1940.

109. William C. Burdett (counselor of U.S. Embassy, Rio de Janeiro) to U.S. Secretary of State, 9 April 1940, 832.55 J/11, NARC-W.

110. Maurício Nabuco (Itamaraty) to Accioly, 4 November 1940, SP/30/558.(99), Maço 12,213 (833), AHI-R; Accioly to Aranha, 4 November 1940, 122, 558.(99), Maço 12,213 (833), AHI-R.

111. Nuncio Micara to Maglione, 21 December 1939, *ADSS* 6:207.

112. Nuncio Micara to Maglione, 21 December 1939, *ADSS* 6:207.

113. Cited in Burdett to Secretary of State, 9 April 1940.

114. Nabuco (Rio de Janeiro) to Vargas, 22 January 1940, PRRE-1940, document 34,516/21–1940a, box 27.667, lata 201, AN-R.

115. Theodore C. Achilles (U.S. embassy, Rio de Janeiro) to Robert Pell (Intergovernmental Committee, London), 20 March 1939, 832.55 J/3, NARC-W.

116. Brazil did regularly give visas to Catholics who could show that "both parents were of the same religion." See visa approval of Konrad Rawski, Ministério do Trabalho, Indústria e Comércio, 11 August 1939, Maço 9,865 (660), AHI-R.

117. Marrus, *The Unwanted,* 266.

118. *New York Times,* 21 October 1941.

6. EPILOGUE: BRAZILIAN JEWS, JEWISH BRAZILIANS

1. A combination of factors caused the drop: a decrease in emigration from Europe based on lack of papers and passenger space, the Vargas regime's lowered desire to accept refugees, decreased U.S. pressure on Brazil on refugee matters, and financial problems that caused Jewish groups to reduce pressure on the Vargas government.

2. Harold S. Tewell to Hull, 12 June 1944, 832.111/319, NARC-W.

3. Tewell to Hull, 12 June 1944.

4. Tewell to Hull, 12 June 1944.

5. Press release from the Wallace Thorsen Organization, 10 November 1944, 832.55/230 IM/HM, NARC-W.

6. Tewell to Hull, 12 June 1944. Concerns were also expressed about the entry of U.S. citizens of African descent.

7. Tewell to Hull, 12 June 1944.

8. Neiva, "Estudos sobre a imigração semita," 215–422.

9. R. A., "A assimilação do elemento estrangeiro," 7.

10. Diégues, *Etnias e cultura no Brasil,* 147. Recent editions of the book have continued to include the cited phrase.

11. Everardo Backheuser, "Comércio ambulante e ocupações de rua no Rio de Janeiro," *Revista Brasileira de Geografia* 6:1 (January–March 1944), 14.

12. Lopes, *O problema judaico,* 49; Martins, *História da inteligência brasileira,* 7:197.

13. *New York Times,* 21 April 1943; John Simmons to Hull, 20 November 1943, 832.55/229 IM/HM, NARC-W; Tewell to Hull, 11 August 1944, 832.111/322, NARC-W.

14. Aranha to Alexandre Marcondes Filho (Interim Minister of Justice), 12 February 1944, Maço 36,311, DPD/81/601.34 (00), AHI-R; [illegible] to Pedro Leão Veloso (Interim Foreign Minister), 4 April 1945, Maço 36,311, 128/601.34 (00) (00), AHI-R.

15. Decree law 7,575 (21 May 1945).

16. Wischnitzer, *To Dwell in Safety,* 293, table 6.

17. Everardo Backheuser, "Geografia carioca: Os guetos da cidade," *Jornal do Brasil,* 13 October 1946. Other examples of postwar anti-Jewish press reports can be found in Werner Nehab, *Anti-semitismo, integralismo, neonazismo* (Rio de Janeiro: Livraria Freitas Bastos, 1988).

18. "Discurso do Deputado Maurício Grabois, Proferido na Sessão do Dia 20–6–47 da Câmara dos Deputados" (photocopy courtesy of John W. F. Dulles); Serebrenick and Lipiner, *Breve história dos judeus,* 149.

19. Leonard Dinnerstein, *America and the Survivors of the Holocaust* (New York: Columbia University Press, 1982), 200.

20. Arthur Hehl Neiva and Manuel Diégues, "The Cultural Assimilation of Immigrants in Brazil," in *The Cultural Integration of Immigrants: A Survey Based upon the Papers and Proceeding of the Unesco Conference Held in Havana, April 1956,* ed. W. D. Borrie (New York: Unesco, 1957), 195.

21. Neiva and Diégues, "Cultural Assimilation," 181–233.

22. Sigue Friesel, *Bror Chail: História do movimento e do kibutz brasileiro* (Jerusalem: Departamento da Juventude e do Chalutz da Organização Sionista Mundial, 1956), 13.

23. Donald L. Herman, *The Latin-American Community of Israel* (New York: Praeger, 1984), 32, table 2.1.

24. Elkin, *Jews of the Latin American Republics,* 94.

25. Jeffrey Lesser, "Challenges to Jewish Life in Latin America," in *Survey of Jewish Affairs,* ed. William Frankel (London: Basil Blackwell, 1991), 232–40; Henrique Rattner, "Economic and Social Mobility of Jews in Brazil," in *The Jewish Presence in Latin America,* ed. Judith Laikin Elkin and Gilbert W. Merkx (Boston: Allen and Unwin, 1987), 199.

26. Herman, *The Latin-American Community,* 33.

27. United Nations Resolution no. 3,379. Cuba, Mexico, and Guyana voted along with Brazil in favor of the measure; a more complete discussion of the subject can be found in *AJYB* (1977), 77:97–126.

28. Sergio DellaPergola, "Demographic Trends of Latin American Jewry," in *Jewish Presence in Latin America*, ed. Elkin and Merkx, 90.

29. Uri Goren, interview by author, Comunidade Shalom (São Paulo), 21 August 1988.

30. Rosa Krausz, "Some Aspects of Intermarriage in the Jewish Community of São Paulo, Brazil," *American Jewish Archives* 34:2 (November 1982), 220; Izaac Gleiser, *Simpósio sobre educação judaica no Rio de Janeiro* (Rio de Janeiro: Instituto Brasileiro Judaico de Cultura e Divulgação, 1966); Rattner, *Tradição*, 61–75.

31. *Latin American Weekly Report*, 20 June 1980.

32. "Brazil: Arms to Libya," *Latin American Political Report*, 4 March 1977.

33. Brazilian constitution of 1988, art. 5, par. 42.

34. Jeffrey Lesser, "Brazil," in *Anti-Semitism World Report—1992*, ed. Antony Lerman and Howard Spier (London: Institute of Jewish Affairs, 1992), 119–21.

35. Haim Avni, *Spain, the Jews, and Franco* (Philadelphia: Jewish Publication Society of America, 1982), 181–83.

36. Levine, *The Vargas Regime*, 233–36; McCann, *The Brazilian American Alliance*, 452–53.

Bibliography

UNPUBLISHED PAPERS

Glick, Thomas F. "Between Science and Zionism: Einstein in Brazil." Used with permission of the author.

Klich, Ignacio. "The Roots of Argentine Abstentionism in the Palestine Question, 1946." Used with permission of the author.

Rabinovitch, Moses (Associação Israelita Brasileira, Rio de Janeiro). "Appello e advertencia aos senhores directores da Associação Israelita de Colonização." 28 March 1935, file 16.152, 1935. Archive of O Estado de São Paulo.

MANUSCRIPT COLLECTIONS

American Jewish Archives. Cincinnati.

Aranha, Oswaldo. Papers. Centro de Pesquisa e Documentação de História Contemporânea. Fundação Getúlio Vargas. Rio de Janeiro.

Archive of Bernhard Wolff. Porto Alegre.

Archive of O Estado de São Paulo. São Paulo.

Archive of Samuel Chwartzman. Porto Alegre.

Archives of Simcha Melon. Porto Alegre.

Archives of the American Jewish Joint Distribution Committee. New York

Archives of the Jewish Colonization Association. London.

Archives of the Lar dos Velhos. São Paulo.

Archives of the St. John's Wood Synagogue. London.

Arquivo Histórico Itamaraty. Rio de Janeiro.

Arquivo Histórico do Rio Grande do Sul. Porto Alegre.

Biblioteca Alfred Hirschberg. Crônica Israelita Collection. Congregação Israelita Paulista. São Paulo.

Board of Deputies of British Jews. Archives. London.

Central Zionist Archives. Brazil File. Jerusalem.

Conselho Nacional de Economia. Collection. Arquivo Nacional. Rio de Janeiro.

D'Avigdor-Goldsmid, Sir Osmond E. Papers. In James G. McDonald Papers. Herbert H. Lehman Papers. Columbia University.

Einstein, Albert. Papers. Einstein Duplicate Archive. Seeley G. Mudd Manuscript Library. Princeton University Archives.

Great Britain. Foreign Office. Records. Public Record Office. Kew.

Gibson, Hugh. Papers. Hoover Institute. Stanford University.

Hebrew Immigrant Aid and Sheltering Society (HIAS). Papers. YIVO—Institute for Jewish Research Archives. New York.

Hospedaria dos Imigrantes. Documentação Administrativo. Archive of the Secretaria de Estado da Promoção Social-Centro Histórico do Imigrante. São Paulo.

Hull, Cordell. Papers. Manuscript Division. Library of Congress. Washington, D.C.

Inman, Samuel Guy. Papers. Archives of the Case Memorial Library of the Hartford Seminary Foundation. Hartford, Conn.

———. Papers. In James G. McDonald Papers. Herbert H. Lehman Papers. Columbia University.

Jewish Colonization Association. Archives. London.

Jewish Colonization Association. Papers. Arquivo Histórico Judaico Brasileiro. São Paulo.

Lemle, Henrique. Papers. American Jewish Archives. Cincinnati.

Lewinsky, Heinz. Interview. Oral History Archives. Instituto Cultural Judaico Marc Chagall. Porto Alegre.

Long, Breckinridge. Papers. Manuscript Division. Library of Congress. Washington, D.C.

McDonald, James G. Papers. Herbert H. Lehman Papers. Columbia University.

Ministério da Justiça e Negócios Interióres. Records. Arquivo Nacional. Rio de Janeiro.

Mocatta Library. Pamphlets Collection. University College. London.

Monteiro, Pedro de Góis. Papers. Arquivo Histórico do Exército. Rio de Janeiro.

———. Papers. Arquivo Nacional. Rio de Janeiro.

Müller, Filinto. Papers. Centro de Pesquisa e Documentação de História Contemporânea. Fundação Getúlio Vargas. Rio de Janeiro.

Neuman, Aaron. Papers. Arquivo Histórico Judaico Brasileiro. São Paulo.

Presidência da República. Collection. Arquivo Nacional. Rio de Janeiro.

Prüfer, Curt Max. Papers. Collection Curt Max Prüfer. Hoover Institute. Stanford University.

Salgado, Plínio. Papers. Arquivo Municipal de Rio Claro.

Salgado Filho, Joaquim Pedro. Papers. Arquivo Nacional. Rio de Janeiro.

Secção de Ordem Social. Collection. Arquivo Municipal de Rio Claro.

United States. Department of State. Record Group 59. General Records of the Department of State. National Archives. Washington, D.C.

———. Record Group 84. Records of Foreign Service Posts. National Archives Branch Depository. Suitland, Md.

Vargas, Getúlio. Papers. Centro de Pesquisa e Documentação de História Contemporânea. Fundação Getúlio Vargas. Rio de Janeiro.
Waldman, Morris. Papers. American Jewish Archives. Cincinnati.

NEWSPAPERS AND JOURNALS

A Ação (São Paulo)
Advance (Calcutta)
American Israelite (Cincinnati)
American Journal of Sociology
Careta (Rio de Janeiro)
O Carioca (Rio de Janeiro)
Christian Science Monitor (Boston)
A Columna (Rio de Janeiro)
Correio da Manhã (Rio de Janeiro)
Crônica Israelita (São Paulo)
Daily Herald (London)
Daily Telegraph (London)
Deutsche Zeitung (São Paulo)
Diário Oficial da República (Rio de Janeiro)
Diário Oficial—Estado de São Paulo
Diário Oficial—Estado do Rio de Janeiro
Diário da Manhã (Niteroi)
Diário da Manhã (Recife)
Diário da Noite (Rio de Janeiro)
Diário de Notícias (Rio de Janeiro)
Diário da Tarde (Rio de Janeiro)
Di Menscheit [Humanity] (Porto Alegre)
Dos Idische Vochenblatt [The Jewish Weekly] (Rio de Janeiro)
O Estado de São Paulo (São Paulo)
A Federação (Porto Alegre)
Folha da Manhã (Rio de Janeiro)
O Globo (Rio de Janeiro)
Idische Folkszeitung [Jewish Gazette] (Rio de Janeiro).
Idische Presse [Jewish Press] (Rio de Janeiro)
Illustração Israelita (Rio de Janeiro)
Indian Daily Mail (Bombay)
Japan Chronicle (Tokyo)
Jewish Chronicle (London)
O Jornal (Rio de Janeiro)
Jewish Week (New York)
Jornal do Comércio (Rio de Janeiro)
Jüdische Rundschau (Berlin)
Kol Yisroel [Voice of Israel] (Belem do Pará)
Latin American Political Report
Latin American Weekly Report
A Lyra (Rezende)

Manchete (Rio de Janeiro)
Meio-Dia (Rio de Janeiro)
Le Monde Diplomatique (Paris)
A Nação (Rio de Janeiro)
Nação Armada (Rio de Janeiro)
New York Times
A Noite (Rio de Janeiro)
A Ofensiva (Rio de Janeiro)
A Opinião (Rezende)
Pester Lloyd (Budapest)
Revista Brasileira (Rio de Janeiro)
Revista Brasileira de Geografia
Revista de Imigração e Colonização (Rio de Janeiro)
Século XX (Rio de Janeiro)
Times (London)
Times Picayune (New Orleans)
A Vanguarda (São Paulo)
Vida Policial (Rio de Janeiro)

BOOKS, ARTICLES, DISSERTATIONS, INTERVIEWS

Abella, Irving, and Harold Troper. *None Is Too Many: Canada and the Jews of Europe, 1933–1948.* New York: Random House, 1982.
Academic American Encyclopedia. Vol. 9. Darien, Conn.: Grolier, 1986.
Adler-Rudel, S. "The Evian Conference on the Refugee Question." *Leo Baeck Institute Yearbook* 13 (1968), 235–76.
———. "Moritz Baron Hirsch." *Leo Baeck Institute Yearbook* 8 (1963), 29–69.
Aguiar, Anésio Frota. *O lenocínio como problema social no Brasil.* Rio de Janeiro: n.p., 1940.
Alexandr, Frida. *Filipson: Memórias da primeira colônia judaica no Rio Grande do Sul.* São Paulo: Editora Fulgor, 1967.
Almeida, Guilherme de. "Cosmópolis: O 'ghetto.' " *O Estado de São Paulo* 31 (March 1929), 4.
———. *Cosmópolis: São Paulo/29.* São Paulo: Companhia Editora Nacional, 1962.
Almeida, J. R. Pires de. *Hygiene moral.* Rio de Janeiro: Laemmert, 1906.
Alvim, Zuleika. *Brava gente: Os italianos em São Paulo, 1870–1920.* São Paulo: Brasiliense, 1986.
Amado, Gilberto. "Momentos de vibração." In *Por que ser anti-semita?: Um inquérito entre intellectuaes brasileiros.* Rio de Janeiro: Civilização Brasileira, 1933.
Amaral, Azevedo. *Getúlio Vargas—estadista.* Rio de Janeiro: Irmãos Pongetti, 1941.
———. "Review of *O Brasil e o anti-semitismo.*" *Revista Brasileira* 2 (August 1934), 77–80.

Amarilio, Júnior. *As vantagens da immigração syria no Brasil (em torno de uma polêmica entre os Snrs. Herbert V. Levy e Salomão Jorge, no "Diário de São Paulo."* Rio de Janeiro: Off. Gr. da S.A. A Noite, 1935.

American Jewish Committee. *American Jewish Yearbook.* Philadelphia: Jewish Publication Society of America, 1899–1950. New York: Jewish Publication Society of America, 1951–.

Americano, Jorge. *São Paulo atual (1935–1962)* São Paulo: Edições Melhoramentos, 1963.

———. *São Paulo nesse tempo (1915–1935).* São Paulo: Edições Melhoramentos, 1962.

Anderson, Benedict. *Imagined Communities: Reflections on the Origin and Spread of Nationalism.* 2d ed. London: Verso, 1991.

Andrews, George Reid. *Blacks and Whites in São Paulo, Brazil, 1888–1988.* Madison: University of Wisconsin Press, 1991.

Annuário do estado do Rio Grande do Sul para o anno de 1906. Porto Alegre: Krabe and Company, 1905.

Appleton, Paul. *La traite des blanches.* Paris: Librairie Nouvelle de Droit et de Jurisprudence, 1903.

Arad, Yitzhak, Yisrael Gutman, and Abraham Margaliot, eds. *Documents on the Holocaust: Selected Sources on the Destruction of the Jews of Germany and Austria, Poland, and the Soviet Union.* Jerusalem: Yad Vashem and KTAV Publishing, 1981.

Araújo, Oscar Egídio de. "Enquistamentos étnicos." *Revista do Arquivo Municipal de São Paulo* 6:65 (March 1940), 227–46.

Araújo, Ricardo Benzaquen de. *Totalitarismo e revolução: O integralismo de Plínio Salgado.* Rio de Janeiro: Jorge Zahar Editor, 1987.

Arinos de Mello Franco, Afonso. *Preparação ao nacionalismo: Cartas aos que tem vinte anos.* Rio de Janeiro: Civilização Brasileira, 1934.

Aschheim, Stephen. *Brothers and Strangers: The East European Jew in German and German-Jewish Consciousness.* Madison: University of Wisconsin Press, 1982.

Associacíon Filantropica Israelita. "La inmigracíon a São Paulo desde 1933 hasta fines de 1942." In *Zehn Jahre Aufbauarbeit in Südamerika: Herausgegeben anlässlich des zehnjährigen Bestehens der Associacíon Filantropica Israelita, 1933–1943,* 207–29. Buenos Aires: Associacíon Filantropica Israelita, 1944.

Avila, Fernando Bastos de. *L'immigration au Brésil: Contribution à une théorie générale de l'immigration.* Rio de Janeiro: AGIR, 1956.

Avni, Haim. *Argentina and the Jews: A History of Jewish Immigration.* Translated by Gila Brand. Tuscaloosa: University of Alabama Press, 1991.

———. *Argentina y la historia de la inmigracíon judía, 1810–1950.* Jerusalem: Editorial Universitaria Magnes, 1983.

———. "Argentine Jewry: Its Socio-Political Status and Organizational Patterns." *Dispersion and Unity,* vol. 12 (1971).

———. "Latin America and the Jewish Refugees: Two Encounters, 1935 and 1938." In *The Jewish Presence in Latin America,* edited by Judith Laikin Elkin and Gilbert W. Merkx, 45–70. Boston: Allen and Unwin, 1987.

————. "Patterns of Jewish Leadership in Latin America during the Holocaust." In *Jewish Leadership During the Nazi Era: Patterns of Behavior in
the Free World,* edited by Randolph L. Braham, 87–125. New York: Columbia University Press, 1985.

————. *Spain, the Jews, and Franco.* Translated by Emanuel Shimoni. Philadelphia: Jewish Publication Society of America, 1982.

Back, Leon. "Imigração judaica no Rio Grande do Sul." In *Enciclopédia rio-
grandense* 5:271–82. Canoas: Editora Regional, 1958.

Backheuser, Everardo. "Comércio ambulante e ocupações de rua no Rio de
Janeiro." *Revista Brasileira de Geografia* 6:1 (January–March 1944), 3–29.

Baily, Samuel L. "The Adjustment of Italian Immigrants in Buenos Aires and
New York, 1870–1914." *American Historical Review* 88: 2 (April 1983),
281–305.

————. "Chain Migration of Italians to Argentina: Case Studies of the Agnonesi and Sirolesi." *Studi Emigrazione* 19 (March 1982), 73–91.

Bakota, Carlos S. "Crisis and the Middle Classes: The Ascendency of Brazilian
Nationalism, 1914–1922." Ph.D. diss., University of California at Los
Angeles, 1973.

Bandeira, Moniz. *Presença dos Estados Unidos no Brasil: Dois séculos de história.* Rio de Janeiro: Civilização Brasileira, 1978.

Barcellos, Rubens de. *Estudos rio grandenses: Motivos de história e literatura.*
Rio de Janeiro: Editora Globo, 1955.

Barretto, Castro. "Seleção e assimilação de imigrantes." *Revista Brasileira de
Medicina Pública* 12 (March–April 1947), 3–28.

Barroso, Gustavo. *Brasil, colônia de banqueiros.* Rio de Janeiro: Civilização
Brasileira, 1934.

————. *Judaismo, maçonaria e comunismo.* Rio de Janeiro: Civilização Brasileira, 1937.

————. *Roosevelt es judío.* Buenos Aires: La Mazorca, 1938.

————. *A sinagoga paulista.* 2d ed. Rio de Janeiro: Empresa Editora ABC,
1937.

Basseches, Bruno. *Bibliografia dos livros, folhetos e artigos referente a história
dos judeus no Brasil, incluindo as obras sobre judaismo publicadas no Brasil.* Rio de Janeiro: n.p., 1961.

Bastide, Roger. *Brasil: Terra de contrastes.* São Paulo: Difel, 1959.

Baumel, Judith Tyler. *Unfulfilled Promise: Rescue and Resettlement of Jewish
Refugee Children in the United States, 1934–1945.* Juneau, Alaska: Denali
Press, 1990.

Becker, Klaus, ed. *Enciclopédia rio-grandense.* Vol. 5, *Imigração.* Canoas: Editora Regional, 1958.

Beloch, Israel, and Alzira Alves de Abreu, eds. *Dicionário histórico-biográfico
brasileiro, 1930–1983.* 4 vols. Rio de Janeiro: Editora Forense-Universitária, 1984.

Berezin, Rifka, Zipora Rubinstein, and Gisele Beiguelman. "Current Research
on the Jews of Brazil." *Latin American Jewish Studies Newsletter* 6 (August
1986), 6.

Berson, Theodore Michael. "A Political Biography of Dr. Oswaldo Aranha of Brazil, 1930–1937." Ph.D. diss., New York University, 1971.

Blakeney, Michael. *Australia and the Jewish Refugees, 1933–1948.* Sydney: Croom Helm Australia, 1985.

Blay, Eva Alterman. "As duas memórias: Pequena história da imigração judaica." *Shalom* 19:223 (August 1984), 4–11.

———. "Inquisição, inquisições: Aspectos da participação dos judeus na vida sócio-política brasileira nos anos 30." *Tempo Social* 1:1 (1989), 105–30.

Bobrow, Henrique. Interview by author. São Paulo, 19 August 1986.

Borges, Vavy Pacheco. *Getúlio Vargas e a oligarquia paulista: História de uma esperança e muitos desenganos, 1926–1932.* São Paulo: Brasiliense, 1979.

Bourgeois, Daniel. "La porte se ferme: La Suisse et le problème de l'immigration juive en 1938." *Relations Internationales* 54 (summer 1988), 181–204.

Bra, Gerardo. *La organizacion negra: La increible historia de la Zwi Migdal.* Buenos Aires: Ediciones Corregidor, 1982.

Braham, Randolph L., ed. *Jewish Leadership during the Nazi Era: Patterns of Behavior in the Free World.* New York: Columbia University Press, 1985.

Brazil. *Collecção das leis da República dos Estados Unidos do Brasil de 1930.* Vol. 2, *Actos da junta governativa provisória e do governo provisório (outubro a dezembro).* Rio de Janeiro: Imprensa Nacional, 1931.

Brazil. Assembléia Nacional Constituinte. *Annaes da assembléia nacional constituinte organizados pela redação das annaes e documentos parlamentares.* Vol. 6. Rio de Janeiro: Imprensa Nacional, 1935.

Brazil. Diretor Geral de Estatística. *Recenseamento do Brasil realizado em 1 de setembro de 1920.* Vol. 4, pt. 1, *População.* Rio de Janeiro: Diretor Geral de Estatística, 1926.

———. *Resultados geraes do rencenseamento do Brasil, 1920: População, agricultura, indústria.* Rio de Janeiro: Diretor Geral de Estatística, 1926.

———. *Sexo, raça e estado civil, nacionalidade, filiação, culto, e analfabetismo da população recenseada em 31 de dezembro de 1890.* Rio de Janeiro: Imprensa Nacional, 1898.

Brazil. Fundação Instituto Brasileiro de Geografia e Estatística. *Estatísticas históricas do Brasil: Séries estatísticas retrospectivas.* Vol. 3, *Séries econômicas, demográficas e sociais de 1550 a 1985.* Rio de Janeiro: IBGE, 1986.

———. *Recenseamento geral do Brasil (1 de setembro de 1940).* 3 vols. Rio de Janeiro: Imprensa Nacional, 1950.

Brazil. Fundação Instituto Brasileiro de Geografia e Estatística. Conselho Nacional de Estatística. Serviço Nacional de Recenseamento. *Recenseamento geral do Brasil, 1950.* 30 vols. Rio de Janeiro: Imprensa Nacional, 1954.

Brazil. Instituto Brasileiro de Geografia e Estatística. *Brazil 1938: A New Survey of Brazilian Life.* Rio de Janeiro: Serviço Gráfico do Instituto Brasileiro de Geografia e Estatística, 1939.

Brazil. Ministério da Justiça e Negócios Interiores. *Estrangeiros: Legislação, 1808–1939.* Rio de Janeiro: Serviço de Documentação, 1950.

———. *Estrangeiros: Legislação, 1940–1949.* Rio de Janeiro: Serviço de Documentação, 1950.

Brazil. Ministério das Relações Exteriores. *Almanque do pessoal.* Rio de Janeiro: Imprensa Nacional, 1928 and 1945.
Brazil. Redação dos Anais e Documentos Parlamentares. *Annães da Assembléia Nacional Constituinte.* Rio de Janeiro: Imprensa Nacional, 1935.
Breitman, Richard, and Alan M. Kraut. *American Refugee Policy and European Jewry, 1933–1945.* Bloomington: Indiana University Press, 1987.
Bristow, Edward J. *Prostitution and Prejudice: The Jewish Fight against the White Slave Trade.* New York: Schocken Books, 1974.
Browne, George P. "Government Immigration Policy in Imperial Brazil, 1822–1870." Ph.D. diss., Catholic University of America, 1972.
Cabral, J. *A questão judaica.* Porto Alegre: Livraria do Globo, 1937.
Caffarelli, Roberto Vergara. "Einstein e o Brasil." *Ciência e Cultura* (São Paulo) 31 (1979), 1436–55.
Câmara, Aristóteles de Lima. "Incompatibilidade étnica?" *Revista de Imigração e Colonização* 1:4 (October 1940), 656–80.
Câmara, Aristóteles de Lima, and Arthur Hehl Neiva. "Colonizações nipônica e germânica no sul do Brasil." *Revista de Imigração e Colonização* 2:1 (January 1941), 39–121.
Camargo, J. F. *Crescimento da população no estado de São Paulo e seus aspectos econômicos.* São Paulo: University of São Paulo, 1952.
Campos, Francisco. *O estado nacional: Sua estructura, seu conteúdo ideológico.* Rio de Janeiro: José Olympio Editora, 1941.
Cancelli, Elizabeth. "O mundo da violência: Repressão e estado policial na era Vargas (1930–1945). Ph.D. diss., Department of History, University of Campinas, 1991.
Carneiro, Maria Luiza Tucci. *O anti-semitismo na era Vargas: Fantasmas de uma geração (1930–1945).* São Paulo: Brasiliense, 1988.
———. *Preconceito racial no Brasil-Colônia: Os Cristãos novos.* São Paulo: Brasiliense, 1983.
Caro, Herbert. "SIBRA 50 anos." In *Sociedade Israelita Brasileira de Cultura e Beneficência, 1936–1986,* 5–36. Porto Alegre: SIBRA, 1986.
Carone, Edgard. *A segunda república (1930–1937).* São Paulo: Corpo e Alma do Brasil-Difusão Européia do Livro, 1973.
———. *O tenentismo: Acontecimentos, personagens, programas.* São Paulo: Difel, 1975.
———. *A terceira república (1937–1945).* São Paulo: Difel/Difusão Editorial, 1976.
Carvalho, Péricles de Mello. "A legislação imigratória do Brasil e sua evolução." *Revista de Imigração e Colonização* 1:4 (October 1940), 719–38.
Castro, Flávio Mendes de Oliveira. *História da organização do ministério das relações exteriores.* Brasília: Editora da Universidade de Brasília, 1983.
Caulfield, Sueann. "Getting into Trouble: Dishonest Women, Modern Girls and Women-Men in the Conceptual Language of *Vida Policial,* 1925–1927." *Signs* 19:1 (fall 1993).
Chiavenato, Júlio José. *O inimigo eleito: Os judeus, o poder e o anti-semitismo.* Porto Alegre: Mercado Aberto, 1985.

Ciano, Galeazzo. *Ciano's Hidden Diary, 1937–1938.* Translated by Andrea Mayor. New York: E. P. Dutton and Co., 1953.

Coelho, Adolfo. *Ópio, cocaína e escravatura branca.* Lisbon: Livraria Clássica Editora, 1931.

Cohen, Jacob X. *Jewish Life in South America: A Survey Study for the American Jewish Congress.* New York: Bloch Publishing, 1941.

Cohen, Jeremy. *The Friars and the Jews: The Evolution of Medieval Anti-Judaism.* Ithaca, N.Y.: Cornell University Press, 1982.

Cohen, Stephen. "Historical Background." In *South African Jewry: A Contemporary Survey,* edited by Marcus Arkin, 1–22. Capetown: Oxford University Press, 1984.

Collor, Lindolfo. *Europa 1939.* Rio de Janeiro: EMIEL Editora, 1939.

Companhole, Adriano, and Hilton Lobo Companhole. *Constituições do Brasil.* São Paulo: Atlas, 1984.

Copstein, Raphael. "O trabalho estrangeiro no município do Rio Grande." *Boletim Gaúcho de Geografia* (Porto Alegre), no. 4 (1975).

Countinho, Lourival. *O general Góis Depõe.* 2d ed. Rio de Janeiro: Livraria Editora Coelho Branco, 1956.

Cytrynowicz, Roney. "Integralismo e anti-semitismo nos textos de Gustavo Barroso na década de 30." Master's thesis, Department of History, University of São Paulo, 1991.

———. *Memória da barbárie: A história do genocídio dos judeus na segunda guerra mundial.* São Paulo: EdUSP/Nova Stella, 1990.

Dahne, Eugenio, ed. *Descriptive Memorial of the State of Rio Grande do Sul, Brazil.* Porto Alegre: Commercial Library, 1904.

Daniels, Roger. *The Politics of Prejudice: The Anti-Japanese Movement in California and the Struggle for Japanese Exclusion.* Berkeley: University of California Press, 1962.

Davis, Moshe, ed. *World Jewry and the State of Israel.* New York: Arno Press, 1977.

Dawidowicz, Lucy S. *The War against the Jews: 1933–1945.* Toronto: Bantam Books, 1976.

Dean, Warren. "Economy." In *Brazil: Empire and Republic, 1822–1930,* edited by Leslie Bethell, 217–56. Cambridge: Cambridge University Press, 1989.

———. *The Industrialization of São Paulo, 1880–1945.* Austin: University of Texas Press, 1969.

Decca, Edgar S. de. *O silêncio dos vencidos.* São Paulo: Brasiliense, 1981.

Deffontaines, Pierre. "Mascates." *Geografia* 2:1 (1936), 26–29.

Degler, Carl. *Neither Black nor White: Slavery and Race Relations in Brazil and the United States.* New York: Macmillan, 1971.

DellaPergola, Sergio. "Demographic Trends of Latin American Jewry." In *The Jewish Presence in Latin America,* edited by Judith Laikin Elkin and Gilbert W. Merkx, 187–200. Boston: Allen and Unwin, 1987.

Didonet, Zilah C. *O positivismo e a constituição rio-grandense de 14 de julho de 1881.* Santa Catarina: Imprensa Universitária, 1977.

Diégues, Manuel, Jr. *Etnias e cultura no Brasil.* 5th ed. São Paulo: Círculo do Livro, 1972.

———. *Imigração, urbanização e industrialização: Estudo sobre alguns aspectos da contribuição cultural do imigrante no Brasil.* Rio de Janeiro: Centro Brasileiro de Pesquisas Educacionais, Instituto Nacional de Estudos Pedagógicos, Ministério da Educação, 1964.

Dines, Alberto. *Morte no paraíso: A tragédia de Stefan Zweig no país do futuro.* Rio de Janeiro: Nova Fronteira, 1981.

Diniz, Eli. "O Estado Novo: Estrutura de poder, relações de classes." In *O Brasil republicano: Sociedade e política (1930–1964)* (part 3, vol. 3 of *História geral da civilização brasileira*), 4th ed., edited by Boris Fausto, 77–120. São Paulo: Difel, 1985.

Dinnerstein, Leonard. *America and the Survivors of the Holocaust.* New York: Columbia University Press, 1982.

Dinnerstein, Leonard, and David M. Reimers. *Ethnic Americans: A History of Immigration and Assimilation.* 2d ed. New York: Harper and Row, 1982.

Duarte, Cândido. *A organização municipal no governo Getúlio Vargas.* Rio de Janeiro: Departamento de Imprensa e Propaganda, 1942.

Dulles, John W. F. *Anarchists and Communists in Brazil, 1900–1935.* Austin: University of Texas Press, 1973.

———. *Brazilian Communism, 1935–1945: Repression during World Upheaval.* Austin: University of Texas Press, 1983.

———. *Carlos Lacerda, Brazilian Crusader.* Vol. 1, *The Years 1914–1960.* Austin: University of Texas Press, 1991.

———. *Vargas of Brazil: A Political Biography.* Austin: University of Texas Press, 1967.

Durand, José Carlos G. "Formação do pequeno empresariado têxtil em São Paulo (1880–1950). In *Pequena empresa: O comportamento empresarial na acumulação e na luta pela sobrevivência*, edited by Henrique Rattner, 1:110–26. São Paulo: Brasiliense, 1985.

Dzidzienyo, Anani. *The Position of Blacks in Brazilian Society.* London: Minority Rights Group, 1971.

Eck, Nathan. "The Rescue of Jews with Aid of Passports and Citizenship Papers of the Latin American States." In *Yad Vashem Studies on the European Jewish Catastrophe and Resistance,* edited by Benzion Dinur and Shaul Esh, 125–52. Jerusalem: Yad Vashem, 1957.

Eisenstadt, Shmuel N. *The Absorption of Immigrants.* London: Routledge and Kegan Paul, 1969.

Eizirik, Moysés. *Imigrantes judeus: Relatos, crônicas e perfis.* Caxias do Sul: Editora da Universidade de Caxias do Sul, 1986.

Elkin, Judith Laikin. *Jews of the Latin American Republics.* Chapel Hill: University of North Carolina Press, 1980.

Elkin, Judith Laikin, and Gilbert W. Merkx, eds. *The Jewish Presence in Latin America.* Boston: Allen and Unwin, 1987.

Elon, Amos. *Herzl.* New York: Holt, Rinehart and Winston, 1975.

Encyclopedia Judaica. 16 vols. Jerusalem: Keter Publishing House, 1971.

Estorick, Eric. "The Evian Conference and the Intergovernmental Committee."

Annals of the American Academy of Political and Social Science 203 (May 1939), 136–41.

Europa World Year Book—1990. London: Europa Publications, 1990.

EZRA. *Ehzreh un Sanitorieh Ehzreh: 25 yohriker yubileitsz oysgohbeh 1916–1941* (EZRA and Sanitorium EZRA: Twenty-fifth year anniversary publication, 1916–1941). São Paulo: EZRA, 1941.

Faermann, Martha Pargendler. *A promessa cumprida.* Porto Alegre: Metrópole, 1990.

Falbel, Nachman. "Early Zionism in Brazil: The Founding Years, 1913–1922." *American Jewish Archives* 38:2 (1986), 123–36.

———. *Estudos sobre a comunidade judaica no Brasil.* São Paulo: Federação Israelita de São Paulo, 1984.

———. "Oswaldo Boxer e o projeto de colonização de judeus no Brasil. *Jornal do Imigrante* 10 (December 1987/January 1988), 18.

Fausto, Boris. "Expansão do café e política cafeeira." In *O Brasil republicano: Estrutura de poder e economia (1889–1930)* (part 3, vol. 1 of *História geral da civilização brasileira*), 4th ed., edited by Boris Fausto, 195–248. São Paulo: Difel, 1985.

———. *A revolução de 1930: Historiografia e história.* São Paulo: Brasiliense, 1986.

———. "Society and Politics." In *Brazil: Empire and Republic, 1822–1930,* edited by Leslie Bethell, 257–308. Cambridge: Cambridge University Press, 1989.

———. *Trabalho urbano e conflito social.* São Paulo: Difel, 1976.

Feffer, Leon. Interview by author. São Paulo, 6 November 1986.

Feingold, Henry L. *The Politics of Rescue: The Roosevelt Administration and the Holocaust, 1938–1945.* New Brunswick, N.J.: Rutgers University Press, 1970.

———. "Roosevelt and the Resettlement Question." In *Rescue Attempts during the Holocaust: Proceedings of the Second Yad Vashem International Historical Conference,* edited by Yisrael Gutman and Efraim Zuroff, 123–81. Jerusalem: Yad Vashem, 1977.

Fernandes, Florestan. "Immigration and Race Relations in São Paulo." In *Race and Class in Latin America,* edited by Magnus Mörner, 122–42. New York: Columbia University Press, 1970.

———. *The Negro in Brazilian Society.* New York: Atheneum, 1971.

Fernandes, Geraldo. "A religião nas constituicões republicanas do Brasil." *Revista Eclesiástica Brasileira* 8:4 (December 1948), 830–57.

Ferreira da Rosa, Francisco. *O lupanar: Estudo sobre o caftismo e a prostituição no Rio de Janeiro.* Rio de Janeiro, n.p., 1896.

Fiola, Jan. *Race Relations in Brazil: A Reassessment of the "Racial Democracy" Thesis.* Program in Latin American Studies Occasional Paper Series, no. 24. Amherst: University of Massachusetts at Amherst, 1990.

Flapan, Simha. *The Birth of Israel: Myths and Realities.* New York: Pantheon Books, 1987.

Fonseca, Guido. *História da prostituição em São Paulo.* São Paulo: Editora Resenha Universitária, 1982.

Fontaine, Pierre-Michel, ed. *Race, Class and Power in Brazil.* Los Angeles: Center for Afro-American Studies, UCLA, 1985.

Ford, Henry. *O judeu internacional.* Translated by Gustavo Barroso. Porto Alegre: Livraria do Globo, 1933.

Frank, Waldo. *South American Journey.* London: Victor Gollancz, 1944.

Frankenstein, Herbert. *Brasilien: Als Aufnahmeland der jüdischen Auswanderung aus Deutschland.* Berlin: Joseph Jastrow Verlagsbuchhandlung, 1936.

Freeman, Mark. *The Yidishe Gauchos.* Berkeley, Calif.: Fine Line Productions, 1989. Documentary film.

Freitas, Jorge Emilio de Souza. "Primeiro ano de trabalhos do conselho de imigração e colonização." *Revista de Imigração e Colonização* 1:1 (January 1940): 5–17.

Freyre, Gilberto. "Brazilian Melting Pot: The Meeting of Race in Portuguese America." In *Perspective of Brazil: An Atlantic Monthly Supplement,* 8–12. New York: Intercultural Publications, 1956.

———. *Ordem e progresso.* 2 vols. Rio de Janeiro: José Olympio Editora, 1959.

———. *Order and Progress: Brazil from Monarchy to Republic.* Translated by Rod W. Horton. New York: Alfred A. Knopf, 1970.

———. *Tempo de aprendiz.* 2 vols. São Paulo: Instituição Brasileira de Difusão Cultural, 1979.

Friedländer, Saul. *Pius XII and the Third Reich: A Documentation.* Translated by Charles Fullman. New York: Alfred A. Knopf, 1966.

Friedman, Saul S. *No Haven for the Oppressed: United States Policy toward Jewish Refugees 1938–1945.* Detroit, Mich.: Wayne State University Press, 1973.

Friesel, Sigue. *Bror Chail: História do movimento e do kibutz brasileiro.* Jerusalem: Departamento da Juventude e do Chalutz da Organização Sionista Mundial, 1956.

Fukunaga, Patrick N. "The Brazilian Experience: The Japanese Immigrants during the Period of the Vargas Regime and Its Immediate Aftermath." Ph.D. diss., University of California at Santa Barbara, 1983.

Gabaglia, Laurita Pessôa Raja. *O Cardeal Leme (1882–1942).* Rio de Janeiro: José Olympio Editora, 1962.

Gambini, Roberto. *O duplo jogo de Getúlio Vargas: Influência americana e alemã no Estado Novo.* São Paulo: Editora Símbolo, 1977.

García-Granados, Jorge. *The Birth of Israel: The Drama As I Saw It.* New York: Alfred A. Knopf, 1949.

Gardolinski, Edmundo. *Escolas da colonização polonesa no Rio Grande do Sul.* Porto Alegre: Escola Superior de Teologia São Lourenço de Brindes, 1976.

Genizi, Haim. *American Apathy: The Plight of Christian Refugees from Nazism.* Ramat Gan, Israel: Bar-Ilan University Press, 1983.

Gertz, René. *O fascismo no sul do Brasil: Germanismo, nazismo, integralismo.* Porto Alegre: Mercado Aberto, 1987.

———. *O perigo alemão.* Porto Alegre: Editora da Universidade Federal do Rio Grande do Sul, 1991.

Gilman, Sander. *The Jew's Body.* New York: Routledge, Chapman and Hall, 1991.

Gleiser, Izaac. *Simpósio sobre educação judaica no Rio de Janeiro.* Rio de Janeiro: Instituto Brasileiro Judaico de Cultura e Divulgação, 1966.

Glick, Edward B. *Latin America and the Palestine Problem.* New York: Theodore Herzl Foundation, 1958.

Gobineau, Arthur, comte de. *The Inequality of Human Races.* Translated by Adrian Collins. Los Angeles: Noontide Press, 1966. Originally published as *Essai sur l'inégalité des races humaines* (Paris: Firmin-Didot, [2d ed.] 1884; Belmond, 1967).

Gold, Arthur, and Robert Fizdale. *The Divine Sarah: A Life of Sarah Bernhardt.* New York: Alfred A. Knopf, 1991.

Gomes, Ângela Maria de Castro, ed. *Regionalismo e centralização política: Partidos e constituinte nos anos 30.* Rio de Janeiro: Nova Fronteira, 1980.

———. "A representação de classes na constituinte de 1934." In *Regionalismo e centralização política: Partidos e constituinte nos anos 30,* 427–91. Rio de Janeiro: Nova Fronteira, 1980.

Gonçalves, Ricardo. "A religião na época da emigração para o Brasil e suas repercussões em nosso país." *Revista de História* 39:80 (1969), 359–77.

Gonzaga, Sergius, and José H. Dacanal, eds. *RS: Imigração e colonização.* Porto Alegre: Mercado Aberto, 1980.

Gonzales Dias, A. *Dicionário da língua Tupy: Chamada língua geral dos indígenas do Brasil.* Leipzig: Brockhaus, 1858.

Goren, Uri. Interview by author. Comunidade Shalom, São Paulo, 21 August 1988.

Goulart, José Alipio. *O mascate no Brasil.* Rio de Janeiro: Editora Conquista, Coleção Terra dos Papagaios, 1967.

Graham, Douglas H. "Migração estrangeira e a questão da oferta de mão-de-obra no crescimento econômico brasileiro, 1880–1930. *Estudos Econômicos* 3:1 (1973), 7–64.

Graham, Douglas H., and Sérgio Buarque Hollanda Filho. *Migration, Regional and Urban Growth, and Development in Brazil: A Selective Analysis of the Historical Record, 1872–1970.* São Paulo: Instituto Pesquisas Econômicas—Universidade de São Paulo, 1971.

Graham, Richard. *Britain and the Onset of Modernization in Brazil, 1850–1914.* Cambridge: Cambridge University Press, 1972.

———, ed. *The Idea of Race in Latin America, 1870–1940.* Austin: University of Texas Press, 1990.

Gritti, Isabel Rosa. "A imigração judaica para o Rio Grande do Sul: A Jewish Colonization Association e a colonização de Quatro Irmãos." Master's thesis, Pontifícia Universidade Católica do Rio Grande do Sul, 1992.

Guinsburg, Solomon L. *A Wandering Jew in Brazil: An Autobiography of Solomon L. Guinsburg.* Nashville: Sunday School Board of the Southern Baptist Convention, 1922.

Gutterman, Itzik. Interview by author. São Paulo, 21 October 1986.

Guy, Donna J. *Sex and Danger in Buenos Aires: Prostitution, Family and Nation in Argentina.* Lincoln: University of Nebraska Press, 1991.

————. "White Slavery, Public Health, and the Socialist Position on Legalized Prostitution in Argentina, 1913–1936." *Latin American Research Review* 23:3 (1988), 60–80.

Hahner, June E. *Poverty and Politics: The Urban Poor in Brazil, 1870–1920.* Albuquerque: University of New Mexico Press, 1986.

Hajjar, Claude Fahd. *Imigração árabe: 100 anos de reflexão.* São Paulo: Editora Cone, 1985.

Hall, Michael M. "New Approaches to Immigration History." In *New Approaches to Latin American History,* edited by Richard Graham and Peter H. Smith, 175–93. Austin: University of Texas Press, 1974.

————. "The Origins of Mass Immigration to Brazil, 1871–1914." Ph. D. diss., Columbia University, 1969.

Henriques, Affonso. *Ascensão e queda de Getúlio Vargas: O Estado Novo.* Rio de Janeiro: Distribuidora Record, 1966.

Herman, Donald L. *The Latin American Jewish Community of Israel.* New York: Praeger, 1984.

Hersch, Leib. "Jewish Migrations during the Last Hundred Years." In Central Yiddish Culture Organization, *The Jewish People: Past and Present,* 407–30. New York: Jewish Encyclopedic Handbooks, 1946.

Herzberg, Rolf. Interview by author. São Paulo, 29 May 1986.

Higham, John. *Strangers in the Land: Patterns of American Nativisim, 1860–1925.* New Brunswick, N.J.: Rutgers University Press, 1955.

Hilton, Stanley E. "Ação Integralista Brasileira: Fascism in Brazil, 1932–1938." *Luso-Brazilian Review* 9:2 (December 1972), 3–29.

————. *Brazil and the Great Powers, 1930–1939: The Politics of Trade Rivalry.* Austin: University of Texas Press, 1975.

————. *Brazil and the Soviet Challenge, 1917–1947.* Austin: University of Texas Press, 1991.

————. *A guerra secreta de Hitler no Brasil.* Rio de Janeiro: Editora Nova Fronteira, 1983.

————. *Hitler's Secret War in South America, 1939–1945: German Military Espionage and Allied Counterespionage in Brazil.* Baton Rouge: Louisiana State University Press, 1981.

————. "The United States and Argentina in Brazil's Wartime Foreign Policy, 1939–1945." In *Argentina between the Great Powers, 1939–1946,* edited by Guido di Tella and D. Cameron Watt, 158–80. Pittsburgh, Pa.: University of Pittsburgh Press, 1990.

Hirsch, Maurice de. "My Views on Philanthropy." *North American Review* 153 (July 1889).

Hirschberg, Alfred. "The Economic Adjustment of Jewish Refugees in São Paulo." *Jewish Social Studies* 7 (January 1945), 31–40.

Hirschberg, Alice Irene. *Desafio e resposta: A história da Congregação Israelita Paulista.* São Paulo: Congregação Israelita Paulista, 1976.

Hirschberg, Eva. Interview by author. São Paulo, 30 May 1986.

Hirschman, Albert O. *Journeys towards Progress: Studies of Economic Policy-Making in Latin America.* New York: Doubleday, 1963.

Holloway, Thomas. *Immigrants on the Land.* Chapel Hill: University of North Carolina Press, 1980.

Hu-DeHart, Evelyn. "Racism and Anti-Chinese Persecution in Sonora, Mexico, 1876–1932." *Amerasia* 9:2 (fall/winter 1982), 1–28.

Hunsche, Carlos E. *O biênio 1824/1825 da imigração e colonização alemã no RS (província de São Pedro)*. Porto Alegre: DAC/SEC, 1975.

Husry, Khaldun S. "The Assyrian Affair of 1933." Parts 1 and 2. *International Journal of Middle East Affairs* 5:2 (1974), 161–76; 5:3 (1974), 348–52.

Hutter, Lucy Maffei. *Imigração italiana em São Paulo, 1880–1889*. São Paulo: Instituto de Estudos Brasileiros, 1972.

Inman, Samuel Guy. "Refugee Settlement in Latin America." *Annals of the American Academy of Political and Social Science* 203 (May 1939), 183–93.

International Emigration Commission. *Report of the Commission, August 1921*. Geneva: International Labour Office, 1921.

International Labour Office. *Yearbook of Labour Statistics, 1940*. Geneva: International Labour Office, 1940.

————. *Yearbook of Labour Statistics, 1949–1950*. Geneva: International Labour Office, 1951.

Jacobina, Eduardo. *Conflictos de duas civilizações*. Rio de Janeiro: Record Editora, 1933.

Jewish Colonization Association. *Annual Report*. Paris: Imprimerie R. Veneziani, 1896–1950.

————. *Atlas des colonies et domaines de la Jewish Colonization Association en république Argentine et au Brésil: Supplément au rapport annuel pour 1913*. Paris: Imprimerie R. Veneziani, 1914.

————. *Jewish Colonization Association: su obra en la república Argentina, 1881–1941*. Buenos Aires: ICA, 1941.

————. *Le baron Maurice de Hirsch et la Jewish Colonization Association (à l'occasion du centenaire de la naissance du baron de Hirsch)*. Paris: Imprimerie R. Veneziani, 1931.

————. *Rapport de l'administration centrale au conseil d'administration*. Paris: Imprimerie R. Veneziani, 1896–1950.

Joffily, José. *Harry Berger*. Rio de Janeiro: Paz e Terra, 1987.

Kalbach, Warren E., and Wayne W. McVey. *The Demographic Bases of Canadian Society*. Toronto: McGraw-Hill, 1971.

Katz, Jacob. *From Prejudice to Destruction: Anti-Semitism, 1700–1933*. Cambridge: Harvard University Press, 1980.

Kellner, Leon. *Theodore Herzl's Lehrjahre, 1860–1895*. Vienna and Berlin: R. Loewit Verlag, 1920.

Klich, Ignacio. "L'essor des relations commericales entre le Brésil et le monde arabe." *Le Monde Diplomatique* (Paris), August 1981.

————. "Latin America, the United States and the Birth of Israel: The Case of Somoza's Nicaragua." *Journal of Latin American Studies* 20:2 (November 1988), 389–432.

Kliemann, Luiza H. Schmitz. "A ferrovia gaúcha e as diretrizes de 'Ordem e progresso,' 1905–1920." *Estudos Íbero-Americanos* (Porto Alegre) 3:2 (December 1977), 159–250.

————. *História da questão agrária*. Porto Alegre: Mercado Aberto, 1986.

Knowlton, Clark. *Sírios e libaneses*. São Paulo: Editora Anhembi, 1960.

Kosminsky, Ethel Volfzon. *Rolândia, a terra prometida: Judeus refugiados do nazismo no norte do Paraná.* São Paulo: Faculdade de Filosofia, Letras, e Ciências Humanas/Centro de Estudos Judaicos-USP, 1985.

Krausz, Rosa R. "Some Aspects of Intermarriage in the Jewish Community of São Paulo, Brazil." *American Jewish Archives* 34:2 (November 1982), 216–30.

Kula, Marcin. "Algumas observações sobre a emigração polonesa para o Brasil." *Estudios Latinoamericanos* (Warsaw) 3 (1976): 171–78.

Kulkes, Marlene, ed. *Histórias de vida: Imigração judaica no Rio Grande do Sul.* Porto Alegre: Instituto Cultural Judaico Marc Chagall, 1989.

La Cava, Gloria. "As origens da emigração italiana para a America Latina após a segunda guerra mundial." *Novos Cadernos* (São Paulo) 2 (1988), 49–78.

Lacerda, Carlos. *A missão da imprensa.* Rio de Janeiro: Livraria AGIR Editora, 1950.

Landman, Isaac. "Jewish Question." In *The Universal Jewish Encyclopedia,* 6:140–41. New York: Universal Jewish Encyclopedia, 1939–43.

Laquer, Walter. *A History of Zionism.* New York: Schocken Books, 1972.

Largman, Esther Regina, and Robert M. Levine. "Jews in the Tropics: Bahian Jews in the Early Twentieth Century." *Americas* 18:2 (October 1986), 159–70.

Lassance Cunha, Ernesto A. *O Rio Grande do Sul: Contribuição para o estudo de suas condições econômicas.* Rio de Janeiro: Imprensa Nacional, 1908.

Lauerhass, Ludwig, Jr. "Getúlio Vargas and the Triumph of Brazilian Nationalism: A Study on the Rise of the Nationalist Generation of 1930." Ph.D. diss., University of California at Los Angeles, 1972.

Layrac, Louis. *La traite des blanches et l'excitation à la débauche.* Paris: V. Girard et F. Briere, 1904.

League of Nations. *Report of the Special Body of Experts on Traffic in Women and Children.* Geneva: League of Nations, 1927.

League of Nations. Office of the High Commissioner for Refugees Coming from Germany. *Fourth Meeting of the Governing Body of the High Commissioner for Refugees (Jewish and Other) Coming from Germany, July 17, 1935 (including the opening remarks of the Chairman, The Rt. Hon. Viscount Cecil of Chelwood, and the Report of the High Commissioner, Mr. James G. McDonald.* London: Office of the High Commissioner, 1935.

Leff, Nathaniel H. *Underdevelopment and Development in Brazil.* Vol. 1, *Economic Structure and Change, 1822–1947.* London: George Allen and Unwin, 1982.

Leite, Solidônio. "O concurso dos judeus na civilização brasileira." In *Por que ser anti-semita?: Um inquérito entre intellectuaes brasileiros,* 179–91. Rio de Janeiro: Civilização Brasileira, 1933.

———. *Os judeus no Brasil.* Rio de Janeiro: J. Leite e Cia., 1923.

Lemos, Renato, and Joana Angélica Melo. "Meira de Vasconcelos." In *Dicionário histórico-biográfico brasileiro, 1930–1983,* edited by Israel Beloch and Alzira Alves de Abreu, 4:3, 517. Rio de Janeiro: Editora Forense-Universitária, 1984.

Lenharo, Alcir. *Sacralização da política*. Campinas: Papiras, 1986.

Lesser, Jeffrey. "Always Outsiders: Asians, Naturalization and the Supreme Court." *Amerasia Journal* 12:1 (1985–86), 83–100.

———. "Are African-Americans African or American? Brazilian Immigration Policy in the 1920s." *Review of Latin American Studies* 4:1 (1991), 115–37. Published in Japanese as "Afurika-kei Amerikajin-wa Afurika-jin nanoka, Amerika-jin nanka?" in *Rekishi Hyoron* (Review of Historical Studies) 501:1 (1992), 54–70.

———. "Brazil." In *Anti-Semitism World Report—1992*, edited by Antony Lerman and Howard Spier, 119–21. London: Institute of Jewish Affairs, 1992.

———. "Challenges to Jewish Life in Latin America." In *Survey of Jewish Affairs*, edited by William Frankel, 232–40. London: Basil Blackwell, 1991.

———. "Continuity and Change within an Immigrant Community: The Jews of São Paulo, 1924–1945." *Luso-Brazilian Review* 25:2 (winter 1988), 45–58.

———. "Diferencias regionales en el desarrollo histórico de las comunidades judeo-brasileñas contemporáneas: San Pablo y Porto Alegre." *Estudios Migratorios Latinoamericanos* 4:11 (April 1989), 71–84. An earlier version appeared as "Historische Entwicklung und regionale Unterscheide der zeitgenössischen brasilianisch-jüdischen Gemeinden: São Paulo und Porto Alegre." Translated by Petra Möbius. In *Europäische Juden in Lateinamerika*, edited by Achim Schrader and Karl H. Rengstorf, 361–77. St. Ingbert: Werner J. Röhrig Verlag, 1989.

———. "From Pedlars to Proprietors: Lebanese, Syrian and Jewish Immigrants in Brazil." In *The Lebanese in the World: A Century of Emigration*, edited by Albert Hourani and Nadim Shehadi, 393–410. London and New York: I. B. Tauris and St. Martin's Press, 1992.

———. "Imigração judaica no Rio de Janeiro." In *Heranças e lembranças: Imigrantes judeus no Rio de Janeiro*, edited by Susane Worcman, 27–32. Rio de Janeiro: ARI/CIEC/MIS, 1991.

———. "Immigration and Shifting Concepts of National Identity in Brazil during the Vargas Era." *Luso-Brazilian Review* 31:2 (winter 1994).

———. *Jewish Colonization in Rio Grande do Sul, 1904–1925*. São Paulo: Centro de Estudos de Demografia Histórica de América Latina, Universidade de São Paulo, 1991.

———. "Pawns of the Powerful: Jewish Immigration to Brazil, 1904–1945." Ph.D. diss., New York University, 1989.

Lestschinsky, Jacob. "The Industrial and Social Structure of the Jewish Population of Interbellum Poland." *YIVO Annual of Jewish Social Science* 11 (1957), 243–69.

———. "Jewish Migrations, 1840–1956." In *The Jews: Their History, Culture and Religion*, 3d ed., edited by Louis Finkelstein, 2:1,536–96. New York: Harper and Brothers, 1960.

———. *De lage fun yidn in lateyn-amerikaner lender* (The situation of Jews in Latin America). New York: World Congress for Jewish Affairs, 1948.

———. "National Groups in Polish Emigration." *Jewish Social Studies* 5:2 (April 1943), 99–114.

Levin, Nora. *The Holocaust: The Destruction of European Jewry, 1933–1945*. New York: Schocken Books, 1968.

Levine, Robert M. "Brazil's Jews during the Vargas Era and After." *Luso-Brazilian Review* 5:1 (June 1968), 45–58.

———. *Race and Ethnic Relations in Latin America and the Caribbean: An Historical Dictionary and Bibliography*. Metuchen, N.J.: Scarecrow Press, 1980.

———. *The Vargas Regime: The Critical Years, 1934–1938*. New York: Columbia University Press, 1970.

Levy, Herbert V. *Problemas actuaes da economia brasileira*. São Paulo: Empresa Gráfica da "Revista dos Tribunaes," 1934.

Levy, Maria Stella Ferreira. "O papel da migração internacional na evolução da população brasileira (1872–1972)." *Revista de Saúde Pública* (São Paulo), supp. 8 (1974), 49–90.

Lévi-Strauss, Claude. *A World on the Wane*. Translated by John Russel. New York: Criterion Books, 1961.

Lewgoi, Wily P. Interview by author. Porto Alegre, 15 July 1986.

Liebman, Seymour B. *New World Jewry, 1493–1825: Requiem for the Forgotten*. New York: KTAV Publishing House, 1982.

Lima, Ivan Lins. *História do positivismo no Brasil*. São Paulo: Editora Nacional, 1967.

Lima, Jorge de. *Os judeus*. Rio de Janeiro: n.p., 1938.

Linfield, Harry S. "Statistics of the Jews." In *American Jewish Yearbook— 5683*, vol. 22. Philadelphia: Jewish Publication Society of America, 1922.

Lobo, Eulália Maria Lahmeyer. *História do Rio de Janeiro: Do capital ao capital industrial e financeiro*. Rio de Janeiro: IBMEC, 1978.

Loewenstamm, Kurt. *Vultos judaicos no Brasil: Uma contribuição a história dos judeus no Brasil*. Vol. 1, *Tempo colonial, 1500–1822*, and vol. 2, *Império, 1822–1899*. Rio de Janeiro: Editora A Noite, 1949 and 1956.

Loewenstein, Kurt. *Brazil under Vargas*. New York: Macmillan, 1942.

Lopes, Osório. *O problema judaico*. Petrópolis: Vozes, 1942.

Love, Joseph L. *Rio Grande do Sul and Brazilian Regionalism, 1882–1930*. Stanford, Calif.: Stanford University Press, 1971.

———. "O Rio Grande do Sul como fator de instabilidade na República Velha." In *O Brasil republicano: Estrutura de poder e economia (1889– 1930)* (part 3, vol. 1 of *História geral da civilização brasileira*), 4th ed., edited by Boris Fausto, 99–121. São Paulo: Difel, 1985.

———. *São Paulo in the Brazilian Federation, 1889–1937*. Stanford, Calif.: Stanford University Press, 1980.

Luebke, Frederick C. *Germans in Brazil: A Comparative History of Cultural Conflict during World War I*. Baton Rouge: Louisiana State University Press, 1987.

Luizetto, Flávio V. "Os constituintes em face da imigração: Estudo sobre o preconceito e a discriminação racial e étnica na constituinte de 1934." Master's thesis, University of São Paulo, 1975.

McAlister, Lyle N. *Spain and Portugal in the New World, 1492–1700*. Minneapolis: University of Minnesota Press, 1984.

Macaulay, Neill. *The Prestes Column: Revolution in Brazil.* New York: New Viewpoints, 1974.

McCann, Frank D., Jr. *The Brazilian American Alliance, 1937–1945.* Princeton, N.J.: Princeton University Press, 1973.

MacDonald, John S., and Leatrice D. MacDonald, "Chain Migration, Ethnic Neighborhood Formation and Social Networks." *Milbank Memorial Fund Quarterly* 13:42 (1964), 82–95.

Maciel, Anor Butler. *Nacionalismo: O problema judaico no mundo e no Brasil: O nacional-socialismo.* Porto Alegre: Livraria do Globo, 1937.

McLain, Douglas, Jr. "Alberto Torres, Ad Hoc Nationalist." *Luso-Brazilian Review* 4:4 (December 1967), 17–34.

MacLean, Annie Marion. *Modern Immigration: A View of the Situation in Immigrant Receiving Countries.* Philadelphia: J. B. Lippincott, 1925.

Magalhaens, Cezar. *Pela brazilidade: Discursos e conferências.* Rio de Janeiro: Typ. A. Pernambucana Hermes Poffes, 1925.

Maier, Max Hermann. *Um advogado de Frankfurt se torna cafeicultor na selva brasileira: Relato de um imigrante (1938–1975).* Translated by Mathilde Maier and Elmar Joenck. Mimeographed. Originally published as *Ein Frankfurter Rechtsanwalt wird Kaffeepflanzer im Urwald Brasiliens: Bericht eines Emigranten (1938–1975)* (Franfurt am Main: Josef Knecht Verlag, 1975).

Maio, Marcos Chor. *Nem Rotschild nem Trotsky: O pensamento anti-semita de Gustavo Barroso.* Rio de Janeiro: Imago, 1992.

Malamud, Samuel. "Contribucíon judía al desarollo del Brasil en las 150 años de la independencia." In *Comunidades judías de Latinoamérica,* 330–39. Buenos Aires: Oficina Sudamerica del Comité Judía Americano, 1971–1972.

———. *Do arquivo e da memória: Fatos, personagems e reflexões sobre o sionismo brasileiro e mundial.* Rio de Janeiro: Bloch Editores, 1983.

———. *Escalas no tempo.* Rio de Janeiro: Editora Record, 1986.

———. *Recordando a Praça Onze.* Rio de Janeiro: Editora Kosmos, 1988.

———. "T'meim: Os judeus impuros." *Shalom* (São Paulo) 13:260 (May 1988), 29–30.

Manfroi, Olívio. *A colonização italiana no RS: Implicações econômicas, políticas e culturais.* Porto Alegre: Grafosul, 1975.

Margaliot, Abraham. "The Problems of the Rescue of German Jewry during the Years 1933–1945." In *Rescue Attempts during the Holocaust: Proceedings of the Second Yad Vashem International Historical Conference, April 1976,* 247–65. Jerusalem: Yad Vashem, 1977.

Margulies, Marcos. *Judaica brasiliensis; Repertório bibliográfico comentando dos livros relacionados com o judaismo.* Rio de Janeiro: Editora Documentário, 1974.

Marr, Phebe. *The Modern History of Iraq.* Boulder, Colo.: Westview Press, 1985.

Marrus, Michael R. *The Unwanted: European Refugees in the Twentieth Century.* New York: Oxford University Press, 1985.

Marson, Adalberto. *A ideologia nacionalista em Alberto Torres.* São Paulo: Duas Cidades, 1979.

Martins, Wilson. *História da inteligência brasileira*. 7 vols. São Paulo: Cultrix, 1978.

Matta, Roberto da. *Carnavais, malandros e heróis*. Rio de Janeiro: Zahar Editores, 1979.

———. *Carnivals, Rogues, and Heroes: An Interpretation of the Brazilian Dilemma*. Translated by John Drury. Notre Dame, Ind.: University of Notre Dame Press, 1991.

Meade, Teresa, and Gregory Alonso Pirio. "In Search of the Afro-American 'Eldorado': Attempts by North American Blacks to Enter Brazil in the 1920s." *Luso-Brazilian Review* 25:1 (summer 1988), 85–109.

Merrick, Thomas W., and Douglas H. Graham. *Population and Economic Development in Brazil, 1800 to Present*. Baltimore, Md.: Johns Hopkins Press, 1979.

Mesquita Filho, Julio de. *Política e cultura*. São Paulo: Livraria Martins, 1969.

Michaels, Meir. *Mussolini and the Jews: German-Italian Relations and the Jewish Question in Italy, 1922–1945*. Oxford: Clarendon Press, 1978.

Milgram, Avraham. "O Brasil e a questão dos refugiados judeus durante a segunda guerra mundial: A tentativa de salvação de católicos não arianos da Alemanha ao Brasil através do Vaticano 1939–1942)." Master's thesis, Hebrew University of Jerusalem, 1989.

———. "A colonização agrícola a refugiados judeus no Brasil, 1936–1939." In *Proceedings of the Tenth World Congress of Jewish Studies*, 583–93. Jerusalem: World Union of Jewish Studies, 1990.

Mindlin, José. Interview by author. São Paulo, 29 October 1986.

Mirelman, Victor A. *Jewish Buenos Aires, 1890–1930: In Search of an Identity*. Detroit, Mich.: Wayne State University Press, 1990.

Monteiro, Norma de Góes. "Esbôço da política imigratória e colonizadora do governo de Minas Gerais, 1889–1930. *Revista Brasileira de Estudos Políticos* 29 (July 1970), 195–216.

Moraes, Evaristo de. *"Judeus sem dinheiro* taes como eu vejo." In *Os judeus na história do Brasil*, edited by Afrânio Peixoto, 101–13. Rio de Janeiro: Uri Zwerling, 1936.

Morais, Fernando. *Olga: A vida de Olga Benário Prestes, judia comunista entregue a Hitler pelo governo Vargas*. São Paulo: Alfa-Ômega, 1986.

Moreira Pinto, Alfredo. *Apontamentos para o dicionário geográfico do Brasil*. Rio de Janeiro: Imprensa Nacional, 1894.

Moritz, Helena. Interview by author. São Paulo, 29 May 1986.

Morley, John F. *Vatican Diplomacy and the Jews during the Holocaust, 1939–1943*. New York: KTAV Publishing House, 1980.

Mörner, Magnus. *Adventurers and Proletarians: The Story of Migrants in Latin America*. Pittsburgh, Pa.: University of Pittsburgh Press, 1985.

———, ed. *Race and Class in Latin America*. New York: Columbia University Press, 1970.

Morse, Richard B. *From Community to Metropolis: A Biography of São Paulo, Brazil*. Gainesville: University of Florida Press, 1958.

Mortara, Giorgio. "Sôbre os métodos aplicados para a reconstituição do movimento da população do Brasil, com a ajuda dos dados dos recenseas-mentos." *Revista Brasileira de Estatística* 11:41 (January–March 1950), 23–30.

Moscovich, Sandra Lemchen, ed. *Histórias de vida: Imigração judaica no Rio Grande do Sul.* Vol. 2. Porto Alegre: Instituto Cultural Judaico Marc Chagall, 1992.

Mosse, George L. *Toward the Final Solution: A History of European Racism.* New York: Howard Fertig, 1978.

Mota, Carlos Guilherme, ed. *Brasil em perspectiva.* 5th ed. São Paulo: Difel, 1985.

Moura, Gerson. *Autonomia na dependência: A política externa brasileira de 1935–1942.* Rio de Janeiro: Editora Nova Fronteira, 1980.

Mourão Filho, Olympio. *Memórias: A verdade de um revolucionário.* Porto Alegre: L and PM Editores, 1978.

———. "Minha defesa." In Hélio Silva et al., *A ameaça vermelha: O plano Cohen,* 75–268. Porto Alegre: L and PM Editores, 1980.

Needell, Jeffrey D. *A Tropical Belle Epoque: Elite Culture and Society in Turn-of-the-Century Rio de Janeiro.* Cambridge: Cambridge University Press, 1987.

Nehab, Werner. *Anti-semitismo, integralismo, neo-nazismo.* Rio de Janeiro: Livraria Freitas Bastos, 1988.

Neiva, Arthur Hehl. "Estudos sobre a imigração semita no Brasil." *Revista de Imigração e Colonização* 5:2 (June 1944): 215–422.

———. "Getúlio Vargas e o problema da imigração e da colonização." In *Revista de Imigração e Colonização* 3:1 (April 1942), 24–70.

Neiva, Arthur Hehl, and Manuel Diégues. "The Cultural Assimilation of Immigrants in Brazil." In *The Cultural Integration of Immigrants: A Survey Based upon the Papers and Proceeding of the Unesco Conference Held in Havana, April 1956,* edited by W. D. Borrie, 181–233. New York: Unesco, 1957.

Nicolaiewsky, Eva. *Israelitas no Rio Grande do Sul.* Porto Alegre: Editora Garatuja, 1975.

Nogueira, Arlinda Rocha. *A imigração japonesa para a lavoura cafeeira paulista, 1908–1922.* São Paulo: Instituto de Estudos Brasileiros, 1973.

Norman, Theodore. *An Outstretched Arm: A History of the Jewish Colonization Association.* London: Routledge and Kegan Paul, 1985.

Novinsky, Anita. *Cristãos novos na Bahia, 1624–1654.* São Paulo: Editora Perspectiva, 1972.

———. "Os israelitas em São Paulo." In *São Paulo: espírito, povo, instituições,* edited by J. V. Freitas Marcondes and Osmar Pimentel, 107–26. São Paulo: Livraria Pioneira Editora, 1968.

———. "The Jewish Roots of Brazil." In *The Jewish Presence in Latin America,* edited by Judith Laikin Elkin and Gilbert W. Merkx, 33–44. Boston: Allen and Unwin, 1987.

Oliveira, Xavier de. *O problema imigratório na constituição brasileira.* Rio de Janeiro: A. Coelho Branco, 1937.

Ornellas, Manoelito de. *Gaúchos e beduínos: A origem étnica e a formação do Rio Grande do Sul*. Rio de Janeiro: Editora José Olympio, 1948.

Os protocolos dos sábios de Sião: O imperialismo de Israel, o plano dos judeus para a conquista do mundo, o código do Anti-Cristo, provas de autenticidade, documentos, notas e comentários. Translated, organized, and annotated by Gustavo Barroso. São Paulo: Editora Agência Minerva, 1936.

Overdyke, W. Darrel. *The Know-Nothing Party in the South*. Baton Rouge: Louisiana State University Press, 1950.

Pace, David. *Claude Lévi-Strauss: The Bearer of Ashes*. Boston: Routledge and Kegan Paul, 1983.

Patai, Daphne. "Minority Status and the Stigma of 'Surplus Visibility.' " *Chronicle of Higher Education* 38:10 (October 30, 1991), A52.

Peixoto, Afrânio, ed. *Os judeus na história do Brasil*. Rio de Janeiro: Uri Zwerling, 1936.

Pereira, Antônio Baptista. *O Brasil e a raça: Conferencia feita na faculdade de direito de São Paulo a 19 de junho de 1928*. São Paulo: Empresa Gráfica Rossetti, 1928.

———. *O Brasil e o anti-semitismo*. Rio de Janeiro: Editora Guanabara, 1934.

Pereira, Luiz Carlos Bresser. "Origens étnicas e sociais do empresário paulista." *Revista de Administração e Emprêsas* 4:11 (June 1964), 83–106.

Pérez, José. *Questão judaica, questão social*. São Paulo: Empresa Gráfica da "Revista dos Tribunaes," 1933.

Peskin, Allan, and Donald Ramos. "An Ohio Yankee at Dom Pedro's Court: Notes on Brazilian Life in the 1850s by an American Diplomat, Robert C. Schenk." *Americas* 38:4 (April 1982), 497–514.

Petrone, Maria Thereza Schorer. "Imigração." In *O Brasil republicano: Sociedade e instituições (1889–1930)* (part 3, vol. 2 of *História geral da civilização brasileira*), 4th ed., edited by Boris Fausto, 93–134. São Paulo: Difel, 1985.

Pinkuss, Fritz. Interview by author. São Paulo, 1 September 1986.

Poncins, Léon de. *As forças secretas da revolução: Maçonaria e judaismo*. Porto Alegre: Livraria do Globo, 1931.

Poppino, Rollie E. *Brazil: The Land and People*. New York: Oxford University Press, 1973.

Por que ser anti-semita?: Um inquérito entre intellectuaes brasileiros. Rio de Janeiro: Civilização Brasileira, 1933.

Price, Charles A. *Southern Europeans in Australia*. Melbourne: Oxford University Press, 1963.

Price, Paul H. "The Polish Immigrant in Brazil: A Study of Immigration, Assimilation and Acculturation." Ph.D. diss., Vanderbilt University, 1950.

Putnam, Samuel "Brazilian Culture under Vargas." *Science and Society* 6:1 (winter 1942), 34–57.

Queiroz, José. *222 anedotas de Getúlio Vargas: Anedotário popular, irreverente e pitoresco. Getúlio no inferno. Getúlio no céu*. Rio de Janeiro: Companhia Brasileira de Artes Gráficas, 1955.

R. A. (initials only). "A assimilação do elemento estrangeiro em São Paulo:

Notas etnológicas sobre os israelitas." *Planalto: Quinzenário de Cultura* (São Paulo) 1:3 (15 June 1941), 7–16.

Rabinovitch, Moses. *Die Iceh fartretersheft in Brazil un ireh zahrgn toyveshakla'l* (The ICA representative in Brazil and the public trust). Rio de Janeiro: n.p., 1933.

Raeders, Georges. *O inimigo cordial do Brasil: O conde de Gobineau no Brasil.* São Paulo: Paz e Terra, 1988. Translated by Rosa Freire d'Aguiar. Originally published as *Le comte de Gobineau au Brésil* (Paris: Nouvelles Editions Latines, 1934).

Raffalovich, Isaiah. *Brazilye: A tsukunftsland far idisher emigratsye* (Brazil: The land of the future for Jewish emigrants). Berlin: HIAS-ICA-EMIGDIRECT, 1928.

———. "The Condition of Jewry and Judaism in South America." In *Central Conference of American Rabbis Yearbook,* 40:414–23. New York: Central Conference of American Rabbis, 1930.

———. *Tsiyunim ve-tamrurim be-shiv'im shenot nedudim: Otobayografiya* (Landmarks and milestones during seventy years of wanderings: An autobiography). Tel Aviv: Defus Sho-Shani, 1952.

Rago, Margareth. *Os prazeres da noite: Prostituição e códigos da sexualidade feminina em São Paulo (1890–1930).* Rio de Janeiro: Paz e Terra, 1991.

Raizman, Itzhak Z. *A fertl yorhundert yiddishe prese in Brazil* (A quarter century of Jewish press in Brazil). Tzfat: Museum le-Omanut ha-Dfus, 1968.

———. *Yiddishe sheferishkeit in lender fun portugalishn loshn: Portugal en Brazil* (Jewish creativity in Portuguese-speaking countries: Portugal and Brazil). Tzfat: Museum of Printing Art, 1975.

Ramos, Arthur. *Guerra e relações de raça.* Rio de Janeiro: Departamento Editorial da União Nacional dos Estudantes, 1943.

Rattner, Henrique. "Economic and Social Mobility of Jews in Brazil." In *The Jewish Presence in Latin America,* edited by Judith Laikin Elkin and Gilbert W. Merkx, 187–200. Boston: Allen and Unwin, 1987.

———. *Tradição e mudança: A comunidade judaica em São Paulo.* São Paulo: Editora Ática, 1977.

Razovsky, Cecilia Davidson. "The Jew Re-discovers America: Jewish Immigration to Latin American Countries." *Jewish Social Service Quarterly* 5:2–3 (December 1928–March 1929), 119–27.

———. *Present Status of Jewish Settlment in Brazil and Argentina.* New York: National Regfugee Service, 1937.

Reale, Miguel. *ABC do integralismo.* Rio de Janeiro: José Olympio, 1935.

———. *O capitalismo internacional: Introdução à economia nova.* Rio de Janeiro: José Olympio, 1935.

Rehfeld, Walter. Interview by author. São Paulo, 27 May 1986.

Reis, Fidelis, and João de Faria. *O problema immigratório e seus aspectos éthnicos: Na camara e fóra de camara.* Rio de Janeiro: Typ. "Revista dos Tribunaes," 1924.

Reutter, Lutz-Eugen. *Katholishe Kirche als Fluchthelfer im Dritten Reich: Die*

Betreuung von Auswanderern durch den St. Raphaels-Verein. Reckling-hausen-Hamburg: Paulus Verlag, 1971.

Revorêdo, Júlio de. *Immigração.* São Paulo: Empresa Gráfica da "Revista dos Tribunaes," 1934.

Richmond, Anthony H. *Immigration and Ethnic Conflict.* New York: St. Martin's Press, 1988.

Rio Grande do Sul. *De província de São Pedro a estado do Rio Grande do Sul, censos do RS: 1803–1950.* Porto Alegre: Fundação de Economia e Estatística, 1986.

Rio Grande do Sul. Assembléia de Representantes. *Anais da assembléia de representantes do estado do Rio Grande do Sul.* Porto Alegre, 1924.

Rio Grande do Sul. Secretaria de Estado dos Negócios das Obras Públicas. *Relatório do secretário de 1906.* Porto Alegre, 1907.

Rissech, Elvira. "Inmigracíon judía a la Argentina, 1938–1942: Entre la aceptacíon e el rechazo." *Rumbos* (Jerusalem) 15 (1986), 91–113.

Robinson, Jacob. *Palestine and the United Nations: Prelude to Solution.* Washington, D.C.: Public Affairs Press, 1947.

Roche, Jean. *A colonização alemã e o Rio Grande do Sul.* Translated by Emery Ruas. Porto Alegre: Editora Globo, 1969.

Rodrigues, Francisca Pereira. *O braço estrangeiro.* São Paulo: Imprensa Oficial do Estado, 1938.

Rodrigues, João Barbosa. *Vocabulário indígena com a orthographia correcta (complemento da poranduba amazonense).* Rio de Janeiro: Typ. de G. Leuzinger & Filhos, 1893.

Rosenstock, Werner. "Exodus 1933–1939: A Survey of Jewish Emigration from Germany." *Leo Baeck Institute Yearbook* 1 (1956), 373–90.

Rozshansky, Shmuel, ed. *Brazilyanish: Antologie: Fragmentn fun farsharbetn tsu der kharakteristik un zikhroynes* (Brazilian Anthology: Fragments of research on characteristics and memories). Buenos Aires: Yoysef Lifshits Fond fun der Literatur Gezelshaft baym YIVO, 1973.

Rose, Peter I. "Ghetto." In *Academic American Encyclopedia,* 9:167. Darien, Conn.: Grolier, 1986.

Ruppin, Arthur. "The Jewish Populations of the World." In Central Yiddish Culture Organization, *The Jewish People: Past and Present,* 348–60. New York: Jewish Encyclopedic Handbooks, 1946.

———. *Los judíos de America del Sur.* Buenos Aires: Editora Darom, 1938.

Sachar, Howard Morley. *The Course of Modern Jewish History,* 2d ed. New York: Dell Publishing Company, 1977.

———. *Diaspora: An Inquiry into the Contemporary Jewish World.* New York: Harper and Row, 1985.

Safa, Elie. *L'émigration libanaise.* Beirut: Université Saint-Joseph, 1960.

Safady, Jamil. *O café e o mascate.* São Paulo: Editora Comercial Safady, 1973.

Safady, Jorge S. "A imigração árabe no Brasil." Ph.D. diss., Department of History, University of São Paulo, 1972.

Saito, Hiroshi. *O japonês no Brasil.* São Paulo: Editora Sociologia e Política, 1962.

Salgado, Plínio. *O estrangeiro*. 5th ed. São Paulo: Companhia Editora Pan-orama, 1948.

Sánchez-Albornoz, Nicolás. *The Population of Latin America: A History*. Berkeley: University of California Press, 1974.

Santos, Francisco Ruas. *Coleção Bibliográfica Militar*. Rio de Janeiro: Biblio-teca do Exército, 1960.

Saxton, Alexander. *The Indispensable Enemy: Labor and the Anti-Chinese Movement in California*. Berkeley: University of California Press, 1971.

Schallman, Lazaro. *Los pioneros de la colonizacíon judía en la Argentina*. Bue-nos Aires: Ejecutivo Sudamericano del Congreso Judío Mundial, 1969.

Schneider, Ronald M. *"Order and Progress": A Political History of Brazil*. Boulder, Colo.: Westview Press, 1991.

Schulman, Bernardo. *Em legítima defeza: A voz de um judeu brasileiro*. 2d ed. Curitiba: n.p., 1937.

Schwartzman, Simon. *A Space for Science: The Development of the Scientific Community in Brazil*. University Park: Pennsylvania State University Press, 1991. Originally published as *Formação da comunidade científica no Brasil* (São Paulo: Compania Editora Nacional, 1979).

Schwarz, Roberto. "Brazilian Culture: Nationalism by Elimination." *New Left Review* 167 (January/February 1988), 77–90.

———. *Que horas são*. São Paulo: Companhia das Letras, 1987.

Schweidson, Jacques. *Judeus de Bombachas e Chimarrão*. Rio de Janeiro: José Olympio Editora, 1985.

Scliar, Moacyr. *Caminhos da esperança: A presença judaica no Rio Grande do Sul*. Porto Alegre: Riocell, 1990.

———. *O ciclo das águas*. Porto Alegre: Editora Globo, 1977.

Scobie, James R. *Revolution on the Pampas*. Austin: University of Texas Press, 1964.

Scott, George Rylel. *A History of Prostitution from Antiquity to the Present Day*. London: T. Werner Laurie, 1936.

Seitenfus, Ricardo Silva. *O Brasil de Getúlio Vargas e a formação dos blocos: 1930–1942*. São Paulo: Companhia Editora Nacional, 1985.

———. "Ideology and Diplomacy: Italian Fascism and Brazil (1935–38). *His-panic American Historical Review* 64:3 (August 1984), 503–34.

Seltzer, Robert M. *Jewish People, Jewish Thought: The Jewish Experience in History*. New York: Macmillan, 1980.

Senkman, Leonardo. "Argentina's Immigration Policy during the Holocaust (1938–1945)." *Yad Vashem Studies* 21 (1991), 155–88.

Sephardic Community of Porto Alegre. Collective interview by author. Porto Alegre, 22 June 1986.

Serebrenick, Salamão, and Elias Lipiner. *Breve história dos judeus no Brasil*. Rio de Janeiro: Edições Biblos, 1962.

Shulman, Abe. "Unclean Burial Place in Brazil." *Jewish Week* 8 (June 1980).

SIBRA. *Sociedade Israelita Brasileira de Cultura e Beneficência, 1936–1986*. Porto Alegre: SIBRA, 1986.

Silva, Hélio. *1934: A constituinte*. Rio de Janeiro: Editora Civilização Brasi-leira, 1969.

————. *1937: Todos os golpes se parecem.* Rio de Janeiro: Editora Civilização Brasileira, 1970.

Silva, Hélio, with Maria Cecília Carneiro and José Augusto Drummond. *A ameaça vermelha: O plano Cohen.* Porto Alegre: L and PM Editores, 1980.

Silva, Hernán Asdrúbal, ed. *Inmigración y politica inmigrante en el cono sur de America.* Vol. 3. Washington, D.C.: CPDP-CAS-PAIGH, 1990.

Sjöberg, Tommie. *The Powers and the Persecuted: The Refugee Problem and the Intergovernmental Committee on Refugees.* Lund: Lund University Press, 1991.

Skidmore, Thomas E. *Black into White: Race and Nationality in Brazilian Thought.* New York: Oxford University Press, 1974.

————. *Fact and Myth: Discovering a Racial Problem in Brazil.* Helen Kellog Institute for International Studies Working Paper no. 173. Notre Dame, Ind.: University of Notre Dame, 1992.

————. *Politics in Brazil, 1930–1964: An Experiment in Democracy.* New York: Oxford University Press, 1967.

————. "Racial Ideas and Social Policy in Brazil, 1870–1940." In *The Idea of Race in Latin America, 1870–1940,* edited by Richard Graham, 7–36. Austin: University of Texas Press, 1990.

Smolana, Krzysztof. "Sobre a gênese do estereótipo do polonês na América Latina: Caso brasileiro." *Estudios Latinoamericanos* (Warsaw) 5 (1979): 69–78.

Sodré, Nelson Werneck. *História da imprensa no Brasil.* Rio de Janeiro: Editora Civilização Brasileira, 1966.

Sofer, Eugene F. *From Pale to Pampa: A Social History of the Jews of Argentina.* New York: Holmes and Meier, 1982.

Soibelmann, Guilherme. *Memórias de Philippson.* São Paulo: Canupus, 1984.

Solberg, Carl. *Immigration and Nationalism: Argentina and Chile, 1890–1914.* Austin: University of Texas Press, 1970.

Spitzer, Leo. *Lives In Between: Assimilation and Marginality in Austria, Brazil, West Africa, 1780–1945.* Cambridge: Cambridge University Press, 1989.

Stawinski, Alberto Victor. *Primórdios da imigração polonesa no Rio Grande do Sul (1875–1975).* Porto Alegre: Escola Superior de Teologia São Lourenço de Brindes, 1976.

Stemplowski, Ryszard. "O diplomata polonês sobre a influência da Segunda Guerra Mundial sobre a situação no Brasil." *Estudios Latinoamericanos* (Warsaw) 5 (1979): 163–69.

Stepan, Nancy Leys. *"The Hour of Eugenics": Race, Gender and Nation in Latin America.* Ithaca, N.Y.: Cornell University Press, 1991.

Stern, J. P. *Hitler: The Führer and the People.* Berkeley: University of California Press, 1988.

Suzigan, Wilson. *Indústria brasileira: Origem e desenvolvimento.* São Paulo: Brasiliense, 1986.

Tartakower, Aryeh, and Kurt R. Grossman. *The Jewish Refugee.* New York: Institute of Jewish Affairs of the World Jewish Congress and American Jewish Congress, 1944.

Topik, Steven. "Middle Class Brazilian Nationalism, 1889–1930: From Radicalism to Reaction." *Social Science Quarterly* 59:1 (June 1978), 101–2.

Torres, Alberto. *A organização nacional*. São Paulo: Companhia Editorial Nacional, 1938.

Trento, Angelo. *Do outro lado do Atlântico: Um século de imigração italiana no Brasil*. Translated by Mariarosaria Fabris and Luiz Eduardo de Lima Brandão. São Paulo: Nobel, 1989.

Trindade, Hélgio. *Integralismo: O fascismo brasileiro na década de 30*. 2d ed. São Paulo: Difel, 1979.

United States. Department of State. *Foreign Relations of the United States: Diplomatic Papers*. Vol. 1, *1938*. Washington, D.C.: Government Printing Office, 1955.

United States. Immigration and Naturalization Service. *Annual Report*. Washington, D.C.: Government Printing Office, 1973.

The Universal Jewish Encyclopedia. Edited by Isaac Landman. 10 vols. New York: Universal Jewish Encyclopedia, 1939–43.

Ussoskin, Moshe. *The Struggle for Survival: A History of Jewish Credit Co-Operatives in Bessarabia, Old-Rumania, Bukovina, and Transylvania*. Jerusalem: Jerusalem Academic Press, 1975.

Vargas, Getúlio. *A nova política do Brasil*. Vol. 6, Realizações do Estado Novo, 1 de agôsto de 1938 a 7 de setembro de 1939. Rio de Janeiro: José Olympio Editora, 1940.

Vasconselos, Gilberto. *Ideologia curupira: Análise do discurso integralista*. São Paulo: Brasiliense, 1979.

Vasconcellos Filho, J. I. Cabral de. *Da revolução de 30 ao terror do Estado Novo: Subsídios para a história de uma época*. Rio de Janeiro: Livraria Editora Cátedra, 1982.

Vatican. Secrétairie d'État de Sa Sainteté. *Actes et documents du Saint Siège relatifs à la seconde guerre mondial*. Edited by Pierre Blet, Robert A. Graham, Angelo Martini, and Burkhart Schneider. 9 vols. Vol. 6, *Le Saint Siège et les victimes de la guerre, mars 1939–décembre 1940*, Vatican City, 1972. Vol. 8, *Le Saint Siège et les victimes de la guerre, janvier 1941–décembre 1942*, Vatican City, 1974.

Vianna, Francisco José Oliveira. *A constituição federal e as constituições dos estados*. Rio de Janeiro: F. Briguiet e Cia. Editores, 1911.

———. "Os imigrantes germânicos e slavos e sua caracterização antropológica." *Revista de Imigração e Colonização* 1:1 (January 1940), 23–32.

———. "Os imigrantes semíticos e mongóis e sua caraterização antropológica." *Revista de Imigração e Colonização* 1:4 (October 1940), 610–16.

———. *Populações meridonais do Brasil*. 5th ed. 2 vols. Rio de Janeiro: José Olympio, 1952. (1st ed. São Paulo: Monteiro Lobato, 1922.)

———. *Raça e assimilação*. São Paulo: Companhia Editora Nacional, 1932.

Vital, David. *The Origins of Zionism*. Oxford: Oxford University Press, 1975.

Waibel, Léo. "Princípios de colonização européia no sul do Brasil." In *Capítulos de geografia tropical e do Brasil*, 2d ed. Rio de Janeiro: IBGE, Supren, 1979.

Wainer, Samuel. *Minha razão de viver: Memórias de um repórter.* Rio de Janeiro: Record, 1987.

Wainstein, Boris. Interview by author. Porto Alegre, 20 June 1986.

Waldman, Maurício, ed. *Política das minorias: O caso dos judeus no Brasil.* Porto Alegre: Mercado Aberto, 1988.

Wasserstein, Bernard. *Britain and the Jews of Europe, 1939–1945.* New York: Oxford University Press, 1979.

Weinstein, Barbara. *The Amazon Rubber Boom, 1850–1920.* Stanford, Calif.: Stanford University Press, 1983.

Weisbord, Robert G., and Wallace P. Sillanpoa. *The Chief Rabbi, the Pope, and the Holocaust.* New Brunswick, N.J.: Transaction Publishers, 1992.

Weisbrot, Robert. *The Jews of Argentina: From the Inquisition to Perón.* Philadelphia: Jewish Publication Society of America, 1979.

Wessel, Bessie Bloom. "Ethnic Factors in the Population of New London, CT." Parts 1 and 2. *American Journal of Sociology* (July 1929), 18–34, 263–70.

White, Paul, and Robert Woods, eds. *The Geographical Impact of Migration.* New York: Longman Press, 1980.

Williams, Margaret Todaro. "The Politicization of the Brazilian Catholic Church: The Catholic Electoral League." *Journal of Interamerican Studies and World Affairs* 16:3 (August 1974), 301–25.

Winsberg, Morton D. *Colonia Baron Hirsch: A Jewish Agricultural Colony in Argentina.* University of Florida Monographs, no. 19. Gainesville: University of Florida Press, 1963.

Wirth, John D. *Minas Gerais in the Brazilian Federation, 1889–1937.* Stanford, Calif.: Stanford University Press, 1977.

Wischnitzer, Mark. "Jewish Emigration from Germany, 1933–1938." *Jewish Social Studies* 2 (January 1940), 23–44.

———. *To Dwell in Safety: The Story of Jewish Migration since 1800.* Philadelphia: Jewish Publication Society of America, 1948.

Witter, José Sebastião. "A política imigratória no Brasil." In *Inmigracíon y politica inmigrante en el cono sur de America,* edited by Hernán Asdrúbal Silva, 3:253–60. Washington, D.C.: CPDP-CAS-PAIGH, 1990.

Wiznitzer, Arnold. *Jews in Colonial Brazil.* New York: Columbia University Press, 1960.

Wolff, Bernhard. Interview by author. Porto Alegre, 21 July 1986.

Wolff, Egon, and Frieda Wolff. *Dicionário biográfico.* Vol. 2, *Judeus no Brasil: Século XIX.* Rio de Janeiro: Egon and Frieda Wolff, 1987.

———. *Guia histórico da comunidade judaica de São Paulo.* São Paulo: Editora B'nei B'rith, 1988.

———. *Os judeus no Brasil imperial.* São Paulo: Centro de Estudos Judaicos, 1975.

———. *Os judeus nos primórdios do Brasil-República, visto especialmente pela documentação no Rio de Janeiro.* Rio de Janeiro: Biblioteca Israelita H. N. Bialik, 1979.

Worcman, Susane, ed. *Heranças e lembranças: Imigrantes judeus no Rio de Janeiro.* Rio de Janeiro: ARI/CIEC/MIS, 1991.

Wrzos, Konrad. *Yerba Mate.* Warsaw: Rój. 1937.

Wyman, David S. *The Abandonment of the Jews: America and the Holocaust, 1941–1945.* New York: Pantheon Books, 1984.
———. *Paper Walls: America and the Refugee Crisis 1938–1941.* Amherst: University of Massachusetts Press, 1968.
Yerushalmi, Yosef Hayim. *Assimilation and Racial Anti-Semitism: The Iberian and the German Models.* Leo Baeck Memorial Lecture no. 26. New York: Leo Baeck Institute, 1982.
Young, Jordan M. *The Brazilian Revolution of 1930 and the Aftermath.* New Brunswick, N.J.: Rutgers University Press, 1967.
Zuccotti, Susan. *The Italians and the Holocaust: Persecution, Rescue and Survival.* New York: Basic Books, 1987.
Zweig, Stefan. *Brazil: Land of the Future.* Translated by Andrew St. James. New York: Viking Press, 1942.

Index

Abravanel, Senor, 173
Ação, A (São Paulo), 59
Ação Integralista Brasileira (AIB), 58–59, 61
Accioly, Hildebrando, 161, 166; announces end to Vatican visa plan, 165
Aché, Atila Monteiro, 170
African Americans, 190 n. 27, 235–36 n. 46, 238 n. 6
Africans, 8, 170
Aguiar, Anésio Frota, 38
aliyah, 172, 173
Almeida, Guilherme de, 33
Almeida, José Américo de, 96
Alsina, S.S., 139
Amaral, A. J. de Azevedo, 50, 61
Amazon: attempts to colonize, 109; North African Jewish colonization in, 15, 41
American Jewish Congress, 143, 233 n. 185
American Jewish Joint Distribution Committee, 101, 107, 140
Americano, Jorge, 65
Amherst College, 84
Anderson, Benedict, 4
Andrade, Carlos Drummond de, 72
anti-Asian movements, 19
anti-foreigner movements, 48
anti-Semites, definition of, 9
anti-Semitic, caricatures and jokes, 90
anti-Semitism: in Brazil, 6, 30, 38; in Brazilian press, 26, 29, 31, 71, 83, 120, 129, 141, 142, 239 n. 17; in Europe, 3; reconceptualization of, 121

Arab nationalism, 172
Arabs, 5, 7, 31, 55, 92
Aranha, Luiza, 122
Aranha, Oswaldo, 85, 86, 88, 96, 166, 176; as ambassador to the U.S., 61, 71, 98; as anti-Semite, 84, 119, 225 n. 4; appointment as foreign minister, 119; attack on Freitas Vale, 133; and Catholic non-Aryans, 148, 152; as champion of U.S.-Brazilian relations, 99, 104, 116; correspondence with Einstein, 130; fear of U.S. Jews, 119; on IGC, 113; ignores complaints about Jews, 143; meeting with relief groups, 101–2; as philo-Semite, 22, 119; as president of U.N. General Assembly, 1; pressure by Vatican, 161; and S.S. *Cabo de Hornos,* 140; stereotypes of Jews, 119; in U.S. to negotiate loans, 121, 126
Argentina, 2, 19, 20, 24, 35, 70, 71, 148; as imperialist, 12; as member of IGC, 114; prostitution in, 33
Arinos de Mello Franco, Afonso, 66; *Preparação ao nacionalismo,* 66
armament industry, 174
Armenians, 55
"aryanization," 49
Aryans, 62, 93, 145, 157
Asians, 5, 7, 170
assimilation, 10, 50, 54, 57, 58, 72, 87, 121, 172; as law, 109, 137
Assyrians, 68–69, 110
authoritarian nationalism, 96, 144
Avanhandava, 108, 221 n. 166

271

Compositer: Maple-Vail
Text: 10/13 Sabon
Display: Sabon
Printer: Maple-Vail
Binder: Maple-Vail